VIRGINIA CONTRACTOR'S LAW

Third Edition   Robert Gregory and Allison Camacho

 **KAPLAN)** AEC EDUCATION

This publication is designed to provide accurate and authoritative information in regard to the subject matter covered. It is sold with the understanding that the publisher is not engaged in rendering legal, accounting, or other professional service. If legal advice or other expert assistance is required, the services of a competent professional person should be sought.

President: Mehul Patel
Executive Director of Product Development: Kate DeVivo
Senior Editorial Project Manager: Laurie McGuire
Director of Production: Daniel Frey
Senior Managing Editor, Production: Jack Kiburz
Creative Director: Lucy Jenkins
Senior Production Artist: Virginia Byrne
Vice President of Product Management: Dave Dufresne
Senior Product Manager: Brian O'Connor

© 2008 by Dearborn Financial Publishing, Inc.®

Published by Kaplan AEC Education
30 South Wacker Drive, Suite 2500
Chicago, IL 60606-7481
(312) 836-4400
www.kaplanAECcontracting.com

Printed in the United States of America.

08   09   10   10   9   8   7   6   5   4   3   2   1

ISBN-13: 978-1-4277-8422-3
ISBN-10:   1-4277-8422-1

CONTENTS

REGULATIONS CONTENTS

4   EROSION AND SEDIMENT CONTROLS

5   VIRGINIA UNIFORM STATEWIDE BUILDING CODE

PART I. GENERAL REGULATIONS

6   VIRGINIA LABOR LAWS

8   MECHANICS' LIEN LAWS

9   VIRGINIA OSHA REGULATIONS

10 UNDERGROUND UTILITIES

INTRODUCTION

Virginia Contractor's Law is a compilation of regulations that a contractor needs to know in order to start a contracting business in the state of Virginia. Each state has unique regulatory requirements and it is strongly suggested that these requirements be completely reviewed before applying for a license, and especially prior to taking the Virginia examination. Contractors who have experience in other states should understand that regulations differ from state to state, and should familiarize themselves with the Virginia regulations.

Study for the exam using this supplement with its companion document, the *Contractor's Business Reference Manual,* which contains information about business operations and federal laws. The two books—a set of tools, each designed to perform a certain task—comprise a complete set of business and law information required to begin work in this profession.

TEST TIPS

License applicants bring to the exam room various levels of experience; however, one thing that many contractors have in common is that it has been a number of years since they have been in a classroom and have been tested on a specific set of knowledge. The licensing exams present unique challenges for adults. Some candidates have not read the state requirements for licensing and have misconceptions about the process; others have exam anxiety. All test candidates can perform better by following certain test strategies.

Study

Success on the exam starts well before entering the exam room. The only way to pass is to be familiar with the reference materials. Open-book exam questions will be quite detailed and can explore tables of information, whereas closed-book exams will be more general in nature. For example:

- Open book—In what year did the number of U-boats sunk exceed the number of Allied ships sunk during WWII?
- Closed book—What year was Pearl Harbor attacked?

The open-book question would require you to find tables in the reference book that listed U-boats sunk and another table that listed Allied ships sunk. The closed-book question is straightforward and requires simple memorization. The test-taker that does not know how to easily find the tables will struggle with the exam.

Following are some tips for preparing for the exam:

- Identify the exam references and where to obtain them. Buy them and read them.

- Read the candidate information brochure to determine which materials are allowed in the exam room and what can be done to the reference materials prior to the exam (such as highlighting, notes, and tabs).
- Review the test outline to determine what must be studied. Obviously, if there are 500 pages of material and only 50 questions, not all of the material will be on the exam.
- Identify study resources such as community colleges, exam preparation companies, contractor associations, or colleagues. Form a study group with another person who has to take the same exam and take time each week to study. Have a friend or family member ask questions each night from the materials.

Most multiple-choice exams break down to about two minutes per question. Searching for information takes time; good preparation saves time.

Attitude

The exam tests the ability to correctly answer a number of questions in a specific period of time. Arguing with a test proctor or getting angry with the exam questions is counterproductive and wastes time and energy. Try to remain calm during the exam and answer the questions to the best of your ability.

How Hard Can It Be?

Exams are complicated and are constructed in accordance with national standards. The development process is carefully structured to make sure that the exam measures at a minimal level of competency. This means that the average, reasonably experienced person should be able to pass the exam. Each person is permitted a few mistakes to allow for a mismarked or misread question, but the exam sorts out those who are not prepared. The exam development process is formally structured and consists of the following:

- Task survey to identify critical elements
- Question development and review
- Scoring and analysis of results
- Maintenance of exam by test developers
- Updating to reflect changes in codes or regulations
- Continuous scrutiny to ensure that both the exam and the administration of the exam are consistent with equal employment opportunity laws and industry practices

Prepare For the Trip to the Exam

Know where the exam location is, how long it will take to get there, and whether parking is available. Assemble all reference materials and supplies and place them in a bag either in the car or by the front door where they cannot be forgotten on test day. Take the admission letter with directions, a photo ID, a spare calculator, and a pencil.

At the Exam Site

- Leave your cell phone and personal items secured in the trunk of your car.
- Use the restroom upon arrival.
- Check in and, when seated, arrange your materials so they are within reach.
- Listen to all directions and ask the proctor to clarify any questions.
- When you receive the exam, make sure that it is the correct exam; even exam companies make mistakes.

Taking the Test

- For best performance, go through the examination quickly the first time, picking out the answers you know to be correct, marking and skipping the hard ones.
- Read and skip math questions. Skipping all the math questions and doing them together on the second attempt organizes your thoughts towards "doing math" rather than shifting focus from text to math to text. If your math answer doesn't match any given answers, try reverse engineering the problem; that is, start with an answer that may be right and work your way back through the problem.
- Read each question carefully; determine what is being asked, and then read (i) all the answers before selecting one. Once the answer has been selected and marked, move on. *Do not doubt your selection.* Only change an answer when you are certain that a mistake has been made.
- If two answers mean the same thing, they are both wrong. Only one answer is correct.
- Go through the exam a second time, answering the harder questions, doing the math problems, and again skipping the most challenging questions.
- Usually all questions on a multiple-choice exam have the same value. The harder ones count the same as the easier ones. A computer-delivered test facilitates marking a question and returning to it later. Even if a question is answered, it can be marked and returned to later for another look.
- Watch exceptions, asterisks, and notes. Test developers are especially fond of exploring remote areas of reference materials.
- When finished, make sure that each question has an answer. Unless stated otherwise in the candidate directions, there is no penalty for guessing and getting a correct answer, but the question is automatically wrong if no answer is selected.

Relax

Remember that this is a test on the knowledge needed to become a contractor and to perform in the profession. This is what contractors do in the business day after day. Test day is just handling a lot of questions in a specific period of time. A contractor can do this!

The profession of contracting is rewarding and not just in a monetary fashion. There is great satisfaction from a job well done and especially from hearing the praise of an owner upon successful completion of a project. May your contracting business be successful and your customers happy.

ACKNOWLEDGMENTS

The publisher would like to thank the Consultant, James L. Guffey, for his invaluable review of material during development. His comments were greatly appreciated.

ABOUT THE AUTHORS

Robert D. Gregory, CPCA, CBO, is President of Contractors Institute, Inc., has served as general manager of a construction company, supervisor of the Virginia State Building Code, and adjunct professor of building code studies in the Virginia Community College System. He has 38 years of experience in construction-related activities, is certified in 14 areas of inspection, and is a Virginia Master Electrician. Bob is the qualifying and designated employee for Contractors Institute, Inc., which is licensed in Virginia as a Class A Building and Electrical contracting company, and he has authored numerous books on contracting and exam preparation. He is a former Marine with service in Vietnam and is a life member of the Disabled American Veterans.

Allison Camacho is the lead instructor for Contractors Institute's Business and Law seminars. She is also President of Alacam, Inc. a test development and administration corporation based in Virginia. Allison is a US Army veteran with extensive background in facilitating briefings and developing training programs. Allison is a life member of the Disabled American Veterans.

READING REGULATIONS

A contractor must comply with a complex set of laws and policies. The federal government has established laws that regulate employment and safety. State and local governments issue laws, ordinances, and policies that further regulate employment and safety laws, as well as how contracts are written, construction methods, and obtaining payment. This chapter details how the United States' system of law was founded, provides terms used to define regulations, and offers suggestions on how to research a legal topic and find it in the law.

DEFINITIONS

bill A document that changes the current law; adds a new law; or deletes an existing law. The idea for a bill may come from general assembly members, their constituents, lobbyists, the governor, or heads of state agencies charged with administering the law.

law A body of rules of action or conduct that has legal force. Laws are developed by state legislatures.

ordinance A law adopted by local jurisdictions. The city may adopt ordinances that govern everyday activities—for example, parking and speed limits.

policy A guideline for operation of an office that does not have the effect of law. For example, the local building department has a policy posted that all inspection requests for the next day must be received by the office no later than 2:00 p.m. the preceding day. This policy helps the office run more smoothly, but no laws are broken and no punishments incurred if the policy is not followed.

> **regulation** A rule or order that has been issued by a government. Regulations are normally adopted by state agencies.

> **rule** A standard or guide for action or conduct. A rule may be issued by a judge.

IN THE BEGINNING

The system of law in the United States is fundamentally based on individual rights and freedoms. This basis of law is clearly defined in the Constitution, but the system has roots dating back much further. It starts with English common law in the year 1215 when the Magna Carta was adopted. The Magna Carta established basic rights for all men and established four principles in written law:

1. The king had to rule in accordance with the desires of the ruled.
2. Government was an unbreakable contract between the people and the king.
3. The king's powers were limited.
4. The rights of the people were defined.

The first English colony in America was in Virginia in the early 1600s. When the New World colonies were established, the settlers brought the English basis of law, the Magna Carta, with them. The colony operated under a system of government consisting of a council of appointed representatives that answered to the king through the governor, and a charter that guaranteed protection to the people based on English law.

This system was modified in 1619 to include a representative assembly that would govern the colony. This new assembly, the House of Burgesses, passed laws about criminal offenses, public conduct, and taxation of residents. The written laws of the assembly were followed by the kings of England until Charles I disregarded the terms. The grievances against Charles were summarized as confiscating property without a hearing; boarding soldiers in private homes; and imprisoning people without a hearing or benefit of a trial.

The Declaration of Independence drafted almost 100 years later lists those same grievances and other continued injustices against the American people by the monarchy. The pattern of intolerable acts continued and resulted in the colonies seceding from English rule, the Revolutionary War, and winning independence.

The new United States assembled a constitutional convention in Philadelphia in May of 1787. The representatives based the new legal system on English common law as evolved from the Magna Carta. The convention proposed a government consisting of a judicial, legislative, and executive branch as outlined in the Constitution. The Bill of Rights in the Constitution is clearly based upon the Magna Carta.

There are a few amendments in the Constitution that are of great interest to the contractor. The Fourth Amendment prohibits unreasonable searches and guarantees the right of the people to be secure in their person and homes. This amendment is of great importance to inspection departments of localities regarding how an inspection is conducted. The Fifth Amendment guarantees due process of law. This means that the government must follow a legal procedure to ensure the rights of an individual. The Tenth Amendment limits the federal power to only what is delegated to it in the Constitution and reserves the rest for the states and the people.

UNDERSTANDING LAWS AND REGULATIONS

States have all the powers not reserved by the federal government, but the Constitution is silent regarding local jurisdictions. The delegation of powers from the state to local governments is dependent on the state constitution. This allowed some cities to operate as independent entities, which resulted in a series of problems and scandals in the 19th century requiring a limit on powers. An interpretation of the control of powers is outlined in a doctrine written in 1868 called Dillon's Rule. Judge John Dillon of Iowa wrote that the power of local jurisdictions was limited to those granted to them by the state. This doctrine, upheld by the Supreme Court in 1903, places great control by the state over the activities of municipalities. In a Dillon Rule state, building codes are based on state regulations and may not be amended by localities other than for geographic conditions.

The other type of delegation of authority is Home Rule, in which cities act in any capacity needed to fulfill their function. A contractor operating in a Home Rule state may find differing laws relating to the practice of their trade in each jurisdiction.

Adoption of Law

A law cannot be adopted until it has gone through a lengthy legal process. The typical process begins with a citizen voicing a concern about some action occurring in the state that can only be rectified by enacting a law. A legislator then drafts a bill and introduces the bill to the legislature. The bill goes to a committee who conducts a public hearing process where citizens may comment. The bill is then heard by both bodies of the legislature, the House of Representatives and the Senate, who may amend the bill, schedule it for further hearings, or reject it. If it is approved by both houses, the bill goes to the governor who may sign it into law, amend it, and send it back to the Senate, or veto it.

Composition of Law

Most of the laws that affect contractors are fairly straightforward and written in a standard format. The format is as follows:

- Definitions that clearly state who is affected by this law.
- The reason for the law and who or what it applies to as well as who will enforce the law.
- Exemptions that define who or what do not have to comply with the law.
- Content that clearly states the requirements of what is regulated and processes for compliance.

Composition of Regulation

Regulations are written to make the law into a workable plan for the enforcing authority. For example, a law may be written that requires all contractors to be licensed by a certain date. Regulations are then written by the enforcing agency that clearly spell out how this licensing will be implemented. Regulations follow the same format as a law but provide much more detail. Ordinances by city government follow this same format.

Finding a Particular Law

Contractors who are looking for a particular law subject are advised to first attempt an Internet search. Most states have an online legislative service that publishes all the laws and regulations of the state. Some municipalities also have this service. The laws have an index by subject area that lists either a page or law number. If it is a law number, it begins with a special character "§" which stands for "section." The number immediately following the symbol is the title, or a broad subdivision of law, and then the number following that is the particular paragraph. A section is a numbered paragraph and is the smallest distinct subdivision of law. For example, looking for an item in the index related to the naming of a business may produce the entry shown in Figure 1.1 on the facing page.

This tells the reader that there is a provision of law governing DBA or "doing business as" and there are several paragraphs indicated by including two section symbols. The laws are found in the body of law under Title 59 of the code and the particular paragraphs are 69 through 76.

For states that do not have an Internet publishing service, the task is a bit more complicated. The local library may have a legal reference section where books can be read but not checked out. The state or commonwealth attorney's office and the city attorney's office also have the books and a cooperative staff person may assist in your search.

Tips for Reading Law

Reading all of the law may be of interest, but if a particular item must be found in a hurry, such as during an exam, first go to the index and find the particular topic in question. Then go to the indicated page and look for a special target word that would be pertinent to the search and skim down the paragraph. For example, if you are trying to find out whom to register an assumed name with, target words could be City Registrar or County Clerk because these agencies are typically charged with the task. One can skip over the details in the law about time frames, fees, and required addresses of applicants, which clutter the search and are sure to be detailed in subsequent paragraphs. Once the target word is found, back up to the beginning of the sentence and start reading. Be advised that at times, regulations can have some very long sentences.

FIGURE 1.1
Names of Parts of Law

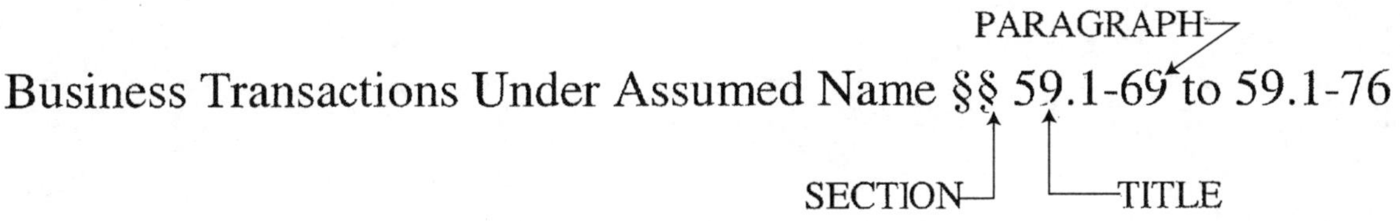

PARAGRAPH

Business Transactions Under Assumed Name §§ 59.1-69 to 59.1-76

SECTION   TITLE

§ 59.1-69. Certificate required of person, partnership, limited liability company or corporation transacting business under assumed name.

A. No person, partnership, limited liability company or corporation shall conduct or transact business in this Commonwealth under any assumed or fictitious name unless such person, partnership, limited liability company or corporation shall sign and acknowledge a certificate setting forth the name under which such business is to be conducted or transacted, and the names of each person, partnership, limited liability company or corporation owning the same, with their respective post-office and residence addresses (and, (i) when the partnership or limited liability company is a foreign limited partnership or limited liability company, the date of the certificate of registration to transact business in this Commonwealth issued to it by the State Corporation Commission, or (ii) when the corporation is a foreign corporation, the date of the certificate of authority to transact business in this Commonwealth issued to it by the State Corporation Commission), and file the same in the office of the clerk of the court in which deeds are recorded in the county or city wherein the business is to be conducted.

B. No person, partnership, limited liability company or corporation shall use an assumed or fictitious name in the conduct of its business to intentionally misrepresent the geographic origin or location of any such person or entity.

C. The clerk with whom the certificate is filed shall keep a book in which all such certificates shall be recorded, with their date of record, and shall keep a register in which shall be entered in alphabetical order the name under which every such business is conducted and the names of every person owning the same. The clerk shall be entitled to a fee of ten dollars for filing and recording such certificate and entering such names. No license shall be issued by the Commissioner of the Revenue until the certificate has been made and filed in the clerk's office and evidence of same produced before him.

STARTING A BUSINESS IN VIRGINIA

E very state has its own requirements for operating businesses within that state, particularly for contracting. This chapter provides basic information about how to start a business in Virginia and how to obtain licensing. It also identifies exceptions for contractors operating within Virginia and resources available to contractors just starting out.

More information about starting a business in Virginia can be found on the Virginia Department of Business Assistance Web site at *www.dba.state.va.us/*. A listing of useful Virginia government Web sites is provided at the end of this chapter. (See Table 2-1.)

CONTRACTOR LICENSING

Virginia requires a contractor license for anyone who wishes to work as a contractor on jobs valued at greater than $1,000; however, if the contracting work is for the purpose of landscape irrigation or the construction of a water well, the contractor must be licensed regardless of the contract amount. Detailed information regarding license classifications and licensure requirements are located in Chapter 3, Contractor Requirements.

Applications and information about licensing and license requirements can be downloaded from the Department of Professional and Occupational Regulation Web site or by contacting them at:

Department of Professional and Occupational Regulation
9960 Mayland Drive, Suite 400
Richmond, VA 23233
(804) 367-8500
www.dpor.virginia.gov

BUSINESS RULES

The first step in establishing a contracting business is to decide on the business type under which the company will operate. Business types include sole proprietorships, partnerships, corporations, and subchapter S corporations. Each business type has advantages and disadvantages. For example, a sole proprietorship is easy to establish but has great personal liability for the contractor. A corporation is more difficult to establish, but provides partners with protection from liability. There are no restrictions in Virginia as to which business entity may be licensed.

Once a business type is selected, there are different steps that must be taken depending on the type selected. The business must be locally registered, a name must be selected, the corporation must be registered, and the employer must be registered.

Local Business Registration

Localities may require local business license registration and may also require special use permits. For example, adding a home office to a home in a residential neighborhood or converting a building from one use to another, such as a factory changed to apartments, may require a special use permit. It is recommended that the building, zoning, and revenue offices and the clerk of the court be contacted to ensure that all appropriate permits and license requirements are met.

Even if the company registers with the state, there may be additional local registration requirements. The Virginia Counties Online Web site can help determine if the business needs any additional permits to operate. (*www.vaco.org/*)

Fictitious Name

Any person, partnership, limited liability company, or corporation may transact business under an assumed or fictitious name by filing an assumed name certificate with the clerk of the circuit court of the county or city where the business will be located. The filing fee is $10. A company that operates under a fictitious name is also commonly referred to as a "Doing Business As" or DBA.

An assumed name certificate form can be downloaded from *www.courts.state.va.us/forms/circuit/cc_1050_1250.pdf.*

Corporate Registration

A company incorporating in Virginia must file articles of incorporation with the State Corporation Commission and pay charter and filing fees. The charter fee is $50 for every 25,000 shares of stock or fraction thereof up to 1,000,000 shares and $2,500 for more than 1,000,000 shares of stock. The charter fee for corporations without stock is $50. The filing fee for filing articles of incorporation is $25. When forming any type of corporation, always seek appropriate legal counsel.

Authority to Transact Business in Virginia.

A corporation incorporated outside Virginia must complete an Application for a Certificate of Authority to Transact Business in Virginia, and file it with the State Corporation Commission (SCC). The filing fee is $25.

An entrance fee is also charged to foreign corporations. The entrance fee for a stock corporation is based on the number of authorized shares of stock shown in the charter. The fee is $50 for every 25,000 shares of stock or fraction thereof up to 1,000,000 shares and $2,500 for more than 1,000,000 shares of stock. A foreign corporation organized without capital stock pays an entrance fee of $50.

Annual Registration. The annual registration fee for a stock corporation is based on the number of authorized shares of stock shown in the charter. The fee is $100 for 5,000 or fewer shares of stock, plus $30 for each additional 5,000 shares or fraction thereof, to a maximum fee of $1,700. Corporations without capital stock pay an annual registration fee of $25. For additional information, contact:

> State Corporation Commission
> Clerk's Office
> Post Office Box 1197
> Richmond, Virginia 23218-1197
> (804) 371-9733
> *www.scc.virginia.gov*

CHAPTER 2
Starting a Business
in Virginia

Non-Corporate Registration

Limited partnerships must file a certificate of limited partnership with the State Corporation Commission. Limited liability companies must also file articles of organization with the State Corporation Commission. The filing fee is $100. The annual registration fee is $50.

Sole proprietors are not required to register with the State Corporation Commission. The only registration required is to file the necessary forms for doing business under an assumed name and to register with the Department of Taxation. General partnerships are not required to file any organizational documents, other than a DBA or a local business registration, and registration with the Department of Taxation.

Employer Registration

All companies doing business in Virginia must register with the Virginia Department of Taxation. All businesses must obtain an employer identification number (EIN) from the Internal Revenue Service to use as a taxpayer identification number.

TAXES

New employers in Virginia are required to pay Virginia unemployment tax at a rate of 2.92 percent to 6.62 percent on the first $8,000 of earnings. The Virginia Department of Taxation will notify the business of the rate it is required to pay. New businesses will typically be charged at the lowest rate while foreign businesses will be charged at the maximum rate.

LABOR LAWS

All employers must comply with state and federal labor laws. Refer to Chapter 6 Virginia Labor Laws for more specific information. More information can also be obtained from the Virginia Department of Labor and Industry Web site.

Workers' Compensation

Virginia law requires workers' compensation insurance be carried by any company with three or more employees. Workers' compensation rules are detailed further in Chapter 6 Virginia Labor Laws.

SAFETY

Virginia has established the Virginia Occupational Safety and Health (VOSH) program to maintain, enforce, and train businesses on federal OSHA standards as well as Virginia OSHA standards. Information about VOSH can be found at the Virginia Department of Labor and Industry Web site at *www.dli.state.va.us/index .html*.

TABLE 2.1

Virginia Government Web Sites

Agency	Topic	Web Site Address
Virginia Department of Business Assistance	Starting a Business	*www.dba.state.va.us/*
Department of Professional and Occupational Regulations	Licensing Requirements	*www.state.va.us/dpor/* *www.dpor.virginia.gov*
Virginia Counties Online	Local Business Registration	*www.vaco.org/*
State Corporation Commission	Corporation Registration	*www.state.va.us/scc* *www.scc.virginia.gov*
Virginia Department of Labor and Industry	Labor Laws and Safety	*www.dli.state.va.us/index.html*

CHAPTER 3

VIRGINIA CONTRACTOR REQUIREMENTS

This chapter provides information for contractors about the Virginia licensing process, maintenance of information supplied to the Board for Contractors, contract requirements, and the Transaction Recovery Fund.

DEFINITIONS

contractor Any person who, for monetary consideration, performs or manages the construction, removal, repair, or improvement of any building or structure.

full-time employee An employee who works a minimum of 30 hours a week.

CONTRACTOR LICENSING

Licensing in Virginia is through the Department of Professional and Occupational Regulation (DPOR). Information about a Virginia contractor's license can be obtained by contacting DPOR at:

Board for Contractor's Licensing Section
Department of Occupational Regulation
9960 Mayland Drive, Suite 400
Richmond, VA 23233
(804) 367-8500
www.dpor.virginia.gov

All pertinent laws may be found in the Code of Virginia, Title 54.1, Chapter 11 Contractor, Article 1 Regulation of Contractors (CoV) and the Virginia Administrative Code, Contractor Regulations (VAC) at the Virginia General Assembly Legislative Information System: *http://leg1.state.va.us/lis.htm* or at the end of this chapter.

Contracting in Virginia encompasses a wide scope of tasks—everything from pool installation to kitchen remodeling to building new homes and highrises. Essentially, a person who writes a contract for an amount over $1,000 needs to be a licensed contractor.

Board for Contractors

The board consists of 13 members who represent the entire spectrum of the contracting profession in Virginia. They have the authority to write regulations and review and issue licenses and renewals. The board has the power to require remedial education and to suspend, revoke, or deny the license of any contractor who has violated any regulation (CoV 54.1-1110).

License Classifications

Virginia has three license classifications for contractors: Class C, Class B, and Class A. All contractor classes are authorized to perform and manage construction, repairs, or improvements to any building or structure if they are licensed in accordance with certain specialties.

All license applicants must complete the required eight-hour pre-license course, fill out a license application, and submit it to DPOR. Information that must be included with the application for each license class is disclosure of:

- all misdemeanor convictions within the past three years
- any felony convictions
- any outstanding tax obligations, or past due debts within the last five years

Class C Contractor Requirements:

- The single contract or project amount for a Class C contractor is limited to amounts that are greater than $1,000 but less than $7,500 and the contract total for a 12-month period is less than $150,000 (CoV 54.1-1100).
- The Class C contractor is not required to take a state exam but must submit an application to DPOR in order to obtain a license.
- A minimum of two years of experience, verified by three individuals, is needed.

Class B Contractor Requirements:

- The single contract or project amount for a Class B contractor is limited to $7,500 or more, but less than $120,000, and the contract total for a 12-month period is less than $750,000 (CoV 54.1-1100).
- The applicant must pass the Virginia and General portions of the contractor exam.
- A minimum of three years of experience is needed.
- The company's net worth must be at least $15,000.

Class A Contractor Requirements:

- The single contract or project amount for a Class A contractor can exceed $120,000 and the contract total may be more than $750,000 (CoV 54.1-1100).

- The applicant must pass the Virginia, General, and Advanced portions of the contractor exam.

- A minimum of five years of experience, verified by three individuals, is needed.

- The company's net worth must be at least $45,000.

A contractor may perform repairs to a dwelling if they are licensed as a home improvement contractor, but may not engage in new construction or repairs that affect structural elements outside the building footprint, other than decks. In order to work on new construction or structural changes, a contractor must be licensed in any one of the A, B, or C categories and also have the designation of building contractor (BLD contractor). There is an additional portion of the exam for the BLD.

License Application

A copy of the license application for a C, B, and A contractor is included at the end of this chapter. The form is downloadable from DPOR in Word format and text can be typed onto the form. A separate short form for a Class C contractor is available but not included in this manual.

Pre-License Education Course

Anyone seeking an A, B, or C license must take an eight-hour class approved by the Board for Contractors. A list of class providers is detailed on the DPOR Web site. If a contractor currently holds a license and is just changing the classification, it is not mandated to take this class; however, it is recommended that anyone with a question contact DPOR for a definitive answer.

Examination

Licenses are issued to companies, not individuals, and a Class A or Class B license application requires successful completion of the examination. The examination is taken by the "designated employee" who is either a full-time employee (30 hours a week) or a member of responsible management. Class C contractors are not required to take an examination; instead they just complete a license application.

Exceptions to Licensing

There are several instances when the work performed will not require a contractor license, such as a property owner building a house on their own property for their own use, or material suppliers dropping off material at a site. A person may perform work for family members without compensation. It is suggested that the law be read thoroughly before deciding that a license is not required and performing the work (CoV 54.1-1101).

License Renewal

Licenses expire two years from the last day of the month that they are issued (18VAC50-22-110). For example, if Builder Bob's license was issued on March 1, 2008, the license will expire on March 31, 2010. DPOR mails a notice of renewal to the licensee at the last known address of record.

To be eligible to renew a license, a contractor must submit an accepted form of payment, made payable to the Treasurer of Virginia, within 30 days of the license expiration date (18VAC50-22-130). DPOR considers the payment made on the day that the payment is received in the office. Contractors should track on their calendars when renewal is required and make sure that the renewal is completed prior to the expiration date. DPOR does not recognize the postmark as the date of payment.

Reinstatement Fees

Should a contractor fail to submit the renewal payment within 30 days of the license expiration date, a reinstatement fee is charged. A reinstatement fee is a late fee and can be significant (18VAC50-22-170). In the case of Builder Bob, if DPOR received the renewal fee on May 1, 2007, the contractor will need to pay a reinstatement fee as well as the renewal fees.

A contractor has one year to submit reinstatement fees from the date that the license expires. If a contractor fails to submit the reinstatement fees, a new application for license will be required (18VAC50-22-170).

DISCIPLINARY ACTIONS

A complaint against a contractor may be filed in writing with DPOR. The Compliance and Investigations Division of the department reviews complaints and determines whether there is legal standing to proceed. Complaints are subject to public disclosure. If there is probable cause to proceed, the complaint may be resolved or subjected to further investigation.

Action against the contractor may include remedial education, a fine, suspension or revocation of the license, or denial of license renewal. Criminal action may be taken if the individual or business is not licensed.

The department may offer mediation as a means of alternative dispute resolution regarding complaints against licensees. An individual or business cannot be required by DPOR to refund money, correct deficiencies, or provide other personal remedies or provide legal advice.

Penalty

A violation of the contractor regulations may incur fines of up to $500 per day per violation and is considered a Class 1 misdemeanor. The maximum monetary amount is limited to $2,500.

Transaction Recovery Fund

The transaction recovery fund was established for persons who have filed a claim in court for any improper or dishonest conduct, or gross negligence against a contractor. The suit must involve residential construction in which a judgment has been awarded but the judgment is not collectible (CoV 54.1-1120).

There are limitations imposed on the amount a person is able to recover. The maximum single claim awarded is $20,000. There is a provision for "aggregate claims" where there are multiple claims against the contractor and reimbursement is limited to $40,000 for all claims during a two-year period. These claims may also include any court costs and attorney's fees (CoV 54.1-1123).

Should a claim be paid out of the Transaction Recovery Fund, the contractor's license is revoked and will not be eligible for reinstatement until the amount of the claim has been repaid in full plus interest (CoV 54.1-1126).

CONTRACT REQUIREMENTS

Most regulatory problems experienced by contractors involve the contents of the contract. The regulations are specific regarding contract contents. A copy of the contract and all documents must be kept for 5 years. Following are the minimum standards for residential contracts (18VAC50-22-260):

- Consumer's name and address
- Description of the property and its location
- Description of the work
- Date the work is to begin and the estimated completion date
- Listing of specific materials and work to be performed that have been requested by the consumer
- Statement of the total cost of the contract and the amounts and schedule for progress payments, including a specific statement on the amount of the down payment
- Identification of drawings and specifications applicable to the project
- "Plain-language" exculpatory clause concerning events beyond the control of the contractor does not constitute abandonment
- Statement that delays caused by events beyond the control of the contractor do not constitute abandonment and are not included in calculating time frames for payment or performance
- Statement of assurance that the contractor will comply with all local requirements for building permits, inspection, and zoning
- Disclosure of the cancellation rights of all parties
- For contracts resulting from door-to-door solicitation, Virginia requires a signed acknowledgment by the consumer (owner) that said consumer has been provided with, read, and understands the right to cancel the contract
- Statement that any modification to the contract that changes the cost, materials, work to be performed, or estimated completion date must be in writing and signed by all parties
- Contractor's name, address, phone number, license number, and the classifications or services authorized under the license
- Signatures of the consumer and contractor, and the date
- Provide consumer a copy of the Statement of Consumer Protection

Statement of Consumer Protections

DPOR has prepared a summary sheet, Statement of Consumer Protections, that provides information a consumer should know before signing a contract. The form is required to be given to a homeowner for residential work and is available for downloading at the DPOR Web site. A copy of the form is included at the end of this chapter.

Warranty

Virginia requires a warranty on new construction for a period of one year from the date of completion.

§55-70.1. Implied warranties on new homes

A. In every contract for the sale of a new dwelling, the vendor shall be held to warrant to the vendee that, at the time of the transfer of record title or the vendee's taking possession, whichever occurs first, the dwelling with all its fixtures is, to the best of the actual knowledge of the vendor or his agents, sufficiently (i) free from structural defects, so as to pass without objection in the trade, and (ii) constructed in a workmanlike manner, so as to pass without objection in the trade.

B. In addition, in every contract for the sale of a new dwelling, the vendor, if he is in the business of building or selling such dwellings, shall be held to warrant to the vendee that, at the time of transfer of record title or the vendee's taking possession, whichever occurs first, the dwelling together with all its fixtures is sufficiently (i) free from structural defects, so as to pass without objection in the trade, (ii) constructed in a workmanlike manner, so as to pass without objection in the trade, and (iii) fit for habitation.

C. The above warranties implied in the contract for sale shall be held to survive the transfer of title. Such warranties are in addition to, and not in lieu of, any other express or implied warranties pertaining to the dwelling, its materials or fixtures. A contract for sale may waive, modify or exclude any or all express and implied warranties and sell a new home "as is" only if the words used to waive, modify or exclude such warranties are conspicuous (as defined by subdivision (10) of §8.1A-201), set forth on the face of such contract in capital letters which are at least two points larger than the other type in the contract and only if the words used to waive, modify or exclude the warranties state with specificity the warranty or warranties that are being waived, modified or excluded. If all warranties are waived or excluded, a contract must specifically set forth in capital letters which are at least two points larger than the other type in the contract that the dwelling is being sold "as is."

D. If there is a breach of warranty under this section, the vendee, or his heirs or personal representatives in case of his death, shall have a cause of action against his vendor for damages; provided, however, for any defect discovered after July 1, 2002, such vendee shall first provide the vendor, by registered or certified mail at his last known address, a written notice stating the nature of the warranty claim. After such notice, the vendor shall have a reasonable period of time, not to exceed six months, to cure the defect that is the subject of the warranty claim.

E. The warranty shall extend for a period of one year from the date of transfer of record title or the vendee's taking possession, whichever occurs first, except that the warranty pursuant to subdivision (i) of subsection B for the foundation of new dwellings shall extend for a period of five years from the date of transfer of record title or the vendee's taking possession, whichever occurs first. Any action for its breach shall be brought within two years after the breach thereof. As used in this section, the term "new dwelling" shall mean a dwelling or house which has not previously been occupied for a period of more than 60 days by anyone other than the vendor or the vendee or which has not been occupied by the original vendor or subsequent vendor for a cumulative period of more than 12 months excluding dwellings constructed solely for lease. The term "new dwelling" shall not include a condominium or condominium units created pursuant to Chapter 4.2 (§55-79.39 et seq.) of this title.

F. The term "structural defects," as used in this section, shall mean a defect or defects that reduce the stability or safety of the structure below accepted standards or that restrict the normal use thereof.

G. In the case of new dwellings where fire-retardant treated plywood sheathing or other roof sheathing materials are used in lieu of fire-retardant treated plywood the vendor shall be deemed to have assigned the manufacturer's warranty, at settlement, to the vendee. The vendee shall have a direct cause of action against the manufacturer of such roof sheathing for any breach of such warranty. To the extent any such manufacturer's warranty purports to limit the right of third parties or prohibit assignment, said provision shall be unenforceable and of no effect.

Larceny

If a contractor accepts a full or partial payment or advance and then does not perform the work or return the money, this is classified as larceny.

§18.2-200.1 Failure to perform promise for construction, etc., in return for advances

If any person obtain from another an advance of money, merchandise or other thing, of value, with fraudulent intent, upon a promise to perform construction, removal, repair or improvement of any building or structure permanently annexed to real property, or any other improvements to such real property, including horticulture, nursery or forest products, and fail or refuse to perform such promise, and also fail to substantially make good such advance, he shall be deemed guilty of the larceny of such money, merchandise or other thing if he fails to return such advance within fifteen days of a request to do so sent by certified mail, return receipt requested, to his last known address or the address listed in the contract.

{Petit Larceny}
§19.2-290. Conviction of petit larceny though thing stolen is worth more than $200
In a prosecution for petit larceny, though the thing stolen be of the value of $200 or more, the jury may find the accused guilty; and upon a conviction under this section or §19.2-289 the accused shall be sentenced for petit larceny.

{Petit Larceny – how punished} §18.2-96 As a Class 1 misdemeanor {$500 fine}
§18.2-95. Grand larceny defined; how punished
Any person who (i) commits larceny from the person of another of money or other thing of value of $5 or more, (ii) commits simple larceny not from the person of another of goods and chattels of the value of $200 or more, or (iii) commits simple larceny not from the person of another of any firearm, regardless of the firearm's value, shall be guilty of grand larceny, punishable by imprisonment in a state correctional facility for not less than one nor more than twenty years or, in the discretion of the jury or court trying the case without a jury, be confined in jail for a period not exceeding twelve months or fined not more than $2,500, either or both.

CODE OF VIRGINIA, TITLE 54.1 CHAPTER 11—CONTRACTORS
ARTICLE 1, REGULATION OF CONTRACTORS

§54.1-1100. Definitions

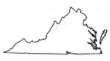

As used in this chapter, unless the context requires a different meaning:

"Board" means the Board for Contractors.

"Class A contractors" perform or manage construction, removal, repair, or improvements when (i) the total value referred to in a single contract or project is $120,000 or more, or (ii) the total value of all such construction, removal, repair, or improvements undertaken by such person within any 12-month period is $750,000 or more.

"Class B contractors" perform or manage construction, removal, repair, or improvements when (i) the total value referred to in a single contract or project is $7,500 or more, but less than $120,000, or (ii) the total value of all such construction, removal, repair, or improvements undertaken by such person within any 12-month period is $150,000 or more, but less than $750,000.

"Class C contractors" perform or manage construction, removal, repair, or improvements when (i) the total value referred to in a single contract or project is over $1,000 but less than $7,500, or (ii) the total value of all such construction, removal, repair, or improvements undertaken by such person within any 12-month period is less than $150,000. The Board shall require a master tradesmen license as a condition of licensure for electrical, plumbing and heating, ventilation and air conditioning contractors.

"Contractor" means any person, that for a fixed price, commission, fee, or percentage undertakes to bid upon, or accepts, or offers to accept, orders or contracts for performing, managing, or superintending in whole or in part, the construction, removal, repair or improvement of any building or structure permanently annexed to real property owned, controlled, or leased by him or another person or any other improvements to such real property.

"Department" means the Department of Professional and Occupational Regulation.

"Designated employee" means the contractor's full-time employee, or a member of the contractor's responsible management, who is at least 18 years of age and who has successfully completed the oral or written examination required by the Board on behalf of the contractor.

"Director" means the Director of the Department of Professional and Occupational Regulation.

"Owner-developer" means any person who, for a third party purchaser, orders or supervises the construction, removal, repair, or improvement of any building or structure permanently annexed to real property owned, controlled, or leased by the owner-developer, or any other improvement to such property and who contracts with a person licensed in accordance with this chapter for the work undertaken.

"Person" means any individual, firm, corporation, association, partnership, joint venture, or other legal entity.

"Value" means fair market value. When improvements are performed or supervised by a contractor, the contract price shall be prima facie evidence of value.

§54.1-1101. Exemptions; failure to obtain certificate of occupancy; penalties

A. The provisions of this chapter shall not apply to:
1. Any governmental agency performing work with its own forces;
2. Work bid upon or undertaken for the armed services of the United States under the Armed Services Procurement Act;

3. Work bid upon or undertaken for the United States government on land under the exclusive jurisdiction of the federal government either by statute or deed of cession;

4. Work bid upon or undertaken for the Department of Transportation on the construction, reconstruction, repair, or improvement of any highway or bridge;

5. Any other persons who may be specifically excluded by other laws but only to such an extent as such laws provide;

6. Any material supplier who renders advice concerning use of products sold and who does not provide construction or installation services;

7. Any person who performs or supervises the construction, removal, repair, or improvement of no more than one primary residence owned by him and for his own use during any 24-month period;

8. Any person who performs or supervises the construction, removal, repair, or improvement of a house upon his own real property as a bona fide gift to a member of his immediate family provided such member lives in the house. For purposes of this section, "immediate family" includes one's mother, father, son, daughter, brother, sister, grandchild, grandparent, mother-in-law, and father-in-law;

9. Any person who performs or supervises the repair or improvement of industrial or manufacturing facilities, or a commercial or retail building, for his own use;

10. Any person who performs or supervises the repair or improvement of residential dwelling units owned by him that are subject to the Virginia Residential Landlord and Tenant Act (§55-248.2 et seq.); and

11. Any owner-developer, provided that any third party purchaser is made a third party beneficiary to the contract between the owner-developer and a licensed contractor whereby the contractor's obligation to perform the contract extends to both the owner-developer and the third party; and

12. Work undertaken by students as part of a career and technical education project as defined in §22.1-228 established by any school board in accordance with Article 5 (§22.1-228 et seq.) of Chapter 13 of Title 22.1 for the construction of portable classrooms or single-family homes.

All other contractors performing work for any government or for any governmental agency are subject to the provisions of this chapter and are required to be licensed as provided herein.

B. Any person who is exempt from the provisions of this chapter as a result of subdivisions 7, 10, 11, or 12 of subsection A shall obtain a certificate of occupancy for any building constructed, repaired, or improved by him prior to conveying such property to a third party purchaser, unless such purchaser has acknowledged in writing that no certificate of occupancy has been issued and that such purchaser consents to acquire the property without a certificate of occupancy.

C. Any person who is exempt from the provisions of this chapter as a result of subdivisions 7, 8, 9, 10, 11, or 12 of subsection A shall comply with the provisions of the Uniform Statewide Building Code (§36-97 et seq.).

D. Any person who violates the provisions of subsections B or C shall be guilty of a Class 1 misdemeanor. The third or any subsequent conviction of violating subsections B or C during a 36-month period shall constitute a Class 6 felony.

§54.1-1102. Board for Contractors membership; offices; meetings; seal; record

A. The Board for Contractors shall be composed of 13 members as follows: one member shall be a licensed Class A general contractor; the larger part of the business of

Code of Virginia
Title 54

one member shall be the construction of utilities; the larger part of the business of one member shall be the construction of commercial and industrial buildings; the larger part of the business of one member shall be the construction of single-family residences; the larger part of the business of one member shall be the construction of home improvements; one member shall be a subcontractor as generally regarded in the construction industry; one member shall be in the business of sales of construction materials and supplies; one member shall be a local building official; one member shall be a licensed plumbing contractor; one member shall be a licensed electrical contractor; one member shall be a licensed heating, ventilation and air conditioning contractor; and two members shall be citizen members. The terms of the Board members shall be four years.

The Board shall meet at least four times each year, once in January, April, July, and October, and at such other times as may be deemed necessary. Annually, the Board shall elect from its membership a chairman and a vice-chairman to serve for a one-year term. Seven members of the Board shall constitute a quorum.

The Board shall promulgate regulations not inconsistent with statute necessary for the licensure of contractors and tradesmen and the certification of backflow prevention device workers, and for the relicensure of contractors and tradesmen and for the recertification of backflow prevention device workers, after license or certificate suspension or revocation. The Board shall include in its regulations a requirement that as a condition for initial licensure as a contractor, the designated employee or a member of the responsible management personnel of the contractor shall have successfully completed a Board-approved basic business course, which shall not exceed eight hours of classroom instruction.

The Board may adopt regulations requiring all Class A, B, and C residential contractors, excluding subcontractors to the contracting parties and those who engage in routine maintenance or service contracts, to use legible written contracts including the following terms and conditions:

1. General description of the work to be performed;
2. Fixed price or an estimate of the total cost of the work, the amounts and schedule of progress payments, a listing of specific materials requested by the consumer and the amount of down payment;
3. Estimates of time of commencement and completion of the work; and
4. Contractor's name, address, office telephone number, and license or certification number and class.

In transactions involving door-to-door solicitations, the Board may require that a statement of protections be provided by the contractor to the homeowner, consumer, or buyer, as the case may be.

The Board shall adopt a seal with the words "Board for Contractors, Commonwealth of Virginia." The Director shall have charge, care, and custody of the seal.

B. The Director shall maintain a record of the proceedings of the Board.

§54.1-1103. Necessity for license; requirements for water well drillers and landscape irrigation contractors; exemption

A. No person shall engage in, or offer to engage in, contracting work in the Commonwealth unless he has been licensed under the provisions of this chapter. The Board may waive any provision of this chapter for Habitat for Humanity, its local affiliates or subsidiaries, and any other nonprofit organization exempt from taxation under §501(c)(3) of the Internal Revenue Code (26 U.S.C. §501(c)(3)) for the purpose of constructing single-family dwellings that will be given to or sold below the appraised value to low-income persons. Prior to a joint venture engaging in, or offering to engage in, contracting work in the Commonwealth, (i) each contracting party of the joint venture shall be licensed under the provisions of this chapter or (ii) a license shall be obtained in the name of the joint venture under the provisions of this chapter.

B. Except as provided in §54.1-1117, the issuance of a license under the provisions of this chapter shall not entitle the holder to engage in any activity for which a special license is required by law.

C. When the contracting work is for the purpose of landscape irrigation or the construction of a water well as defined in §62.1-255, the contractor shall be licensed, regardless of the contract amount, as follows:

1. A Class C license is required when the total value referred to in a single contract or project is no more than $7,500, or the total value of all such water well or landscape irrigation contracts undertaken within any 12-month period is no more than $150,000;

2. A Class B license is required when the total value referred to in a single contract is $7,500 or more, but less than $120,000, or the total value of all such water well or landscape irrigation contracts undertaken within any 12-month period is $150,000 or more, but less than $750,000; and

3. A Class A license is required when the total value referred to in a single contract or project is $120,000 or more, or when the total value of all such water well or landscape irrigation contracts undertaken within any 12-month period is $750,000 or more.

D. Notwithstanding the other provisions of this section, an architect or professional engineer who is licensed pursuant to Chapter 4 (§54.1-400 et seq.) of this title shall not be required to be licensed or certified to engage in, or offer to engage in, contracting work or operate as an owner-developer in the Commonwealth in accordance with this chapter when bidding upon or negotiating design-build contracts or performing services other than construction services under a design-build contract. However, the construction services offered or rendered in connection with such contracts shall only be rendered by a contractor licensed or certified in accordance with this chapter.

E. Notwithstanding the other provisions of this section, any person licensed under the provisions of Article 4 (§9.1-138 et seq.) of Chapter 1 of Title 9.1 as a private security services business shall not be required to be licensed or certified to engage in, or offer to engage in, contracting work in the Commonwealth in accordance with this chapter when bidding upon or performing services to install, service, maintain, design, or consult in the design of any electronic security equipment as defined in §9.1-138 including but not limited to, low voltage cabling, network cabling, and computer or systems integration.

§54.1-1104. Register of applicants

The Director shall keep a register of all applicants showing their date of application, name, qualifications, place of business, place of residence, and whether such application was approved or refused. The books and register of the Board shall be prima facie evidence of all matters recorded therein.

§54.1-1105. Repealed by Acts 1991, c. 151

§54.1-1106. Application for Class A license; fees; examination; issuance

A. Any person desiring to be licensed as a Class A contractor shall file with the Department a written application on a form prescribed by the Board. The application shall be accompanied by a fee set by the Board pursuant to §54.1-201. The application shall contain the name, place of employment, and business address of the proposed designated employee, and information on the knowledge, skills, abilities, and financial position of the applicant. The Board shall determine whether the past performance record of the applicant, including his reputation for paying material bills and carrying out other contractual obligations, satisfies the purposes and intent of this chapter. The Board shall also determine whether the applicant has complied with the laws of the Commonwealth pertaining to the domestication of foreign corporations and all other laws affecting those engaged in the practice of contracting as set forth in this chapter. If the Board determines that sufficient questions or ambiguities exist in an individual applicant's presentation of his financial information, the Board may require the applicant to provide a balance sheet reviewed by a certified public accountant licensed in accordance with §54.1-4409. In addition, if the applicant is a sole proprietor, he shall furnish to the Board his name and address. If the applicant is a member of a partnership, he shall furnish to the Board the names and addresses of all of the general partners of the partnership. If the applicant is a member of an association, he shall furnish to the Board the names and addresses of all of the members of the association. If the applicant is a corporation, it shall furnish to the Board the names and addresses of all officers of the corporation. If the applicant is a joint venture, it shall furnish to the Board the names and addresses of (i) each member of the joint venture and (ii) any sole proprietor, general partner of any partnership, member of any association, or officer of any corporation who is a member of the joint venture. The applicant shall thereafter keep the Board advised of any changes in the above information.

B. If the application is satisfactory to the Board, the proposed designated employee shall be required by Board regulations to take an oral or written examination to determine his general knowledge of contracting, including the statutory and regulatory requirements governing contractors in the Commonwealth. If the proposed designated employee successfully completes the examination and the applicant meets or exceeds the other entry criteria established by Board regulations, a Class A contractor license shall be issued to the applicant. The license shall permit the applicant to engage in contracting only so long as the designated employee is in the full-time employment of the contractor or is a member of the contractor's responsible management. No examination shall be required where the licensed Class A contractor changes his form of business entity provided he is in good standing with the Board. In the event the designated employee leaves the full-time employ of the licensed contractor or is no longer a member of the contractor's responsible management, no additional examination shall be required of such designated employee, except in accordance with §54.1-1110.1, and the contractor shall within 90 days of that departure provide to the Board the name of the new designated employee.

C. The Board may grant a Class A license in any of the following classifications: (i) building contractor, (ii) highway/heavy contractor, (iii) electrical contractor, (iv) plumbing contractor, (v) heating, ventilation, and air conditioning contractor, and (vi) specialty contractor.

§54.1-1106.1. Violations of certain State Board of Health regulations; penalty

The Board for Contractors shall consider violations of regulations of the State Board of Health relating to water wells as violations of this chapter, punishable by a fine of not more than $1,000 or suspension or revocation of license. No contractor shall be subject to the monetary penalties provided by this section if he has been assessed a civil penalty for such violation pursuant to §32.1-27.

§§54.1-1107, 54.1-1107.1. Repealed by Acts 1990, c. 911, effective January 1, 1991

§54.1-1108. Application for Class B license; fees; examination; issuance

A. Any person desiring to be licensed as a Class B contractor shall file with the Department a written application on a form prescribed by the Board. The application shall be accompanied by a fee set by the Board pursuant to §54.1-201. The application shall contain the name, place of employment, and business address of the proposed designated employee; information on the knowledge, skills, abilities, and financial position of the applicant; and evidence of holding a current local license pursuant to local ordinances adopted pursuant to §54.1-1117. The Board shall determine whether the past performance record of the applicant, including his reputation for paying material bills and carrying out other contractual obligations, satisfies the purpose and intent of this chapter. The Board shall also determine whether the applicant has complied with the laws of the Commonwealth pertaining to the domestication of foreign corporations and all other laws affecting those engaged in the practice of contracting as set forth in this chapter. In addition, if the applicant is a sole proprietor, he shall furnish to the Board his name and address. If the applicant is a member of a partnership, he shall furnish to the Board the names and addresses of all of the general partners of that partnership. If the applicant is a member of an association, he shall furnish to the Board the names and addresses of all of the members of the association. If the applicant is a corporation, it shall furnish to the Board the name and address of all officers of the corporation. If the applicant is a joint venture, it shall furnish to the Board the names and addresses of (i) each member of the joint venture and (ii) any sole proprietor, general partner of any partnership, member of any association, or officer of any corporation who is a member of the joint venture. The applicant shall thereafter keep the Board advised of any changes in the above information.

B. If the application is satisfactory to the Board, the proposed designated employee shall be required by Board regulations to take an oral or written examination to determine his general knowledge of contracting, including the statutory and regulatory requirements governing contractors in the Commonwealth. If the proposed designated employee successfully completes the examination and the applicant meets or exceeds the other entry criteria established by Board regulations, a Class B contractor license shall be issued to the applicant. The license shall permit the applicant to engage in contracting only so long as the designated employee is in the full-time employment of the contractor and only in the counties, cities, and towns where such person has complied with all local licensing requirements and for the type of work to be performed. No examination shall be required where the licensed Class B contractor changes his form of business entity provided he is in good standing with the Board. In the event the designated employee leaves the full-time employ of the licensed contractor, no additional examination shall be required of such designated employee, except in accordance with §54.1-1110.1, and the contractor shall within 90 days of that departure provide to the Board the name of the new designated employee.

C. The Board may grant a Class B license in any of the following classifications: (i) building contractor, (ii) highway/heavy contractor, (iii) electrical contractor, (iv) plumbing contractor, (v) HVAC contractor, and (vi) specialty contractor.

§54.1-1108.1. Waiver of examination; designated employee

Any Class A contractor licensed in the Commonwealth of Virginia prior to January 1, 1991, and in business on December 31, 1990, shall provide to the Board in writing the name of one full-time employee or member of the contractor's responsible management who is at least 18 years of age and that employee shall be deemed to have fulfilled the requirement for examination in §54.1-1106, so long as he remains a full-time employee of the contractor or remains a member of the contractor's responsible management. The designated employee shall not be required to take an examination if the Class A contractor changes his form of business entity and is in good standing with the Board. Upon his leaving the employ of the contractor or his leaving as a member of the contractor's responsible management, the contractor shall name another full-time employee or member of the contractor's responsible management in accordance with §54.1-1106.

Any Class B contractor registered in the Commonwealth prior to January 1, 1991, and in business on December 31, 1990, shall, within its current period of registration, provide on a form prescribed by the Board satisfactory information on the financial position, and knowledge, skills and abilities of the registered firm; and the name of a full-time employee who is at least 18 years of age and that employee shall be deemed to have fulfilled the requirement for examination in §54.1-1108, so long as he remains a full-time employee of the contractor. The designated employee shall not be required to take an examination if the Class B contractor changes his form of business entity and is in good standing with the Board. If such employee leaves the employ of the contractor, the contractor shall name another full-time employee in accordance with §54.1-1108.

§54.1-1108.2. Application for Class C license; fees; issuance

A. Any person desiring to be licensed as a Class C contractor shall file with the Department a written application on a form prescribed by the Board. The application shall be accompanied by a fee set by the Board pursuant to §54.1-201. The application shall contain information concerning the name, location, nature, and operation of the business, and information demonstrating that the applicant possesses the character and minimum skills to properly engage in the occupation of contracting.

B. The Board may grant a Class C license in any of the following classifications: (i) building contractor, (ii) highway/heavy contractor, (iii) electrical contractor, (iv) plumbing contractor, (v) heating, ventilation, and air conditioning contractor, and (vi) specialty contractor.

§54.1-1109. Expiration and renewal of license or certificate

A license or certificate issued pursuant to this chapter shall expire as provided in Board regulations. Application for renewal of a license or certificate may be made as provided by Board regulations. The application shall be accompanied by a fee set by the Board pursuant to §54.1-201.

§54.1-1110. Grounds for denial or revocation of license or certificate

The Board shall have the power to require remedial education, suspend, revoke, or deny renewal of the license or certificate of any contractor who is found to be in violation of the statutes or regulations governing the practice of licensed or certified contractors in the Commonwealth.

The Board may suspend, revoke, or deny renewal of an existing license or certificate, or refuse to issue a license or certificate, to any contractor who is shown to have a substantial identity of interest with a contractor whose license or certificate has been revoked or not renewed by the Board. A substantial identity of interest includes but is not limited to (i) a controlling financial interest by the individual or corporate principals of the contractor whose license or certificate has been revoked or nonrenewed, (ii) substantially identical principals or officers, or (iii) the same designated employee as the contractor whose license or certificate has been revoked or not renewed by the Board.

Additionally, the Board may suspend, revoke or deny renewal of an existing license or certificate, or refuse to issue a license or certificate to any contractor who violates the provisions of Chapter 5 (§60.2-500 et seq.) of Title 60.2 and Chapter 8 (§65.2-800 et seq.) of Title 65.2.

Any person whose license is suspended or revoked by the Board shall not be eligible for a license or certificate under any circumstances or under any name, except as provided by regulations of the Board pursuant to §54.1-1102.

§54.1-1110.1. Re-examination of designated employee

The Board shall have the power to require remedial education or may require a designated employee to retake the examination required by this chapter, in any case where the conduct of the designated employee, while in the employ of a licensed Class A or Class B contractor, has resulted in any disciplinary action by the Board against such contractor.

§54.1-1111. Prerequisites to obtaining building, etc., permit

Any person applying to the building inspector or any other authority of a county, city, or town in this Commonwealth, charged with the duty of issuing building or other permits for the construction of any building, highway, sewer, or structure, or any removal, grading, or improvement shall furnish prior to the issuance of the permit, either (i) satisfactory proof to such inspector or authority that he is duly licensed or certified under the terms of this chapter to carry out or superintend the same, or (ii) file a written statement, supported by an affidavit, that he is not subject to licensure or certification as a contractor or subcontractor pursuant to this chapter. The applicant shall also furnish satisfactory proof that the taxes or license fees required by any county, city, or town have been paid so as to be qualified to bid upon or contract for the work for which the permit has been applied.

It shall be unlawful for the building inspector or other authority to issue or allow the issuance of such permits unless the applicant has furnished his license or certificate number issued pursuant to this chapter or evidence of being exempt from the provisions of this chapter.

The building inspector, or other such authority, violating the terms of this section shall be guilty of a Class 3 misdemeanor.

§54.1-1112. Invitations to bid and specifications to refer to law

All architects and engineers preparing plans and specifications for work to be contracted in Virginia shall include in their invitations to the bidder and in their specifications a reference to this chapter so as to convey to the invited bidder prior to the consideration of the bid (i) whether such person is a resident or nonresident of the Commonwealth, (ii) whether the proper license or certificate has been issued to the bidder, and (iii) the information required of the bidder to show evidence of proper licensure or certification under the provisions of this chapter.

§54.1-1113. Nonresident bidders to appoint statutory agent for service of process

Before any nonresident person or any foreign corporation bids on any work in this Commonwealth, the nonresident person or foreign corporation, by written power of attorney, shall appoint the Director as his agent upon whom all lawful process against or notice to such nonresident person or foreign corporation may be served, and authorize the Director to enter an appearance on his behalf. Upon the filing of the power of attorney the provisions of §§13.1-763 through 13.1-766, with reference to service of process and notice, and judgments, decrees, and orders, shall be applicable as to such nonresident person or foreign corporation.

§54.1-1114. Filing and hearing of charges

Any person may file complaints against any contractor licensed or certified pursuant to this chapter. The Director shall investigate complaints and the Board may take appropriate disciplinary action if warranted. Disciplinary proceedings shall be conducted in accordance with the Administrative Process Act (§2.2-4000 et seq.). The Board shall immediately notify the Director and the clerk and building official of each city, county, or town in the Commonwealth of its findings in the case of the revocation of a license or certificate, or of the reissuance of a revoked license or certificate.

§54.1-1115. Prohibited acts

A. The following acts are prohibited and shall constitute the commission of a Class 1 misdemeanor:

1. Contracting for, or bidding upon the construction, removal, repair, or improvements to or upon real property owned, controlled, or leased by another person without a license or certificate, or without the proper class of license as defined in §54.1-1100 for the value of work to be performed.
2. Attempting to practice contracting in the Commonwealth, except as provided for in this chapter.
3. Presenting or attempting to use the license or certificate of another.
4. Giving false or forged evidence of any kind to the Board or any member thereof in an application for the issuance or renewal of a license or certificate.
5. Impersonating another or using an expired or revoked license or certificate.
6. Receiving or considering as the awarding authority a bid from anyone whom the awarding authority knows is not properly licensed or certified under this chapter. The awarding authority shall require a bidder to submit his license or certificate number prior to considering a bid.

B. Any person who undertakes work without (i) any valid Virginia contractor's license or certificate when a license or certificate is required by this chapter or (ii) the proper class of license as defined in §54.1-1100 for the work undertaken, shall be fined an amount not to exceed $500 per day for each day that such person is in violation, in addition to the authorized penalties for the commission of a Class 1 misdemeanor.

C. No person shall be entitled to assert the lack of licensure or certification as required by this chapter as a defense to any action at law or suit in equity if the party who seeks to recover from such person gives substantial performance within the terms of the contract in good faith and without actual knowledge that a license or certificate was required by this chapter to perform the work for which he seeks to recover payment.

Failure to renew a license or certificate issued in accordance with this chapter shall create a rebuttable presumption of actual knowledge of such licensing or certification requirements.

§54.1-1115.1. Evidence of violation of the Virginia Uniform Statewide Building Code

In any proceeding pursuant to §54.1-1114, the Board shall consider any written documentation of a violation of the Uniform Statewide Building Code (§36-97 et seq.) provided by a local building official as evidence of a violation of such building code. Such written documentation shall not be prima facie evidence of a building code violation.

§54.1-1116. Repealed by Acts 1993, c. 717

§54.1-1117. Licensing of certain contractors by cities, counties, and towns; qualifications and procedure; registration of certain persons engaged in business of home improvement

A. Except as to contractors currently licensed under the provisions of §54.1-1106, the governing body of every city, county, or town shall have the power and authority to adopt ordinances, not inconsistent with the provisions of this chapter, requiring every person who engages in, or offers to engage in, the business of home improvement or the business of constructing single- or multi-family dwellings, in such city, county, or town, to obtain a license from such city, county, or town.

B. The governing body of every city, county, or town adopting ordinances pursuant to this section may require every applicant for such license, other than those currently licensed under the provisions of §54.1-1106, (i) to furnish evidence of his ability and proficiency; and (ii) to successfully complete an examination to determine his qualifications. The governing body may designate or establish an agent or board and establish the procedures for an examination according to the standards set forth in this chapter and in the regulations of the Board for Contractors. Except contractors currently licensed under the provisions of §54.1-1106, licensure may be refused to any person found not to be qualified. Persons not currently licensed pursuant to §54.1-1106 may be required to furnish bond in a reasonable penal sum, with reasonable condition, and with surety as the governing body deems necessary. The governing body may provide for the punishment of violations of such ordinances, provided that no such punishment shall exceed that provided for misdemeanors generally.

C. For the purpose of this section the business of home improvement shall mean the contracting for and/or providing labor and material or labor only for repairs, improvements, and additions to residential buildings or structures accessory thereto where any payment of money or other thing of value is required.

VIRGINIA ADMINISTRATIVE CODE—CONTRACTORS' REGULATIONS

18VAC50-22-10. General definitions

The following words and terms when used in this chapter, unless a different meaning is provided or is plainly required by the context, shall have the following meanings:

"Affidavit" means a written statement of facts, made voluntarily, and confirmed by the oath or affirmation of the party making it, taken before a notary or other person having the authority to administer such oath or affirmation.

"Business entity" means a sole proprietorship, partnership, corporation, limited liability company, limited liability partnership, or any other form of organization permitted by law.

"Controlling financial interest" means the direct or indirect ownership or control of more than 50% ownership of a firm.

"Firm" means any business entity recognized under the laws of the Commonwealth of Virginia.

"Formal vocational training" means courses in the trade administered at an accredited educational facility; or formal training, approved by the department, conducted by trade associations, businesses, military, correspondence schools or other similar training organizations.

"Full-time employee" means an employee who spends a minimum of 30 hours a week carrying out the work of the licensed contracting business.

"Helper" or "laborer" means a person who assists a licensed tradesman and who is not an apprentice as defined in 18VAC50-30-10.

"Licensee" means a firm holding a license issued by the Board for Contractors to act as a contractor, as defined in §54.1-1100 of the Code of Virginia.

"Net worth" means assets minus liabilities. For purposes of this chapter, assets shall not include any property owned as tenants by the entirety.

"Reciprocity" means an arrangement by which the licensees of two states are allowed to practice within each other's boundaries by mutual agreement.

"Reinstatement" means having a license restored to effectiveness after the expiration date has passed.

"Renewal" means continuing the effectiveness of a license for another period of time.

"Responsible management" means the following individuals:

1. The sole proprietor of a sole proprietorship;
2. The partners of a general partnership;
3. The managing partners of a limited partnership;
4. The officers of a corporation;
5. The managers of a limited liability company;
6. The officers or directors of an association or both; and
7. Individuals in other business entities recognized under the laws of the Commonwealth as having a fiduciary responsibility to the firm.

"Sole proprietor" means any individual, not a corporation, who is trading under his own name, or under an assumed or fictitious name pursuant to the provisions of §59.1-69 through 59.1-76 of the Code of Virginia.

"Supervision" means providing guidance or direction of a delegated task or procedure by a tradesman licensed in accordance with Chapter 11 (§54.1-1100 et seq.) of Title 54.1 of the Code of Virginia, being accessible to the helper or laborer, and periodically observing and evaluating the performance of the task or procedure.

"Supervisor" means the licensed master or journeyman tradesman who has the responsibility to ensure that the installation is in accordance with the applicable provisions of the Virginia Uniform Statewide Building Code and provides supervision to helpers and laborers as defined in this chapter.

"Tenants by the entirety" means a tenancy which is created between a husband and wife and by which together they hold title to the whole with right of survivorship so that, upon death of either, the other takes whole to exclusion of the deceased's remaning heirs.

18VAC50-22-20. Definitions of license classifications

The following words and terms, when used in this chapter unless a different meaning is provided or is plainly required by the context shall have the following meanings:

"Building contractors" (Abbr: BLD) means those individuals whose contracts include construction on real property owned, controlled or leased by another person of commercial, industrial, institutional, governmental, residential (single-family, two-family or multifamily), and accessory use buildings or structures. This classification also provides for remodeling, repair, improvement or demolition of these buildings and structures. A holder of this license can do general contracting.

If the BLD contractor performs specialty services, all required specialty designations shall be obtained. The building classification includes but is not limited to the functions carried out by the following specialties:

Billboard/sign contracting	Landscape service contracting
Commercial improvement contracting	Marine facility contracting
	Modular/manufactured building contracting
Farm improvement contracting	
Home improvement contracting	Recreational facility contracting

"Electrical contractors" (Abbr: ELE) means those individuals whose contracts include the construction, repair, maintenance, alteration, or removal of electrical systems under the National Electrical Code. This classification provides for all work covered by the National Electrical Code including electrical work covered by the alarm/security systems contracting (ALS), electronic/communication service contracting (ESC), and fire alarm systems contracting (FAS) specialties. A firm holding an electrical license is responsible for meeting all applicable tradesman licensing standards.

"Highway/heavy contractors" (Abbr: H/H) means those individuals whose contracts include construction, repair, improvement, or demolition of the following:

Bridges	Rail roads
Dams	Roads
Drainage systems	Runways
Foundations	Streets
Parking lots	Structural signs and lights
Public transit systems	Tanks

The functions carried out by these contractors include but are not limited to the following:

Building demolition	Nonwater well drilling
Clearing	Paving
Concrete work	Pile driving
Excavating	Road marking
Grading	

These contractors also install, maintain, or dismantle the following:

1. Power systems for the generation and primary and secondary distribution of electric current ahead of the customer's meter;
2. Pumping stations and treatment plants;
3. Telephone, telegraph, or signal systems for public utilities; and
4. Water, gas, and sewer connections to residential, commercial, and industrial sites, subject to local ordinances.

This classification may also install backflow prevention devices incidental to work in this classification when the installer has received formal vocational training approved by the board that included instruction in the installation of backflow prevention devices.

"HVAC contractors" (Abbr: HVA) means those individuals whose work includes the installation, alteration, repair, or maintenance of heating systems, ventilating systems, cooling systems, steam and hot water heaters, boilers, process piping, and mechanical refrigeration systems, including tanks incidental to the system. This classification does not provide for fire suppression installations, sprinkler system installations, or gas piping. A firm holding a HVAC license is responsible for meeting all applicable tradesman licensure standards. This classification may install backflow prevention devices incidental to work in this classification.

"Plumbing contractors" (Abbr: PLB) means those individuals whose contracts include the installation, maintenance, extension, or alteration, or removal of all piping, fixtures, appliances, and appurtenances in connection with any of the following:

Backflow prevention devices	Public-private water supply systems within
Boilers	or adjacent to any building, structure
Hot water baseboard heating systems	or conveyance
Hot water heaters	Sanitary or storm drainage facilities
Hydronic systems	Steam heating systems
Limited area sprinklers (as defined by	Storage tanks incidental to the installation
BOCA)	of related systems
Process piping	Venting systems related to plumbing

These contractors also install, maintain, extend or alter the following:

Liquid waste systems	Sewerage systems
Storm water systems	Water supply systems

This classification does not provide for gas piping or the function of fire sprinkler contracting as noted above. A firm holding a plumbing license is responsible for meeting all applicable tradesman licensure standards.

"Specialty contractors" means those individuals whose contracts are for specialty services which do not generally fall within the scope of any other classification within this chapter.

18VAC50-22-30. Definitions of specialty services

The following words and terms when used in this chapter unless a different meaning is provided or is plainly required by the context shall have the following meanings:

"Alternative energy system contracting" (Abbr: AES) means that service which provides for the installation, repair or improvement, from the customer's meter, of alternative energy generation systems, supplemental energy systems and associated equipment annexed to real property. No other classification or specialty service provides this function. This specialty does not provide for electrical, plumbing, gas fitting, or HVAC functions.

"Asbestos contracting" (Abbr: ASB) means that service which provides for the installation, removal, or encapsulation of asbestos containing materials annexed to real property. No other classification or specialty service provides for this function.

"Asphalt paving and sealcoating contracting" (Abbr: PAV) means that service which provides for the installation of asphalt paving and/or sealcoating on subdivision streets and adjacent intersections, driveways, parking lots, tennis courts, running tracks, and play areas, using materials and accessories common to the industry. This includes height adjustment of existing sewer manholes, storm drains, water valves, sewer cleanouts and drain grates, and all necessary excavation and grading. The H/H classification also provides for this function.

"Billboard/sign contracting" (Abbr: BSC) means that service which provides for the installation, repair, improvement, or dismantling of any billboard or structural sign permanently annexed to real property. H/H and BLD are the only other classifications that can perform this work except that a contractor in this specialty may connect or disconnect signs to existing electrical circuits. No trade related plumbing, electrical, or HVAC work is included in this function.

"Blast/explosive contracting" (Abbr: BEC) means that service which provides for the use of explosive charges for the repair, improvement, alteration, or demolition of any real property or any structure annexed to real property.

"Commercial improvement contracting" (Abbr: CIC) means that service which provides for repair or improvement to nonresidential property and multifamily property as defined in the Virginia Uniform Statewide Building Code. The BLD classification also provides for this function. The CIC classification does not provide for the construction of new buildings, accessory buildings, electrical, plumbing, HVAC, or gas work.

"Concrete contracting" (Abbr: CEM) means that service which provides for all work in connection with the processing, proportioning, batching, mixing, conveying and placing of concrete composed of materials common to the concrete industry. This includes but is not limited to finishing, coloring, curing, repairing, testing, sawing, grinding, grouting, placing of film barriers, sealing and waterproofing. Construction and assembling of forms, molds, slipforms, pans, centering, and the use of rebar is also included. The BLD and H/H classifications also provide for this function.

"Electronic/communication service contracting" (Abbr: ESC) means that service which provides for the installation, repair, improvement, or removal of electronic or communications systems annexed to real property including telephone wiring, computer cabling, sound systems, data links, data and network installation, television and cable TV wiring, antenna wiring, and fiber optics installation, all of which operate at 50 volts or less. A firm holding an ESC license is responsible for meeting all applicable tradesman licensure standards. The ELE classification also provides for this function.

"Elevator/escalator contracting" (Abbr: EEC) means that service which provides for the installation, repair, improvement or removal of elevators or escalators permanently annexed to real property. A firm holding an EEC license is responsible for meeting all applicable tradesman licensure standards. No other classification or specialty service provides for this function.

"Environmental monitoring well contracting" (Abbr: EMW) means that service which provides for the construction of a well to monitor hazardous substances in the ground.

"Environmental specialties contracting" (Abbr: ENV) means that service which provides for installation, repair, removal, or improvement of pollution control and remediation devices. No other specialty provides for this function. This specialty does not provide for electrical, plumbing, gas fitting, or HVAC functions.

"Equipment/machinery contracting" (Abbr: EMC) means that service which provides for the installation or removal of equipment or machinery including but not limited to conveyors or heavy machinery. Boilers exempted by the Virginia Uniform Statewide Building Code but regulated by the Department of Labor and Industry are also included in this specialty. This specialty does not provide for any electrical, plumbing, process piping or HVAC functions.

"Farm improvement contracting" (Abbr: FIC) means that service which provides for the installation, repair or improvement of a nonresidential farm building or structure, or nonresidential farm accessory-use structure, or additions thereto. The BLD classification also provides for this function. The FIC specialty does not provide for any electrical, plumbing, HVAC, or gas fitting functions.

"Fire alarm systems contracting" (Abbr: FAS) means that service which provides for the installation, repair, or improvement of fire alarm systems which operate at 50 volts or less. The ELE classification also provides for this function. A firm with an FAS license is responsible for meeting all applicable tradesman licensure standards.

"Fire sprinkler contracting" (Abbr: SPR) means that service which provides for the installation, repair, alteration, addition, testing, maintenance, inspection, improvement, or removal of sprinkler systems using water as a means of fire suppression when annexed to real property. This specialty does not provide for the installation, repair, or maintenance of other types of fire suppression systems. The PLB classification allows for the installation of limited area sprinklers as defined by BOCA. This specialty may engage in the installation of backflow prevention devices in the fire sprinkler supply main and sprinkler system when the installer has received formal vocational training approved by the board that included instruction in the installation of backflow prevention devices.

"Fire suppression contracting" (Abbr: FSP) means that service which provides for the installation, repair, improvement, or removal of fire suppression systems including but not limited to halon and other gas systems; dry chemical systems; and carbon dioxide systems annexed to real property. No other classification provides for this function. The FSP specialty does not provide for the installation, repair, or maintenance of water sprinkler systems.

"Gas fitting contracting" (Abbr: GFC) means that service which provides for the installation, repair, improvement, or removal of gas piping and appliances annexed to real property. A firm with a GFC license is responsible for meeting all applicable tradesman licensure standards.

"Home improvement contracting" (Abbr: HIC) means that service which provides for repairs or improvements to one-family and two-family residential buildings or structures annexed to real property. The BLD classification also provides for this function. The HIC specialty does not provide for electrical, plumbing, HVAC, or gas fitting functions. It does not include high rise buildings, buildings with more than two dwelling units, or new construction functions beyond the existing building structure other than decks, patios, driveways and utility out buildings.

"Landscape irrigation contracting" (Abbr: ISC) means that service which provides for the installation, repair, improvement, or removal of irrigation sprinkler systems or outdoor sprinkler systems. The PLB and H/H classifications also provide for this function. This specialty may install backflow prevention devices incidental to work in this specialty when the installer has received formal vocational training approved by the board that included instruction in the installation of backflow prevention devices.

"Landscape service contracting" (Abbr: LSC) means that service which provides for the alteration or improvement of a land area not related to any other classification or service activity by means of excavation, clearing, grading, construction of retaining walls for landscaping purposes, or placement of landscaping timbers. The BLD classification also provides for this function.

"Lead abatement contracting" (Abbr: LAC) means that service which provides for the removal or encapsulation of lead-containing materials annexed to real property. No other classification or specialty service provides for this function, except that the PLB and HVA classifications may provide this service incidental to work in those classifications.

"Liquefied petroleum gas contracting" (Abbr: LPG) means that service which includes the installation, maintenance, extension, alteration, or removal of all piping, fixtures, appliances, and appurtenances used in transporting, storing or utilizing liquefied petroleum gas. This excludes hot water heaters, boilers, and central heating systems that require a HVA or PLB license. The GFC specialty also provides for this function. A firm holding a LPG license is responsible for meeting all applicable tradesman licensure standards.

"Marine facility contracting" (Abbr: MCC) means that service which provides for the construction, repair, improvement, or removal of any structure the purpose of which is to provide access to, impede, or alter a body of surface water. The BLD and H/H classifications also provide for this function. The MCC specialty does not provide for the construction of accessory structures or electrical, HVAC or plumbing functions.

"Masonry contracting" (Abbr: BRK) means that service which includes the installation of brick, concrete block, stone, marble, slate or other units and products common to the masonry industry, including mortarless type masonry products. This includes installation of grout, caulking, tuck pointing, sand blasting, mortar washing, parging and cleaning and welding of reinforcement steel related to masonry construction. The BLD classification and HIC and CIC specialties also provide for this function.

"Modular/manufactured building contracting" (Abbr: MBC) means that service which provides for the installation or removal of a modular or manufactured building manufactured under ANSI standards. This classification does not cover foundation work; however, it does allow installation of piers covered under HUD regulations. It does allow a licensee to do internal tie ins of plumbing, gas and electrical or HVAC equipment. It does not allow for installing additional plumbing, electrical, or HVAC work such as installing the service meter, or installing the outside compressor for the HVAC system. The H/H and BLD classifications also provide for this function.

"Natural gas fitting provider contracting" (Abbr: NGF) means that service which provides for the incidental repair, testing, or removal of natural gas piping or fitting annexed to real property. This does not include new installation of gas piping for hot water heaters, boilers, central heating systems, or other natural gas equipment which requires a HVA or PLB license. The GFC specialty also provides for this function. A firm holding a NGF license is responsible for meeting all applicable tradesman licensure standards.

"Painting and wallcovering contracting" (Abbr: PTC) means that service which provides for the application of materials common to the painting and decorating industry for protective or decorative purposes, the installation of surface coverings such as vinyls, wall papers, and cloth fabrics. This includes surface preparation, caulking, sanding and cleaning preparatory to painting or coverings and includes both interior and exterior surfaces. The BLD classification and the HIC and CIC specialties also provide for this function.

"Radon mitigation contracting" (Abbr: RMC) means that service which provides for additions, repairs or improvements to buildings or structures, for the purpose of mitigating or preventing the effects of radon gas. This function can only be performed by a firm holding the BLD classification or CIC (for other than one-family and two-family dwellings), FIC (for nonresidential farm buildings) or HIC (for one-family and two-family dwellings) specialty services. No electrical, plumbing, gas fitting, or HVAC functions are provided by this specialty.

"Recreational facility contracting" (Abbr: RFC) means that service which provides for the construction, repair, or improvement of any recreational facility, excluding paving and the construction of buildings, plumbing, electrical, and HVAC functions. The BLD classification also provides for this function.

"Refrigeration contracting" (Abbr: REF) means that service which provides for installation, repair, or removal of any refrigeration equipment (excluding HVAC equipment). No electrical, plumbing, gas fitting, or HVAC functions are provided by this specialty. This specialty is intended for those contractors who repair or install coolers, refrigerated casework, ice-making machines, drinking fountains, cold room equipment, and similar hermetic refrigeration equipment. The HVAC classification also provides for this function.

"Roofing contracting" (Abbr: ROC) means that service which provides for the installation, repair, removal or improvement of materials common to the industry that form a watertight, weather resistant surface for roofs and decks. This includes roofing system components when installed in conjunction with a roofing project, application of dampproofing or waterproofing, and installation of roof insulation panels and other roof insulation systems above roof deck. The BLD classification and the HIC and CIC specialties also provide for this function.

"Sewage disposal systems contracting" (Abbr: SDS) means that service which provides for the installation, repair, improvement, or removal of septic tanks, septic systems, and other on-site sewage disposal systems annexed to real property.

"Swimming pool construction contracting" (Abbr: POL) means that service which provides for the construction, repair, improvement or removal of in-ground swimming pools. The BLD classification and the RFC specialty also provide for this function. No trade related plumbing, electrical, backflow or HVAC work is included in this specialty.

"Vessel construction contracting" (Abbr: VCC) means that service which provides for the construction, repair, improvement, or removal of nonresidential vessels, tanks, or piping that hold or convey fluids other than sanitary, storm, waste, or potable water supplies. The H/H classification also provides for this function.

"Water well/pump contracting" (Abbr: WWP) means that service which provides for the installation of a water well system, which includes construction of a water well to reach groundwater, as defined in §62.1-255 of the Code of Virginia, and the installation of the well pump and tank, including pipe and wire, up to and including the point of connection to the plumbing and electrical systems. No other classification or specialty service provides for construction of water wells. This regulation shall not exclude PLB, ELE or HVAC from installation of pumps and tanks.

Note: Specialty contractors engaging in construction which involves the following activities or items or similar activities or items may fall under the CIC, HIC, and/or FIC specialty services, or they may fall under the BLD classification.

Appliances	Fiberglass	Rigging
Awnings	Fireplaces	Rubber Linings
Blinds	Fireproofing	Sandblasting
Bricks	Fixtures	Scaffolding
Bulkheads	Floor Coverings	Screens
Cabinetry	Flooring	Sheet Metal

Carpentry	Floors	Shutters
Carpeting	Glass	Siding
Casework	Glazing	Skylights
Ceilings	Grouting	Storage bins and lockers
Chimneys	Grubbing	Stucco
Chutes	Guttering	Temperature controls
Conduit rodding	Insulation	Terrazzo
Curtains	Interior decorating	Tile
Curtain walls	Lubrication	Vaults
Decks	Metal work	Vinyl flooring
Doors	Millwrighting	Wall Panels
Drapes	Mirrors	Wall tile
Drywall	Miscellaneous iron	Waterproofing
Epoxy	Ornamental iron	Weatherstripping
Exterior decoration	Partitions	Welding
Facings	Protective coatings	Windows
Fences	Railings	Wood floors

Entry

18VAC50-22-40. Requirements for a Class C license

A. A firm applying for a Class C license must meet the requirements of this section.

B. For every classification or specialty in which the firm seeks to be certified, the firm shall name a qualified individual who meets the following requirements:

   1. Is at least 18 years old;

   2. Has a minimum of two years experience in the classification or specialty for which he is the qualifier;

   3. Is a full-time employee of the firm as defined in this chapter or is a member of the responsible management of the firm; and :

   4. Where appropriate, has passed the trade-related examination or has completed an education and training program approved by the board and required for the specialties listed belo w:

Blast/explosive contracting	HVAC contracting
Electrical contracting	Plumbing contracting
Fire sprinkler contracting	Radon mitigation contracting
Gas fitting contracting	Water well drilling contracting

   5. Has obtained, pursuant to the tradesman regulations, a master tradesman license as required for those classifications and specialties listed in 18 VAC 50- 22-20 and 18 VAC 50-22-30.

C. The firm shall provide information for the past five years prior to application on any outstanding, past-due debts and judgments, outstanding tax obligations, defaults on bonds or pending or past bankruptcies. The firm, its qualified individual or individuals, and all members of the responsible management of the firm shall submit information on any past-due debts and judgments or defaults on bonds directly related to the practice of contracting as defined in Chapter 11 (§54.1-1100 et seq.)*{definitions}* of Title 54.1 of the Code of Virginia.

D. The firm, the qualified individual, and all members of the responsible management of the firm shall disclose at the time of application any current or previous contractor licenses held in Virginia or in other jurisdictions and any disciplinary actions taken on these licenses. This includes but is not limited to any monetary penalties, fines, suspension, revocation or surrender of a license in connection with a disciplinary action or voluntary termination of a license in Virginia or any other jurisdiction.

E. In accordance with *§54.1-204 {prior convictions not to abridge rights}* of the Code of Virginia, each applicant shall disclose the following information about the firm, any member of the responsible management, and the qualified individual or individuals for the firm:
   1. All misdemeanor convictions within three years of the date of application; and
   2. All felony convictions during their lifetime.

   Any plea of nolo contendere shall be considered a conviction for purposes of this subsection. The record of a conviction received from a court shall be accepted as prima facie evidence of a conviction or finding of guilt. The board, in its discretion, may deny certification to any applicant in accordance with *§54.1-204* of the Code of Virginia.

F. A member of responsible management shall have successfully completed a board approved basic business course.

18VAC50-22-50. Requirements for a Class B license

A. A firm applying for a Class B license must meet the requirements of this section.

B. A firm shall name a designated employee who meets the following requirements:
   1. Is at least 18 years old;
   2. Is a full-time employee of the firm as defined in this chapter, or is a member of responsible management as defined in this chapter;
   3. Has passed a board-approved examination as required by §54.1-1108 of the Code of Virginia or has been exempted from the exam requirement in accordance with §54.1-1108.1 of the Code of Virginia; and
   4. Has followed all rules established by the board or by the testing service acting on behalf of the board with regard to conduct at the examination. Such rules shall include any written instructions communicated prior to the examination date and any oral or written instructions given at the site on the date of the exam.

C. For every classification or specialty in which the firm seeks to be licensed, the firm shall name a qualified individual who meets the following requirements:
   1. Is at least 18 years old;
   2. Has a minimum of three years experience in the classification or specialty for which he is the qualifier;
   3. Is a full-time employee of the firm as defined in this chapter or is a member of the responsible management of the firm; and
   4. Where appropriate, has passed the trade-related examination approved by the board and required for the classifications and specialties listed below:

Blast/explosive contracting	HVAC contracting
Electrical contracting	Plumbing contracting
Fire sprinkler contracting	Radon mitigation contracting
Gas fitting contracting	Water well drilling contracting

5. Has obtained, pursuant to the tradesman regulations, a master tradesman license as required for those classifications and specialties listed in 18 VAC 50- 22-20 and 18 VAC 50-22-30.

D. Each firm shall submit information on its financial position. Excluding any property owned as tenants by the entirety, the firm shall state a net worth or equity of $15,000 or more.

E. Each firm shall provide information for the five years prior to application on any outstanding, past-due debts and judgments, outstanding tax obligations, or defaults on bonds or pending or past bankrupcies. The firm, its designated employee, qualified individual or individuals, and all members of the responsible management of the firm shall submit information on any past-due debts and judgments or defaults on bonds directly related to the practice of contracting as defined in Chapter 11 (§54.1-1100 et seq.) of Title 54.1 of the Code of Virginia.

F. The firm, the designated employee, the qualified individual, and all members of the responsible management of the firm shall disclose at the time of application any current or previous substantial identities of interest with any contractor licenses issued in Virginia or in other jurisdictions and any disciplinary actions taken on these licenses. This includes but is not limited to any monetary penalties, fines, suspension, revocation, or surrender of a license in connection with a disciplinary action. The board, in its discretion, may deny licensure to any applicant when any of the parties listed above have had a substantial identity of interest (as deemed in §54.1-1110 of the Code of Virginia) with any firm that has had a license suspended, revoked, voluntarily terminated or surrendered in connection with a disciplinary action in Virginia or any other jurisdiction.

G. In accordance with *§54.1-204* of the Code of Virginia, each applicant shall disclose the following information about the firm, designated employee, any member of the responsible management, and the qualified individual or individuals for the firm:
    1. All misdemeanor convictions within three years of the date of application; and
    2. All felony convictions during their lifetime.

    Any plea of nolo contendere shall be considered a conviction for purposes of this subsection. The record of a conviction received from a court shall be accepted as prima facie evidence of a conviction or finding of guilt. The board, in its discretion, may deny certification to any applicant in accordance with *§54.1-204* of the Code of Virginia.

H. The designated employee or a member of responsible management shall have successfully completed a board approved basic business course.

18VAC50-22-60. Additional requirements for a Class A license

A. A firm applying for a Class A license shall meet all of the requirements of this section.

B. A firm shall name a designated employee who meets the following requirements:
    1. Is a least 18 years old;
    2. Is a full-time employee of the firm as defined in this chapter or is a member of the responsible management of the firm; and
    3. Has passed a board-approved examination as required by §54.1-1108 of the Code of Virginia or has been exempted from the exam requirement in accordance with §54.1-1108.1 of the Code of Virginia; and

4. Has followed all rules established by the board or by the testing service acting on behalf of the board with regard to conduct at the examination. Such rules shall include any written instructions communicated prior to the examination date and any oral or written instructions given at the site on the date of the exam.

C. For every classification or specialty in which the firm seeks to be licensed, the firm shall name a qualified individual who meets the following requirements:

1. Is a least 18 years old;

2. Has a minimum of five years of experience in the classification or specialty for which he is the qualifier;

3. Is a full-time employee of the firm as defined in this chapter or is a member of the firm as defined in this chapter or is a member of the responsible management of the firm;

4. Where appropriate, has passed the trade-related examination or has completed an education and training program approved by the board and required for the classifications and specialties listed below, and

Blast/explosive contracting	HVAC contracting
Electrical contracting	Plumbing contracting
Fire sprinkler contracting	Radon mitigation contracting
Gas fitting contracting	Water well drilling contracting

5. Has obtained, pursuant to the tradesman regulations, a master tradesman license as required for those classifications and specialties listed in 18 VAC 50- 22-20 and 18 VAC 50-22-30.

D. Each firm shall submit information on its financial position. Excluding any property owned as tenants by the entirety, the firm shall state a net worth or equity of $45,000.

E. Each firm shall provide information for the five years prior to application on any outstanding, past-due debts and judgments, outstanding tax obligations, or defaults on bonds or pending or past bankruptcies. The firm, its designated employee, qualified individual or individuals, and all members of the responsible management of the firm shall submit information on any past-due debts and judgments or defaults on bonds directly related to the practice of contracting as defined in Chapter 11 (§54.1-1100 et seq.) of Title 54.1 of the Code of Virginia.

F. The firm, the designated employee, the qualified individual, and all members of the responsible management of the firm shall disclose at the time of application any current or previous substantial identities of interest with any contractor licenses issued in Virginia or in other jurisdictions and any disciplinary actions taken on these licenses. This includes but is not limited to any monetary penalties, fines, suspension, revocation, or surrender of a license in connection with a disciplinary action. The board, in its discretion, may deny licensure to any applicant when any of the parties listed above have had a substantial identity of interest (as deemed in §54.1-1110 of the Code of Virginia) with any firm that has had a license suspended, revoked, voluntarily terminated or surrendered in connection with a disciplinary action in Virginia or any other jurisdiction.

G. In accordance with *§54.1-204* of the Code of Virginia, each applicant shall disclose the following information about the firm, designated employee, any member of the responsible management, and the qualified individual or individuals for the firm:

1. All misdemeanor convictions within three years of the date of application; and

2. All felony convictions during their lifetime.

Any plea of nolo contendere shall be considered a conviction for purposes of this subsection. The record of a conviction received from a court shall be accepted as prima facie evidence of a conviction or finding of guilt. The board, in its discretion, may deny certification to any applicant in accordance with §*54.1-204* of the Code of Virginia.

H. The designated employee or a member of responsible management shall have successfully completed a board approved basic business course.

18VAC50-22-70. Qualifications for licensure by reciprocity

Firms originally licensed in a state with which the board has a reciprocal agreement may obtain a Virginia contractor's license in accordance with the terms of that agreement.

18VAC50-22-80. Examinations

All examinations required for licensure shall be approved by the board and provided by the board or a testing service acting on behalf of the board, or another governmental agency or organization. The examination fee shall consist of the administration expenses of the Department of Professional and Occupational Regulation ensuing from the board's examination procedures and contract charges. Exam service contracts shall be established through competitive negotiation in compliance with the Virginia Public Procurement Act (§11-35 et seq. of the Code of Virginia). The current examination shall not exceed a cost of $100 per element to the candidate.

18VAC50-22-90. Past due recovery fund assessments

No license shall be issued to an applicant whose previous license or registration was suspended for nonpayment of a Virginia Contractor Transaction Recovery Fund assessment until all past-due assessments have been paid.

18VAC50-22-100. Fees

Each check or money order shall be made payable to the Treasurer of Virginia. All fees required by the board are nonrefundable. In the event that a check, money draft, or similar instrument for payment of a fee required by statute or regulation is not honored by the bank or financial institution named, the applicant or regulant shall be required to remit fees sufficient to cover the original fee, plus an additional processing charge set by the Department:

Fee Type	When Due	Amount Due
Class C Initial License	With certificate application	$150
Class B Initial License	With license application	$175
Class A Initial License	With license application	$200
Declaration of Designated Employee	With license application	$40
Qualified Individual Exam Fee	With exam application	$20
Class B Exam Fee	With exam application ($20 per section)	$40
Class A Exam Fee	With exam application ($20 per section)	$60
Water Well Exam Fee	With exam application	$40

Note: A $25 Recovery Fund assessment is also required with each initial license application. If the applicant does not meet all requirements and does not become licensed, this assessment will be refunded. The examination fees approved by the board but administered by another governmental agency or organization shall be determined by that agency or organization.

Renewal
18VAC50-22-110. Renewal required
Licenses issued under this chapter shall expire two years from the last day of the month in which they were issued, as indicated on the license.

18VAC50-22-120. Procedures for renewal
The Department of Professional and Occupational Regulation will mail a notice of renewal to the licensee at the last known address of record. Failure to receive this notice shall not relieve the licensee of the obligation to renew. If the licensee does not receive the renewal application, a copy of the license may be substituted with the required fee.

18VAC50-22-130. Qualifications for renewal
The license holder's completed renewal form and appropriate fees must be received within 30 days of the license expiration date in order to renew the license. Applications and fees received after the 30-day period will be processed in accordance with Part IV (18 VAC 50-20-160 et seq.) of this chapter.

Applicants for renewal of a Class C license shall continue to meet all of the qualifications for certification set forth in 18 VAC 50-22-40. Applicants for renewal of a Class B license shall continue to meet all of the qualifications for licensure set forth in 18 VAC 50-22-50. Applicants for renewal of a Class A license shall continue to meet all of the qualifications for licensure set forth in 18 VAC 50-22-60.

18VAC50-22-140. Renewal fees
Each check or money order should be made payable to the Treasurer of Virginia. All fees required by the board are nonrefundable. In the event that a check, money draft, or similar instrument for payment of a fee required by statute or regulation is not honored by the bank or financial institution named, the applicant or regulant shall be required to remit fees sufficient to cover the original fee, plus an additional processing charge set by the Department:

Fee Type	When Due	Amount Due
Class C Renewal	With renewal application	$110
Class B Renewal	With renewal application	$150
Class A Renewal	With renewal application	$165

The date on which the renewal fee is received by the Department or its agent shall determine whether the licensee is eligible for renewal or must apply for reinstatement.

18VAC50-22-150. Board discretion to deny renewal
A. The board may deny renewal of a license for the same reasons as it may refuse initial licensure or discipline a licensee. The licensee has a right to appeal any such action by the board under the Administrative Process Act (§*9-6.14:1* et seq. of the Code of Virginia).

B. Failure to timely pay any monetary penalty, reimbursement of cost, or other fee assessed by consent order or final order shall result in delaying or withholding services provided by the department such as, but not limited to, renewal, reinstatement, processing a new application, or exam administration.

Reinstatement

18VAC50-22-160. Reinstatement required

Should the Department of Professional and Occupational Regulation fail to receive a licensee's renewal application or fees within 30 days of the license expiration date, the licensee shall be required to reinstate the license. Applicants for reinstatement of a Class C license shall meet the requirements of 18 VAC 50-22-130. Applicants for reinstatement of a Class B license shall continue to meet the qualifications for licensure set forth in 18 VAC 50-22-50. Applicants for reinstatement of a Class A license shall continue to meet all the qualifications for licensure set forth in 18 VAC 50-22-60.

18VAC50-22-170. Reinstatement fees

Each check or money order should be made payable to the Treasurer of Virginia. All fees required by the board are nonrefundable. In the event that a check, money draft, or similar instrument for payment of a fee required by statute or regulation is not honored by the bank or financial institution named, the applicant or regulant shall be required to remit fees sufficient to cover the original fee, plus an additional processing charge set by the Department:

Fee Type	When Due	Amount Due
Class C Reinstatement	With reinstatement application	$260*
Class B Reinstatement	With reinstatement application	$325*
Class A Reinstatement	With reinstatement application	$365*

* in addition to the renewal fee listed in 18 VAC 22-140 of these regulations

The date on which the reinstatement fee is received by the department or its agent shall determine whether the licensee is eligible for reinstatement or must apply for a new license and meet the entry requirements in place at the time of that application. In order to ensure that licensees holders are qualified to practice as contractors, no reinstatement will be permitted one year from the expiration date of the license has passed.

18VAC50-22-180. Status of licensee during the period prior to reinstatement

A. When a license is reinstated, the licensee shall continue to have the same license number and shall be assigned an expiration date two years from the previous expiration date of the license.

B. A contractor who reinstates his license shall be regarded as having been continuously licensed without interruption. Therefore:

  1. The contractor shall remain under the disciplinary authority of the board during this entire period and may be held accountable for his activities during this period.

  2. A consumer who contracts with a contractor during the period between the expiration of the license and the reinstatement of the license shall not be prohibited from making a claim on the Virginia Contractor Transaction Recovery Fund.

  A contractor who fails to reinstate his license shall be regarded as unlicensed from the expiration date of the license forward.

  Nothing in this chapter shall divest the board of its authority to discipline a contractor for a violation of the law or regulations during the period of time for which the contractor was licensed.

18VAC50-22-190. Board discretion to deny reinstatement

A. The board may deny reinstatement of a license for the same reasons as it may refuse initial licensure or discipline a licensee. The licensee has a right to appeal any such action by the board under the Administrative Process Act (§*9-6.14:1* et seq. of the Code of Virginia).

B. Failure to timely pay any monetary penalty, reimbursement of cost or other fee assessed by consent order or final order shall result in delaying or withholding services provided by the department such as, but not limited to, renewal, reinstatement, processing of a new application, or exam administration.

Standards of Practice and Conduct
18VAC50-22-200. Remedial education, revocation or suspension; fines
The board may require remedial education, revoke or suspend a license or fine a licensee when a licensee has been found to have violated or cooperated with others in violating any provision of Chapter 11 (§*54.1-1100* et seq.) of Title 54.1 of the Code of Virginia, or any regulation of the board.

18VAC50-22-210. Change of business entity requires a new license
Licenses are issued to firms as defined in this chapter and are not transferable. Whenever the legal business entity holding the license is dissolved or altered to form a new business entity, the firm shall apply for a new license, on a form provided by the board, within 30 days of the change in the business entity. Such changes include but are not limited to:

1. Death of a sole proprietor;
2. Death or withdrawal of a general partner in a general partnership or the managing partner in a limited partnership; and
3. Formation or dissolution of a corporation, a limited liability company, or an association, or any other business entity recognized under the laws of the Commonwealth of Virginia.

18VAC50-22-220. Change of responsible management, designated employee, or qualified individual
A. Any change in the officers of a corporation, managers of a limited liability company, or officers or directors of an association shall be reported to the board in writing within 90 days of the change.

B. Any change of designated employee shall be reported on a form provided by the board within 90 days of the change. The new designated employee for a Class B licensee shall meet the requirements of 18 VAC 50-22-50 B. The new designated employee for a Class A licensee shall meet the requirements of 18 VAC 50-22-60 B.

C. Any change of qualified individual shall be reported on a form provided by the board within 45 days of the change. The new qualified individual for a Class C licensee shall meet the requirements of 18 VAC 50-22-40 B. The new qualified individual for a Class B licensee shall meet the requirements of 18 VAC 50-22-50 C. The new qualified individual for a Class A licensee shall meet the requirements of 18 VAC 50-22-60 C.

18VAC50-22-230. Change of name or address
A. A licensee must operate under the name in which the license is issued. Any name change shall be reported in writing to the board within 30 days of the change. The board shall not be responsible for the licensee's failure to receive notices or correspondence due to the licensee's not having reported a change of name.

B. Any change of address shall be reported in writing to the board within 30 days of the change. The board shall not be responsible for the licensee's failure to receive notices or correspondence due to the licensee's not having reported a change of address.

18VAC50-22-240. Deletion or addition of a classification or specialty

A. A licensee wishing to delete a classification or specialty from its license shall notify the board in writing. If a licensee has only one classification or specialty, deletion of that classification or specialty will result in termination of the license.

B. A licensee wishing to add a classification or specialty to its license shall complete a form provided by the board. A Class C licensee seeking an additional classification or specialty shall meet the requirements of 18 VAC 50-22-40 B for the new classification or specialty. A Class B licensee seeking an additional classification or specialty shall meet the requirements of 18 VAC 50-22-50 C for the new classification or specialty. A Class A licensee seeking an additional classification or specialty shall meet the requirements of 18 VAC5 0-22-60 C for the new classification or specialty.

18VAC50-22-250. Fees

Each check or money order should be made payable to the Treasurer of Virginia. All fees required by the board are nonrefundable. In the event that a check, money draft, or similar instrument for payment of a fee required by statute or regulation is not honored by the bank or financial institution named, the applicant or regulant shall be required to remit fees sufficient to cover the original fee, plus an additional processing charge set by the Department:

Fee Type	When Due	Amount Due
Change of Designated Employee	With change form	$40
Change of Qualified Individual	With change form	$40
Addition of Classification or Specialty	With addition application	$40

18VAC50-22-260. Filing of charges; prohibited acts

A. All complaints against contractors may be filed with the Department of Professional and Occupational Regulation at any time during business hours, pursuant to §*54.1-1114* of the Code of Virginia.

B. The following are prohibited acts:

1. Failure in any material way to comply with provisions of Chapter 1 (§*54.1-100 {Authority to regulate professions}* et seq.) or Chapter 11 (§*54.1-1100* et seq.) of Title 54.1 of the Code of Virginia or the regulations of the board.

2. Furnishing substantially inaccurate or incomplete information to the board in obtaining, renewing, reinstating, or maintaining a license.

3. Failure of the responsible management, designated employee, or qualified individual to report to the board, in writing, the suspension or revocation of a contractor license by another state or his conviction in a court of competent jurisdiction of a building code violation.

4. Publishing or causing to be published any advertisement relating to contracting which contains an assertion, representation, or statement of fact that is false, deceptive, or misleading.

5. Negligence and/or incompetence in the practice of contracting.

6. Misconduct in the practice of contracting.

7. A finding of improper or dishonest conduct in the practice of his profession by a court of competent jurisdiction.

8. Failure of all those who engage in residential contracting, excluding subcontractors to the contracting parties and those who engage in routine maintenance or service contracts, to make use of a legible written contract clearly specifying the terms and conditions of the work to be performed. For the purposes

of this chapter, residential contracting means construction, removal, repair, or improvements to single-family or multiple-family residential buildings, including accessory-use structures as defined in §54.1-1100 of the Code of Virginia. Prior to commencement of work or acceptance of payments, the contract shall be signed by both the consumer and the licensee or his agent.

9. Failure of those engaged in residential contracting as defined in this chapter to comply with the terms of a written contract which contains the following minimum requirements:

   a. When work is to begin and the estimated completion date;
   b. A statement of the total cost of the contract and the amounts and schedule for progress payments including a specific statement on the amount of the down payment;
   c. A listing of specified materials and work to be performed, which is specifically requested by the consumer;
   d. A "plain-language" exculpatory clause concerning events beyond the control of the contractor and a statement explaining that delays caused by such events do not constitute abandonment and are not included in calculating time frames for payment or performance;
   e. A statement of assurance that the contractor will comply with all local requirements for building permits, inspections, and zoning;
   f. Disclosure of the cancellation rights of the parties;
   g. For contracts resulting from a door-to-door solicitation, a signed acknowledgment by the consumer that he has been provided with and read the Department of Professional and Occupational Regulation statement of protection available to him through the Board for Contractors;
   h. Contractor's name, address, license number, class of license, and classifications or specialty services; and
   i. Statement providing that any modification to the contract, which changes the cost, materials, work to be performed, or estimated completion date, must be in writing and signed by all parties.

10. Failure to make prompt delivery to the consumer before commencement of work of a fully executed copy of the contract as described in subdivision 8 and 9 of this section for construction or contracting work.

11. Failure of the contractor to maintain for a period of five years from the date of contract a complete and legible copy of all documents relating to that contract, including, but not limited to, the contract and any addenda or change orders.

12. Refusing or failing, upon request or demand, to produce to the board, or any of its agents, any document, book, record, or copy of it in the licensee's possession concerning a transaction covered by this chapter or for which the licensee is required to maintain records.

13. Failing to respond to an investigator seeking information in the investigation of a complaint filed with the board against the contractor.

14. Abandonment (defined as the unjustified cessation of work under the contract for a period of 30 days or more.

15. The intentional and unjustified failure to complete work contracted for, and/or to comply with the terms in the contract.

16. The retention or misapplication of funds paid, for which work is either not performed or performed only in part.

17. Making any misrepresentation or making a false promise of a character likely to influence, persuade, or induce.

18. Assisting another to violate any provision of Chapter 1 (§*54.1-100* et seq.) or Chapter 11 (§*54.1-1100* et seq.) of Title 54.1 of the Code of Virginia, or this chapter; or combining or conspiring with or acting as agent, partner, or associate for another.

19. Allowing a firm's license to be used by another.

20. Acting as or being an ostensible licensee for undisclosed persons who do or will control or direct, directly or indirectly, the operations of the licensee's business.

21. Action by the firm, responsible management as defined in this chapter, designated employee or qualified individual offer, give, or promise anything of value or benefit to any federal, state, or local employee for the purpose of influencing that employee to circumvent, in the performance of his duties, any federal, state, or local law, regulation, or ordinance governing the construction industry.

22. Where the firm, responsible management as defined in this chapter, designated employee or qualified individual has been convicted or found guilty, after initial licensure, regardless of adjudication, in any jurisdiction, of any felony or of any misdemeanor, there being no appeal pending therefrom or the time of appeal having elapsed. Any plea of guilty or nolo contendere shall be considered a conviction for the purposes of this subdivision. The record of a conviction received from a court shall be accepted as prima facie evidence of a conviction or finding of guilt.

23. Failure to inform the board in writing, within 30 days, that the firm, a member of responsible management as defined in this chapter, its designated employee, or its qualified individual has pleaded guilty or nolo contendere or was convicted and found guilty of any felony or of a Class 1 misdemeanor or any misdemeanor conviction for activities carried out while engaged in the practice of contracting.

24. Having been disciplined by any county, city, town, or any state or federal governing body including action by the Virginia Department of Health, which action shall be reviewed by the board before it takes any disciplinary action of its own.

25. Failure to abate a violation of the Virginia Uniform Statewide Building Code, as amended.

26. Failure of a contractor to comply with the notification requirements of the Virginia Underground Utility Prevention Act, Chapter 10.3 (§*56-265.14* et seq.) of Title 56 of the Code of Virginia (Underground Utility).

27. Practicing in a classification, specialty service, or class of license for which the contractor is not licensed.

28. Failure to satisfy any judgments.

29. Contracting with an unlicensed or improperly licensed contractor or subcontractor in the delivery of contracting services.

30. Failure to honor the terms and conditions of a warranty.

31. Failure to obtain written change orders, which are signed by both the consumer and the licensee or his agent, to an already existing contract.

18VAC50-22-270. Repealed

18VAC50-22-300. Pre-license education courses

All courses offered by pre-license education providers must be approved by the Board, prior to the initial offering of the course, and shall cover business principles related to the standards of conduct found in 18VAC50-22-260 B and other applicable requirements of continued licensure set forth in this chapter. Courses must be eight hours in length. Correspondence and other distance learning courses must include appropriate testing procedures to verify completion of the course.

18VAC50-22-310. Requirements for pre-license education providers

A. Each provider of a pre-license education course shall submit an application for course approval on a form provided by the Board. The application shall include but is not limited to:

1. The name of the provider
2. Provider contact person, address and telephone number
3. Course contact hours
4. Schedule of courses, if established, including dates, time, and locations
5. Instructor information, including name, license number(s), if applicable, and a list of other appropriate trade designations
6. Course and material fees
7. Course syllabus

B. All providers must establish and maintain a record for each student. The record shall include: the student's name and address; Social Security number or DMV control number; the course name and clock hours attended; the course syllabus or outline; the name or names of the instructor; the date of successful completion; and the Board's course code. Records shall be available for inspection during normal business hours by authorized representatives of the Board. Providers must maintain class records for a minimum of five years.

18VAC50-22-320. Reporting of course completion

All pre-license education providers shall electronically transmit course completion data, to the Board, in an approved format, within 7 days of the completion of each individual course. The transmittal will include: each student's name; Social Security number or DMV control number; the date of successful completion of the course; and the Board's course code.

18VAC50-22-330. Posting pre-license education course certificates of approval

Copies of pre-license education course certificates of approval must be available at the location a course is taught.

18VAC50-30-340. Reporting of changes

Any change in the information provided in 18VAC50-22-310 A must be reported to the board within 30 days of the change with the exception of changes in the schedule of courses, which must be reported within 10 days of the change. Failure to report the changes as required may result in the withdrawal of approval of a pre-license education provider by the board.

18VAC50-30-350. Denial or withdrawal of approval

The Board may deny or withdraw approval of any pre-license education provider for the following reasons:

1. The courses being offered no longer meet the standards established by the Board.
2. The provider, through an agent or otherwise, advertises its services in a fraudulent or deceptive way.
3. The provider, instructor, or designee of the provider falsifies any information relating to the application for approval, course information, student records, or fails to produce records required by 18VAC50-30-210 C.

ARTICLE 2—VIRGINIA CONTRACTOR TRANSACTION RECOVERY ACT

§54.1-1118. Definitions

As used in this article, unless the context requires a different meaning:

"Act" means the Virginia Contractor Transaction Recovery Act.

"Biennium" means a two-year period beginning on July 1 of an even-numbered year and continuing through June 30 of the next even-numbered year.

"Claimant" means any person with an unsatisfied judgment involving residential construction against a regulant, who has filed a verified claim under this Act.

"Fund" means the Contractor Transaction Recovery Fund.

"Improper or dishonest conduct" includes only the wrongful taking or conversion of money, property, or other things of value which involves fraud, material misrepresentation or conduct constituting gross negligence, continued incompetence, or intentional violation of the Uniform Statewide Building Code (§*36-97* et seq.). The term "improper or dishonest conduct" does not include mere breach of contract.

"Judgment" includes an order of a United States Bankruptcy Court (i) declaring a claim against a regulant who is in bankruptcy to be a "Debt Nondischargeable in Bankruptcy" or (ii) extinguishing a claim against a regulant who is in bankruptcy and for which claim no distribution was made from the regulant's bankruptcy estate but excluding any such claim disallowed by order of the bankruptcy court.

"Regulant" means any individual, person, firm, corporation, association, partnership, joint venture, or any other legal entity licensed by the Board for Contractors. "Regulant" shall not include tradesmen or backflow prevention device workers licensed or certified in accordance with Article 3 (§54.1-1128 et seq.) of this chapter.

§54.1-1119. Assessments by Director; assignment to Fund; minimum balance; notice; penalties; costs of administration

A. Each initial regulant, at the time of application, shall be assessed twenty-five dollars, which shall be specifically assigned to the Fund. Initial payments may be incorporated in any application fee payment and transferred to the Fund by the Director within thirty days.

   All assessments, except initial assessments, for the Fund shall be deposited within three work days after their receipt by the Director, in one or more federally insured banks, savings and loan associations or savings banks located in the Commonwealth. Funds deposited in banks, savings institutions or savings banks, to the extent in excess of insurance afforded by the Federal Deposit Insurance Corporation or other federal insurance agency, shall be secured under the Security for Public Deposits Act (§*2.1-359* et seq.). The deposit of these funds in federally insured banks, savings and loan associations or savings banks located in the Commonwealth shall not be considered investment of such funds for purposes of this section. Funds maintained by the Director may be invested in securities that are legal investments for fiduciaries under the provisions of §*26-40.01*.

B. The minimum balance of the Fund shall be $400,000. Whenever the Director determines that the balance of the Fund is or will be less than this minimum balance, the Director shall immediately inform the Board, which shall assess each regulant at the time of his license renewal a sum sufficient to bring the balance of the Fund to an amount of not less than $400,000, when combined with similar assessments of other regulants. No regulant shall be assessed a total amount of more than fifty dollars during any biennium.

   Notice to regulants of these assessments shall be by first-class mail, and payment of such assessments shall be made by first-class mail addressed to the Director within forty-five days after the mailing of the notice to regulants.

C. If any regulant fails to remit the required assessment mailed in accordance with subsection B within forty-five days of such mailing, the Director shall notify such regulant by first-class mail at the latest address of record filed with the Board. If no payment has been received by the Director within thirty days after mailing the second notice, the license of the regulant shall be automatically suspended and shall be restored only upon the actual receipt by the Director of the delinquent assessment.

Interest earned on the deposits constituting the Fund shall be used for administering the Fund. The remainder of this interest may be used for the purposes of providing educational programs about the Uniform Statewide Building Code (§*36-97* et seq.), for providing education on subjects of benefit to licensees or members of the public relating to contracting, or shall accrue to the Fund.

§54.1-1120. Recovery from Fund generally

A. Whenever any person is awarded a judgment in a court of competent jurisdiction in the Commonwealth of Virginia against any individual or entity which involves improper or dishonest conduct occurring (i) during a period when such individual or entity was a regulant and (ii) in connection with a transaction involving contracting, the claimant may file a verified claim with the Director to obtain a directive ordering payment from the Fund of the amount unpaid upon the judgment, subject to the following conditions:

1. If any action is instituted against a regulant by any person, such person shall serve a copy of the process upon the Board in the manner prescribed by law. Included in such service shall be an affidavit stating all acts constituting improper or dishonest conduct. The provisions of §*8.01-288* shall not be applicable to the service of process required by this subdivision.

2. A copy of any pleading or document filed subsequent to the initial service of process in the action against a regulant shall be provided to the Board. The claimant shall submit such copies to the Board by certified mail, or the equivalent, upon his receipt of the pleading or document.

3. For judgments entered on or after July 1, 1996, a verified claim shall be filed with the Director no later than twelve months after the judgment became final. Such verified claim shall be accompanied by the copies of the order for the underlying judgment, and evidence of compliance with subdivisions 6 and 7 below.

4. The claimant shall be (i) an individual whose contract with the regulant involved contracting for the claimant's residence(s) located in the Commonwealth or (ii) a property owners' association as defined in §*55-509* whose contract with the regulant involved contracting for improvements to the common area owned by such association.

5. The claimant shall not himself be (i) an employee of such judgment debtor, (ii) a vendor of such judgment debtor, (iii) another licensee, (iv) the spouse or child of such judgment debtor nor the employee of such spouse or child, or (v) any financial or lending institution nor anyone whose business involves the construction or development of real property.

6. No directive ordering payment from the fund to the claimant the amount remaining unpaid on the judgment, subject to the limitations set forth in §*54.1- 1123*. The claimant shall be notified in writing of the findings of the Board. The Board's findings shall be considered a "case decision" and judicial review of these findings shall be in accordance with §*2.2-4025* of the Administrative Process Act (§*2.2-4000* et seq.). Notwithstanding any other provision

of law, the Board shall have the right to appeal a decision of any court which is contrary to any distribution recommended or authorized by it.

    a. That the claimant has conducted debtor's interrogatories to determine whether the judgment debtor has any assets which may be sold or applied in satisfaction of the judgment.

    b. A description of the assets disclosed by such interrogatories.

    c. That all legally available actions have been taken for the sale, or application of the disclosed assets and the amount realized therefrom.

    d. The balance remaining due the claimant after the sale or application of such assets.

  7. A claimant shall not be denied recovery from the Fund due to the fact the order for the judgment filed with the verified claim does not contain a specific finding of "improper or dishonest conduct." Any language in the order which supports the conclusion that the court found that the conduct of the regulant involved improper or dishonest conduct may be used by the Board to determine eligibility for recovery from the Fund.

B. If the regulant has filed bankruptcy, the claimant shall file a claim with the proper bankruptcy court. If no distribution is made, the claimant may then file a claim with the Board. The Board shall determine (i) whether the conduct that gave rise to the claim was improper or dishonest and (ii) what amount, if any, such claimant is entitled to recover from the Fund.

§54.1-1121. Investigations

Upon receipt of the notice of proceedings against the regulant, the Board may cause its own investigation to be conducted.

§54.1-1122. Consideration of applications for payment

A. The Department shall promptly consider the verified claim of the claimant administratively. If it appears that a prima facie case has been made for payment of the claim, the Department shall provide the regulant with a notice offering the opportunity to be heard at an informal fact-finding conference pursuant to **§2.2-4019** of the Administrative Process Act (**§2.2-4000**, et seq.). Such notice shall state that if the regulant does not request an informal fact-finding conference within 30 days, with three days added in instances where the notice is sent by mail, the Department shall present the claim to the Board with a recommendation to pay the verified claim.

B. If the Board finds there has been compliance with the required conditions, the Board shall issue a directive ordering payment from the fund to the claimant the amount remaining unpaid on the judgment, subject to the limitations set forth in **§54.1-1123**. The claimant shall be notified in writing of the findings of the Board. The Board's findings shall be considered a "case decision" and judicial review of these findings shall be in accordance with **§2.2-4025** of the Administrative Process Act (**§2.2-4000** et seq.). Notwithstanding any other provision of law, the Board shall have the right to appeal a decision of any court which is contrary to any distribution recommended or authorized by it.

§54.1-1123. Limitations upon recovery from Fund; certain actions not a bar to recovery

A. The maximum claim of one claimant against the Fund based upon an unpaid judgment arising out of the improper or dishonest conduct of one regulant in connection with a single transaction involving contracting, is limited to $20,000, regardless of the amount of the unpaid judgment of the claimant.

VAC
Transaction Recovery Act

B. The aggregate of claims against the Fund based upon unpaid judgments arising out of the improper or dishonest conduct of any one regulant involving contracting, is limited by the Board to $40,000 during any biennium. If a claim has been made against the Fund, and the Board has reason to believe there may be additional claims against the Fund from other transactions involving the same regulant, the Board may withhold any payment(s) from the Fund involving such regulant for a period of not more than one year from the date on which the claimant is awarded in a court of competent jurisdiction in the Commonwealth the final judgment on which his claim against the Fund is based. After this one-year period, if the aggregate of claims against the regulant exceeds $40,000, during a biennium, $40,000 shall be prorated by the Board among the claimants and paid from the Fund in proportion to the amounts of their judgments against the regulant remaining unpaid.

C. Excluded from the amount of any unpaid judgment upon which a claim against the Fund is based shall be any sums representing interest, or punitive or exemplary damages, or any amounts that do not constitute actual monetary loss to the claimants. Such claim against the Fund may include court costs and attorneys' fees.

D. If, at any time, the amount of the Fund is insufficient to fully satisfy any claims or claim filed with the Board and authorized by this Act, the Board shall pay such claims, claim, or portion thereof to the claimants in the order that the claims were filed with the Board.

E. Failure of a claimant to comply with the provisions of subdivisions 1, 2, and 7 of *§54.1-1120* and the provisions of *§54.1-1124* shall not be a bar to recovery under this Act if the claimant is otherwise entitled to such recovery.

F. The Board shall have the authority to deny any claim which otherwise appears to meet the requirements of the Act if it finds by clear and convincing evidence that the claimant has presented false information or engaged in collusion to circumvent any of the requirements of the Act.

§54.1-1124. Participation by Board or Director in proceeding

Upon service of process as provided in subdivision 1 of *§54.1-1120*, the Board, the Director, or duly authorized representatives of the Board shall then have the right to request leave of court to intervene.

§54.1-1125. Assignment of claimant's rights to Board; payment of claim

Subject to the provisions of *§54.1-1123* upon the claimant's execution and delivery to the Director of an assignment to the Board of his rights against the regulant, to the extent he received satisfaction from the Fund, the Director shall pay the claimant from the Fund the amount ordered by the Board.

§54.1-1126. Revocation of license upon payment from Fund

Upon payment by the Director to a claimant from the Fund as provided in *§54.1-1125*, the Board shall immediately revoke the license of the regulant whose improper or dishonest conduct resulted in this payment. Any regulant whose license is revoked shall not be eligible to apply for a license as a contractor until the regulant has repaid in full the amount paid from the Fund on his account, plus interest at the judgment rate of interest from the date of payment.

§54.1-1127. No waiver by Board of disciplinary action against regulant

This article shall not limit the authority of the Board to take disciplinary action against any regulant for any violation of this title or the regulations of the Board. Full repayment of the amount paid from the Fund on a regulant's account shall not nullify or modify the effect of any disciplinary proceeding against that regulant for any violation.

RBC-9.1(8/01/05)

DEPARTMENT OF PROFESSIONAL AND OCCUPATIONAL REGULATION
STATEMENT OF CONSUMER PROTECTIONS

THIS CONSUMER INFORMATION SHEET IS PROVIDED THROUGH
THE BOARD FOR CONTRACTORS AND MAY BE
REPRODUCED BUT NOT ALTERED

If you are about to engage the services of a contractor in the Commonwealth of Virginia, you should be aware of the state's program for the regulation of this occupation by licensing or certifying these businesses.

Any contractor who undertakes a project the total value of which is $120,000 or more is required to have a valid Class A license issued by the Board for Contractors. Any contractor who undertakes a project the total value of which is over $7,500 but less than $120,000 must have a valid Class B license. A licensed contractor has met standards established by the Board for Contractors to ensure that the licensee possesses the character, knowledge, and skills necessary to practice without harm to the public.

Any contractor who undertakes a project the total value of which is more than $1,000 but no more than $7,500 is required to have a valid Class C license. Class C licensure requires that the contractor submit information to the Board for Contractors concerning the location, nature, and operation of the business, as well as evidence of experience and information on the applicant's credit history. **Contractors who work in the plumbing, electrical, heating/ventilation/air-conditioning or gas-fitting trades must have either a Class A, Class B , or Class C license, according to project amount.**

Before signing any contract, you should ask to see the license or the pocket card issued with the license number and check to be sure that it has not expired and that the contractor is working within the limits of his licensure.

The authority of the Board for Contractors to discipline the licensed contractors is limited to specific violations of the law and/or regulations of the board, such as written citations from the local Building Inspectors for violations of the Virginia Uniform Statewide Building Code or practices which constitute abandonment, gross negligence, continued incompetence, or misconduct in the practice of the profession. In such cases disciplinary action by the board is limited to fines and/or revocation or suspension of the contractor's license, and such action can only be taken after a hearing or with the consent of the license holder and his agreement to waive his right to a hearing.

The board does not have the authority to order a license holder to make restitution to you for losses you may have incurred due to the contractor's poor performance; efforts to recover such funds must be made through the civil courts. If you are planning to take such action against the contractor, you should contact the Board for Contractors at (804) 367-1559 in order to receive information about the Virginia Contractors Transaction Recovery Fund and the procedures for applying to recover from the fund if you are unable to collect after judgment is awarded in court. Issues involving cosmetic defects in workmanship must be resolved by negotiation between you and your contractor or civil action to enforce the terms of your contract if necessary. **You should be careful in reviewing the contract before signing it in order to be sure that the terms of the agreement are clear and acceptable to you.** You should know that, customarily, the initial down payment is no more than 30% of the total value of the contract and that, if you are dissatisfied with the work performed by the sub-contractors, you may hold the general contractor responsible. Finally, remember that, in accordance with the Virginia Home Solicitation Sales Act (Code of Virginia, Section 59.1-21.1 et seq.), you have a three-day right to cancel a contract which you have negotiated in your home. (For more precise information about the application of this law, see the Code of Virginia or seek legal advice.)

Should you have reason to believe that your contractor may not have complied with the rules and regulations of the Board for Contractors, you should notify the Department of Professional and Occupational Regulation by calling (804) 367-8504 or write to the following address:

> Department of Professional and Occupational Regulation
> Compliance & Investigations Division
> 3600 West Broad Street
> Richmond, Virginia 23230-4917

The aforementioned information is not intended to be an exhaustive list of the remedies available to you through your local government or other agencies. If you need additional assistance, call the Virginia Department of Agriculture and Consumer Services, Citizens Assistance number at (804) 786-2042, or write to the following address:

> Department of Agriculture and Consumer Services
> Washington Building - Capitol Square
> 1100 Bank Street, Room 101
> Richmond, Virginia 23219

VAC
Transaction Recovery Act

Commonwealth of Virginia
Department of Professional and Occupational Regulation
Post Office Box 11066
Richmond, Virginia 23230-1066
(804) 367-8511
www.dpor.virginia.gov

Board for Contractors
LICENSE APPLICATION

A check or money order payable to the <u>TREASURER OF VIRGINIA</u>, *or*
a completed credit card insert must be mailed with your application package.
APPLICATION FEES ARE NOT REFUNDABLE.

Select the **one** license you are requesting.

Type of License	Fee	X
Class **A** License	$ 265.00	☐
Class **B** License	$ 240.00	☐
Class **C** License	$ 175.00	☐

FINANCIAL REQUIREMENTS

Class **A** Applicants: Must submit an annual report, balance sheet <u>OR</u> financial statement showing a CPA review to provide proof of your firm's net worth of at least $45,000. A **Class A Financial Statement** is included on page 6 of this application.

Class **B** Applicants: Does your firm meet the net worth requirement of $15,000?

Yes ☐
No ☐   If no, your firm is <u>not eligible</u> for a Class B Contractor License.

1. Business Entity/Sole Proprietor's Name

2. Trade or "Fictitious" Name

3. Federal Employer Identification Number

    Sole Proprietor's Social Security No. *

4. Street Address (PO Box <u>not</u> accepted)
    City, State, Zip Code

5. Mailing Address
    City, State, Zip Code

6. E-mail Address

7. Telephone & Facsimile Numbers

    (   )   -   (   )   -   (   )   -
    Telephone   Facsimile   Beeper/Cellular

8. Type of business entity (select only <u>one</u>)

    Sole Proprietorship ☐   Limited Partnership ☐   Limited Liability Company ☐
    General Partnership ☐   Association ☐   Corporation ☐

OFFICE USE ONLY	DATE	FEE	CLASS OF FEE	LICENSE NUMBER		ISSUE DATE

SCC	ETS	CLASS A	CLASS B	VIRGINIA	TECHNICAL

27LIC (8/01/07)

Board for Contractors/LICENSE APPLICATION

9. Does your business have another current or expired license issued by the Board for Contractors?

    NO   ☐

    YES   ☐   License Number _____   Expiration Date _____

10. Effective with all applications received on or after August 21, 2006, all business entities applying for a license, that are not applying for a change of license class only, are required to have their Designated Employee (Class A or B only) **_or_** a member of Responsible Management complete an eight hour business class approved by the Board for Contractors. Complete the following information on the individual who has successfully completed this requirement.

Name _____

                First   Middle   Last   Generation   Birth Date

Social Security Number*   ☐☐☐ - ☐☐ - ☐☐☐☐   Course Provider _____

Completion Date _____

11. All Class A & Class B (**not Class C**) license applicants are required to declare a Designated Employee who has successfully completed the appropriate licensure examination and is either a bona fide full-time employee of the applicant or a member of Responsible Management. If no one at your business entity has passed the licensure exam, contact PSI Examination Services at 3210 East Tropicana, Las Vegas, NV 89121; www.psiexams.com; telephone 800-733-9267 or facsimile 818-247-3853. Complete the following information on the individual selected to be the Designated Employee of this firm.

Designated Employee's Name _____

                First   Middle   Last   Generation

Social Security Number*   ☐☐☐ - ☐☐ - ☐☐☐☐   Birth Date _____   Exam Date _____

In addition to the class of a license (A, B & C) all contractor license must have at least one license classification or specialty diesignation. Below is a list of the license classifications and specialty designations issued by the Virginia Board for Contractors and the **three-letter code** to be entered when completing the Qualified Individual table #12. A definition of the type of work that each of these classifications and designations may perform is available in the *Board for Contractors Regulations*. A license may have more than one classification or specialty designation.

AES	Alternative energy systems	FIC	Farm improvement	BRK	Masonry
ASB⌇	Asbestos	FAS	Fire alarm systems	MBC	Modular/manufactured bldg
PAV	Asphalt paving & seal coating	SPR⌇	Fire sprinkler	NGF⌇	Natural gas fitting provider
BSC	Billboard/sign	FSP	Fire suppression	PTC	Painting & wall covering
BEC⌇	Blast/explosive	GFC⌇	Gas fitting	PLB⌇	Plumbing
BLD⌇	Building	H/H	Highway/Heavy	RMC⌇	Radon mitigation
CIC	Commercial improvement	HIC	Home improvement	RFC	Recreational facility
CEM	Concrete	HVA⌇	HVAC	REF	Refrigeration
ELE⌇	Electrical	ISC	Landscape irrigation	ROC	Roofing
ESC	Electronic/communication service	LSC	Landscape service	SDS	Sewage disposal systems
EEC⌇	Elevator/escalator	LAC⌇	Lead abatement	POL	Swimming pool construction
EMW	Environmental monitoring well	LPG⌇	Liquefied petroleum gas	VCC	Vessel construction
ENV	Environmental specialties	MCC	Marine facility	WWP⌇	Waterwell/Pump
EMC	Equipment/machinery				

⌇ Indicates that additional certification, licensure and/or testing may be required for the classification/specialty.

12. List the classification/designation for which you are applying and <u>one</u> Qualified Individual for each classification/designation. The Qualified Individual must possess the minimum number of years of relevant experience required for the type of license being requested (i.e., 2 years for a Class C License, 3 years for a Class B License and 5 years for a Class A License).

♦ *Qualified Individuals for the electrical, plumbing, HVAC, gas fitting, liquefied petroleum gas fitting and natural gas fitting provider classifications must hold a current Master Tradesman Card issued by the Virginia Board for Contractors Tradesman Program. This individual must be a full-time employee (working 30 hours or more for the business or one of the persons listed as Responsible Management in item #14).*

3-letter Code	Last Name	First Name	MI	Years of Experience	Social Security No. *	(if applicable) VA Tradesman License No.	Birth Date
						2710	
						2710	
						2710	
						2710	
						2710	

13. Three references that will attest to the Qualified Individual's satisfactory completion of contracting work in their license classification(s) and/or specialty designation(s). If your business employs more than one Qualified Individual, please attach an **Additional Qualified Individual Experience Reference Form (27qiexp)** for each additional Qualified Individual.

Name	Street Address, City, State, Zip Code	Telephone Number
		( ) -
		( ) -
		( ) -

14. Responsible Management (sole proprietor, partners of a general partnership, managing partner of a limited partnership, officers/directors of an association, managers/members of a limited liability company, or officers of a corporation)

Individual's Full Legal Name	Title	Address	Social Security No.

15. Does your business have a current or expired contractors license, certification or registration in another state?

No ☐
Yes ☐ If yes, complete the following table.

Business Name	State	License, Certification or Registration No.	Expiration Date

16. Does your Designated Employee, Qualified Individual(s) or Responsible Management have a current or expired contractor's license, certification or registration in another state?

No ☐
Yes ☐   If yes, complete the following table.

Individual's Full Legal Name	Business Name	State	License, Certification or Registration No.	Expiration Date

17. Has your business, Designated Employee, Qualified Individual(s) or Responsible Management been subject to a disciplinary action imposed by <u>any</u> (including Virginia) local, state or national regulatory body?

No ☐
Yes ☐   If yes, please provide a certified copy of the final order, decree or case decision by a court or regulatory agency with lawful authority to issue such order, decree or case decision.

18. A. Has your business, Designated Employee, Qualified Individual(s) or Responsible Management ever been convicted in any jurisdiction of **any felony**? *Any guilty plea or plea of nolo contendere must be disclosed on this application. Do not disclose violations that were adjudicated as a minor in the juvenile court system.*

No ☐
Yes ☐   If yes, please provide the information requested in #18.C.

B. Has your business, Designated Employee, Qualified Individual(s) or Responsible Management ever been convicted in any jurisdiction of **any misdemeanor** within the last three years? *Any guilty plea or plea of nolo contendere must be disclosed on this application. Do not disclose violations that were adjudicated as a minor in the juvenile court system.*

No ☐
Yes ☐   If yes, please provide the information requested in #18.C.
Please read the following instructions carefully!

C. If you answered "yes" to either question #18.A. or #18.B., list the felony and/or misdemeanor conviction(s). Attach your original criminal history record and any other information you wish to have considered with this application (i.e., information on the status of incarceration, parole or probation; reference letters; documentation of rehabilitation; etc.). If necessary, you may attach a separate sheet of paper.

Original criminal history records may be obtained by contacting the state police in the jurisdiction in which you were convicted. Virginia residents *__must__* obtain complete a criminal history record from the Virginia State Police. You may obtain a request form from the Department of State Police, Central Criminal Records Exchange, Post Office Box 27472, Midlothian, Virginia 23261-7472 or by contacting your local State Police Division. *Certified copies of court records* may be obtained by writing to the Clerk of the Court in the jurisdiction in which you were convicted. The address is available from your local police department.

_____

_____

_____

19. During the past five years, has your business, Designated Employee, Qualified Individual(s), or Responsible Management had any outstanding/past-due debts or judgments; outstanding tax obligations; or defaults on bonds?

No ☐
Yes ☐   IF YES, YOU MUST PROVIDE AN EXPLANATION OF THE SITUATION, INCLUDING

DOCUMENTATION OF THE BEGINNING BALANCE, CURRENT BALANCE AND PAYMENT ARRANGEMENTS. Failure to provide adequate documentation may result in a delay in the processing of your application.

20. Does your Responsible Management understand that all Class A, Class B and Class C Contractors must comply with the local licensing requirements of all counties, cities and towns in which work is performed?

Yes ☐

No ☐ **IF NO, THIS APPLICATION CANNOT BE PROCESSED.**

By signing this application, you acknowledge that if you are not a Virginia resident, or move outside of Virginia while you hold a Virginia Contractors License, you understand that this application serves as a written power of attorney, whereby you appoint the Director of the Department of Professional and Occupational Regulation, and his/her successors in office, to be your true and lawful agency and attorney-in-fact, in your stead, upon whom all legal process against and notice to you may be served and who is hereby authorized to enter an appearance in your behalf in any case or proceedings arising out of the trade or profession practiced; and that by submitting this application, you hereby agree that any lawful process against you which is duly served on said agent and attorney-in-fact shall be of the same legal force and validity as if served upon you.

21 I, the undersigned, certify that the foregoing statements and answers are true, and I have not suppressed any information that might affect the Board's decision to approve this application. I certify that I will notify the Department if the business, the designated employee, the qualified individual(s), or any member of responsible management are subject to any disciplinary action; judgments or past due debts; or convicted of any felony or misdemeanor charges (in any jurisdiction) prior to the receipt of the requested license. I certify that I am a member of responsible management as defined in 18 VAC 50-22-10 of the Board for Contractors regulations and am authorized to bind the applicant to contracts and other legal obligations. I also certify that I understand, and have complied with, all the laws of Virginia related to contractor licensure under the provisions of Title 54.1, Chapter 11 of the *Code of Virginia*, and the *Board for Contractors Regulations*.

Responsible Management (sole proprietor, partners of a general partnership, managing partner of a limited partnership, officers/directors of an association, managers/members of a limited liability company, or officers of a corporation)

Name _____ SS # _____ DOB _____

Signature _____ Title _____ Date _____

* State law requires every applicant for a license, certificate, registration or other authorization to engage in a business, trade, profession or occupation issued by the Commonwealth to provide a social security number or a control number issued by the Virginia Department of Motor Vehicles.

Commonwealth of Virginia
Department of Professional and Occupational Regulation
3600 West Broad Street
Post Office Box 11066
Richmond, Virginia 23230-1066
(804) 367-8511

Board for Contractors
FINANCIAL STATEMENT

ONLY <u>CLASS A</u> APPLICANTS ARE REQUIRED TO COMPLETE THIS SECTION OF THE CONTRACTOR LICENSE APPLICATION.

All applicants are required to furnish proof of financial responsibility. Excluding any property owned as tenants by the entirety, applicants for a Class A license must document a net worth or equity of $45,000 or more *and* a current ratio of assets to liabilities.

A current financial statement that essentially duplicates the information included on this form may be substituted, however **the net worth and current ratio information must be entered on lines 10, 20, 21, and 23**. Please note that the information reported on the financial statement must not be more than one year old. All assets and liabilities must be in the name of the business entity applying for the license.

Balance Sheet as of   _____

Contracting Business Name   _____

	ASSETS	
1.	**Current Assets**	
2.	Cash and Investments	
3.	Accounts Receivable (Net)	
4.	Inventories	
5.	Prepaid Expenses	
6.	Other Current Assets	
7.	**Total Current Assets** (sum of lines 2 through 6)	
8.	Land, Buildings and Equipment (Net)	
9.	Other Non-Current Assets	
10.	**TOTAL ASSETS** (sum of lines 7 through 9)	

	LIABILITIES AND OWNER'S EQUITY	
11.	**Current Liabilities**	
12.	Accounts Payable	
13.	Current Portion of Long-term Debt (payable within the next 12 months)	
14.	Accrued Taxes	
15.	Accrued Payroll	
16.	Other Current Liabilities	
17.	**Total Current Liabilities** (sum of lines 12 through 16)	
18.	Long-term Debt	
19.	Other Long-term Liabilities	
20.	**TOTAL LIABILITIES** (sum of lines 17 through 19)	
21.	**OWNER'S EQUITY (NET WORTH)** (line 10 minus line 20)	
22.	**TOTAL LIABILITIES & OWNER'S EQUITY** (sum of lines 20 and 21)	
23.	**CURRENT RATIO** (line 7 divided by line 17)	

Is a substitute Financial Statement attached?   Yes ☐   No ☐

EROSION AND SEDIMENT CONTROLS

Virginia has established statewide regulations to require control of water and sediment debris leaving a work site. This chapter explains which areas must be controlled, how to file a plan, and methods of containment. The state codes governing this program are the Code of Virginia (CoV), Title 10.1, Chapter 5, Article 4 and the Virginia Administration Code (VAC), Title 4, Conservation and Natural Resources. These codes can be found at the end of this chapter and may also be viewed online at *http://leg1.state.va.us/*. More information about the ESC program can be downloaded from the Department of Conservation and Recreation Web site at *www.dcr.state.va.us*.

EROSION AND SEDIMENT CONTROL

Soil erosion is the removal of material from a site by water, wind, or gravity. Erosion and sediment control measures will prevent problems with soil erosion and movement. While construction activities are not a major cause of sediment deposition, they are a major cause of accelerated erosion. Erosion problems associated with construction activities include water pollution, flooding, stream channel damage, decreased groundwater storage, slope failures, and damage to adjacent properties.

Erosion and sediment control (ESC) programs regulate construction activities that constitute land-disturbing activities. A **land-disturbing activity** is any change to the land that may result in soil erosion from water or wind and the movement of sediments into state waters or onto other land. The ESC program applies to both public and private lands in the commonwealth, and covers land-disturbing activities including, but not limited to, the clearing, grading, excavating, transporting, and filling of land (CoV 10.1-560). This definition includes land-disturbing activities equal to or exceeding 10,000 square feet in area; however, the following 13 activities are specifically *exempt* from the definition:

1. Disturbed land areas of less than 10,000 square feet in size. A local ESC program may reduce this exception to a smaller area of disturbed land or qualify the conditions under which this exception shall apply;

2. Minor land-disturbing activities and individual home landscaping, repairs, and maintenance work;

3. Individual service connections;

4. Installation, maintenance, or repair of underground public utility lines when such activity is confined to an existing hard-surfaced road, street, or sidewalk;

5. Septic tank lines or drainage fields unless included in an overall plan for land-disturbing activity relating to construction of the building to be served by the septic tank system;

6. Surface or deep mining;

7. Exploration or drilling for oil and gas including the well site, roads, feeder lines, and off-site disposal areas;

8. Tilling, planting, or harvesting of agricultural, horticultural, or forest crops, or livestock feedlot operations; including a specific list of engineering operations;

9. Repair or rebuilding of the tracks, right-of-way, bridges, communication facilities, and other related structures, and facilities of a railroad company;

10. Agricultural engineering operations including but not limited to the construction of terraces, terrace outlets, check dams, desilting basins, dikes, ponds not required to comply with the provisions of the Virginia Dam Safety Act, ditches, strip-cropping, lister furrowing, contour cultivating, contour furrowing, land drainage, and land irrigation;

11. Installation of fence, sign, telephone, electric, or other kinds of posts or poles;

12. Shore erosion control projects on tidal waters when the projects are approved by local wetlands boards, the Marine Resources Commission, or the U. S. Army Corps of Engineers; and

13. Emergency work to protect life, limb, or property, and emergency repairs.

Responsible Land Disturber

Virginia requires that anyone performing excavation be certified as a Responsible Land Disturber (RLD). The responsible land disturber program was established as a component of the Virginia Erosion and Sediment Control (ESC) Program.

In order to submit an erosion and sediment control plan for approval, the person responsible for carrying out the plan must provide the name of the individual holding an RLD certificate who will be in charge of and responsible for carrying out the regulated land-disturbing activity. The Department of Conservation and Recreation operates the RLD Certificate of Competence Program.

Registration for the computer exam is available online and the exam can be taken anywhere. Study materials can be downloaded and used during the open-book exam. The exam is multiple choice and test-takers are allotted one hour to complete it. Information about the exam can be found on the Department of Conservation and Recreation Web site at *www.dcr.virginia.gov/sw/es_rld.htm.*

Erosion and Sediment Control Plans

There are 19 minimum standards that must be met to comply with the erosion and sediment control regulations. These standards are outlined in VAC 50-30-40, which is included at the end of this chapter. Acceptable plans require extensive detail about soil type, surface runoff, retention, silt fencing, seeding, and maintenance. A typical plan is several pages long and includes much technical detail. The technical detail needed requires that the plans be prepared by an individual who has extensive knowledge and training in the field of Virginia erosion and sediment control measures.

The statewide regulations require erosion and sediment control for areas larger than 10,000 square feet, but this may be amended by localities, and usually is much less than 10,000 square feet. If a contractor is going to perform any land-disturbing activity, it is recommended that local officials be contacted to determine compliance requirements.

CODE OF VIRGINIA (COV)
TITLE 10.1, CHAPTER 5, ARTICLE 4

§10.1-560. Definitions

As used in this article, unless the context requires a different meaning:

"Agreement in lieu of a plan" means a contract between the plan-approving authority and the owner that specifies conservation measures that must be implemented in the construction of a single-family residence; this contract may be executed by the plan-approving authority in lieu of a formal site plan.

"Applicant" means any person submitting an erosion and sediment control plan for approval or requesting the issuance of a permit, when required, authorizing land-disturbing activities to commence.

"Certified inspector" means an employee or agent of a program authority who (i) holds a certificate of competence from the Board in the area of project inspection or (ii) is enrolled in the Board's training program for project inspection and successfully completes such program within one year after enrollment.

"Certified plan reviewer" means an employee or agent of a program authority who (i) holds a certificate of competence from the Board in the area of plan review, (ii) is enrolled in the Board's training program for plan review and successfully completes such program within one year after enrollment, or (iii) is licensed as a professional engineer, architect, certified landscape architect or land surveyor pursuant to Article 1 (§54.1-400 et seq.) of Chapter 4 of Title 54.1.

"Certified program administrator" means an employee or agent of a program authority who (i) holds a certificate of competence from the Board in the area of program administration or (ii) is enrolled in the Board's training program for program administration and successfully completes such program within one year after enrollment.

"Conservation plan," "erosion and sediment control plan," or "plan" means a document containing material for the conservation of soil and water resources of a unit or group of units of land. It may include appropriate maps, an appropriate soil and water plan inventory and management information with needed interpretations, and a record of decisions contributing to conservation treatment. The plan shall contain all major conservation decisions to assure that the entire unit or units of land will be so treated to achieve the conservation objectives.

"District" or "soil and water conservation district" means a political subdivision of the Commonwealth organized in accordance with the provisions of Article 3 (§10.1-506 et seq.) of this chapter.

"Erosion impact area" means an area of land not associated with current land-disturbing activity but subject to persistent soil erosion resulting in the delivery of sediment onto neighboring properties or into state waters. This definition shall not apply to any lot or parcel of land of 10,000 square feet or less used for residential purposes or to shorelines where the erosion results from wave action or other coastal processes.

"Land-disturbing activity" means any land change that may result in soil erosion from water or wind and the movement of sediments into state waters or onto lands in the Commonwealth, including, but not limited to, clearing, grading, excavating, transporting and filling of land, except that the term shall not include:

1. Minor land-disturbing activities such as home gardens and individual home landscaping, repairs and maintenance work;

2. Individual service connections;

3. Installation, maintenance, or repair of any underground public utility lines when such activity occurs on an existing hard surfaced road, street or sidewalk

provided the land-disturbing activity is confined to the area of the road, street or sidewalk which is hard surfaced;

4. Septic tank lines or drainage fields unless included in an overall plan for land-disturbing activity relating to construction of the building to be served by the septic tank system;

5. Surface or deep mining activities authorized under a permit issued by the Department of Mines, Minerals and Energy;

6. Exploration or drilling for oil and gas including the well site, roads, feeder lines and off-site disposal areas;

7. Tilling, planting, or harvesting of agricultural, horticultural, or forest crops, or livestock feedlot operations; including engineering operations as follows: construction of terraces, terrace outlets, check dams, desilting basins, dikes, ponds, ditches, strip cropping, lister furrowing, contour cultivating, contour furrowing, land drainage and land irrigation; however, this exception shall not apply to harvesting of forest crops unless the area on which harvesting occurs is reforested artificially or naturally in accordance with the provisions of Chapter 11 (§10.1-1100 et seq.) of this title or is converted to bona fide agricultural or improved pasture use as described in subsection B of §10.1-1163;

8. Repair or rebuilding of the tracks, right-of-way, bridges, communication facilities and other related structures and facilities of a railroad company;

9. Agricultural engineering operations including but not limited to the construction of terraces, terrace outlets, check dams, desilting basins, dikes, ponds not required to comply with the provisions of the Dam Safety Act, Article 2 (§10.1-604 et seq.) of Chapter 6 of this title, ditches, strip cropping, lister furrowing, contour cultivating, contour furrowing, land drainage and land irrigation;

10. Disturbed land areas of less than 10,000 square feet in size; however, the governing body of the program authority may reduce this exception to a smaller area of disturbed land or qualify the conditions under which this exception shall apply;

11. Installation of fence and sign posts or telephone and electric poles and other kinds of posts or poles;

12. Shoreline erosion control projects on tidal waters when all of the land disturbing activities are within the regulatory authority of and approved by local wetlands boards, the Marine Resources Commission or the United States Army Corps of Engineers; however, any associated land that is disturbed outside of this exempted area shall remain subject to this article and the regulations adopted pursuant thereto; and

13. Emergency work to protect life, limb or property, and emergency repairs; however, if the land-disturbing activity would have required an approved erosion and sediment control plan, if the activity were not an emergency, then the land area disturbed shall be shaped and stabilized in accordance with the requirements of the plan-approving authority.

"Local erosion and sediment control program" or "local control program" means an outline of the various methods employed by a program authority to regulate land-disturbing activities and thereby minimize erosion and sedimentation in compliance with the state program and may include such items as local ordinances, policies and guidelines, technical materials, inspection, enforcement and evaluation.

"Natural channel design concepts" means the utilization of engineering analysis and fluvial geomorphic processes to create, rehabilitate, restore, or stabilize an open conveyance system for the purpose of creating or recreating a stream that conveys its bankfull storm event within its banks and allows larger flows to access its bankfull bench and its floodplain.

"Owner" means the owner or owners of the freehold of the premises or lesser estate therein, a mortgagee or vendee in possession, assignee of rents, receiver, executor, trustee, lessee or other person, firm or corporation in control of a property.

"Peak flow rate" means the maximum instantaneous flow from a given storm condition at a particular location.

"Permittee" means the person to whom the permit authorizing land-disturbing activities is issued or the person who certifies that the approved erosion and sediment control plan will be followed.

"Person" means any individual, partnership, firm, association, joint venture, public or private corporation, trust, estate, commission, board, public or private institution, utility, cooperative, county, city, town, or other political subdivision of the Commonwealth, any interstate body, or any other legal entity.

"Plan-approving authority" means the Board, the program authority, or a department of a program authority, responsible for determining the adequacy of a conservation plan submitted for land-disturbing activities on a unit or units of lands and for approving plans.

"Program authority" means a district, county, city, or town that has adopted a soil erosion and sediment control program that has been approved by the Board.

"Runoff volume" means the volume of water that runs off the land development project from a prescribed storm event.

"State erosion and sediment control program" or "state program" means the program administered by the Board pursuant to this article, including regulations designed to minimize erosion and sedimentation.

"State waters" means all waters on the surface and under the ground wholly or partially within or bordering the Commonwealth or within its jurisdiction.

"Town" means an incorporated town.

"Water quality volume" means the volume equal to the first one-half inch of runoff multiplied by the impervious surface of the land development project.

§10.1-561. State Erosion and Sediment Control Program

A. The Board shall develop a program and promulgate regulations for the effective control of soil erosion, sediment deposition, and nonagricultural runoff that must be met in any control program to prevent the unreasonable degradation of properties, stream channels, waters and other natural resources in accordance with the Administrative Process Act (§2.2-4000 et seq.). Stream restoration and relocation projects that incorporate natural channel design concepts are not man-made channels and shall be exempt from any flow rate capacity and velocity requirements for natural or man-made channels as defined in any regulations promulgated pursuant to this section, §10.1-562, or 10.1-570. Any land-disturbing activity that provides for stormwater management intended to address any flow rate capacity and velocity requirements for natural or man-made channels shall satisfy the flow rate capacity and velocity requirements for natural or man-made channels if the practices are designed to (i) detain the water quality volume and to release it over 48 hours; (ii) detain and release over a 24-hour period the expected rainfall resulting from the one year, 24-hour storm; and (iii) reduce the allowable peak flow rate resulting from the 1.5, 2, and 10-year, 24-hour storms to a level that is less than or equal to the peak flow rate from the site assuming it was in a good forested condition, achieved through multiplication of the forested peak flow rate by a reduction factor that is equal to the runoff volume from the site when it was in a good forested condition divided by the runoff volume from the site in its proposed condition, and shall be exempt from any flow rate capacity and velocity requirements for natural or man-made channels as defined in any regulations promulgated pursuant to §10.1-562 or 10.1-570.

The regulations shall:

1. Be based upon relevant physical and developmental information concerning the watersheds and drainage basins of the Commonwealth, including, but not limited to, data relating to land use, soils, hydrology, geology, size of land area being disturbed, proximate water bodies and their characteristics, transportation, and public facilities and services;

2. Include such survey of lands and waters as may be deemed appropriate by the Board or required by any applicable law to identify areas, including multijurisdictional and watershed areas, with critical erosion and sediment problems; and

3. Contain conservation standards for various types of soils and land uses, which shall include criteria, techniques, and methods for the control of erosion and sediment resulting from land-disturbing activities.

B. The Board shall provide technical assistance and advice to, and conduct and supervise educational programs for, districts and localities that have adopted local control programs.

C. The program and regulations shall be available for public inspection at the Department.

D. The Board shall promulgate regulations establishing minimum standards of effectiveness of erosion and sediment control programs, and criteria and procedures for reviewing and evaluating the effectiveness of erosion and sediment control programs. In developing minimum standards for program effectiveness, the Board shall consider information and standards on which the regulations promulgated pursuant to subsection A of this section are based.

E. The Board shall periodically conduct a comprehensive review and evaluation to ensure that all erosion and sediment control programs operating under the jurisdiction of this article meet minimum standards of effectiveness in controlling soil erosion, sediment deposition and nonagricultural runoff. The Board shall develop a schedule for conducting periodic reviews and evaluations of the effectiveness of erosion and sediment control programs.

F. The Board shall issue certificates of competence concerning the content, application and intent of specified subject areas of this chapter and accompanying regulations, including program administration, plan review, and project inspection, to personnel of program authorities and to any other persons who have completed training programs or in other ways demonstrated adequate knowledge. The Department shall administer education and training programs for specified subject areas of this chapter and accompanying regulations, and is authorized to charge persons attending such programs reasonable fees to cover the costs of administering the programs.

G. As of December 31, 2004, any Department personnel conducting inspections pursuant to this chapter shall hold a certificate of competence as provided in subsection F.

§10.1-561.1. Certification of Local Program Personnel

A. The minimum standards of local program effectiveness established by the Board pursuant to subsection D of §10.1-561 shall provide that within one year following the adoption of amendments to the local program adding the provisions of this section, (i) a conservation plan shall not be approved until it is reviewed by a certified plan reviewer; (ii) inspections of land-disturbing activities are conducted by a certified inspector; and (iii) a local program shall contain a certified program administrator, a certified plan reviewer, and a certified project inspector, who may be the same person.

B. Any person who holds a certificate of competence from the Board in the areas of plan review, project inspection, or program administration which was attained prior to the adoption of the mandatory certification provisions of subsection A of this section shall be deemed to satisfy the requirements of that area of certification.

§10.1-562. Local erosion and sediment control programs

A. Each district in the Commonwealth shall adopt and administer an erosion and sediment control program for any area within the district for which a county, city, or town does not have an approved erosion and sediment control program.

    To carry out its program the district shall adopt regulations consistent with the state program. The regulations may be revised from time to time as necessary. Before adopting or revising regulations, the district shall give due notice and conduct a public hearing on the proposed or revised regulations except that a public hearing shall not be required when the district is amending its program to conform to revisions in the state program. However, a public hearing shall be held if a district proposes or revises regulations that are more stringent than the state program. The program and regulations shall be available for public inspection at the principal office of the district.

B. In areas where there is no district, a county, city, or town shall adopt and administer an erosion and sediment control program.

C. Any county, city, or town within a district may adopt and administer an erosion and sediment control program.

    Any town, lying within a county which has adopted its own erosion and sediment control program, may adopt its own program or become subject to the county program. If a town lies within the boundaries of more than one county, the town shall be considered for the purposes of this article to be wholly within the county in which the larger portion of the town lies. Any county, city, or town with an erosion and sediment control program may designate its department of public works or a similar local government department as the plan-approving authority or may designate the district as the plan-approving authority for all or some of the conservation plans.

D. Any erosion and sediment control program adopted by a district, county, city, or town shall be approved by the Board if it is consistent with the state program and regulations for erosion and sediment control.

E. If a comprehensive review conducted by the Board of a local control program indicates that the program authority has not administered, enforced or conducted its program in a manner that satisfies the minimum standards of effectiveness established pursuant to subsection D of §10.1-561, the Board shall notify the program authority in writing, which notice shall identify corrective action required to attain the minimum standard of effectiveness and shall include an offer to provide technical assistance to implement the corrective action. If the program authority has not implemented the corrective action identified by the Board within 30 days following receipt of the notice, or such additional period as is necessary to complete the implementation of the corrective action, then the Board shall have the authority to (i) issue a special order to any locality that has failed to enter into a corrective action agreement or, where such corrective action agreement exists, has failed to initiate or has not made substantial and consistent progress towards implementing an approved corrective action agreement within the deadline established by the Board to pay a civil penalty not to exceed $5,000 per day with the maximum amount not to exceed $20,000 per violation for noncompliance with the state program, to be paid into the state treasury and deposited in the Virginia Stormwater Management Fund established by §10.1-603.4:1 or (ii) revoke its approval of the program. Prior to issuing a special order or revoking its approval of any local control program, the Board shall conduct a formal hearing pursuant to §2.2-4020 of the Administrative Process Act. Judicial review of any order of the Board issuing a civil penalty pursuant to this section or revoking its approval of a local control program shall be made in accordance with Article 5 (§2.2-4025 et seq.) of the Administrative Process Act.

F. If the Board revokes its approval of a local control program of a county, city, or town, and the locality is in a district, the district shall adopt and administer an erosion and sediment control program for the locality.

G. If the Board (i) revokes its approval of a local control program of a district, or of a county, city, or town not in a district, or (ii) finds that a local program consistent with the state program and regulations has not been adopted by a district or a county, city, or town which is required to adopt and administer a local program, the Board shall, after such hearings or consultations as it deems appropriate with the various local interests involved, develop, adopt, and administer an appropriate program to be carried out within such district, county, city, or town, as applicable, by the Board.

H. If the Board has revoked its approval of any local control program, the program authority may request that the Board approve a replacement program, and the Board shall approve the replacement program if it finds that (i) the program authority is capable of administering the program in accordance with the minimum standards of effectiveness and (ii) the replacement program otherwise meets the requirements of the state program and regulations. The Board shall conduct a formal hearing pursuant to §2.2-4020 of the Administrative Process Act on any request for approval of a replacement program.

I. Any program authority which administers an erosion and sediment control program may charge applicants a reasonable fee to defray the cost of program administration. A program authority shall hold a public hearing prior to enacting an ordinance establishing a schedule of fees. The fee shall not exceed an amount commensurate with the services rendered, taking into consideration the time, skill and administrators' expense involved.

J. The governing body of any county, city or town which (i) is in a district which has adopted a local control program, (ii) has adopted its own local control program, (iii) is subject to a local control program adopted by the Board, or (iv) administers a local control program, may adopt an ordinance providing that violations of any regulation or order of the Board, any provision of its program, any condition of a permit, or any provision of this article shall be subject to a civil penalty. The civil penalty for any one violation shall be not less than $100 nor more than $1,000, except that the civil penalty for commencement of land-disturbing activities without an approved plan as provided in §10.1-563 shall be $1,000. Each day during which the violation is found to have existed shall constitute a separate offense. In no event shall a series of specified violations arising from the same operative set of facts result in civil penalties which exceed a total of $10,000, except that a series of violations arising from the commencement of land-disturbing activities without an approved plan for any site shall not result in civil penalties which exceed a total of $10,000. Adoption of such an ordinance providing that violations are subject to a civil penalty shall be in lieu of criminal sanctions and shall preclude the prosecution of such violation as a misdemeanor under subsection A of §10.1-569.

§10.1-563. Regulated Land-Disturbing Activities; Submission and Approval of Control Plan

A. Except as provided in §10.1-564, no person may engage in any land-disturbing activity until he has submitted to the district or locality an erosion and sediment control plan for the land-disturbing activity and the plan has been reviewed and approved by the plan-approving authority. Where land-disturbing activities involve lands under the jurisdiction of more than one local control program an erosion and sediment control plan may, at the option of the applicant, be submitted to the Board for review and approval rather than to each jurisdiction concerned. Where the land-disturbing activity results from the construction of a single-family residence, an agreement in lieu of a plan may be substituted for an erosion and sediment control plan if executed by the plan-approving authority.

B. The plan-approving authority shall review conservation plans submitted to it and grant written approval within 45 days of the receipt of the plan if it determines that the plan meets the requirements of the Board's regulations and if the person responsible for carrying out the plan certifies that he will properly perform the conservation measures included in the plan and will conform to the provisions of this article. In addition, as a prerequisite to engaging in the land-disturbing activities shown on the approved plan, the person responsible for carrying out the plan shall provide the name of an individual holding a certificate of competence to the program authority, as provided by §10.1-561, who will be in charge of and responsible for carrying out the land-disturbing activity. However, any plan-approving authority may waive the certificate of competence requirement for an agreement in lieu of a plan for construction of a single family residence. If a violation occurs during the land-disturbing activity, then the person responsible for carrying out the agreement in lieu of a plan shall correct the violation and provide the name of an individual holding a certificate of competence, as provided by §10.1-561. Failure to provide the name of an individual holding a certificate of competence prior to engaging in land-disturbing activities may result in revocation of the approval of the plan and the person responsible for carrying out the plan shall be subject to the penalties provided in this article.

When a plan is determined to be inadequate, written notice of disapproval stating the specific reasons for disapproval shall be communicated to the applicant within 45 days. The notice shall specify the modifications, terms and conditions that will permit approval of the plan. If no action is taken by the plan-approving authority within the time specified above, the plan shall be deemed approved and the person authorized to proceed with the proposed activity.

C. An approved plan may be changed by the authority that approved the plan in the following cases:

1. Where inspection has revealed that the plan is inadequate to satisfy applicable regulations; or

2. Where the person responsible for carrying out the approved plan finds that because of changed circumstances or for other reasons the approved plan cannot be effectively carried out, and proposed amendments to the plan, consistent with the requirements of this article, are agreed to by the plan-approving authority and the person responsible for carrying out the plan.

D. Electric, natural gas and telephone utility companies, interstate and intrastate natural gas pipeline companies and railroad companies shall file general erosion and sediment control specifications annually with the Board for review and approval. The specifications shall apply to:

1. Construction, installation or maintenance of electric transmission, natural gas and telephone utility lines and pipelines; and

2. Construction of the tracks, rights-of-way, bridges, communication facilities and other related structures and facilities of the railroad company.

The Board shall have 60 days in which to approve the specifications. If no action is taken by the Board within 60 days, the specifications shall be deemed approved. Individual approval of separate projects within subdivisions 1 and 2 of this subsection is not necessary when approved specifications are followed. Projects not included in subdivisions 1 and 2 of this subsection shall comply with the requirements of the appropriate local erosion and sediment control program. The Board shall have the authority to enforce approved specifications.

E. Any person engaging in the creation and operation of wetland mitigation banks in multiple jurisdictions, which have been approved and are operated in accordance with applicable federal and state guidance, laws, or regulations for the establishment, use, and operation of mitigation banks, pursuant to a permit issued by the Department of Environmental Quality, the Marine Resources Commission, or the U.S. Army Corps of Engineers, may, at the option of that person, file general erosion and sediment control specifications for wetland mitigation banks annually with the Board for review and approval consistent with guidelines established by the Board.

The Board shall have 60 days in which to approve the specifications. If no action is taken by the Board within 60 days, the specifications shall be deemed approved. Individual approval of separate projects under this subsection is not necessary when approved specifications are implemented through a project-specific erosion and sediment control plan. Projects not included in this subsection shall comply with the requirements of the appropriate local erosion and sediment control program. The Board shall have the authority to enforce approved specifications. Approval of general erosion and sediment control specifications by the Board does not relieve the owner or operator from compliance with any other local ordinances and regulations including requirements to submit plans and obtain permits as may be required by such ordinances and regulations.

F. In order to prevent further erosion a local program may require approval of a conservation plan for any land identified in the local program as an erosion impact area.

G. For the purposes of subsections A and B of this section, when land-disturbing activity will be required of a contractor performing construction work pursuant to a construction contract, the preparation, submission and approval of an erosion and sediment control plan shall be the responsibility of the owner.

§10.1-564. State agency projects

A. A state agency shall not undertake a project involving a land-disturbing activity unless (i) the state agency has submitted annual specifications for its conduct of land-disturbing activities which have been reviewed and approved by the Department as being consistent with the state program or (ii) the state agency has submitted a conservation plan for the project which has been reviewed and approved by the Department.

B. The Department shall not approve a conservation plan submitted by a federal or state agency for a project involving a land-disturbing activity (i) in any locality which has not adopted a local program with more stringent regulations than those of the state program or (ii) in multiple jurisdictions with separate local programs, unless the conservation plan is consistent with the requirements of the state program.

C. The Department shall not approve a conservation plan submitted by a federal or state agency for a project involving a land-disturbing activity in one locality with a local program with more stringent regulations than those of the state program unless the conservation plan is consistent with the requirements of the local program. If a locality has not submitted a copy of its local program regulations to the Department, the provisions of subsection B of this section shall apply.

D. The Department shall have sixty days in which to comment on any specifications or conservation plan submitted to it for review, and its comments shall be binding on the state agency and any private business hired by the state agency.

E. As on-site changes occur, the state agency shall submit changes in a conservation plan to the Department.

F. The state agency responsible for the land-disturbing activity shall ensure compliance with the approved plan or specifications.

§10.1-565. Approved Plan Required for Issuance of Grading, Building, or Other Permits; Security for Performance

Agencies authorized under any other law to issue grading, building, or other permits for activities involving land-disturbing activities may not issue any such permit unless the applicant submits with his application an approved erosion and sediment control plan and certification that the plan will be followed. Prior to issuance of any permit, the agency may also require an applicant to submit a reasonable performance bond with surety, cash escrow, letter of credit, any combination thereof, or such other legal arrangement acceptable to the agency, to ensure that measures could be taken by the agency at the applicant's expense should he fail, after proper notice, within the time specified to initiate or maintain appropriate conservation action which may be required of him by the approved plan as a result of his land-disturbing activity. The amount of the bond or other security for performance shall not exceed the total of the estimated cost to initiate and maintain appropriate conservation action based on unit price for new public or private sector construction in the locality and a reasonable allowance for estimated administrative costs and inflation which shall not exceed twenty-five percent of the estimated cost of the conservation action. If the agency takes such conservation action upon such failure by the permittee, the agency may collect from the permittee for the difference should the amount of the reasonable cost of such action exceed the amount of the security held. Within sixty days of the achievement of adequate stabilization of the land-disturbing activity in any project or section thereof, the bond, cash escrow, letter of credit or other legal arrangement, or the unexpended or unobligated portion thereof, shall be refunded to the applicant or terminated based upon the percentage of stabilization accomplished in the project or section thereof. These requirements are in addition to all other provisions of law relating to the issuance of such permits and are not intended to otherwise affect the requirements for such permits.

§10.1-566. Monitoring, Reports, and Inspections

A. The plan-approving authority or, if a permit is issued in connection with land-disturbing activities which involve the issuance of a grading, building, or other permit, the permit-issuing authority (i) shall provide for periodic inspections of the land-disturbing activity and require that an individual holding a certificate of competence, as provided by §10.1-561, who will be in charge of and responsible for carrying out the land-disturbing activity and (ii) may require monitoring and reports from the person responsible for carrying out the plan, to ensure compliance with the approved plan and to determine whether the measures required in the plan are effective in controlling erosion and sediment. The owner, permittee, or person responsible for carrying out the plan shall be given notice of the inspection. If the permit-issuing authority or plan-approving authority determines that there is a failure to comply with the plan, notice shall be served upon the permittee or person responsible for carrying out the plan by registered or certified mail to the address specified in the permit application or in the plan certification, or by delivery at the site of the land-disturbing activities to the agent or employee supervising such activities. Where the plan-approving authority serves notice, a copy of the notice shall also be sent to the issuer of the permit. The notice shall specify the measures needed to comply with the plan and shall specify the time within which such measures shall be completed. Upon failure to comply within the time specified, the permit may be revoked and the permittee or person responsible for carrying out the plan shall be deemed to be in violation of this article and shall be subject to the penalties provided by §10.1-569.

B. Notwithstanding the above provisions of this section the following may be applied:

1. Where a county, city, or town administers the local control program and the permit-issuing authority and the plan-approving authority are not within the same local government department, the locality may designate one department to inspect, monitor, report and ensure compliance. In the event a district has been designated as the plan-approving authority for all or some of the conservation plans, the enforcement of the program shall be with the local government department; however, the district may inspect, monitor and make reports for the local government department.

2. Where a district adopts the local control program and permit-issuing authorities have been established by a locality, the district by joint resolution with the appropriate locality may exercise the responsibilities of the permit-issuing authorities with respect to monitoring, reports, inspections and enforcement.

3. Where a permit-issuing authority has been established, and such authority is not vested in an employee or officer of local government but in the commissioner of revenue or some other person, the locality shall exercise the responsibilities of the permit-issuing authority with respect to monitoring, reports, inspections and enforcement unless such responsibilities are transferred as provided for in this section.

Code of Virginia
Title 10.1

C. Upon receipt of a sworn complaint of a violation of this section, §10.1-563 or §10.1-564 from the representative of the program authority or the Board responsible for ensuring program compliance, the chief administrative officer, or his designee, of the program authority or the Board may, in conjunction with or subsequent to a notice to comply as specified in subsection A above, issue an order requiring that all or part of the land-disturbing activities permitted on the site be stopped until the specified corrective measures have been taken or, if land-disturbing activities have commenced without an approved plan as provided in §10.1-563, requiring that all of the land-disturbing activities be stopped until an approved plan or any required permits are obtained. Where the alleged noncompliance is causing or is in imminent danger of causing harmful erosion of lands or sediment deposition in waters within the watersheds of the Commonwealth, or where the land-disturbing activities have commenced without an approved plan or any required permits, such an order may be issued whether or not the alleged violator has been issued a notice to comply as specified in subsection A above. Otherwise, such an order may be issued only after the alleged violator has failed to comply with a notice to comply. The order shall be served in the same manner as a notice to comply, and shall remain in effect for seven days from the date of service pending application by the enforcing authority or alleged violator for appropriate relief to the circuit court of the jurisdiction wherein the violation was alleged to have occurred. If the alleged violator has not obtained an approved plan or any required permits within seven days from the date of service of the order, the chief administrative officer or his designee may issue an order to the owner requiring that all construction and other work on the site, other than corrective measures, be stopped until an approved plan and any required permits have been obtained. Such an order shall be served upon the owner by registered or certified mail to the address specified in the permit application or the land records of the locality in which the site is located. The owner may appeal the issuance of an order to the circuit court of the jurisdiction wherein the violation was alleged to have occurred. Any person violating or failing, neglecting or refusing to obey an order issued by the chief administrative officer or his designee may be compelled in a proceeding instituted in the circuit court of the jurisdiction wherein the violation was alleged to have occurred to obey same and to comply therewith by injunction, mandamus or other appropriate remedy. Upon completion and approval of corrective action or obtaining an approved plan or any required permits, the order shall immediately be lifted. Nothing in this section shall prevent the chief administrative officer or his designee from taking any other action specified in §10.1-569.

§10.1-567. Cooperation with Federal and State Agencies

The districts and localities operating their own programs, and the Board are authorized to cooperate and enter into agreements with any federal or state agency in connection with plans for erosion and sediment control with respect to land-disturbing activities.

§10.1-568. Appeals

A. Final decisions of counties, cities or towns under this article shall be subject to review by the court of record of the county or city, provided that an appeal is filed within thirty days from the date of any written decision adversely affecting the rights, duties or privileges of the person engaging in or proposing to engage in land-disturbing activities.

B. Final decisions of the districts shall be subject to an administrative review by the Board, provided that an appeal is filed within thirty days from the date of the written decision.

C. Final decisions of the Board either upon its own action or upon the review of the action of a district shall be subject to judicial review in accordance with the provisions of the Administrative Process Act (§2.2-4000 et seq.).

§10.1-569. Penalties, Injunctions, and Other Legal Actions

A. Violators of §§10.1-563, 10.1-564 or §10.1-566 shall be guilty of a Class 1 misdemeanor.

B. If a locality has adopted an ordinance establishing a uniform schedule of civil penalties as permitted by subsection J of §10.1-562, any person who violates any regulation or order of the Board, any condition of a permit, any provision of its program, or any provision of this article shall, upon a finding of an appropriate general district court, be assessed a civil penalty in accordance with the schedule. The erosion and sediment control administrator, his deputy or a certified inspector for the locality wherein the land lies may issue a summons for collection of the civil penalty and the action may be prosecuted by the locality wherein the land lies. In any trial for a scheduled violation, it shall be the burden of the locality to show the liability of the violator by a preponderance of the evidence. An admission or finding of liability shall not be a criminal conviction for any purpose. Any civil penalties assessed by a court shall be paid into the treasury of the locality wherein the land lies, except that where the violator is the locality itself, or its agent, the court shall direct the penalty to be paid into the state treasury.

C. The appropriate permit-issuing authority, the program authority, the Board, or the owner of property which has sustained damage or which is in imminent danger of being damaged, may apply to the circuit court in any jurisdiction wherein the land lies to enjoin a violation or a threatened violation under §§10.1-563, 10.1-564 or §10.1-566 without the necessity of showing that an adequate remedy at law does not exist; however, an owner of property shall not apply for injunctive relief unless (i) he has notified in writing the person who has violated the local program, and the program authority, that a violation of the local program has caused, or creates a probability of causing, damage to his property, and (ii) neither the person who has violated the local program nor the program authority has taken corrective action within fifteen days to eliminate the conditions which have caused, or create the probability of causing, damage to his property.

D. In addition to any criminal or civil penalties provided under this chapter, any person who violates any provision of this chapter may be liable to the program authority, or the Board, as appropriate, in a civil action for damages.

E. Without limiting the remedies which may be obtained in this section, any person violating or failing, neglecting or refusing to obey any injunction, mandamus or other remedy obtained pursuant to this section shall be subject, in the discretion of the court, to a civil penalty not to exceed $2,000 for each violation. A civil action for such violation or failure may be brought by the locality wherein the land lies. Any civil penalties assessed by a court shall be paid into the treasury of the locality wherein the land lies, except that where the violator is the locality itself, or its agent, the court shall direct the penalty to be paid into the state treasury.

F. With the consent of any person who has violated or failed, neglected or refused to obey any regulation or order of the Board, or any condition of a permit or any provision of this article, the Board, the Director, or plan-approving or permit-issuing authority may provide, in an order issued by the Board or plan-approving or permit-issuing authority against such person, for the payment of civil charges for violations in specific sums, not to exceed the limit specified in subsection E of this section. Such civil charges shall be instead of any appropriate civil penalty which could be imposed under subsection B or E.

G.   Upon request of a program authority, or the permit-issuing authority, the attorney for the Commonwealth shall take legal action to enforce the provisions of this article. Upon request of the Board, the Attorney General shall take appropriate legal action on behalf of the Board to enforce the provisions of this article.

H.   Compliance with the provisions of this article shall be prima facie evidence in any legal or equitable proceeding for damages caused by erosion or sedimentation that all requirements of law have been met and the complaining party must show negligence in order to recover any damages.

§10.1-569.1. Stop Work Orders by Board; Civil Penalties

A.   An aggrieved owner of property sustaining pecuniary damage resulting from a violation of an approved plan or required permit, or from the conduct of land-disturbing activities commenced without an approved plan or required permit, may give written notice of the alleged violation to the program authority and to the Director.

B.   Upon receipt of the notice from the aggrieved owner and notification to the program authority, the Director shall conduct an investigation of the aggrieved owner's complaint.

C.   If the program authority has not responded to the alleged violation in a manner which causes the violation to cease and abates the damage to the aggrieved owner's property within thirty days following receipt of the notice from the aggrieved owner, the aggrieved owner may request that the Director require the violator to stop the violation and abate the damage to his property.

D.   If (i) the Director's investigation of the complaint indicates that the program authority has not responded to the alleged violation as required by the local program, (ii) the program authority has not responded to the alleged violation within thirty days from the date of the notice given pursuant to subsection A of this section, and (iii) the Director is requested by the aggrieved owner to require the violator to cease the violation, then the Director shall give written notice to the program authority that the Director will request the Board to issue an order pursuant to subsection E of this section.

E.   If the program authority has not instituted action to stop the violation and abate the damage to the aggrieved owner's property within ten days following receipt of the notice from the Director, the Board is authorized to issue an order requiring the owner, permittee, person responsible for carrying out an approved plan, or person conducting the land-disturbing activities without an approved plan or required permit to cease all land-disturbing activities until the violation of the plan or permit has ceased, or an approved plan and required permits are obtained, as appropriate, and specified corrective measures have been completed.

F.   Such orders are to be issued only after a hearing with reasonable notice to the affected person of the time, place and purpose thereof, and they shall become effective upon service on the person by certified mail, return receipt requested, sent to his address specified in the land records of the locality, or by personal delivery by an agent of the Director. However, if the Board finds that any such violation is grossly affecting or presents an imminent and substantial danger of causing harmful erosion of lands or sediment deposition in waters within the watersheds of the Commonwealth, it may issue, without advance notice or hearing, an emergency order directing such person to cease all land-disturbing activities on the site immediately and shall provide an opportunity for a hearing, after reasonable notice as to the time and place thereof, to such person, to affirm, modify, amend or cancel such emergency order.

G. If a person who has been issued an order or emergency order is not complying with the terms thereof, the Board may institute a proceeding in the appropriate circuit court for an injunction, mandamus, or other appropriate remedy compelling the person to comply with such order.

H. Any person violating or failing, neglecting or refusing to obey any injunction, mandamus or other remedy obtained pursuant to subsection G of this section shall be subject, in the discretion of the court, to a civil penalty not to exceed $2,000 for each violation. Any civil penalties assessed by a court shall be paid into the state treasury.

§10.1-570. Authorization for More Stringent Regulations

A district or locality is authorized to adopt more stringent soil erosion and sediment control regulations than those necessary to ensure compliance with the Board's regulations. However, this section shall not be construed to authorize any district or locality to impose any more stringent regulations for plan approval or permit issuance than those specified in §§10.1-563 and 10.1-565.

§10.1-571. No Limitation on Authority of Water Control Board or Department of Mines, Minerals, and Energy

The provisions of this article shall not limit the powers or duties presently exercised by the State Water Control Board under Chapter 3.1 (§62.1-44.2 et seq.) of Title 62.1, or the powers or duties of the Department of Mines, Minerals and Energy as they relate to strip mine reclamation under Chapters 16 (§45.1-180 et seq.), 17 (§45.1-198 et seq.) and 19 (§45.1-226 et seq.) of Title 45.1 or oil or gas exploration under the Virginia Oil and Gas Act (§45.1-361.1 et seq.).

VIRGINIA ADMINISTRATIVE CODE (VAC)
TITLE 4 CONSERVATION AND NATURAL RESOURCES

4VAC50-30-10. Definitions

The following words and terms, when used in this chapter, shall have the following meanings, unless the context clearly indicates otherwise. In addition, some terms not defined herein are defined in §10.1-560 of the Erosion and Sediment Control Law.

"Act" means the Erosion and Sediment Control Law, Article 4 (§10.1-560 et seq.) of Chapter 5 of Title 10.1 of the Code of Virginia.

"Adequate channel" means a watercourse that will convey the designated frequency storm event without overtopping its banks or causing erosive damage to the bed, banks and overbank sections of the same.

"Agreement in lieu of a plan" means a contract between the program authority and the owner which specifies conservation measures which must be implemented in the construction of a single-family residence; this contract may be executed by the program authority in lieu of an erosion and sediment control plan.

"Applicant" means any person submitting an erosion and sediment control plan or an agreement in lieu of a plan for approval or requesting the issuance of a permit, when required, authorizing land-disturbing activities to commence.

"Board" means the Virginia Soil and Water Conservation Board.

"Causeway" means a temporary structural span constructed across a flowing watercourse or wetland to allow construction traffic to access the area without causing erosion damage.

"Channel" means a natural stream or manmade waterway.

"Cofferdam" means a watertight temporary structure in a river, lake, etc., for keeping the water from an enclosed area that has been pumped dry so that bridge foundations, dams, etc., may be constructed.

"Dam" means a barrier to confine or raise water for storage or diversion, to create a hydraulic head, to prevent gully erosion, or to retain soil, rock or other debris.

"Denuded" means a term applied to land that has been physically disturbed and no longer supports vegetative cover.

"Department" means the Department of Conservation and Recreation.

"Development" means a tract or parcel of land developed or to be developed as a single unit under single ownership or unified control which is to be used for any business or industrial purpose or is to contain three or more residential dwelling units.

"Dike" means an earthen embankment constructed to confine or control water, especially one built along the banks of a river to prevent overflow of lowlands; levee.

"Director" means the Director of the Department of Conservation and Recreation.

"District" or "soil and water conservation district" means a political subdivision of the Commonwealth organized in accordance with the provisions of Article 3 (§10.1-506 et seq.) of Chapter 5 of Title 10.1 of the Code of Virginia.

"Diversion" means a channel with a supporting ridge on the lower side constructed across or at the bottom of a slope for the purpose of intercepting surface runoff.

"Dormant" refers to denuded land that is not actively being brought to a desired grade or condition.

"Energy dissipator" means a nonerodible structure which reduces the velocity of concentrated flow to reduce its erosive effects.

"Erosion and Sediment Control Plan," "conservation plan" or "plan," means a document containing material for the conservation of soil and water resources of a unit or group of units of land. It may include appropriate maps, an appropriate soil and water plan inventory and management information with needed interpretations, and a record of decisions contributing to conservation treatment. The plan shall contain all major conservation decisions and all information deemed necessary by the plan-approving authority to assure that the entire unit or units of land will be so treated to achieve the conservation objectives.

"Flume" means a constructed device lined with erosion-resistant materials intended to convey water on steep grades.

"Live watercourse" means a definite channel with bed and banks within which concentrated water flows continuously.

"Locality" means a county, city or town.

"Natural stream" means nontidal waterways that are part of the natural topography. They usually maintain a continuous or seasonal flow during the year and are characterized as being irregular in cross-section with a meandering course. Constructed channels such as drainage ditches or swales shall not be considered natural streams.

"Nonerodible" means a material, e.g., riprap, concrete, plastic, etc., that will not experience surface wear due to natural forces.

"Person" means any individual, partnership, firm, association, joint venture, public or private corporation, trust, estate, commission, board, public or private institution, utility, cooperative, county, city, town or other political subdivision of the Commonwealth, any interstate body, or any other legal entity.

"Plan approving authority" means the board, the program authority, a department of a program authority, or an agent of the program authority responsible for determining the adequacy of a conservation plan submitted for land-disturbing activities on a unit or units of land and for approving plans.

"Post-development" refers to conditions that may be reasonably expected or anticipated to exist after completion of the land development activity on a specific site or tract of land.

"Program administrator" means the person or persons responsible for administering and enforcing the erosion and sediment control program of a program authority.

"Program authority" means a district, county, city, or town which has adopted a soil erosion and sediment control program which has been approved by the board.

"Pre-development" refers to conditions at the time the erosion and sediment control plan is submitted to the plan approving authority. Where phased development or plan approval occurs (preliminary grading, roads and utilities, etc.), the existing conditions at the time the erosion and sediment control plan for the initial phase is submitted for approval shall establish pre-development conditions.

"Sediment basin" means a temporary impoundment build to retain sediment and debris with a controlled stormwater release structure.

"Sediment trap" means a temporary impoundment built to retain sediment and debris which is formed by constructing an earthen embankment with a stone outlet.

"Sheet flow" (also called overland flow) means shallow, unconcentrated and irregular flow down a slope. The length of strip for overland flow usually does not exceed 200 feet under natural conditions.

"Shore erosion control project" means an erosion control project approved by local wetlands boards, the Virginia Marine Resources Commission, the Virginia Department of Environmental Quality or the United States Army Corps of Engineers and located on tidal waters and within nonvegetated or vegetated wetlands as defined in Title 28.2 of the Code of Virginia.

"Slope drain" means tubing or conduit made of nonerosive material extending from the top to the bottom of a cut or fill slope with an energy dissipator at the outlet end.

"Stabilized" means land that has been treated to withstand normal exposure to natural forces without incurring erosion damage.

"Storm sewer inlet" means a structure through which stormwater is introduced into an underground conveyance system.

"Stormwater detention" means the process of temporarily impounding runoff and discharging it through a hydraulic outlet structure to a downstream conveyance system.

"Temporary vehicular stream crossing" means a temporary nonerodible structural span installed across a flowing watercourse for use by construction traffic. Structures may include bridges, round pipes or pipe arches constructed on or through nonerodible material.

"Ten-year storm" means a storm that is capable of producing rainfall expected to be equaled or exceeded on the average of once in 10 years. It may also be expressed as an exceedence probability with a 10% chance of being equaled or exceeded in any given year.

"Two-year storm" means a storm that is capable of producing rainfall expected to be equaled or exceeded on the average of once in two years. It may also be expressed as an exceedence probability with a 50% chance of being equaled or exceeded in any given year.

"Twenty-five-year storm" means a storm that is capable of producing rainfall expected to be equaled or exceeded on the average of once in 25 years. It may also be expressed as exceedence probability with a 4.0% chance of being equaled or exceeded in any given year.

4VAC50-30-20. Purpose

The purpose of this chapter is to form the basis for the administration, implementation and enforcement of the Act. The intent of this chapter is to establish the framework for compliance with the Act while at the same time providing flexibility for innovative solutions to erosion and sediment control concerns.

4VAC50-30-30. Scope and Applicability

A. This chapter sets forth minimum standards for the effective control of soil erosion, sediment deposition and nonagricultural runoff that must be met:

1. In erosion and sediment control programs adopted by districts and localities under §10.1-562 of the Act;
2. In erosion and sediment control plans that may be submitted directly to the board pursuant to §10.1-563 A of the Act;
3. In annual general erosion and sediment control specifications that electric and telephone utility companies and railroad companies are required to file with the board pursuant to §10.1-563 D of the Act;
4. In conservation plans and annual specifications that state agencies are required to file with the department pursuant to §10.1-564 of the Act; and
5. By federal agencies that enter into agreements with the board.

B. The submission of annual specifications to the board or the department by any agency or company does not eliminate the need for a project specific Erosion and Sediment Control Plan.

C. This chapter must be incorporated into the local erosion and sediment control program within one year of its effective date.

4VAC50-30-40. Minimum Standards

An erosion and sediment control program adopted by a district or locality must be consistent with the following criteria, techniques and methods:

1. Permanent or temporary soil stabilization shall be applied to denuded areas within seven days after final grade is reached on any portion of the site. Temporary soil stabilization shall be applied within seven days to denuded areas that may not be at final grade but will remain dormant for longer than 30 days. Permanent stabilization shall be applied to areas that are to be left dormant for more than one year.

2. During construction of the project, soil stock piles and borrow areas shall be stabilized or protected with sediment trapping measures. The applicant is responsible for the temporary protection and permanent stabilization of all soil stockpiles on site as well as in borrow areas and soil intentionally transported from the project site.

3. A permanent vegetative cover shall be established on denuded areas not otherwise permanently stabilized. Permanent vegetation shall not be considered established until a ground cover is achieved that is uniform, mature enough to survive and will inhibit erosion.

4. Sediment basins and traps, perimeter dikes, sediment barriers and other measures intended to trap sediment shall be constructed as a first step in any land-disturbing activity and shall be made functional before upslope land disturbance takes place.

5. Stabilization measures shall be applied to earthen structures such as dams, dikes and diversions immediately after installation.

6. Sediment traps and sediment basins shall be designed and constructed based upon the total drainage area to be served by the trap or basin.

   a. The minimum storage capacity of a sediment trap shall be 134 cubic yards per acre of drainage area and the trap shall only control drainage areas less than three acres.

   b. Surface runoff from disturbed areas that is comprised of flow from drainage areas greater than or equal to three acres shall be controlled by a sediment basin. The minimum storage capacity of a sediment basin shall be 134 cubic yards per acre of drainage area. The outfall system shall, at a minimum, maintain the structural integrity of the basin during a 25-year storm of 24-hour duration. Runoff coefficients used in runoff calculations shall correspond to a bare earth condition or those conditions expected to exist while the sediment basin is utilized.

7. Cut and fill slopes shall be designed and constructed in a manner that will minimize erosion. Slopes that are found to be eroding excessively within one year of permanent stabilization shall be provided with additional slope stabilizing measures until the problem is corrected.

8. Concentrated runoff shall not flow down cut or fill slopes unless contained within an adequate temporary or permanent channel, flume or slope drain structure.

9. Whenever water seeps from a slope face, adequate drainage or other protection shall be provided.

10. All storm sewer inlets that are made operable during construction shall be protected so that sediment-laden water cannot enter the conveyance system without first being filtered or otherwise treated to remove sediment.

11. Before newly constructed stormwater conveyance channels or pipes are made operational, adequate outlet protection and any required temporary or permanent channel lining shall be installed in both the conveyance channel and receiving channel.

VAC Title 4
Conservation and
Natural Resources

12. When work in a live watercourse is performed, precautions shall be taken to minimize encroachment, control sediment transport and stabilize the work area to the greatest extent possible during construction. Nonerodible material shall be used for the construction of causeways and cofferdams. Earthen fill may be used for these structures if armored by nonerodible cover materials.

13. When a live watercourse must be crossed by construction vehicles more than twice in any six-month period, a temporary vehicular stream crossing constructed of nonerodible material shall be provided.

14. All applicable federal, state and local chapters pertaining to working in or crossing live watercourses shall be met.

15. The bed and banks of a watercourse shall be stabilized immediately after work in the watercourse is completed.

16. Underground utility lines shall be installed in accordance with the following standards in addition to other applicable criteria:

    a. No more than 500 linear feet of trench may be opened at one time.

    b. Excavated material shall be placed on the uphill side of trenches.

    c. Effluent from dewatering operations shall be filtered or passed through an approved sediment trapping device, or both, and discharged in a manner that does not adversely affect flowing streams or off-site property.

    d. Material used for backfilling trenches shall be properly compacted in order to minimize erosion and promote stabilization.

    e. Restabilization shall be accomplished in accordance with this chapter.

    f. Applicable safety chapters shall be complied with.

17. Where construction vehicle access routes intersect paved or public roads, provisions sall be made to minimize the transport of sediment by vehicular tracking onto the paved surface. Where sediment is transported onto a paved or public road surface, the road surface shall be cleaned thoroughly at the end of each day. Sediment shall be removed from the roads by shoveling or sweeping and transported to a sediment control disposal area. Street washing shall be allowed only after sediment is removed in this manner. This provision shall apply to individual development lots as well as to larger land-disturbing activities.

18. All temporary erosion and sediment control measures shall be removed within 30 days after final site stabilization or after the temporary measures are no longer needed, unless otherwise authorized by the local program authority. Trapped sediment and the disturbed soil areas resulting from the disposition of temporary measures shall be permanently stabilized to prevent further erosion and sedimentation.

19. Properties and waterways downstream from development sites shall be protected from sediment deposition, erosion and damage due to increases in volume, velocity and peak flow rate of stormwater runoff for the stated frequency storm of 24-hour duration in accordance with the following standards and criteria:

    a. Concentrated stormwater runoff leaving a development site shall be discharged directly into an adequate natural or man-made receiving channel, pipe or storm sewer system. For those sites where runoff is discharged into a pipe or pipe system, downstream stability analyses at the outfall of the pipe or pipe system shall be performed.

    b. Adequacy of all channels and pipes shall be verified in the following manner:

        (1) The applicant shall demonstrate that the total drainage area to the point of analysis within the channel is one hundred times greater than the contributing drainage area of the project in question; or

(2) (a) Natural channels shall be analyzed by the use of a two-year storm to verify that stormwater will not overtop channel banks nor cause erosion of channel bed or banks.

(b) All previously constructed man-made channels shall be analyzed by the use of a ten-year storm to verify that stormwater will not overtop its banks and by the use of a two-year storm to demonstrate that stormwater will not cause erosion of channel bed or banks; and

(c) Pipes and storm sewer systems shall be analyzed by the use of a ten-year storm to verify that stormwater will be contained within the pipe or system.

c. If existing natural receiving channels or previously constructed man-made channels or pipes are not adequate, the applicant shall:

(1) Improve the channels to a condition where a ten-year storm will not overtop the banks and a two-year storm will not cause erosion to channel the bed or banks; or

(2) Improve the pipe or pipe system to a condition where the ten-year storm is contained within the appurtenances;

(3) Develop a site design that will not cause the pre-development peak runoff rate from a two-year storm to increase when runoff outfalls into a natural channel or will not cause the pre-development peak runoff rate from a ten-year storm to increase when runoff outfalls into a man-made channel; or

(4) Provide a combination of channel improvement, stormwater detention or other measures which is satisfactory to the plan approving authority to prevent downstream erosion.

d. The applicant shall provide evidence of permission to make the improvements.

e. All hydrologic analyses shall be based on the existing watershed characteristics and the ultimate development condition of the subject project.

f. If the applicant chooses an option that includes stormwater detention, he shall obtain approval from the locality of a plan for maintenance of the detention facilities. The plan shall set forth the maintenance requirements of the facility and the person responsible for performing the maintenance.

g. Outfall from a detention facility shall be discharged to a receiving channel, and energy dissipators shall be placed at the outfall of all detention facilities as necessary to provide a stabilized transition from the facility to the receiving channel.

h. All on-site channels must be verified to be adequate.

i. Increased volumes of sheet flows that may cause erosion or sedimentation on adjacent property shall be diverted to a stable outlet, adequate channel, pipe or pipe system, or to a detention facility.

j. In applying these stormwater management criteria, individual lots or parcels in a residential, commercial or industrial development shall not be considered to be separate development projects. Instead, the development, as a whole, shall be considered to be a single development project. Hydrologic parameters that reflect the ultimate development condition shall be used in all engineering calculations.

k. All measures used to protect properties and waterways shall be employed in a manner which minimizes impacts on the physical, chemical and biological integrity of rivers, streams and other waters of the state.

4VAC50-30-50. Variances

The plan approving authority may waive or modify any of the chapters that are deemed inappropriate or too restrictive for site conditions, by granting a variance. A variance may be granted under these conditions:

1. At the time of plan submission, an applicant may request a variance to become part of the approved erosion and sediment control plan. The applicant shall explain the reasons for requesting variances in writing. Specific variances which are allowed by the plan approving authority shall be documented in the plan.

2. During construction, the person responsible for implementing the approved plan may request a variance in writing from the plan approving authority. The plan approving authority shall respond in writing either approving or disapproving such a request. If the plan approving authority does not approve a variance within 10 days of receipt of the request, the request shall be considered to be disapproved. Following disapproval, the applicant may resubmit a variance request with additional documentation.

3. The plan approving authority shall consider variance requests judiciously, keeping in mind both the need of the applicant to maximize cost effectiveness and the need to protect off-site properties and resources from damage.

4VAC50-30-60. Maintenance and Inspections

A. All erosion and sediment control structures and systems shall be maintained, inspected and repaired as needed to insure continued performance of their intended function. A statement describing the maintenance responsibilities of the permittee shall be included in the approved erosion and sediment control plan.

B. Periodic inspections are required on all projects by the program authority. The program authority shall either:

1. Provide for an inspection during or immediately following initial installation of erosion and sediment controls, at least once in every two-week period, within 48 hours following any runoff producing storm event, and at the completion of the project prior to the release of any performance bonds; or

2. Establish an alternative inspection program which ensures compliance with the approved erosion and sediment control plan. Any alternative inspection program shall be:
   - Approved by the board prior to implementation;
   - Established in writing;
   - Based on a system of priorities that, at a minimum, address the amount of disturbed project area, site conditions and stage of construction; and
   - Documented by inspection records.

4VAC50-30-70. Developments

A. An erosion and sediment control plan shall be filed for a development and the buildings constructed within, regardless of the phasing of construction.

B. If individual lots or sections in a residential development are being developed by different property owners, all land-disturbing activities related to the building construction shall be covered by an erosion and sediment control plan or an "Agreement in Lieu of a Plan" signed by the property owner.

C. Land-disturbing activity of less than 10,000 square feet on individual lots in a residential development shall not be considered exempt from the provisions of the Act and this chapter if the total land-disturbing activity in the development is equal to or greater than 10,000 square feet.

4VAC50-30-80. Criteria for Determining Status of Land-Disturbing Activity

A. The program administrator shall determine the validity of a claim of exempt status by a property owner who disturbs 10,000 square feet or more. As soon as a nonexempt status is determined, the requirements of the Act shall be immediately enforced.

B. Should a land-disturbing activity not begin during the 180-day period following plan approval or cease for more than 180 days, the plan-approval authority or the permit issuing authority may evaluate the existing approved erosion and sediment control plan to determine whether the plan still satisfies local and state erosion and sediment control criteria and to verify that all design factors are still valid. If the authority finds the previously filed plan to be inadequate, a modified plan shall be submitted and approved prior to the resumption of land-disturbing activity.

C. Shore erosion control projects are not subject to this chapter. However, land-disturbing activity immediately outside the limits of the shore erosion project is subject to the Act and this chapter.

D. Whenever land-disturbing activity involves activity at a separate location (including but not limited to borrow and disposal areas), the program authority may either:

   1. Consider the off-site activity as being part of the proposed land-disturbing activity; or

   2. If the off-site activity is already covered by an approved erosion and sediment control plan, the program authority may require the applicant to provide proof of the approval and to certify that the plan will be implemented in accordance with a the Act and this chapter.

4VAC50-30-90. Review and Evaluation of Local Programs: Minimum Program Standards

A. This section sets forth the criteria that will be used by the department to determine whether a local program operating under authority of the Act, satisfies minimum standards of effectiveness, as follows.

   Each local program must contain an ordinance or other appropriate document or documents adopted by the governing body. Such document or documents must be consistent with the Act, this chapter, and 4VAC50-40-10 et seq., including the following criteria:

   1. The document or documents shall include or reference the definition of land-disturbing activity including exemptions, as well as any other significant terms, as necessary to produce an effective local program.

   2. The document or documents shall identify the plan-approving authority and other positions of authority within the program, and must include the chapters and design standards to be used in the program.

   3. The document or documents shall include procedures for submission and approval of plans, issuance of permits, monitoring and inspections of land-disturbing activities. The position, agency, department, or other party responsible for conducting inspections shall be identified. The local program authority shall maintain, either on-site or in local program files, a copy of the approved plan and a record of inspections for each active land-disturbing activity.

   4. The local program authority must take appropriate enforcement actions to achieve compliance with the program and maintain a record of enforcement actions for all active land-disturbing activities.

B.   The department staff, under authority of the board, shall periodically conduct a comprehensive review and evaluation of local programs. The review and evaluation of a local program shall consist of the following: (i) personal interview between the department staff and the local program administrator or designee or designees; (ii) review of the local ordinance and other applicable documents; (iii) review of plans approved by the program; (iv) inspection of regulated activities; and (v) review of enforcement actions.

C.   Local programs shall be reviewed and evaluated for effectiveness in carrying out the Act using the criteria in this section. However, the director is not limited to the consideration of only these items when assessing the overall effectiveness of a local program.

D.   If the director determines that the deficiencies noted in the review will cause the local erosion and sediment control program to be inconsistent with the state program and chapters, the director shall notify the local program authority concerning the deficiencies and provide a reasonable period of time for corrective action to be taken. If the program authority fails to take the corrective action within the specified time, the director may formally request board action pursuant to §10.1-562 of the Code of Virginia.

E.   Review and evaluation of local programs shall be conducted according to a schedule adopted by the board.

4VAC50-30-100. State Agency Projects

A.   All state agency land-disturbing activities that are not exempt and that have commenced without an approved erosion and sediment control plan shall immediately cease until an erosion and sediment control plan has been submitted to and approved by the department. A formal "Notice of Plan Requirement" will be sent to the state agency under whose purview the project lies since that agency is responsible for compliance with the Act.

B.   Where inspections by department personnel reveal deficiencies in carrying out an approved plan, the person responsible for carrying out the plan, as well as the state agency responsible, will be issued a notice to comply with specific actions and the deadlines that shall be met. Failure to meet the prescribed deadlines can result in the issuance of a stop work order for all land-disturbing activities on the project at the discretion of the Chief Administrative Officer of the board, who is authorized to sign such an order. The stop work order will be lifted once the required erosion and sediment control measures are in place and inspected by department staff.

C.   Whenever the Commonwealth or any of its agencies fails to comply within the time provided in an appropriate final order, the director of the department may petition for compliance as follows: For violations in the Natural Resources Secretariat, to the secretary of Natural Resources; for violations in other secretariats, to the appropriate Secretary; for violations in other state agencies, to the head of such agency. Where the petition does not achieve timely compliance, the director shall bring the matter to the Governor for resolution.

D.   Where compliance will require the appropriation of funds, the director shall cooperate with the appropriate agency head in seeking such an appropriation; where the director determines that an emergency exists, he shall petition the Governor for funds from the Civil Contingency Fund or other appropriate source.

4VAC50-30-110. Document or Documents Adopted Local Erosion and Sediment Control Programs

A. To carry out its duties under §10.1-562 of the Code of Virginia, the board shall develop, adopt, and administer an appropriate local erosion and sediment control program for the locality under consideration. In fulfilling these duties, the board shall assume the full powers of the local erosion and sediment control program granted by law.

B. The board shall develop, adopt and administer a local erosion and sediment control program based on the minimum program standards established by this chapter and, as deemed appropriate by the board, may include any or all of the provisions provided by law and chapter including administrative fees and performance securities.

C. Upon adoption of a local erosion and sediment control program by the board, payment of moneys, including fees, securities, and penalties, shall be made to the state treasury.

D. When administering a local erosion and sediment control program the board may delegate to the director such operational activities as necessary. Further, the board may enter into agreements with other public or private entities to accomplish certain program responsibilities as it deems necessary to administer the local program.

CHAPTER 5

VIRGINIA UNIFORM STATEWIDE BUILDING CODE

V irginia is a Dillon Rule state which means that any regulation adopted by a locality must be authorized by the General Assembly. The Virginia Uniform Statewide Building Code (VUSBC) is the result of this rule and is the one code that governs all construction. Construction as it relates to the VUSBC is a general term that includes renovation, repair, demolition, change of use, and maintenance of a building.

VIRGINIA UNIFORM STATEWIDE BUILDING CODE

The VUSBC is an administrative document that adopts model codes (VUSBC Section 101.2) and then makes changes to them. Basically, all of the administrative chapters of the model codes are deleted and replaced with state specific language. Technical changes to the model codes are included in the VUSBC. The VUSBC and changes are included at the end of the chapter.

The VUSBC is divided into three "Parts". Part I contains regulations specific to the construction of new buildings and structures including alterations, additions, and changes of occupancy in existing buildings. It is referred to as the Virginia Construction Code. Part II contains optional regulations relating to the rehabilitation of existing buildings and may be used as an acceptable alternative to the Virginia Construction Code. Part II is referred to as the Virginia Rehabilitation Code. Part III contains regulations for the maintenance of existing structures and is enforced at the option of local governments. Part III is referred to as the Virginia Maintenance Code.

While the title "Virginia Uniform Statewide Building Code" may lead one to believe that this is the only document needed as a construction guide, the VUSBC only details the title of other codes to be used, and when permits and inspections are required. It is an administrative document and does not detail specific construction requirements such as the number of nails or the size of boards and beams required. That information is found in the adopted model codes.

Changes to the VUSBC by Localities

Localities may only make changes to the code based on regional differences of geography. The snow load in the mountain region is much heavier than that of the Atlantic coastline and roofs must be designed to accommodate the loads. Frost depths are greater in the mountains and less on the coastlines. The coast requires unique wind load considerations and structures must be designed to withstand severe winds. Wind loads also require unique precautions that may not be plainly detailed in the code. For example, a roof covering replacement in residential occupancies is generally exempt from requiring a building permit (VUSBC Section 108.2, Exceptions, 8.2); however, if a roof covering is replaced in the coastal region, localities may require a building permit to ensure that the installation meets wind load requirements. To obtain the specific geographic and permit requirements, the local building department should be contacted before proceeding with any contract work on a building.

Permit Requirements

A permit application to a local jurisdiction may require a review by a number of offices before the permit is issued (VUSBC Section 108.1). These offices usually include the Virginia Highway Department for a curb cut and driveway consideration and the Health Department for septic, sewage, and occupancy. If the building is to be on a septic system, the occupancy load of the building may be determined by the size of the septic system rather than the square footage of the building.

The zoning office determines if the proposed building use is consistent with the neighborhood, and the engineering office determines compliance with local erosion and sediment control regulations as well as property storm water runoff containment. Another local consideration is historical districts that may restrict changes to a building or require unique architectural features such as window grids, brick facades, or color choice restrictions. Contractors should inquire about deed restrictions that may impose limits on what can be done to a building based on a subdivision ordinance.

The code provides for the building official to accept the use of an alternate form of construction if the case can be made that the proposed method is consistent with a recognized standard of performance (VUSBC Section 112.2).

When all of the various agencies and offices have signed off on the application, the building department issues a permit. One set of plans, stamped "Approved," is returned to the applicant and this set is kept on the job site (Section 109.5).

Inspections

Inspectors inspect the project as it progresses through various stages. The locality lists the required inspections on the building permit. A list of minimum inspections is found in Section 113.3 of the VUSBC. Virginia allows the use of private inspection agencies that are approved by the building department (VUSBC Section 113.7).

Appeals

Disagreements about a violation or an alternative form of construction can be resolved by contacting the local building official. If the issue is not resolved at that level, an appeals procedure is detailed in the code (VUSBC Section 106.0).

This requires a written application to be filed with the building official no later than 14 days after the issuance of the decision by the building official. The appeals board will then meet within 30 days of the filing. The appeals procedure is not looked upon as a confrontation with the inspection department, and may often be a recommendation of the building official who may not want to make a decision involving an alternative method of construction. In any case, if a violation notice is issued to a contractor, it must be resolved. Ignoring a violation triggers legal action by the building department and it also creates a violation of state contractor regulations which requires compliance with the building code.

Violations

A **violation** a misdemeanor that incurs a civil penalty (Section 115). Local jurisdictions are authorized to adopt ordinances that establish a uniform schedule of penalties for violations of provisions of the code that are not corrected after receiving a written notice of violation from the local enforcement officer. The violation notice is to be delivered to the owner, permit holder, or tenants.

VIRGINIA CONSTRUCTION CODE

PART I OF THE VIRGINIA UNIFORM STATEWIDE BUILDING CODE

2006

Effective May 1, 2008

PREFACE

Introduction

The Virginia Uniform Statewide Building Code (USBC) is a state regulation promulgated by the Virginia Board of Housing and Community Development, a Governor-appointed board, for the purpose of establishing minimum regulations to govern the construction and maintenance of buildings and structures.

The provisions of the USBC are based on nationally recognized model building and fire codes published by the International Code Council, Inc.. The model codes are made part of the USBC through a regulatory process known as incorporation by reference. The USBC also contains administrative provisions governing the use of the model codes and establishing requirements for the enforcement of the code by the local building departments and other code enforcement agencies.

In keeping with the designations of the USBC used previously, since the 2006 editions of the International Codes are incorporated by reference into this version of the USBC, it is known as the 2006 edition of the USBC.

Arrangement

The USBC is part of the Virginia Administrative Code (VAC), the official compilation of state regulations published under the authority and guidance of the Virginia Code Commission. Due to the difference in the section numbering system between the VAC and the model codes incorporated by reference into the USBC, the UBSC utilizes a dual section numbering system. In the USBC, the VAC section numbers are listed first, followed by a section number matching the model code system. In this printing of the USBC, the VAC section numbers are omitted and only the model code numbering system is utilized. The version of the USBC containing both the VAC section numbers and the model code numbering is available from the Virginia Department of Housing and Community Development and may also be accessed through the website of the Virginia Code Commission or by subscription to the VAC.

Overview

The USBC is divided into three stand-alone parts. Part I contains regulations specific to the construction of new buildings and structures and alterations, additions and change of occupancy in existing buildings and structures and is known as the Virginia Construction Code. Part II contains optional regulations specific to the rehabilitation of existing buildings that may be used as an acceptable alternative to the Virginia Construction Code. Part II is known as the Virginia Rehabilitation Code. Part III of the USBC contains the regulations for the maintenance of existing structures which is enforced at the option of the local governments. It is known as the Virginia Maintenance Code.

State Pamphlets and Codes Purchased from ICC

The 2006 edition of the USBC is being made available in pamphlet form as in past editions of the USBC. In the state pamphlet version, a single line is placed in the margin to delineate changes between the 2003 edition of the USBC and the 2006 edition of the USBC.

New for the 2006 edition are versions of the Virginia Construction Code, Virginia Rehabilitation Code, Virginia Maintenance Code and a series of Virginia specific trade codes published by the International Code Council (ICC). In the ICC published versions, marginal markings are provided to distinguish between text which is part of the International Codes and text which is part of the state regulations. Double vertical lines in the margins within the body of the codes indicate state amendments to the International Codes. As in the standard printings of the International Codes, a single vertical line in the margins within the body of the code indicates a technical change from the previous edition of the International Codes. Deletions from the previous editions of the International Codes are indicated in the form of an arrow (→) in the margin where an entire section, paragraph, exception or table has been deleted or an item in a list of items or a table has been deleted.

Technical Assistance

The local building departments and enforcing agencies may be contacted for further information concerning the USBC. Contact information for the Virginia Department of Housing and Community Development is below.

Virginia Department of Housing and Community Development
Division of Building and Fire Regulation
501 North 2nd Street
Richmond, Virginia 23219-1321
Phone: (804) 371-7150 – Email: usbc@dhcd.virginia.gov

TABLE OF CONTENTS

2006 VIRGINIA CONSTRUCTION CODE (Part I of the Virginia Uniform Statewide Building Code) – Effective May 1, 2008

CHAPTER 1

ADMINISTRATION

SECTION 101
GENERAL

101.1 Short title. The Virginia Uniform Statewide Building Code, Part I, Construction, may be cited as the Virginia Construction Code. The term "USBC" shall mean the Virginia Construction Code unless the context in which the term is used clearly indicates it to be an abbreviation for the entire Virginia Uniform Statewide Building Code or for a different part of the Virginia Uniform Statewide Building Code.

101.2 Incorporation by reference. Chapters 2 – 35 of the 2006 International Building Code, published by the International Code Council, Inc., are adopted and incorporated by reference to be an enforceable part of the USBC. The term "IBC" means the 2006 International Building Code, published by the International Code Council, Inc. Any codes and standards referenced in the IBC are also considered to be part of the incorporation by reference, except that such codes and standards are used only to the prescribed extent of each such reference. In addition, any provisions of the appendices of the IBC specifically identified to be part of the USBC are also considered to be part of the incorporation by reference.

> **Note 1:** The IBC references the whole family of International Codes including the following major codes:
>
> 2006 International Plumbing Code
> 2006 International Mechanical Code
> 2005 National Electrical Code
> 2006 International Fuel Gas Code
> 2006 International Energy Conservation Code
> 2006 International Residential Code
>
> **Note 2:** The International Residential Code is applicable to the construction of detached one- and two-family dwellings and townhouses as set out in Section 310.

101.3 Numbering system. A dual numbering system is used in the USBC to correlate the numbering system of the Virginia Administrative Code with the numbering system of the IBC. IBC numbering system designations are provided in the catch-lines of the Virginia Administrative Code sections. Cross references between sections or chapters of the USBC use only the IBC numbering system designations. The term "chapter" is used in the context of the numbering system of the IBC and may mean a chapter in the USBC, a chapter in the IBC or a chapter in a referenced code or standard, depending on the context of the use of the term. The term "chapter" is not used to designate a chapter of the Virginia Administrative Code, unless clearly indicated.

101.4 Arrangement of code provisions. The USBC is comprised of the combination of (i) the provisions of Chapter 1, Administration, which are established herein, (ii) Chapters 2 – 35 of the IBC, which are incorporated by reference in Section 101.2, and (iii) the changes to the text of the incorporated chapters of the IBC that are specifically identified. The terminology "changes to the text of the incorporated chapters of the IBC that are specifically identified" shall also be referred to as the "state amendments to the IBC." Such state amendments to the IBC are set out using corresponding chapter and section numbers of the IBC numbering system. In addition, since Chapter 1 of the IBC is not incorporated as part of the USBC, any reference to a provision of Chapter 1 of the IBC in the provisions of Chapters 2 - 35 of the IBC is generally invalid. However, where the purpose of such a reference would clearly correspond to a provision of Chapter 1 established herein, then the reference may be construed to be a valid reference to such corresponding Chapter 1 provision.

101.5 Use of terminology and notes. The term "this code," or "the code," where used in the provisions of Chapter 1, in Chapters 2 – 35 of the IBC or in the state amendments to the IBC means the USBC, unless the context clearly indicates otherwise. The term "this code," or "the code," where used in a code or standard referenced in the IBC means that code or standard, unless the context clearly indicates otherwise. The use of notes in Chapter 1 is to provide information only and shall not be construed as changing the meaning of any code provision. Notes in the IBC, in the codes and standards referenced in the IBC and in the state amendments to the IBC may modify the content of a related provision and shall be considered to be a valid part of the provision, unless the context clearly indicates otherwise.

2006 VIRGINIA CONSTRUCTION CODE (Part I of the Virginia Uniform Statewide Building Code) – Effective May 1, 2008

101.6 Order of precedence. The provisions of Chapter 1 of this code supersede any conflicting provisions of Chapters 2 – 35 of the IBC and any conflicting provisions of the codes and standards referenced in the IBC. In addition, the state amendments to the IBC supersede any conflicting provisions of Chapters 2 – 35 of the IBC and any conflicting provisions of the codes and standards referenced in the IBC. Further, the provisions of Chapters 2 – 35 of the IBC supersede any conflicting provisions of the codes and standards referenced in the IBC.

101.7 Administrative provisions. The provisions of Chapter 1 establish administrative requirements, which include but are not limited to provisions relating to the scope of the code, enforcement, fees, permits, inspections and disputes. Any provisions of Chapters 2 – 35 of the IBC or any provisions of the codes and standards referenced in the IBC that address the same subject matter and impose differing requirements are deleted and replaced by the provisions of Chapter 1. Further, any administrative requirements contained in the state amendments to the IBC shall be given the same precedence as the provisions of Chapter 1. Notwithstanding the above, where administrative requirements of Chapters 2 – 35 of the IBC or of the codes and standards referenced in the IBC are specifically identified as valid administrative requirements in Chapter 1 of this code or in the state amendments to the IBC, then such requirements are not deleted and replaced.

> **Note:** The purpose of this provision is to eliminate overlap, conflicts and duplication by providing a single standard for administrative, procedural and enforcement requirements of this code.

101.8 Definitions. The definitions of terms used in this code are contained in Chapter 2 along with specific provisions addressing the use of definitions. Terms may be defined in other chapters or provisions of the code and such definitions are also valid.

> **Note:** The order of precedence outlined in Section 101.6 may be determinative in establishing how to apply the definitions in the IBC and in the referenced codes and standards.

SECTION 102
PURPOSE AND SCOPE

102.1 Purpose. In accordance with Section 36-99 of the Code of Virginia, the purpose of the USBC is to protect the health, safety and welfare of the residents of the Commonwealth of Virginia, provided that buildings and structures should be permitted to be constructed at the least possible cost consistent with recognized standards of health, safety, energy conservation and water conservation, including provisions necessary to prevent overcrowding, rodent or insect infestation, and garbage accumulation; and barrier-free provisions for the physically handicapped and aged.

102.2 Scope. This section establishes the scope of the USBC in accordance with Section 36-98 of the Code of Virginia. The USBC shall supersede the building codes and regulations of the counties, municipalities and other political subdivisions and state agencies. This code also shall supersede the provisions of local ordinances applicable to single-family residential construction that (i) regulate dwelling foundations or crawl spaces, (ii) require the use of specific building materials or finishes in construction, or (iii) require minimum surface area or numbers of windows; however, this code shall not supersede proffered conditions accepted as a part of a rezoning application, conditions imposed upon the grant of special exceptions, special or conditional use permits or variances, conditions imposed upon a clustering of single-family homes and preservation of open space development through standards, conditions, and criteria established by a locality pursuant to subdivision 8 of Section 15.2-2242 of the Code of Virginia or subdivision A 12 of Section 15.2-2286 of the Code of Virginia, or land use requirements in airport or highway overlay districts, or historic districts created pursuant to Section 15.2-2306 of the Code of Virginia, or local flood plain regulations adopted as a condition of participation in the National Flood Insurance Program.

> **Note:** Requirements relating to functional design are contained in Section 103.11 of this code.

> **102.2.1 Invalidity of provisions.** To the extent that any provisions of this code are in conflict with Chapter 6 (Section 36-97 et seq.) of Title 36 of the Code of Virginia or in conflict with the scope of the USBC, those provisions are considered to be invalid to the extent of such conflict.

102.3 Exemptions. The following are exempt from this code:

1. Equipment and related wiring installed by a provider of publicly regulated utility service or a franchised cable television operator and electrical equipment and related wiring used for radio, broadcast or cable television,

2006 VIRGINIA CONSTRUCTION CODE (Part I of the Virginia Uniform Statewide Building Code) – Effective May 1, 2008

telecommunications or information service transmission. The exemption shall apply only if under applicable federal and state law the ownership and control of the equipment and wiring is by the service provider or its affiliates. Such exempt equipment and wiring shall be located on either public rights-of-way or private property for which the service provider has rights of occupancy and entry; however, the structures, including their service equipment, housing or supporting such exempt equipment and wiring shall be subject to the USBC. The installation of equipment and wiring exempted by this section shall not create an unsafe condition prohibited by the USBC.

2.   Manufacturing and processing machines, including all of the following service equipment associated with the manufacturing or processing machines.

2.1.   Electrical equipment connected after the last disconnecting means.

2.2.   Plumbing piping and equipment connected after the last shutoff valve or backflow device and before the equipment drain trap.

2.3.   Gas piping and equipment connected after the outlet shutoff valve.

3.   Parking lots and sidewalks, which are not part of an accessible route.

4.   Nonmechanized playground or recreational equipment such as swing sets, sliding boards, climbing bars, jungle gyms, skateboard ramps, and similar equipment where no admission fee is charged for its use or for admittance to areas where the equipment is located.

5.   Industrialized buildings subject to the Virginia Industrialized Building Safety Regulations (13 VAC 5-91) and manufactured homes subject to the Virginia Manufactured Home Safety Regulations (13 VAC 5-95); except as provided for in Section 421.

6.   Farm buildings and structures, except for a building or a portion of a building located on a farm that is operated as a restaurant as defined in Section 35.1-1 of the Code of Virginia and licensed as such by the Virginia Board of Health pursuant to Chapter 2 (Section 35.1-11 et. seq.) of Title 35.1 of the Code of Virginia. However, farm buildings and structures lying within a flood plain or in a mudslide-prone area shall be subject to flood-proofing regulations or mudslide regulations, as applicable.

SECTION 103
APPLICATION OF CODE

103.1 General. In accordance with Section 36-99 of the Code of Virginia, the USBC shall prescribe building regulations to be complied with in the construction and rehabilitation of buildings and structures, and the equipment therein.

103.2 When applicable to new construction. Construction for which a permit application is submitted to the local building department after May 1, 2008, shall comply with the provisions of this code, except for permit applications submitted during a one-year period after May 1, 2008. The applicant for a permit during such one-year period shall be permitted to choose whether to comply with the provisions of this code or the provisions of the code in effect immediately prior to May 1, 2008. This provision shall also apply to subsequent amendments to this code based on the effective date of such amendments. In addition, when a permit has been properly issued under a previous edition of this code, this code shall not require changes to the approved construction documents, design or construction of such a building or structure, provided the permit has not been suspended or revoked.

103.3 Change of occupancy. No change shall be made in the existing occupancy classification of any structure when the current USBC requires a greater degree of structural strength, fire protection, means of egress, ventilation or sanitation. When such a greater degree is required, the owner or the owner's agent shall make written application to the local building department for a new certificate of occupancy and shall obtain the new certificate of occupancy prior to the use of the structure under the new occupancy classification. When impractical to achieve compliance with this code for the new occupancy classification, the building official shall consider modifications upon application and as provided for in Section 106.3.

Exception: This section shall not be construed to permit noncompliance with any applicable flood load or flood-resistant construction requirements of this code.

103.4 Additions. Additions to buildings and structures shall comply with the requirements of this code for new construction and an existing building or structure plus additions shall comply with the height and area provisions of Chapter 5. Further, this code shall not require changes to the design or construction of any portions of the building or structure not altered or affected by an addition, unless the addition has the effect of lowering the current level of safety.

Exception: This section shall not be construed to permit noncompliance with any applicable flood load or flood-resistant construction requirements of this code.

103.5 Reconstruction, alteration or repair. The following criteria is applicable to reconstruction, alteration or repair of buildings or structures:

1. Any reconstruction, alteration or repair shall not adversely affect the performance of the building or structure, or cause the building or structure to become unsafe or lower existing levels of health and safety.

2. Parts of the building or structure not being reconstructed, altered or repaired shall not be required to comply with the requirements of this code applicable to newly constructed buildings or structures.

3. The installation of material or equipment, or both, that is neither required nor prohibited shall only be required to comply with the provisions of this code relating to the safe installation of such material or equipment.

4. Material or equipment, or both, may be replaced in the same location with material or equipment of a similar kind or capacity.

Exceptions:

1. This section shall not be construed to permit noncompliance with any applicable flood load or flood-resistant construction requirements of this code.

2. Reconstructed decks, balconies, porches and similar structures located 30 inches (762 mm) or more above grade shall meet the current code provisions for structural loading capacity, connections and structural attachment. This requirement excludes handrails and guardrails.

103.6. Use of rehabilitation code. Compliance with Part II of the Virginia Uniform Statewide Building Code, also known as the "Virginia Rehabilitation Code," shall be an acceptable alternative to compliance with this code for the rehabilitation of such existing buildings and structures within the scope of that code. For the purposes of this section, the term "rehabilitation" shall be as defined in the Virginia Rehabilitation Code.

103.7. Retrofit requirements. The local building department shall enforce the provisions of Section 3411, which require certain existing buildings to be retrofitted with fire protection systems and other safety equipment. Retroactive fire protection system requirements contained in the International Fire Code shall not be applicable unless required for compliance with the provisions of Section 3411.

103.8 Non-required equipment. The following criteria for non-required equipment is in accordance with Section 36-103 of the Code of Virginia. Building owners may elect to install partial or full fire alarms or other safety equipment that was not required by the edition of the USBC in effect at the time a building was constructed without meeting current requirements of the code, provided the installation does not create a hazardous condition. Permits for installation shall be obtained in accordance with this code. In addition, as a requirement of this code, when such non-required equipment is to be installed, the building official shall notify the appropriate fire official or fire chief.

103.8.1 Reduction in function or discontinuance of nonrequired fire protection systems. When a nonrequired fire protection system is to be reduced in function or discontinued, it shall be done in such a manner so as not to create a false sense of protection. Generally, in such cases, any features visible from interior areas shall be removed, such as sprinkler heads, smoke detectors or alarm panels or devices, but any wiring or piping hidden within the construction of the building may remain. Approval of the proposed method of reduction or discontinuance shall be obtained from the building official.

2006 VIRGINIA CONSTRUCTION CODE (Part I of the Virginia Uniform Statewide Building Code) – Effective May 1, 2008

103.9 Equipment changes. Upon the replacement or new installation of any fuel-burning appliances or equipment in existing buildings, an inspection or inspections shall be conducted to ensure that the connected vent or chimney systems comply with the following:

1. Vent or chimney systems are sized in accordance with either the International Residential Code, the International Mechanical Code or the International Fuel Gas Code, depending on which is applicable based on the fuel source and the occupancy classification of the structure.

2. Vent or chimney systems are clean, free of any obstruction or blockages, defects or deterioration and are in operable condition.

Where not inspected by the local building department, persons performing such changes or installations shall certify to the building official that the requirements of Items 1 and 2 of this section are met.

103.10 Use of certain provisions of referenced codes. The following provisions of the IBC and of other indicated codes or standards are to be considered valid provisions of this code. Where any such provisions have been modified by the state amendments to the IBC, then the modified provisions apply.

1. Special inspection requirements in Chapters 2 – 35.

2. Chapter 34, Existing Structures, except that Section 3410, Compliance Alternatives, shall not be used to comply with the retrofit requirements identified in Section 103.7 and shall not be construed to permit noncompliance with any applicable flood load or flood-resistant construction requirements of this code.

3. Testing requirements and requirements for the submittal of construction documents in any of the ICC codes referenced in Chapter 35.

4. Section R301.2 of the International Residential Code authorizing localities to determine climatic and geographic design criteria.

5. Flood load or flood-resistant construction requirements in the IBC or the International Residential Code, including, but not limited to, any such provisions pertaining to flood elevation certificates which are located in Chapter 1 of those codes. Any required flood elevation certificate pursuant to such provisions shall be prepared by a land surveyor licensed in Virginia or an RDP.

103.11 Functional design. The following criteria for functional design is in accordance with Section 36-98 of the Code of Virginia. The USBC shall not supersede the regulations of other state agencies which require and govern the functional design and operation of building related activities not covered by the USBC including but not limited to (i) public water supply systems, (ii) waste water treatment and disposal systems, (iii) solid waste facilities. Nor shall state agencies be prohibited from requiring, pursuant to other state law, that buildings and equipment be maintained in accordance with provisions of this code. In addition, as established by this code, the building official may refuse to issue a permit until the applicant has supplied certificates of functional design approval from the appropriate state agency or agencies. For purposes of coordination, the locality may require reports to the building official by other departments or agencies indicating compliance with their regulations applicable to the functional design of a building or structure as a condition for issuance of a building permit or certificate of occupancy. Such reports shall be based upon review of the plans or inspection of the project as determined by the locality. All enforcement of these conditions shall not be the responsibility of the building official, but rather the agency imposing the condition.

Note: Identified state agencies with functional design approval are listed in the "Related Laws Package" which is available from DHCD.

103.12 Amusement devices and inspections. In accordance with Section 36-98.3 of the Code of Virginia, to the extent they are not superseded by the provisions of Section 36-98.3 of the Code of Virginia and the VADR, the provisions of the USBC shall apply to amusement devices. In addition, as a requirement of this code, inspections for compliance with the VADR shall be conducted either by local building department personnel or private inspectors provided such persons are certified as amusement device inspectors under the VCS.

103.13 State buildings and structures. This section establishes the application of the USBC to state-owned buildings and structures in accordance with Section 36-98.1 of the Code of Virginia. The USBC shall be applicable to all state-owned buildings and structures, with the exception that Sections 2.2-1159, 2.2-1160 and 2.2-1161 of the Code of Virginia shall provide the standards for ready access to and use of state-owned buildings by the physically handicapped.

Any state-owned building or structure for which preliminary plans were prepared or on which construction commenced after the initial effective date of the USBC, shall remain subject to the provisions of the USBC that were in effect at the time such plans were completed or such construction commenced. Subsequent reconstruction, renovation or demolition of such building or structure shall be subject to the pertinent provisions of this code.

Acting through the Division of Engineering and Buildings, the Virginia Department of General Services shall function as the building official for state-owned buildings. The Department shall review and approve plans and specifications, grant modifications, and establish such rules and regulations as may be necessary to implement this section. It shall provide for the inspection of state-owned buildings and enforcement of the USBC and standards for access by the physically handicapped by delegating inspection and USBC enforcement duties to the State Fire Marshal's Office, to other appropriate state agencies having needed expertise, and to local building departments, all of which shall provide such assistance within a reasonable time and in the manner requested. State agencies and institutions occupying buildings shall pay to the local building department the same fees as would be paid by a private citizen for the services rendered when such services are requested by the Department. The Department may alter or overrule any decision of the local building department after having first considered the local building department's report or other rationale given for its decision. When altering or overruling any decision of a local building department, the Department shall provide the local building department with a written summary of its reasons for doing so.

Notwithstanding any provision of this code to the contrary, roadway tunnels and bridges owned by the Virginia Department of Transportation shall be exempt from this code. The Virginia Department of General Services shall not have jurisdiction over such roadway tunnels, bridges and other limited access highways; provided, however, that the Department of General Services shall have jurisdiction over any occupied buildings within any Department of Transportation rights-of-way that are subject to this code.

Except as provided in Section 23-38.109 D of the Code of Virginia, and notwithstanding any provision of this code to the contrary, at the request of a public institution of higher education, the Virginia Department of General Services, as further set forth in this provision, shall authorize that institution of higher education to contract with a building official of the locality in which the construction is taking place to perform any inspection and certifications required for the purpose of complying with this code. The Department shall publish administrative procedures that shall be followed in contracting with a building official of the locality. The authority granted to a public institution of higher education under this provision to contract with a building official of the locality shall be subject to the institution meeting the conditions prescribed in Section 23-38.88 B of the Code of Virginia.

Note: In accordance with Section 36-98.1 of the Code of Virginia, roadway tunnels and bridges shall be designed, constructed and operated to comply with fire safety standards based on nationally recognized model codes and standards to be developed by the Virginia Department of Transportation in consultation with the State Fire Marshal and approved by the Virginia Commonwealth Transportation Board. Emergency response planning and activities related to the standards approved by the Commonwealth Transportation Board shall be developed by the Department of Transportation and coordinated with the appropriate local officials and emergency service providers. On an annual basis, the Department of Transportation shall provide a report on the maintenance and operability of installed fire protection and detection systems in roadway tunnels and bridges to the State Fire Marshal.

SECTION 104
ENFORCEMENT, GENERALLY

104.1 Scope of enforcement. This section establishes the requirements for enforcement of the USBC in accordance with Section 36-105 of the Code of Virginia. Enforcement of the provisions of the USBC for construction and rehabilitation shall be the responsibility of the local building department. Whenever a county or municipality does not have such a building department, the local governing body shall enter into an agreement with the local governing body of another county or municipality or with some other agency, or a state agency approved by DHCD for such enforcement. For the purposes of this section, towns with a population of less than 3,500 may elect to administer and enforce the USBC; however, where the town does not elect to administer and enforce the code, the county in which the town is situated shall

2006 VIRGINIA CONSTRUCTION CODE (Part I of the Virginia Uniform Statewide Building Code) – Effective May 1, 2008

administer and enforce the code for the town. In the event such town is situated in two or more counties, those counties shall administer and enforce the USBC for that portion of the town which is situated within their respective boundaries.

Upon a finding by the local building department, following a complaint by a tenant of a residential rental unit that is the subject of such complaint, that there may be a violation of the unsafe structures provisions of Part III of the Virginia Uniform Statewide Building Code, also known as the "Virginia Maintenance Code," the local building department shall enforce such provisions.

If the local building department receives a complaint that a violation of the Virginia Maintenance Code exists that is an immediate and imminent threat to the health or safety of the owner or tenant of a residential dwelling unit or a nearby residential dwelling unit, and the owner or tenant of the residential dwelling unit that is the subject of the complaint has refused to allow the local building official or his agent to have access to the subject dwelling, the local building official or his agent may present sworn testimony to a court of competent jurisdiction and request that the court grant the local building official or his agent an inspection warrant to enable the building official or his agent to enter the subject dwelling for the purpose of determining whether violations of the Virginia Maintenance Code exist. The local building official or his agent shall make a reasonable effort to obtain consent from the owner or tenant of the subject dwelling prior to seeking the issuance of an inspection warrant under this section.

The local governing body shall inspect and enforce the provisions of the Virginia Maintenance Code for elevators except for elevators in single and two-family homes and townhouses. Such inspection and enforcement shall be carried out by an agency or department designated by the local governing body.

104.2 Interagency coordination. When any inspection functions under this code are assigned to a local agency other than the local building department, such agency shall coordinate its reports of inspection with the local building department.

104.3 Transfer of ownership. If the local building department has initiated an enforcement action against the owner of a building or structure and such owner subsequently transfers the ownership of the building or structure to an entity in which the owner holds an ownership interest greater than 50%, the pending enforcement action shall continue to be enforced against the owner.

SECTION 105
LOCAL BUILDING DEPARTMENT

105.1 Appointment of building official. Every local building department shall have a building official as the executive official in charge of the department. The building official shall be appointed in a manner selected by the local governing body. After permanent appointment, the building official shall not be removed from office except for cause after having been afforded a full opportunity to be heard on specific and relevant charges by and before the appointing authority. DHCD shall be notified by the appointing authority within 30 days of the appointment or release of a permanent or acting building official.

Note: Building officials are subject to sanctions in accordance with the VCS.

105.1.1 Qualifications of building official. The building official shall have at least five years of building experience as a licensed professional engineer or architect, building, fire or trade inspector, contractor, housing inspector or superintendent of building, fire or trade construction or at least five years of building experience after obtaining a degree in architecture or engineering, with at least three years in responsible charge of work. Any combination of education and experience that would confer equivalent knowledge and ability shall be deemed to satisfy this requirement. The building official shall have general knowledge of sound engineering practice in respect to the design and construction of structures, the basic principles of fire prevention, the accepted requirements for means of egress and the installation of elevators and other service equipment necessary for the health, safety and general welfare of the occupants and the public. The local governing body may establish additional qualification requirements.

105.1.2 Certification of building official. An acting or permanent building official shall be certified as a building official in accordance with the VCS within one year after being appointed as acting or permanent building official.

Exception: A building official in place prior to April 1, 1983, shall not be required to meet the certification requirements in this section while continuing to serve in the same capacity in the same locality.

105.1.3 Noncertified building official. Except for a building official exempt from certification under the exception to Section 105.1.2, any acting or permanent building official who is not certified as a building official in accordance with the VCS shall attend the core module of the Virginia Building Code Academy or an equivalent course in an individual or regional code academy accredited by DHCD within 180 days of appointment. This requirement is in addition to meeting the certification requirement in Section 105.1.2.

105.1.4 Continuing education requirements. Building officials shall attend 16 hours every two years of continuing education and periodic training courses approved or required by DHCD. Additional continuing education hours shall not be required if more than one certificate is held.

105.2 Technical assistants. The building official, subject to any limitations imposed by the locality, shall be permitted to utilize technical assistants to assist the building official in the enforcement of the USBC. DHCD shall be notified by the building official within 60 days of the employment of, contracting with or termination of all technical assistants.

Note: Technical assistants are subject to sanctions in accordance with the VCS.

105.2.1 Qualifications of technical assistants. A technical assistant shall have at least three years of experience and general knowledge in at least one of the following areas: building construction; building, fire or housing inspections; plumbing, electrical or mechanical trades; or fire protection, elevator or property maintenance work. Any combination of education and experience that would confer equivalent knowledge and ability shall be deemed to satisfy this requirement. The locality may establish additional qualification requirements.

105.2.2 Certification of technical assistants. A technical assistant shall be certified in the appropriate subject area within 18 months after becoming a technical assistant. When required by local policy to have two or more certifications, a technical assistant shall obtain the additional certifications within three years from the date of such requirement.

Exception: A technical assistant in place prior to March 1, 1988 shall not be required to meet the certification requirements in this section while continuing to serve in the same capacity in the same locality.

105.2.3 Continuing education requirements. Technical assistants shall attend 16 hours every two years of continuing education and periodic training courses approved or required by DHCD. Additional continuing education hours shall not be required if more than one certificate is held.

105.3 Conflict of interest. The standards of conduct for building officials and technical assistants shall be in accordance with the provisions of the State and Local Government Conflict of Interests Act, Chapter 31 (Section 2.2-3100 et seq.) of Title 2.2 of the Code of Virginia.

105.4 Records. The local building department shall retain a record of applications received, permits, certificates, notices and orders issued, fees collected and reports of inspection in accordance with The Library of Virginia's General Schedule Number Six.

SECTION 106
POWERS AND DUTIES OF THE BUILDING OFFICIAL

106.1 Powers and duties, generally. The building official shall enforce this code as set out herein and as interpreted by the State Review Board.

106.2 Delegation of authority. The building official may delegate powers and duties except where such authority is limited by the local government. When such delegations are made, the building official shall be responsible for assuring that they are carried out in accordance with the provisions of this code.

106.3 Issuance of modifications. Upon written application by an owner or an owner's agent, the building official may approve a modification of any provision of the USBC provided the spirit and functional intent of the code are observed and public health, welfare and safety are assured. The decision of the building official concerning a modification shall be made in writing and the application for a modification and the decision of the building official concerning such modification shall be retained in the permanent records of the local building department.

2006 VIRGINIA CONSTRUCTION CODE (Part I of the Virginia Uniform Statewide Building Code) – Effective May 1, 2008

Note: The USBC references nationally recognized model codes and standards. Future amendments to such codes and standards are not automatically included in the USBC; however the building official should give them due consideration in deciding whether to approve a modification.

106.3.1 Substantiation of modification. The building official may require or may consider a statement from an RDP or other person competent in the subject area of the application as to the equivalency of the proposed modification. In addition, the building official may require the application to include construction documents sealed by an RDP.

106.3.2 Use of performance code. Compliance with the provisions of a nationally recognized performance code when approved as a modification shall be considered to constitute compliance with this code. All documents submitted as part of such consideration shall be retained in the permanent records of the local building department.

SECTION 107
FEES

107.1 Authority for charging fees. In accordance with Section 36-105 of the Code of Virginia, fees may be levied by the local governing body in order to defray the cost of enforcement of the USBC.

107.1.1 Fee schedule. The local governing body shall establish a fee schedule incorporating unit rates, which may be based on square footage, cubic footage, estimated cost of construction or other appropriate criteria. A permit or any amendments to an existing permit shall not be issued until the designated fees have been paid, except that the building official may authorize the delayed payment of fees.

107.1.2 Refunds. When requested in writing by a permit holder, the locality shall provide a fee refund in the case of the revocation of a permit or the abandonment or discontinuance of a building project. The refund shall not be required to exceed an amount which correlates to work not completed.

107.2 Code Academy fee levy. In accordance with subdivision 7 of Section 36-137 of the Code of Virginia, the local building department shall collect a 1.75% levy of fees charged for building permits issued under this code and transmit it quarterly to DHCD to support training programs of the Virginia Building Code Academy. The foregoing levy shall remain effective until July 1, 2009, after which time the fee levy shall be increased to 2%. Localities which maintain individual or regional training academies accredited by DHCD shall retain such levy.

SECTION 108
APPLICATION FOR PERMIT

108.1 When applications are required. Application for a permit shall be made to the building official and a permit shall be obtained prior to the commencement of any of the following activities, except that applications for emergency construction, alterations or equipment replacement shall be submitted by the end of the first working day that follows the day such work commences. In addition, the building official may authorize work to commence pending the receipt of an application or the issuance of a permit.

1. Construction or demolition of a building or structure. Installations or alterations involving (i) the removal or addition of any wall, partition or portion thereof, (ii) any structural component, (iii) the repair or replacement of any required component of a fire or smoke rated assembly, (iv) the alteration of any required means of egress system, (v) water supply and distribution system, sanitary drainage system or vent system, (vi) electric wiring, (vii) fire protection system, mechanical systems or fuel supply systems or (viii) any equipment regulated by the USBC.

2. For change of occupancy, application for a permit shall be made when a new certificate of occupancy is required under Section 103.3.

3. Movement of a lot line that increases the hazard to or decreases the level of safety of an existing building or structure in comparison to the building code under which such building or structure was constructed.

4. Removal or disturbing of any asbestos containing materials during the construction or demolition of a building or structure, including additions.

2006 VIRGINIA CONSTRUCTION CODE (Part I of the Virginia Uniform Statewide Building Code) – Effective May 1, 2008

108.2 Exemptions from application for permit. Notwithstanding the requirements of Section 108.1, application for a permit and any related inspections shall not be required for the following; however, this section shall not be construed to exempt such activities from other applicable requirements of this code. In addition, when an owner or an owner's agent requests that a permit be issued for any of the following, then a permit shall be issued and any related inspections shall be required.

1. Installation of wiring and equipment that (i) operates at less than 50 volts, (ii) is for network powered broadband communications systems, or (iii) is exempt under Section 102.3(1), except when any such installations are located in a plenum, penetrate fire rated or smoke protected construction or are a component of any of the following.

    1.1. Fire alarm system.

    1.2. Fire detection system.

    1.3. Fire suppression system.

    1.4. Smoke control system.

    1.5. Fire protection supervisory system.

    1.6. Elevator fire safety control system.

    1.7. Access or egress control system or delayed egress locking or latching system.

    1.8. Fire damper.

    1.9. Door control system.

2. Detached accessory structures used as tool and storage sheds, playhouses or similar uses, provided the floor area does not exceed 150 square feet (14 m²) and the structures are not accessory to a Group F or H occupancy.

3. Detached pre-fabricated buildings housing the equipment of a publicly regulated utility service, provided the floor area does not exceed 150 square feet (14 m²).

4. Tents or air-supported structures, or both, that cover an area of 900 square feet (84 m²) or less, including within that area all connecting areas or spaces with a common means of egress or entrance, provided such tents or structures have an occupant load of 50 or less persons.

5. Fences and privacy walls not part of a building, structure or of the barrier for a swimming pool, provided such fences and privacy walls do not exceed six feet in height above the finished grade. Ornamental post caps shall not be considered to contribute to the height of the fence or privacy wall and shall be permitted to extend above the six feet height measurement.

6. Retaining walls supporting less than two feet of unbalanced fill. This exemption shall not apply to any wall impounding Class I, II or III-A liquids or supporting a surcharge other than ordinary unbalanced fill.

7. Swimming pools that have a surface area not greater than 150 square feet (13.95 m²), do not exceed 5,000 gallons (19 000 L) and are less than 24 inches (610 mm) deep.

8. Signs under the conditions in Section H101.2 of Appendix H.

9. Replacement of above-ground existing LP-gas containers of the same capacity in the same location and associated regulators when installed by the serving gas supplier.

10. Ordinary repairs that include the following.

    10.1. Replacement of windows and doors that are not required to be fire rated in Group R-2 where serving a single dwelling unit and in Groups R-3, R-4 and R-5.

2006 VIRGINIA CONSTRUCTION CODE (Part I of the Virginia Uniform Statewide Building Code) – Effective May 1, 2008

10.2.   Replacement of plumbing fixtures in all groups without alteration of the water supply and distribution systems, sanitary drainage systems or vent systems.

10.3.   Replacement of general use snap switches, dimmer and control switches, 125 volt-15 or 20 ampere receptacles, luminaries (lighting fixtures) and ceiling (paddle) fans in Group R-2 where serving a single dwelling unit and in Groups R-3, R-4 and R-5.

10.4.   Replacement of mechanical appliances provided such equipment is not fueled by gas or oil in Group R-2 where serving a single family dwelling and in Groups R-3, R-4 and R-5.

10.5.   Replacement of an unlimited amount of roof covering or siding in Groups R-3, R-4 or R-5 provided the building or structure is not in an area where the design (3 second gust) wind speed is greater than 100 miles per hour (160 km/hr) and replacement of 100 square feet (9.29 m^2) or less of roof covering in all groups and all wind zones.

10.6.   Replacement of 100 square feet (9.29 m^2) or less of roof decking in Groups R-3, R-4 or R-5 unless the decking to be replaced was required at the time of original construction to be fire-retardant-treated or protected in some other way to form a fire-rated wall termination.

10.7.   Installation or replacement of floor finishes in all occupancies.

10.8.   Replacement of Class C interior wall or ceiling finishes installed in Groups A, E and I and replacement of all classes of interior wall or ceiling finishes in other groups.

10.9.   Installation of replacement cabinetry or trim.

10.10. Application of paint or wallpaper.

10.11. Other repair work deemed by the building official to be minor and ordinary which does not adversely affect public health or general safety.

Exception: Application for a permit may be required by the building official for the installation of replacement siding, roofing and windows in buildings within a historic district designated by a locality pursuant to Section 15.2-2306 of the Code of Virginia.

108.3 Applicant information, processing by mail. Application for a permit shall be made by the owner or lessee of the relevant property or the agent of either or by the Registered Design Professional, contractor or subcontractor associated with the work or any of their agents. The full name and address of the owner, lessee and applicant shall be provided in the application. If the owner or lessee is a corporate body, when and to the extent determined necessary by the building official, the full name and address of the responsible officers shall also be provided.

A permit application may be submitted by mail and such permit applications shall be processed by mail, unless the permit applicant voluntarily chooses otherwise. In no case shall an applicant be required to appear in person.

The building official may accept applications for a permit through electronic submissions provided the information required by this section is obtained.

108.4 Prerequisites to obtaining permit. In accordance with Section 54.1-1111 of the Code of Virginia, any person applying to the building department for the construction, removal or improvement of any structure shall furnish prior to the issuance of the permit, either (i) satisfactory proof to the building official that he is duly licensed or certified under the terms or Chapter 11 (Section 54.1-1000 et seq.) of Title 54.1 of the Code of Virginia to carry out or superintend the same, or (ii) file a written statement, supported by an affidavit, that he is not subject to licensure or certification as a contractor or subcontractor pursuant to Chapter 11 of Title 54.1 of the Code of Virginia. The applicant shall also furnish satisfactory proof that the taxes or license fees required by any county, city, or town have been paid so as to be qualified to bid upon or contract for the work for which the permit has been applied.

2006 VIRGINIA CONSTRUCTION CODE (Part I of the Virginia Uniform Statewide Building Code) – Effective May 1, 2008

108.5 Mechanics' lien agent designation. In accordance with Section 36-98.01 of the Code of Virginia, a building permit issued for any one- or two-family residential dwelling shall at the time of issuance contain, at the request of the applicant, the name, mailing address, and telephone number of the mechanics' lien agent as defined in Section 43-1 of the Code of Virginia. If the designation of a mechanics' lien agent is not so requested by the applicant, the building permit shall at the time of issuance state that none has been designated with the words "None Designated."

108.6 Application form, description of work. The application for a permit shall be submitted on a form or forms supplied by the local building department. The application shall contain a general description and location of the proposed work and such other information as determined necessary by the building official.

108.7 Amendments to application. An application for a permit may be amended at any time prior to the completion of the work governed by the permit. Additional construction documents or other records may also be submitted in a like manner. All such submittals shall have the same effect as if filed with the original application for a permit and shall be retained in a like manner as the original filings.

108.8 Time limitation of application. An application for a permit for any proposed work shall be deemed to have been abandoned six months after the date of filing unless such application has been pursued in good faith or a permit has been issued, except that the building official is authorized to grant one or more extensions of time if a justifiable cause is demonstrated.

SECTION 109
CONSTRUCTION DOCUMENTS

109.1 Submittal of documents. Construction documents shall be submitted with the application for a permit. The number of sets of such documents to be submitted shall be determined by the locality. Construction documents for one- and two-family dwellings may have floor plans reversed provided an accompanying site plan is approved.

Exception: Construction documents do not need to be submitted when the building official determines the proposed work is of a minor nature.

Note: Information on the types of construction required to be designed by an RDP is included in the "Related Laws Package" available from DHCD.

109.2 Site plan. When determined necessary by the building official, a site plan shall be submitted with the application for a permit. The site plan shall show to scale the size and location of all proposed construction, including any associated wells, septic tanks or drain fields. The site plan shall also show to scale the size and location of all existing structures on the site, the distances from lot lines to all proposed construction, the established street grades and the proposed finished grades. When determined necessary by the building official, the site plan shall contain the elevation of the lowest floor of any proposed buildings. The site plan shall also be drawn in accordance with an accurate boundary line survey. When the application for a permit is for demolition, the site plan shall show all construction to be demolished and the location and size of all existing structures that are to remain on the site.

Note: Site plans are generally not necessary for alterations, renovations, repairs or the installation of equipment.

109.3 Engineering details. When determined necessary by the building official, construction documents shall include adequate detail of the structural, mechanical, plumbing or electrical components. Adequate detail may include computations, stress diagrams or other essential technical data and when proposed buildings are more than two stories in height, adequate detail may specifically be required to include where floor penetrations will be made for pipes, wires, conduits, and other components of the electrical, mechanical and plumbing systems and how such floor penetrations will be protected to maintain the required structural integrity or fire-resistance rating, or both. All engineered documents, including relevant computations, shall be sealed by the RDP responsible for the design.

109.4 Examination of documents. The building official shall examine or cause to be examined all construction documents or site plans, or both, within a reasonable time after filing. If such documents or plans do not comply with the provisions of this code, the permit applicant shall be notified in writing of the reasons, which shall include any adverse construction document review comments or determinations that additional information or engineering details need to be submitted. The review of construction documents for new one- and two-family dwellings for determining compliance with the technical provisions of this code not relating to the site, location or soil conditions associated with the dwellings shall not be required when identical construction documents for identical dwellings have been previously approved in the same locality under the same edition of the code and such construction documents are on file with the local building department.

109.4.1 Expedited construction document review. The building official may accept reports from an approved person or agency that the construction documents have been examined and conform to the requirements of the USBC and may establish requirements for the person or agency submitting such reports. In addition, where such reports have been submitted, the building official may expedite the issuance of the permit.

109.5 Approval of construction documents. The approval of construction documents shall be limited to only those items within the scope of the USBC. Either the word "Approved" shall be stamped on all required sets of approved construction documents or an equivalent endorsement in writing shall be provided. One set of the approved construction documents shall be retained for the records of the local building department and one set shall be kept at the building site and shall be available to the building official at all reasonable times.

109.6 Phased approval. The building official is authorized to issue a permit for the construction of foundations or any other part of a building or structure before the construction documents for the whole building or structure have been submitted, provided that adequate information and detailed statements have been filed complying with pertinent requirements of this code. The holder of such permit for the foundation or other parts of a building or structure shall proceed at the holder's own risk with the building operation and without assurance that a permit for the entire structure will be granted.

SECTION 110
PERMITS

110.1 Approval and issuance of permits. The building official shall examine or cause to be examined all applications for permits or amendments to such applications within a reasonable time after filing. If the applications or amendments do not comply with the provisions of this code or all pertinent laws and ordinances, the permit shall not be issued and the permit applicant shall be notified in writing of the reasons for not issuing the permit. If the application complies with the applicable requirements of this code, a permit shall be issued as soon as practicable. The issuance of permits shall not be delayed in an effort to control the pace of construction of new detached one- or two-family dwellings.

110.2 Types of permits. Separate or combined permits may be required for different areas of construction such as building construction, plumbing, electrical, and mechanical work, or for special construction as determined appropriate by the locality. In addition, permits for two or more buildings or structures on the same lot may be combined. Annual permits may also be issued for any construction regulated by this code. The annual permit holder shall maintain a detailed record of all construction under the annual permit. Such record shall be available to the building official and shall be submitted to the local building department if requested by the building official.

110.3 Asbestos inspection in buildings to be renovated or demolished; exceptions. In accordance with Section 36-99.7 of the Code of Virginia, the local building department shall not issue a building permit allowing a building for which an initial building permit was issued before January 1, 1985, to be renovated or demolished until the local building department receives certification from the owner or his agent that the affected portions of the building have been inspected for the presence of asbestos by an individual licensed to perform such inspections pursuant to Section 54.1-503 of the Code of Virginia and that no asbestos-containing materials were found or that appropriate response actions will be undertaken in accordance with the requirements of the Clean Air Act National Emission Standard for the Hazardous Air Pollutant (NESHAPS) (40 CFR Part 61, Subpart M), and the asbestos worker protection requirements established by the U.S. Occupational Safety and Health Administration for construction workers (29 CFR 1926.1101). Local educational agencies that are subject to the requirements established by the Environmental Protection Agency under the Asbestos Hazard Emergency Response Act (AHERA) shall also certify compliance with 40 CFR 763 and subsequent amendments thereto.

To meet the inspection requirements above, except with respect to schools, asbestos inspection of renovation projects consisting only of repair or replacement of roofing, floorcovering, or siding materials may be satisfied by a statement that the materials to be repaired or replaced are assumed to contain friable asbestos and that asbestos installation, removal, or encapsulation will be accomplished by a licensed asbestos contractor.

The provisions of this section shall not apply to single-family dwellings or residential housing with four or fewer units, unless the renovation or demolition of such buildings is for commercial or public development purposes. The provisions of this section shall not apply if the combined amount of regulated asbestos-containing material involved in the renovation or demolition is less than 260 linear feet on pipes or less than 160 square feet on other facility components or less than 35 cubic feet off facility components where the length or area could not be measured previously.

An abatement area shall not be reoccupied until the building official receives certification from the owner that the response actions have been completed and final clearances have been measured. The final clearance levels for reoccupancy of the abatement area shall be 0.01 or fewer asbestos fibers per cubic centimeter if determined by Phase Contrast Microscopy analysis (PCM) or 70 or fewer structures per square millimeter if determined by Transmission Electron Microscopy analysis (TEM).

110.4 Fire apparatus access road requirements. The permit applicant shall be informed of any requirements for providing or maintaining fire apparatus access roads prior to the issuance of a building permit.

110.5 Signature on and posting of permits; limitation of approval. The signature of the building official or authorized representative shall be on or affixed to every permit. A copy of the permit shall be posted on the construction site for public inspection until the work is completed. Such posting shall include the street or lot number if one has been assigned, to be readable from a public way. In addition, each building or structure to which a street number has been assigned shall, upon completion, have the number displayed so as to be readable from the public way.

A permit shall be considered authority to proceed with construction in accordance with this code, the approved construction documents, the permit application and any approved amendments or modifications. The permit shall not be construed to otherwise authorize the omission or amendment of any provision of this code.

110.6 Abandonment of work. A building official shall be permitted to revoke a permit if work on the site authorized by the permit is not commenced within six months after issuance of the permit, or if the authorized work on the site is suspended or abandoned for a period of six months after the permit is issued; however, permits issued for plumbing, electrical and mechanical work shall not be revoked if the building permit is still in effect. It shall be the responsibility of the permit applicant to prove to the building official that authorized work includes substantive progress, characterized by approved inspections as specified in Section 113.3 of at least one inspection within a period of six months or other evidence that would indicate substantial work has been performed. Upon written request, the building official may grant one or more extensions of time, not to exceed one year per extension.

110.7 Single-family dwelling permits. The building official shall be permitted to require a three year time limit to complete construction of new detached single-family dwellings, additions to detached single-family dwellings and residential accessory structures. The time limit shall begin from the issuance date of the permit. The building official may grant extensions of time if the applicant can demonstrate substantive progress, characterized by approved inspections as specified in Section 113.3 of at least one inspection within a period of six months or other evidence that would indicate substantial work has been performed.

110.8 Revocation of a permit. The building official may revoke a permit or approval issued under this code in the case of any false statement, misrepresentation of fact, abandonment of work, failure to complete construction as required by Section 110.7 or incorrect information supplied by the applicant in the application or construction documents on which the permit or approval was based.

SECTION 111
RDP SERVICES

111.1 When required. In accordance with Section 54.1-410 of the Code of Virginia and under the general authority of this code, the local building department shall establish a procedure to ensure that construction documents under Section 109 are prepared by an RDP in any case in which the exemptions contained in Sections 54.1-401, 54.1-402 or Section 54.1-402.1 of the Code of Virginia are not applicable or in any case where the building official determines it necessary. When required under Section 54.1-402 of the Code of Virginia or when required by the building official, or both, construction documents shall bear the name and address of the author and his occupation.

Note: Information on the types of construction required to be designed by an RDP is included in the "Related Laws Package" available from DHCD.

111.2 Special inspection requirements. Special inspections shall be conducted when required by Section 1704. Individuals or agencies, or both, conducting special inspections shall meet the qualification requirements of Sections 1703

2006 VIRGINIA CONSTRUCTION CODE (Part I of the Virginia Uniform Statewide Building Code) – Effective May 1, 2008

and 1704.1. The permit applicant shall submit a completed statement of special inspections with the permit application. The building official shall review, and if satisfied that the requirements have been met, approve the statement of special inspections as required in Sections 1704.1.1 and 1705 as a requisite to the issuance of a building permit. The building official may require interim inspection reports. The building official shall receive, and if satisfied that the requirements have been met, approve a final report of special inspections as specified in Section 1704.1.2. All fees and costs related to the special inspections shall be the responsibility of the building owner.

SECTION 112
WORKMANSHIP, MATERIALS AND EQUIPMENT

112.1 General. It shall be the duty of any person performing work covered by this code to comply with all applicable provisions of this code and to perform and complete such work so as to secure the results intended by the USBC.

112.2 Alternative methods or materials. In accordance with Section 36-99 of the Code of Virginia, where practical, the provisions of this code are stated in terms of required level of performance, so as to facilitate the prompt acceptance of new building materials and methods. When generally recognized standards of performance are not available, this section and other applicable requirements of this code provide for acceptance of materials and methods whose performance is substantially equal in safety to those specified on the basis of reliable test and evaluation data presented by the proponent. In addition, as a requirement of this code, the building official shall require that sufficient technical data be submitted to substantiate the proposed use of any material, equipment, device, assembly or method of construction.

112.3 Documentation and approval. In determining whether any material, equipment, device, assembly or method of construction complies with this code, the building official shall approve items listed by nationally recognized testing laboratories (NRTL), when such items are listed for the intended use and application, and in addition, may consider the recommendations of RDPs. Approval shall be issued when the building official finds that the proposed design is satisfactory and complies with the intent of the provisions of this code and that the material, equipment, device, assembly or method of construction offered is, for the purpose intended, at least the equivalent of that prescribed by the code. Such approval is subject to all applicable requirements of this code and the material, equipment, device, assembly or method of construction shall be installed in accordance with the conditions of the approval and their listings. In addition, the building official may revoke such approval whenever it is discovered that such approval was issued in error or on the basis of incorrect information, or where there are repeated violations of the USBC.

112.3.1 Conditions of listings. Where conflicts between this code and conditions of the listing or the manufacturer's installation instructions occur, the provisions of this code shall apply.

Exception: Where a code provision is less restrictive than the conditions of the listing of the equipment or appliance or the manufacturer's installation instructions, the conditions of the listing and the manufacturer's installation instructions shall apply.

112.4 Used material and equipment. Used materials, equipment and devices may be approved provided they have been reconditioned, tested or examined and found to be in good and proper working condition and acceptable for use by the building official.

SECTION 113
INSPECTIONS

113.1 General. In accordance with Section 36-105 of the Code of Virginia, any building or structure may be inspected at any time before completion, and shall not be deemed in compliance until approved by the inspecting authority. Where the construction cost is less than $2,500, however, the inspection may, in the discretion of the inspecting authority, be waived. The building official shall coordinate all reports of inspections for compliance with the USBC, with inspections of fire and health officials delegated such authority, prior to the issuance of an occupancy permit.

113.1.1 Equipment required. Any ladder, scaffolding or test equipment necessary to conduct or witness a requested inspection shall be provided by the permit holder.

113.1.2 Duty to notify. When construction reaches a stage of completion which requires an inspection, the permit holder shall notify the building official.

113.1.3 Duty to inspect. Except as provided for in Section 113.7, the building official shall perform the requested inspection in accordance with Section 113.6 when notified in accordance with Section 113.1.2.

113.2 Prerequisites. The building official may conduct a site inspection prior to issuing a permit. When conducting inspections pursuant to this code, all personnel shall carry proper credentials.

113.3 Minimum inspections. The following minimum inspections shall be conducted by the building official when applicable to the construction or permit:

1. Inspection of footing excavations and reinforcement material for concrete footings prior to the placement of concrete.

2. Inspection of foundation systems during phases of construction necessary to assure compliance with this code.

3. Inspection of preparatory work prior to the placement of concrete.

4. Inspection of structural members and fasteners prior to concealment.

5. Inspection of electrical, mechanical and plumbing materials, equipment and systems prior to concealment.

6. Inspection of energy conservation material prior to concealment.

7. Final inspection.

113.4 Additional inspections. The building official may designate additional inspections and tests to be conducted during the construction of a building or structure and shall so notify the permit holder.

113.5 In-plant and factory inspections. When required by the provisions of this code, materials, equipment or assemblies shall be inspected at the point of manufacture or fabrication. The building official shall require the submittal of an evaluation report of such materials, equipment or assemblies. The evaluation report shall indicate the complete details of the assembly including a description of the assembly and its components, and describe the basis upon which the assembly is being evaluated. In addition, test results and other data as necessary for the building official to determine conformance with the USBC shall be submitted. For factory inspections, an identifying label or stamp permanently affixed to materials, equipment or assemblies indicating that a factory inspection has been made shall be acceptable instead of a written inspection report, provided the intent or meaning of such identifying label or stamp is properly substantiated.

113.6 Approval or notice of defective work. The building official shall either approve the work in writing or give written notice of defective work to the permit holder. Upon request of the permit holder, the notice shall reference the USBC section that serves as the basis for the defects and such defects shall be corrected and reinspected before any work proceeds that would conceal such defects. A record of all reports of inspections, tests, examinations, discrepancies and approvals issued shall be maintained by the building official and shall be communicated promptly in writing to the permit holder. Approval issued under this section may be revoked whenever it is discovered that such approval was issued in error or on the basis of incorrect information, or where there are repeated violations of the USBC.

113.7 Approved inspection agencies. The building official may accept reports of inspections and tests from individuals or inspection agencies approved in accordance with the building official's written policy required by Section 113.7.1. The individual or inspection agency shall meet the qualifications and reliability requirements established by the written policy. Under circumstances where the building official is unable to make the inspection or test required by Section 113.3 or 113.4 within two working days of a request or an agreed upon date or if authorized for other circumstances in the building official's written policy, the building official shall accept reports for review. The building official shall approve the report from such approved individuals or agencies unless there is cause to reject it. Failure to approve a report shall be in writing within two working days of receiving it stating the reason for the rejection. Reports of inspections conducted by approved third-party inspectors or agencies shall be in writing, shall indicate if compliance with the applicable provisions of the USBC have been met and shall be certified by the individual inspector or by the responsible officer when the report is from an agency.

Note: Photographs, videotapes or other sources of pertinent data or information may be considered as constituting such reports and tests.

2006 VIRGINIA CONSTRUCTION CODE (Part I of the Virginia Uniform Statewide Building Code) – Effective May 1, 2008

113.7.1 Third-party inspectors. Each building official charged with the enforcement of the USBC shall have a written policy establishing the minimum acceptable qualifications for third-party inspectors. The policy shall include the format and time frame required for submission of reports, any prequalification or pre-approval requirements before conducting a third-party inspection and any other requirements and procedures established by the building official.

113.7.2 Qualifications. In determining third-party inspector qualifications, the building official may consider such items as DHCD certification, other state and national certifications, state professional registrations, related experience, education and any other factors that would demonstrate competency and reliability to conduct inspections.

113.8 Final inspection. Upon completion of a building or structure and before the issuance of a certificate of occupancy, a final inspection shall be conducted to ensure that any defective work has been corrected and that all work complies with the USBC and has been approved, including any work associated with modifications under Section 106.3. The approval of a final inspection shall be permitted to serve as the new certificate of occupancy required by Section 116.1 in the case of additions or alterations to existing buildings or structures that already have a certificate of occupancy.

SECTION 114
STOP WORK ORDERS

114.1 Issuance of order. When the building official finds that work on any building or structure is being executed contrary to the provisions of this code or any pertinent laws or ordinances, or in a manner endangering the general public, a written stop work order may be issued. The order shall identify the nature of the work to be stopped and be given either to the owner of the property involved, to the owner's agent or to the person performing the work. Following the issuance of such an order, the affected work shall cease immediately. The order shall state the conditions under which such work may be resumed.

114.2 Limitation of order. A stop work order shall apply only to the work identified in the order, provided that other work on the building or structure may be continued if not concealing the work covered by the order.

SECTION 115
VIOLATIONS

115.1 Violation a misdemeanor; civil penalty. In accordance with Section 36-106 of the Code of Virginia, it shall be unlawful for any owner or any other person, firm or corporation, on or after the effective date of any code provisions, to violate any such provisions. Any locality may adopt an ordinance which establishes a uniform schedule of civil penalties for violations of specified provisions of the code which are not abated or remedied promptly after receipt of a notice of violation from the local enforcement officer.

Note: See the full text of Section 36-106 of the Code of Virginia for additional requirements and criteria pertaining to legal action relative to violations of the code.

115.2 Notice of violation. The building official shall issue a written notice of violation to the responsible party if any violations of this code or any directives or orders of the building official have not been corrected or complied with in a reasonable time. The notice shall reference the code section upon which the notice is based and direct the discontinuance and abatement of the violation or the compliance with such directive or order. The notice shall be issued by either delivering a copy to the responsible party by mail to the last known address or delivering the notice in person or by leaving it in the possession of any person in charge of the premises, or by posting the notice in a conspicuous place if the person in charge of the premises cannot be found. The notice of violation shall indicate the right of appeal by referencing the appeals section. When the owner of the building or structure, or the permit holder for the construction in question, or the tenants of such building or structure, are not the responsible party to whom the notice of violation is issued, then a copy of the notice shall also be delivered to the such owner, permit holder or tenants.

115.2.1 Notice not to be issued under certain circumstances. When violations are discovered more than two years after the certificate of occupancy is issued or the date of initial occupancy, whichever occurred later, or more than two years after the approved final inspection for an alteration or renovation, a notice of violation shall only be issued upon advice from the legal counsel of the locality that action may be taken to compel correction of the violation. When compliance can no longer be compelled by prosecution under Section 36-106 of the Code of Virginia, the building

2006 VIRGINIA CONSTRUCTION CODE (Part I of the Virginia Uniform Statewide Building Code) – Effective May 1, 2008

official, when requested by the owner, shall document in writing the existence of the violation noting the edition of the USBC the violation is under.

115.3 Further action when violation not corrected. If the responsible party has not complied with the notice of violation, the building official shall submit a written request to the legal counsel of the locality to institute the appropriate legal proceedings to restrain, correct or abate the violation or to require the removal or termination of the use of the building or structure involved. In cases where the locality so authorizes, the building official may issue or obtain a summons or warrant. Compliance with a notice of violation notwithstanding, the building official may request legal proceedings be instituted for prosecution when a person, firm or corporation is served with three or more notices of violation within one calendar year for failure to obtain a required construction permit prior to commencement of work subject to this code.

Note: See Section 19.2-8 of the Code of Virginia concerning the statute of limitations for building code prosecutions.

115.4 Penalties and abatement. Penalties for violations of the USBC shall be as set out in Section 36-106 of the Code of Virginia. The successful prosecution of a violation of the USBC shall not preclude the institution of appropriate legal action to require correction or abatement of a violation.

SECTION 116
CERTIFICATES OF OCCUPANCY

116.1 General; when to be issued. A certificate of occupancy indicating completion of the work for which a permit was issued shall be obtained prior to the occupancy of any building or structure, except as provided for in this section generally and as specifically provided for in Section 113.8 for additions or alterations. The certificate shall be issued after completion of the final inspection and when the building or structure is in compliance with this code and any pertinent laws or ordinances, or when otherwise entitled. The building official shall, however, issue a certificate of occupancy within five working days after being requested to do so, provided the building or structure meets all of the requirements for a certificate.

Exception: A certificate of occupancy is not required for an accessory structure as defined in the International Residential Code.

116.1.1 Temporary certificate of occupancy. Upon the request of a permit holder, a temporary certificate of occupancy may be issued before the completion of the work covered by a permit, provided that such portion or portions of a building of structure may be occupied safely prior to full completion of the building or structure without endangering life or public safety.

116.2 Contents of certificate. A certificate of occupancy shall specify the following:

1.   The edition of the USBC under which the permit is issued.

2.   The group classification and occupancy in accordance with the provisions of Chapter 3.

3.   The type of construction as defined in Chapter 6.

4.   If an automatic sprinkler system is provided and whether or not such system was required.

5.   Any special stipulations and conditions of the building permit and if any modifications were issued under the permit, there shall be a notation on the certificate that modifications were issued.

116.3 Suspension or revocation of certificate. A certificate of occupancy may be revoked or suspended whenever the building official discovers that such certificate was issued in error or on the basis of incorrect information, where there are repeated violations of the USBC after the certificate has been issued or when requested by the code official under Section 105.7 of the Virginia Maintenance Code. The revocation or suspension shall be in writing and shall state the necessary corrections or conditions for the certificate to be reissued or reinstated in accordance with Section 116.3.1.

116.3.1 Reissuance of reinstatement of certificate of occupancy. When a certificate of occupancy has been revoked or suspended, it shall be reissued or reinstated upon correction of the specific condition or conditions cited as the cause of the revocation or suspension and the revocation or suspension of a certificate of occupancy shall not be used as

2006 VIRGINIA CONSTRUCTION CODE (Part I of the Virginia Uniform Statewide Building Code) – Effective May 1, 2008

justification for requiring a building or structure to be subject to a later edition of the code than that under which such building or structure was initially constructed.

116.4 Issuance of certificate for existing buildings or structures. Upon written request from the owner or the owner's agent, or as otherwise determined necessary by the building official, a certificate of occupancy shall be issued for an existing building or structure provided there are no current violations of the Virginia Maintenance Code or the Virginia Statewide Fire Prevention Code (13 VAC 5-51) and the occupancy classification of the building or structure has not changed. An inspection shall be performed prior to the issuance of the certificate and such buildings and structures shall not be prevented from continued use.

SECTION 117
TEMPORARY AND MOVED BUILDINGS AND STRUCTURES; DEMOLITION

117.1 Temporary building and structures. The building official is authorized to issue a permit for temporary buildings or structures. Such permits shall be limited as to time of service, but shall not be permitted for more than one year, except that upon the permit holder's written request, the building official may grant one or more extensions of time, not to exceed one year per extension. The building official is authorized to terminate the approval and order the demolition or removal of temporary buildings or structures during the period authorized by the permit when determined necessary.

117.2 Moved buildings and structures. Any building or structure moved into a locality or moved to a new location within a locality shall not be occupied or used until a certification of occupancy is issued for the new location. Such moved buildings or structures shall be required to comply with the requirements of this code for a newly constructed building or structure unless meeting all of the following requirements relative to the new location:

1. There is no change in the occupancy classification from its previous location.

2. The building or structure was in compliance with all state and local requirements applicable to it in its previous location and is in compliance with all state and local requirements applicable if originally constructed in the new location.

3. The building or structure did not become unsafe during the moving process due to structural damage or for other reasons.

4. Any alterations, reconstruction, renovations or repairs made pursuant to the move are in compliance with applicable requirements of this code.

117.3 Demolition of buildings and structures. Prior to the issuance of a permit for the demolition of any building or structure, the owner or the owner's agent shall provide certification to the building official that all service connections of utilities have been removed, sealed or plugged satisfactorily and a release has been obtained from the associated utility company. The certification shall further provide that written notice has been given to the owners of adjoining lots and any other lots that may be affected by the temporary removal of utility wires or the temporary disconnection or termination of other services or facilities relative to the demolition. In addition, the requirements of Chapter 33 of the IBC for any necessary retaining walls or fences during demolition shall be applicable and when a building or structure is demolished or removed, the established grades shall be restored.

SECTION 118
BUILDINGS AND STRUCTURES BECOMING UNSAFE DURING CONSTRUCTION

118.1 Applicability. This section applies to buildings and structures for which a construction permit has been issued under this code and construction has not been completed or a certificate of occupancy has not been issued, or both. In addition, this section applies to any building or structure that is under construction or that was constructed without obtaining the required permits under this edition or any edition of the USBC.

Note: Existing buildings and structures other than those under construction or subject to this section are subject to the Virginia Maintenance Code that also has requirements for unsafe conditions.

118.2 Repair or removal of unsafe buildings or structures. Any building or structure subject to this section that is either deteriorated, improperly maintained, of faulty construction, deficient in adequate exit facilities, a fire hazard or dangerous

2006 VIRGINIA CONSTRUCTION CODE (Part I of the Virginia Uniform Statewide Building Code) – Effective May 1, 2008

to life or the public welfare, or both, or any combination of the foregoing, is an unsafe building or structure and shall be made safe through compliance with this code or shall be taken down and removed if determined necessary by the building official.

118.3 Inspection report and notice of unsafe building or structure. The building official shall inspect any building or structure reported to be unsafe and shall prepare a report to be filed in the records of the local building department. In addition to a description of any unsafe conditions found, the report shall include the occupancy classification of the building or structure and the nature and extent of any damages caused by collapse or failure of any building components. If the building or structure is determined by the building official to be unsafe, a notice of unsafe building or structure shall be issued in person to the owner and any permit holder. The notice shall describe any unsafe conditions and specify any repairs or improvements necessary to make the building or structure safe, or alternatively, when determined necessary by the building official, require the unsafe building or structure, or any portion of it, to be taken down and removed. The notice shall stipulate a time period for the repair or demolition of the unsafe building or structure and contain a statement requiring the person receiving the notice to determine whether to accept or reject the terms of the notice. If any persons to which the notice of unsafe building or structure is to be issued cannot be found after diligent search, as equivalent service, the notice shall be sent by registered or certified mail to the last known address of such persons and a copy of the notice posted in a conspicuous place on the premises.

118.4 Vacating the unsafe building or structure. If any portion of an unsafe building or structure has collapsed or fallen, or if the building official determines there is actual and immediate danger of any portion collapsing or falling, and when life is endangered by the occupancy of the unsafe building or structure, the building official shall be authorized to order the occupants to immediately vacate the unsafe building or structure. When an unsafe building or structure is ordered to be vacated, the building official shall post a notice at each entrance that reads as follows:

"This Building (or Structure) is Unsafe and its Occupancy (or Use) is Prohibited by the Building Official."

After posting, occupancy or use of the unsafe structure shall be prohibited except when authorized to enter to conduct inspections, make required repairs or as necessary to demolish the building or structure.

118.5 Emergency repairs and demolition. To the extent permitted by the locality, the building official may authorize emergency repairs to unsafe buildings or structures when it is determined that there is an immediate danger of any portion of the unsafe building or structure collapsing or falling and when life is endangered. Emergency repairs may also be authorized when there is a code violation resulting in the immediate, serious and imminent threat to the life and safety of the occupants. The building official shall be permitted to authorize the necessary work to make the building or structure temporarily safe whether or not legal action to compel compliance has been instituted.

In addition, whenever an owner of an unsafe building or structure fails to comply with a notice to demolish issued under Section 118.3 in the time period stipulated, the building official shall be permitted to cause the unsafe building or structure to be demolished. In accordance with Sections 15.2-906 and 15.2-1115 of the Code of Virginia , the legal counsel of the locality may be requested to institute appropriate action against the property owner to recover the costs associated with any such emergency repairs or demolition and every such charge that remains unpaid shall constitute a lien against the property on which the emergency repairs or demolition were made and shall be enforceable in the same manner as provided in Articles 3 (Section 58.1-3940 et seq.) and 4 (Section 58.1-3965 et seq.) of Chapter 39 of Title 58.1 of the Code of Virginia.

Note: Building officials and local governing bodies should be aware that other statutes and court decisions may impact on matters relating to demolition, in particular whether newspaper publication is required if the owner cannot be located and whether the demolition order must be delayed until the owner has been given the opportunity for a hearing.

SECTION 119
APPEALS

119.1 Establishment of appeals board. In accordance with Section 36-105 of the Code of Virginia, there shall be established within each local building department a LBBCA. Whenever a county or a municipality does not have such a LBBCA, the local governing body shall enter into an agreement with the local governing body of another county or municipality or with some other agency, or a state agency approved by DHCD for such appeals resulting therefrom. Fees may be levied by the local governing body in order to defray the cost of such appeals. In addition, as an authorization in

2006 VIRGINIA CONSTRUCTION CODE (Part I of the Virginia Uniform Statewide Building Code) – Effective May 1, 2008

this code, separate LBBCAs may be established to hear appeals of different enforcement areas such as electrical, plumbing or mechanical requirements. Each such LBBCA shall comply with the requirements of this section.

119.2 Membership of board. The LBBCA shall consist of at least five members appointed by the locality for a specific term of office established by written policy. Alternate members may be appointed to serve in the absence of any regular members and as such, shall have the full power and authority of the regular members. Regular and alternate members may be reappointed. Written records of current membership, including a record of the current chairman and secretary shall be maintained in the office of the locality. In order to provide continuity, the terms of the members may be of different length so that less than half will expire in any one-year period.

119.3 Officers and qualifications of members. The LBBCA shall annually select one of its regular members to serve as chairman. When the chairman is not present at an appeal hearing, the members present shall select an acting chairman. The locality or the chief executive officer of the locality shall appoint a secretary to the LBBCA to maintain a detailed record of all proceedings. Members of the LBBCA shall be selected by the locality on the basis of their ability to render fair and competent decisions regarding application of the USBC and shall to the extent possible, represent different occupational or professional fields relating to the construction industry. At least one member should be an experienced builder; at least one member should be an RDP, and at least one member should be an experienced property manager. Employees or officials of the locality shall not serve as members of the LBBCA.

119.4 Conduct of members. No member shall hear an appeal in which that member has a conflict of interest in accordance with the State and Local Government Conflict of Interests Act (Section 2.2-3100 et seq. of the Code of Virginia). Members shall not discuss the substance of an appeal with any other party or their representatives prior to any hearings.

119.5 Right of appeal; filing of appeal application. The owner of a building or structure, the owner's agent or any other person involved in the design or construction of a building or structure may appeal a decision of the building official concerning the application of the USBC to such building or structure and may also appeal a refusal by the building official to grant a modification to the provisions of the USBC pertaining to such building or structure. The applicant shall submit a written request for appeal to the LBBCA within 30 calendar days of the receipt of the decision being appealed. The application shall contain the name and address of the owner of the building or structure and in addition, the name and address of the person appealing, when the applicant is not the owner. A copy of the building official's decision shall be submitted along with the application for appeal and maintained as part of the record. The application shall be marked by the LBBCA to indicate the date received. Failure to submit an application for appeal within the time limit established by this section shall constitute acceptance of a building official's decision.

> **Note:** To the extent that a decision of a building official pertains to amusement devices there may be a right of appeal under the VADR.

119.6 Meetings and postponements. The LBBCA shall meet within 30 calendar days after the date of receipt of the application for appeal, except that a longer time period shall be permitted if agreed to by all the parties involved in the appeal. A notice indicating the time and place of the hearing shall be sent to the parties in writing to the addresses listed on the application at least 14 calendar days prior to the date of the hearing, except that a lesser time period shall be permitted if agreed to by all the parties involved in the appeal. When a quorum of the LBBCA is not present at a hearing to hear an appeal, any party involved in the appeal shall have the right to request a postponement of the hearing. The LBBCA shall reschedule the appeal within 30 calendar days of the postponement, except that a longer time period shall be permitted if agreed to by all the parties involved in the appeal.

119.7 Hearings and decision. All hearings before the LBBCA shall be open meetings and the appellant, the appellant's representative, the locality's representative and any person whose interests are affected by the building official's decision in question shall be given an opportunity to be heard. The chairman shall have the power and duty to direct the hearing, rule upon the acceptance of evidence and oversee the record of all proceedings. The LBBCA shall have the power to uphold, reverse or modify the decision of the official by a concurring vote of a majority of those present. Decisions of the LBBCA shall be final if no further appeal is made. The decision of the LBBCA shall be by resolution signed by the chairman and retained as part of the record of the appeal. Copies of the resolution shall be sent to all parties by certified mail. In addition, the resolution shall contain the following wording:

> "Any person who was a party to the appeal may appeal to the State Review Board by submitting an application to such Board within 21 calendar days upon receipt by certified mail of this resolution. Application forms are available from the Office of the State Review Board, 501 North Second Street, Richmond, Virginia 23219, (804) 371-7150."

119.8 Appeals to the State Review Board. After final determination by the LBBCA in an appeal, any person who was a party to the appeal may further appeal to the State Review Board. In accordance with Section 36-98.2 of the Code of Virginia for state-owned buildings and structures, appeals by an involved state agency from the decision of the building official for state-owned buildings or structures shall be made directly to the State Review Board. The application for appeal shall be made to the State Review Board within 21 calendar days of the receipt of the decision to be appealed. Failure to submit an application within that time limit shall constitute an acceptance of the building official's decision. For appeals from a LBBCA, a copy of the building official's decision and the resolution of the LBBCA shall be submitted with the application for appeal to the State Review Board. Upon request by the office of the State Review Board, the LBBCA shall submit a copy of all pertinent information from the record of the appeal. In the case of appeals involving state-owned buildings or structures, the involved state agency shall submit a copy of the building official's decision and other relevant information with the application for appeal to the State Review Board. Procedures of the State Review Board are in accordance with Article 2 (Section 36-108 et seq.) of Chapter 6 of Title 36 of the Code of Virginia. Decisions of the State Review Board shall be final if no further appeal is made.

CHAPTER 2

DEFINITIONS

Add the following definitions to Section 202 of the IBC to read:

BUILDING REGULATIONS. Any law, rule, resolution, regulation, ordinance or code, general or special, or compilation thereof, heretofore or hereafter enacted or adopted by the Commonwealth or any county or municipality, including departments, boards, bureaus, commissions, or other agencies thereof, relating to construction, reconstruction, alteration, conversion, repair, maintenance, or use of structures and buildings and installation of equipment therein. The term does not include zoning ordinances or other land use controls that do not affect the manner of construction or materials to be used in the erection, alteration or repair of a building or structure.

CONSTRUCTION. The construction, reconstruction, alteration, repair, or conversion of buildings and structures.

DAY-NIGHT AVERAGE SOUND LEVEL (LDN). See Section 1202.1.

DHCD. The Virginia Department of Housing and Community Development.

EMERGENCY COMMUNICATION EQUIPMENT. See Section 902.1.

EMERGENCY PUBLIC SAFETY PERSONNEL. See Section 902.1

EQUIPMENT. Plumbing, heating, electrical, ventilating, air-conditioning and refrigeration equipment, elevators, dumbwaiters, escalators, and other mechanical additions or installations.

FARM BUILDING OR STRUCTURE. A building or structure not used for residential purposes, located on property where farming operations take place, and used primarily for any of the following uses or combination thereof:

1. Storage, handling, production, display, sampling or sale of agricultural, horticultural, floricultural or silvicultural products produced in the farm.

2. Sheltering, raising, handling, processing or sale of agricultural animals or agricultural animal products.

3. Business or office uses relating to the farm operations.

4. Use of farm machinery or equipment or maintenance or storage of vehicles, machinery or equipment on the farm.

5. Storage or use of supplies and materials used on the farm.

6. Implementation of best management practices associated with farm operations.

2006 VIRGINIA CONSTRUCTION CODE (Part I of the Virginia Uniform Statewide Building Code) – Effective May 1, 2008

INDUSTRIALIZED BUILDING. A combination of one or more sections or modules, subject to state regulations and including the necessary electrical, plumbing, heating, ventilating and other service systems, manufactured off-site and transported to the point of use for installation or erection, with or without other specified components, to comprise a finished building. Manufactured homes shall not be considered industrialized buildings for the purpose of this code.

LOCAL BOARD OF BUILDING CODE APPEALS (LBBCA). See Section 119.1.

LOCAL BUILDING DEPARTMENT. The agency or agencies of any local governing body charged with the administration, supervision, or enforcement of this code, approval of construction documents, inspection of buildings or structures, or issuance of permits, licenses, certificates or similar documents.

LOCAL GOVERNING BODY. The governing body of any city, county or town in this Commonwealth.

LOCALITY. A city, county or town in this Commonwealth.

MANUFACTURED HOME. A structure subject to federal regulation, which is transportable in one or more sections; is eight body feet or more in width and 40 body feet or more in length in the traveling mode, or is 320 or more square feet when erected on site; is built on a permanent chassis; is designed to be used as a single-family dwelling, with or without a permanent foundation, when connected to the required utilities; and includes the plumbing, heating, air-conditioning, and electrical systems contained in the structure.

NIGHT CLUB. Any building in which the main use is a place of public assembly that provides exhibition, performance or other forms of entertainment; serves alcoholic beverages; and provides music and space for dancing.

SKIRTING. A weather-resistant material used to enclose the space from the bottom of the manufactured home to grade.

SOUND TRANSMISSION CLASS (STC) RATING. See Section 1202.1.

STATE REGULATED CARE FACILITY (SRCF). A building with an occupancy in Group R-2, R-3, R-4 or R-5 occupied by persons in the care of others where program oversight is provided by the Virginia Department of Social Services, the Virginia Department of Mental Health, Mental Retardation and Substance Abuse Services, the Virginia Department of Education or the Virginia Department of Juvenile Justice.

STATE REVIEW BOARD. The Virginia State Building Code Technical Review Board as established under Section 36-108 of the Code of Virginia.

TECHNICAL ASSISTANT. Any person employed by or under an extended contract to a local building department or local enforcing agency for enforcing the USBC. For the purposes of this definition, an extended contract shall be a contract with an aggregate term of 18 months or longer.

VADR. The Virginia Amusement Device Regulations (13 VAC 5-31).

VCS. The Virginia Certification Standards (13 VAC 5-21).

WORKING DAY. A day other than Saturday, Sunday or a legal local, state or national holiday.

Change the following definitions in Section 202 of the IBC to read:

BUILDING. A combination of materials, whether portable or fixed, having a roof to form a structure for the use or occupancy by persons, or property. The word "building" shall be construed as though followed by the words "or part or parts thereof" unless the context clearly requires a different meaning. "Building" shall not include roadway tunnels and bridges owned by the Virginia Department of Transportation, which shall be governed by construction and design standards approved by the Virginia Commonwealth Transportation Board.

For application of this code, each portion of a building which is completely separated from other portions by fire walls complying with Section 705 shall be considered as a separate building (see Section 503.1).

2006 VIRGINIA CONSTRUCTION CODE (Part I of the Virginia Uniform Statewide Building Code) – Effective May 1, 2008

CANOPY. A structure or architectural projection of rigid construction over which a covering is attached that provides weather protection, identity or decoration and may be structurally independent or supported by attachment to a building on one end by not less than one stanchion on the outer end.

OWNER. The owner or owners of the freehold of the premises or lesser estate therein, a mortgagee or vendee in possession, assignee of rents, receiver, executor, trustee or lessee in control of a building or structure.

REGISTERED DESIGN PROFESSIONAL (RDP). An architect or professional engineer, licensed to practice architecture or engineering, as defined under Section 54.1-400 of the Code of Virginia.

STRUCTURE. An assembly of materials forming a construction for occupancy or use including stadiums, gospel and circus tents, reviewing stands, platforms, stagings, observation towers, radio towers, water tanks, storage tanks (underground and aboveground), trestles, piers, wharves, swimming pools, amusement devices, storage bins, and other structures of this general nature but excluding water wells. The word "structure" shall be construed as though followed by the words "or part or parts thereof" unless the context clearly requires a different meaning. "Structure" shall not include roadway tunnels and bridges owned by the Virginia Department of Transportation, which shall be governed by construction and design standards approved by the Virginia Commonwealth Transportation Board.

Delete the following definitions from Section 202 of the IBC:

AGRICULTURAL, BUILDING.

EXISTING STRUCTURE.

CHAPTER 3

USE AND OCCUPANCY CLASSIFICATION

Change exception 15 of Section 307.1 of the IBC to read:

15. The storage of black powder, smokeless propellant and small arms primers in Groups M, R-3 and R-5 and special industrial explosive devices in Groups B, F, M and S, provided such storage conforms to the quantity limits and requirements prescribed in the *International Fire Code*, as amended in Section 307.9.

Add Section 307.9 to the IBC to read:

307.9 Amendments. The following changes shall be made to the *International Fire Code* (IFC) for the use of Exception 15 in Section 307.1:

1. Change Section 314.1 of the IFC to read as follows:

    314.1 General. Indoor displays constructed within any building or structure shall comply with Sections 314.2 through 314.5.

2. Add new Section 314.5 to the IFC to read as follows:

    314.5 Smokeless powder and small arms primers. Vendors shall not store, display or sell smokeless powder or small arms primers during trade shows inside exhibition halls except as follows:

    1. The amount of smokeless powder each vender may store is limited to the storage arrangements and storage amounts established in Section 3306.5.2.1.

    2. Smokeless powder shall remain in the manufacturer's original sealed container and the container shall remain sealed while inside the building. The repackaging of smokeless powder shall not be performed inside the building. Damaged containers shall not be repackaged inside the building and shall be immediately removed from the building in such manner to avoid spilling any powder.

    3.   There shall be at least 50 feet separation between vendors and 20 feet from any exit.

    4.   Small arms primers shall be displayed and stored in the manufacturer's original packaging and in accordance with the requirements of Section 3306.5.2.3.

3. Change Exception 4 and add Exceptions 10 and 11 to Section 3301.1 of the IFC as follows:

    4.   The possession, storage and use of not more than 15 pounds (6.75 kg) of commercially manufactured sporting black powder, 20 pounds (9 kg) of smokeless powder and any amount of small arms primers for hand loading of small arms ammunition for personal consumption.

    10. The display of small arms primers in Group M when in the original manufacturer's packaging.

    11. The possession, storage and use of not more than 50 pounds (23 kg) of commercially manufactured sporting black powder, 100 pounds (45 kg) of smokeless powder, and small arms primers for hand loading of small arms ammunition for personal consumption in Group R-3 or R-5, or 200 pounds (91 kg) of smokeless powder when stored in the manufacturer's original containers in detached Group U structures at least 10 feet (3048 mm) from inhabited buildings and are accessory to Group R-3 or R-5.

4. Change the definition of Smokeless Propellants in Section 3302.1 of the IFC as follows:

SMOKELESS PROPELLANTS. Solid propellants, commonly referred to as smokeless powders, or any propellants classified by DOTn as smokeless propellants in accordance with NA3178 (Smokeless Powder for Small Arms), used in small arms ammunition, firearms, cannons, rockets, propellant-actuated devices and similar articles.

5. Change Section 3306.4 of the IFC to read as follows:

3306.4 Storage in residences. Propellants for personal use in quantities not exceeding 50 pounds (23 kg) of black powder or 100 pounds (45 kg) of smokeless powder shall be stored in original containers in occupancies limited to Group R-3 and R-5 or 200 pounds (91 kg) of smokeless powder when stored in the manufacturer's original containers in detached Group U structures at least 10 feet (3048 mm) from inhabited buildings and are accessory to Group R-3 or R-5. In other than Group R-3 or R-5, smokeless powder in quantities exceeding 20 pounds (9 kg) but not exceeding 50 pounds (23 kg) shall be kept in a wooden box or cabinet having walls of at least one inch (25 mm) nominal thickness or equivalent.

6. Delete Sections 3306.4.1 and 3306.4.2 of the IFC.

7. Change Section 3306.5.1.1 of the IFC to read as follows:

3306.5.1.1 Smokeless propellant. No more than 100 pounds (45 kg) of smokeless propellants in containers of eight pounds (3.6 kg) or less capacity shall be displayed in Group M occupancies.

8. Delete Section 3306.5.1.3 of the IFC.

9. Change Section 3306.5.2.1 of the IFC as follows:

3306.5.2.1 Smokeless propellant. Commercial stocks of smokeless propellants shall be stored as follows:

    1.   Quantities exceeding 20 pounds (9 kg), but not exceeding 100 pounds (45 kg) shall be stored in portable wooden boxes having walls of at least one inch (25 mm) nominal thickness or equivalent.

    2.   Quantities exceeding 100 pounds (45 kg), but not exceeding 800 pounds (363 kg), shall be stored in storage cabinets having walls at least one inch (25 mm) nominal thickness or equivalent. Not more than 400 pounds (182 kg) shall be stored in any one cabinet, and cabinets shall be separated by a distance of at least 25 feet (7620 mm) or by a fire partition having a fire-resistance rating of at least one hour.

3. Storage of quantities exceeding 800 pounds (363 kg), but not exceeding 5,000 pounds (2270 kg) in a building shall comply with all of the following:

   3.1. The storage is inaccessible to unauthorized personnel.

   3.2. Smokeless propellant shall be stored in nonportable storage cabinets having wood walls at least one inch (25 mm) nominal thickness or equivalent and having shelves with no more than three feet (914 mm) of vertical separation between shelves.

   3.3. No more than 400 pounds (182 kg) is stored in any one cabinet.

   3.4. Cabinets shall be located against walls with at least 40 feet (12 192 mm) between cabinets. The minimum required separation between cabinets may be reduced to 20 feet (6096 mm) provided that barricades twice the height of the cabinets are attached to the wall, midway between each cabinet. The barricades must extend a minimum of 10 feet (3048 mm) outward, be firmly attached to the wall, and be constructed of steel not less than 0.25 inch thick (6.4 mm), 2-inch (51 mm) nominal thickness wood, brick, or concrete block.

   3.5. Smokeless propellant shall be separated from materials classified as combustible liquids, flammable liquids, flammable solids, or oxidizing materials by a distance of 25 feet (7620 mm) or by a fire partition having a fire-resistance rating of 1 hour.

   3.6. The building shall be equipped throughout with an automatic sprinkler system installed in accordance with Section 903.3.1.1.

4. Smokeless propellants not stored according to Item 1, 2, or 3 above shall be stored in a Type 2 or 4 magazine in accordance with Section 3304 and NFPA 495.

Change Section 308.5.2 of the IBC to read:

308.5.2 Child care facility. A facility other than family day homes under Section 310.4 that provides supervision and personal care on less than a 24-hour basis for more than five children 2½ years of age or less shall be classified as Group I-4.

   Exception: A child day care facility that provides care for more than five but no more than 100 children 2½ years or less of age, when the rooms where such children are cared for are located on the level of exit discharge and each of these child care rooms has an exit door directly to the exterior, shall be classified as Group E.

Change occupancy classifications "R-1" and "R-4" and add new occupancy classification "R-5" to Section 310 of the IBC to read:

R-1 Residential occupancies containing sleeping units where the occupants are primarily transient in nature, including:

   Boarding houses (transient)
   Hotels (transient)
   Motels (transient)

   Exceptions:

   1. Non-proprietor occupied bed and breakfast and other transient boarding facilities not more than three stories above grade plane in height with a maximum of 10 occupants total are permitted to be classified as either Group R-3 or Group R-5 provided that smoke alarms are installed in compliance with Section 907.2.10.1.2 for Group R-3 or Section 313.1 of the *International Residential Code* for Group R-5.

   2. Proprietor occupied bed and breakfast and other transient boarding facilities not more than three stories above grade plane in height, that are also occupied as the residence of the proprietor, with a

2006 VIRGINIA CONSTRUCTION CODE (Part I of the Virginia Uniform Statewide Building Code) – Effective May 1, 2008

maximum of 5 guest room sleeping units provided for the transient occupants are permitted to be classified as either Group R-3 or R-5 provided that smoke alarms are installed in compliance with Section 907.2.10.1.2 for Group R-3 or Section 313.1 of the *International Residential Code* for Group R-5.

R-4 Residential occupancies shall include buildings arranged for occupancy as residential care/assisted living facilities including more than five but not more than 16 occupants, excluding staff.

Group R-4 occupancies shall meet the requirements for construction as defined for Group R-3, except as otherwise provided for in this code, or shall comply with the *International Residential Code* with the additional requirement to provide an automatic sprinkler system in accordance with Section 903.2.7.

> **Exception:** Group homes licensed by the Virginia Department of Mental Health, Mental Retardation and Substance Abuse Services or the Virginia Department of Social Services that house no more than eight persons with one or more resident counselors shall be classified as Group R-2, R-3, R-4 or R-5. Not more than five of the persons may require physical assistance from staff to respond to an emergency situation.

R-5 Residential occupancies in detached one- and two-family dwellings, townhouses and accessory structures within the scope of the *International Residential Code*, also referred to as the "IRC."

Add Section 310.3 to the IBC to read:

310.3 Group R-5. The construction of Group R-5 structures shall comply with the IRC. The amendments to the IRC set out in Section 310.6 shall be made to the IRC for its use as part of this code. In addition, all references to Section 101.2 in the IBC relating to the construction of such structures subject to the IRC shall be considered to be references to this section.

Add Section 310.3.1 to the IBC to read:

310.3.1 Additional requirements. Methods of construction, materials, systems, equipment or components for Group R-5 structures not addressed by prescriptive or performance provisions of the IRC shall comply with applicable IBC requirements.

Add Section 310.4 to the IBC to read:

310.4 Family day homes. Family day homes where program oversight is provided by the Virginia Department of Social Services shall be classified as Group R-2, R-3 or R-5.

> **Note:** Family day homes may generally care for up to 12 children. See the DHCD Related Laws Package for additional information.

Add Section 310.5 to the IBC to read:

310.5 Radon-resistant construction in Group R-3 and R-4 structures. Group R-3 and R-4 structures shall be subject to the radon-resistant construction requirements in Appendix F in localities enforcing such requirements pursuant to Section R324 of the IRC.

Add Section 310.6 to the IBC to read:

310.6 Amendments to the IRC. The following changes shall be made to the IRC for its use as part of this code.

1.   Add the following definitions to Section R202 to read:

> **AIR-IMPERMEABLE INSULATION.** An insulation having an air permanence equal to or less than 0.02 L/s-m^2 at 75 Pa pressure differential tested according to ASTM E 2178 or E 283.

> **SUBSOIL DRAIN.** A drain that collects subsurface water or seepage water and conveys such water to a place of disposal.

2. Change the definition of "Story Above Grade" in Section R202 to read:

   STORY ABOVE GRADE. Any story having its finished floor surface entirely above grade, except that a basement shall be considered as a story above grade where the finished surface of the floor above the basement meets any one of the following:

   1. Is more than 6 feet (1829 mm) above the grade plane.

   2. Is more than 6 feet (1829 mm) above the finished ground level for more than 50% of the total building perimeter.

   3. Is more than 12 feet (3658 mm) above the finished ground level at any point.

3. Change Section R301.2.1 to read:

   R301.2.1 Wind limitations. Buildings and portions thereof shall be limited by wind speed, as defined in Table R301.2(1), and construction methods in accordance with this code. Basic wind speeds shall be determined from Figure R301.2(4). Where different construction methods and structural materials are used for various portions of a building, the applicable requirements of this section for each portion shall apply. Where loads for wall coverings, curtain walls, roof coverings, exterior windows, skylights, garage doors and exterior doors are not otherwise specified, the loads listed in Table R301.2(2) adjusted for height and exposure using Table R301.2(3) shall be used to determine design load performance requirements for wall coverings, curtain walls, roof coverings, exterior windows, skylights, garage doors and exterior doors. Asphalt shingles shall be designed for wind speeds in accordance with Section R905.2.6. Wind speeds for localities in special wind regions, near mountainous terrain and near gorges shall be based on elevation. Areas at 4,000 feet in elevation or higher shall use 110 V mph (48.4 m/s) and areas under 4,000 feet in elevation shall use 90 V mph (39.6 m/s). Gorge areas shall be based on the highest recorded speed per locality or in accordance with local jurisdiction requirements determined in accordance with Section 6.5.4 of ASCE 7.

4. Change Section R301.2.1.1 to read:

   R301.2.1.1 Design criteria. Construction in regions where the basic wind speeds from Figure R301.2(4) equal or exceed 110 miles per hour (49m/s) shall be designed in accordance with one of the following:

   1. American Forest and Paper Association (AF&PA) *Wood Frame Construction Manual for One- and Two-Family Dwellings* (WFCM); or

   2. *Southern Building Code Congress International Standard for Hurricane Resistant Residential Construction* (SSTD 10); or

   3. *Minimum Design Loads for Buildings and Other Structures* (ASCE-7); or

   4. American Iron and Steel Institute (AISI), *Standard for Cold-Formed Steel Framing—Prescriptive Method For One- and Two-Family Dwellings (COFS/PM) with Supplement to Standard for Cold-Formed Steel Framing—Prescriptive Method For One- and Two-Family Dwellings.*

   5. Concrete construction shall be designed in accordance with the provisions of this code.

5. Change Table R301.7 to read:

TABLE R301.7
ALLOWABLE DEFLECTION OF STRUCTURAL MEMBERS[a,b,c,d]

STRUCTURAL MEMBER	ALLOWABLE DEFLECTION
Rafters having slopes greater than 3/12 with no finished ceiling attached to rafters	L/180
Interior walls and partitions	H/180
Floors and plastered ceilings	L/360
All other structural members	L/240

Exterior walls with plaster or stucco finish	H/360
Exterior walls–wind loads[a] with brittle finishes	H/240
Exterior walls–wind loads[a] with flexible finishes	H/120[d]
Veneer masonry walls	L/600

Note: L = span length, H = span height.

a. The wind load shall be permitted to be taken as 0.7 times the Component and Cladding loads for the purpose of determining deflection limits herein.

b. For cantilever members, L shall be taken as twice the length of the cantilever.

c. For aluminum structural members or panels used in roofs or walls of sunroom additions or patio covers, not supporting edge of glass or sandwich panels, the total load deflection shall not exceed L/60. For sandwich panels used in roofs or walls of sunroom additions or patio covers, the total load deflection shall not exceed L/120.

d. Deflection for exterior walls with interior gypsum board finish shall be limited to an allowable deflection of H/180.

6. Change Section R302.1 to read:

R302.1 Exterior walls. Construction, projections, openings and penetrations of exterior walls of dwellings and accessory buildings shall comply with Table R302.1.

Exceptions:

1. Walls, projections, openings or penetrations in walls perpendicular to the line used to determine the fire separation distance.

2. Walls of dwellings and accessory structures located on the same lot.

3. Detached tool sheds and storage sheds, playhouses and similar structures exempted from permits are not required to provide wall protection based on location on the lot. Projections beyond the exterior wall shall not extend over the lot line.

4. Detached garages accessory to a dwelling located within 2 feet (610 mm) of a lot line are permitted to have roof eave projections not exceeding 4 inches (102 mm).

5. Foundation vents installed in compliance with this code are permitted.

7. Add an exception to Section R303.8 to read:

Exception: Seasonal structures not used as a primary residence for more than 90 days per year, unless rented, leased or let on terms expressed or implied to furnish heat, shall not be required to comply with this section.

8. Add Section R303.8.1 to read:

R303.8.1 Nonowner occupied required heating. Every dwelling unit or portion thereof which is to be rented, leased or let on terms either expressed or implied to furnish heat to the occupants thereof shall be provided with facilities in accordance with Section R303.8 during the period from October 15 to May 1.

9. Add Section R303.9 to read:

R303.9 Insect screens. Every door, window and other outside opening required for ventilation purposes shall be supplied with approved tightly fitted screens of not less than 16 mesh per inch (16 mesh per 25 mm) and every screen door used for insect control shall have a self-closing device.

10. Add Section R306.5 to read:

R306.5 Water supply sources and sewage disposal systems. The water and drainage system of any building or premises where plumbing fixtures are installed shall be connected to a public or private water-supply and a public or private sewer system. As provided for in Section 103.11 for functional design, water supply sources and sewage disposal systems are regulated and approved by the Virginia Department of Health and the Virginia Department of Environmental Quality.

2006 VIRGINIA CONSTRUCTION CODE (Part I of the Virginia Uniform Statewide Building Code) – Effective May 1, 2008

Note: See also the Memorandums of Agreement in the "Related Laws Package" which is available from the Virginia Department of Housing and Community Development.

11. Change Section R310.1 to read:

R310.1 Emergency escape and rescue required. Basements and each sleeping room designated on the construction documents shall have at least one openable emergency escape and rescue opening. Such opening shall be directly to the exterior of the building or to a deck, screen porch or egress court, all of which shall provide access to a public street, public alley or yard. Where emergency escape and rescue openings are provided, they shall have a sill height of not more than 44 inches (1118 mm) above the floor. Where a door opening having a threshold below the adjacent ground elevation serves as an emergency escape and rescue opening and is provided with a bulkhead enclosure, the bulkhead enclosure shall comply with Section R310.3. The net clear opening dimensions required by this section shall be obtained by the normal operation of the emergency escape and rescue opening from the inside, except that tilt-out or removable sash designed windows shall be permitted to be used. Emergency escape and rescue openings with a finished height below the adjacent ground elevation shall be provided with a window well in accordance with Section R310.2.

Exceptions:

1. Dwelling units equipped throughout with an approved automatic sprinkler system installed in accordance with NFPA 13, 13R or 13D.

2. Basements used only to house mechanical equipment and not exceeding total floor area of 200 square feet (18.58 m^2).

12. Change Section R310.1.1 to read:

R310.1.1 Minimum opening area. All emergency escape and rescue openings shall have a minimum net clear opening of 5.7 square feet (0.530 m^2), including the tilting or removal of the sash as the normal operation to comply with sections R310.1.2 and R310.1.3.

Exception: Grade floor openings shall have a minimum net clear opening of 5 square feet (0.465 m^2).

13. Change Section R311.5.3.1 to read:

R311.5.3.1 Riser height. The maximum riser height shall be 8-1/4 inches (210 mm). The riser shall be measured vertically between the leading edges of the adjacent treads. The greatest riser height within any flight of stairs shall not exceed the smallest by more than 3/8 inch (9.5 mm).

14. Change Section R311.5.3.2 to read:

R311.5.3.2 Tread depth. The minimum tread depth shall be 9 inches (229 mm). The tread depth shall be measured horizontally between the vertical planes of the foremost projection of adjacent treads and at a right angle to the tread's leading edge. The greatest tread depth within any flight of stairs shall not exceed the smallest by more than 3/8 inch (9.5 mm). Winder treads shall have a minimum tread depth of 10 inches (254 mm) measured as above at a point 12 inches (305 mm) from the side where the treads are narrower. Winder treads shall have a minimum tread depth of 6 inches (152 mm) at any point. Within any flight of stairs, the greatest winder tread depth at the 12 inch (305 mm) walk line shall not exceed the smallest by more than 3/8 inch (9.5 mm).

15. Change Section R311.5.5 to read:

R311.5.5 Stairway walking surface. The walking surface of treads and landings of stairways shall be level or sloped no steeper than one unit vertical in 48 inches horizontal (two-percent slope).

16. Change Section R317.1 to read:

2006 VIRGINIA CONSTRUCTION CODE (Part I of the Virginia Uniform Statewide Building Code) – Effective May 1, 2008

R317.1 Two-family dwellings. Dwelling units in two-family dwellings shall be separated from each other by wall and/or floor assemblies having not less than a 1-hour fire-resistance rating when tested in accordance with ASTM E 119. Fire-resistance- rated floor-ceiling and wall assemblies shall extend to and be tight against the exterior wall, and wall assemblies shall extend to and be tight against the underside of the roof sheathing. Dwelling unit separation wall assemblies, which are constructed on a lot line, shall be constructed as required in Section R317.1 for townhouses.

Exceptions:

1. A fire-resistance rating of ½ hour shall be permitted in buildings located entirely on the same lot and equipped throughout with an automatic sprinkler system installed in accordance with NFPA 13.

2. For two-family dwellings located on the same lot, wall assemblies need not extend through attic spaces when the ceiling is protected by not less than ⅝-inch (15.9 mm) Type X gypsum board and an attic draft stop constructed as specified in Section R502.12.1 is provided above and along the wall assembly separating the dwellings. The structural framing supporting the ceiling shall also be protected by not less than ½-inch (12.7 mm) gypsum board or equivalent.

17. Add Section R325 Radon-Resistant Construction.

18. Add Section R325.1 to read:

R325.1 Local enforcement of radon requirements. Following official action under Article 7 (Section 15.2-2280 et seq.) of Chapter 22 of Title 15.2 of the Code of Virginia by a locality in areas of high radon potential, as indicated by Zone 1 on the U.S. EPA Map of Radon Zones (IRC Figure AF101), such locality shall enforce the provisions contained in Appendix F.

Exception: Buildings or portions thereof with crawl space foundations which are ventilated to the exterior, shall not be required to provide radon-resistant construction.

19. Add Section R326 Swimming Pools, Spas and Hot Tubs.

20. Add Section R326.1 to read:

R326.1 Use of Appendix G for swimming pools, spas and hot tubs. In addition to other applicable provisions of this code, swimming pools, spas and hot tubs shall comply with the provisions in Appendix G.

21. Add Section R327 Patio Covers.

22. Add Section R327.1 to read:

R327.1 Use of Appendix H for patio covers. Patio covers shall comply with the provisions in Appendix H.

23. Add Section R328 Sound Transmission.

24. Add Section R328.1 to read:

R328.1 Sound transmission between dwelling units. Construction assemblies separating dwelling units shall provide airborne sound insulation as required in Appendix K.

25. Add Section R328.2 to read:

R328.2 Airport noise attenuation. This section applies to the construction of the exterior envelope of detached one- and two-family dwellings and multiple single-family dwellings (townhouses) not more than three stories high with separate means or egress within airport noise zones when enforced by a locality pursuant to Section 15.2-2295 of the Code of Virginia. The exterior envelope of such structures shall comply with Section 1207.4 of the state amendments to the IBC.

26. Change Section R401.4 to read:

R401.4 Soil tests. Where quantifiable data created by sound soil science methodologies indicate expansive, compressible, shifting or unknown soil characteristics are likely to be present, the building official shall determine whether to require a soil test to determine the soil's characteristics at a particular location. This test shall be made by an approved agency using an approved method.

27. Change Section R403.1 to read:

R403.1 General. All exterior walls shall be supported on continuous solid or fully grouted masonry or concrete footings, wood foundations, or other approved structural systems which shall be of sufficient design to accommodate all loads according to Section R301 and to transmit the resulting loads to the soil within the limitations as determined from the character of the soil. Footings shall be supported on undisturbed natural soils or engineered fill.

> **Exception:** One-story detached accessory structures used as tool and storage sheds, playhouses and similar uses, not exceeding 256 square feet (23.7824 m²) of building area, provided all of the following conditions are met:
>
> 1. The building eave height is 10 feet or less.
>
> 2. The maximum height from the finished floor level to grade does not exceed 18 inches.
>
> 3. The supporting structural elements in direct contact with the ground shall be placed level on firm soil and when such elements are wood they shall be approved pressure preservative treated suitable for ground contact use.
>
> 4. The structure is anchored to withstand wind loads as required by this code.
>
> 5. The structure shall be of light-frame construction with walls and roof of light weight material, not slate, tile, brick or masonry.

28. Change Section R404.1 to read as follows and delete Tables R404.1(1), R404.1(2) and R404.1(3):

R404.1 Concrete and masonry foundation walls. Concrete and masonry foundation walls shall be selected and constructed in accordance with Section R404 or in accordance with ACI 318, ACI 332, NCMA TR68-A or ACI 530/ASCE 5/TMS 402 or other approved structural standards.

29. Change Section R408.1 to read:

R408.1 Ventilation. The under-floor space between the bottom of the floor joists and the earth under any building (except space occupied by a basement) shall have ventilation openings through foundation walls or exterior walls. The minimum net area of ventilation openings shall not be less than 1 square foot (0.0929 m²) for each 150 square feet (14 m²) of under-floor space area. One such ventilating opening shall be within 3 feet (914 mm) of each corner of the building.

> **Exception:** When the exposed earth is covered with a continuous vapor barrier, the minimum net area of ventilation openings shall be not less than 1 square foot (0.0929 m²) for each 1500 square feet (139 m²) of under-floor space area. Joints of the vapor retarder shall overlap by 6 inches (152 mm).

30. Change Section R408.2 to read:

R408.2 Openings for under-floor ventilation. Ventilation openings shall be covered for their height and width with any of the following materials provided that the least dimension of the covering shall not exceed ¼ inch (6.4 mm):

1. Perforated sheet metal plates not less than 0.070 inch (1.8 mm) thick.

2. Expanded sheet metal plates not less than 0.047 inch (1.2 mm) thick.

3. Cast-iron grill or grating.

4. Extruded load-bearing brick vents.

5. Hardware cloth of 0.035 inch (0.89 mm)wire or heavier.

6. Corrosion-resistant wire mesh, with the least dimension being 1/8 inch (3.2 mm).

31. Add Section R502.2.2.1 to read:

R502.2.2.1 Deck ledger connection to band joist. For residential applications and a total design load of 50 psf, the connection between a pressure preservative treated southern pine (or approved decay-resistant species) deck ledger and a two-inch nominal band joist bearing on a sill plate or wall plate shall be constructed with 1/2-inch lag screws or bolts with washers per Table R502.2.2.1.

32. Add Table R502.2.2.1 to read:

TABLE R502.2.2.1
FASTENER SPACING FOR A RESIDENTIAL SOUTHERN PINE DECK LEDGER
AND A 2-INCH NOMINAL SOLID-SAWN BAND JOIST (50 PSF TOTAL LOAD)[c]

JOIST SPAN (ft)	6' AND LESS	6'-1" TO 8'	8'-1" TO 10'	10'-1" TO 12'	12'-1" TO 14'	14'-1" TO 16'	16'-1" TO 18'
	On-Center Spacing of Fasteners[d,e]						
½" x 4" Lag Screw[a,b]	30	23	18	15	13	11	10
½" Bolt with washers	36	36	34	29	24	21	19

a. The maximum gap between the face of the ledger board and face of the house band joist shall be 1/2 inch.
b. The tip of the lag screw shall fully extend beyond the inside face of the band joist.
c. Ledgers shall be flashed to prevent water from contacting the house band joist.
d. Lag screws and bolts shall be staggered as set out in Section R502.2.2.1.1.
e. Deck ledger shall be 2x8 PPT No. 2 Southern Pine (minimum) or other approved method and material as established by standard engineering practice.

33. Add Section R502.2.2.1.1 to read:

R502.2.2.1.1 Placement of lag screws or bolts in residential deck ledgers. The lag screws or bolts shall be placed two inches in from the bottom or top of the deck ledgers and two inches in from the ends. The lag screws or bolts shall be staggered from the top to the bottom along the horizontal run of the deck ledger.

34. Change Section R506.2.1 to read:

R506.2.1 Fill. Fill material shall be free of vegetation and foreign material and shall be natural nonorganic material that is not susceptible to swelling when exposed to moisture. The fill shall be compacted to assure uniform support of the slab, and except where approved, the fill depth shall not exceed 24 inches (610 mm) for clean sand or gravel and 8 inches (203 mm) for earth.

Exception: Material other than natural material may be used as fill material when accompanied by a certification from an RDP and approved by the building official.

35. Change Section R506.2.2 to read:

R506.2.2 Base. A 4-inch-thick (102 mm) base course consisting of clean graded sand, gravel or crushed stone passing a 2-inch (51 mm) sieve shall be placed on the prepared subgrade when the slab is below grade.

Exception: A base course is not required when the concrete slab is installed on well drained or sand-gravel mixture soils classified as Group I according to the United Soil Classification System in accordance with Table R405.1. Material other than natural material may be used as base course material when accompanied by a certification from an RDP and approved by the building official.

2006 VIRGINIA CONSTRUCTION CODE (Part I of the Virginia Uniform Statewide Building Code) – Effective May 1, 2008

36. Replace Section R602.10, including all subsections, with the following:

   R602.10 Wall bracing. The use of this section is subject to the following clarification of cross-references:

   1. In Sections R301.2.2.1.1 and R301.2.2.4.1, delete the references to Table R602.10.1.

   2. In Section R301.3, delete the exception to Item 1.

   3. References to Table R602.10.1 in all other provisions of the IRC except those in Items 1 and 2 above shall be references to Table R602.10.1.5 of this section.

   4. In Section R403.1.6, delete the sentence which reads, "In Seismic Design Categories D0, D1 and D2, anchor bolts shall be spaced at 6 feet (1829 mm) on center and located within 12 inches (304 mm) of the ends of each plate section at interior braced wall lines when required by Section R602.10.9 to be supported on a continuous foundation." In addition, all references to Figure R602.10.5 in Section R403.1.6 shall be references to Figure R602.10.3.3(1) of this section.

   5. Change the reference in Section R502.2.1 from Section R602.10.8 to Section R602.10.5 of this section.

   All new buildings, additions and conversions shall be braced in accordance with this section. Where a building, or portion thereof, does not comply with one or more of the bracing requirements in this section, those portions shall be designed and constructed in accordance with the International Building Code. For structures in areas where the wind speed from Table R301.2(1) is 110 mph or greater, an engineered design is required.

   The building official may require the permit applicant to identify and locate on the construction documents the bracing methods utilized.

   R602.10.1 Braced wall lines. Braced wall lines shall be straight lines through the building plan at each level provided with braced wall panels to resist lateral load. The percentage, location and construction of braced wall panels shall be as specified in this section.

   R602.10.1.1 Spacing of braced wall lines. In each story, spacing of parallel braced wall lines shall not exceed 50 feet (15 240 mm) as shown in Figure R602.10.1.1. When braced wall lines exceed a spacing of 50 feet (15 240 mm), intermediate braced wall line(s) shall be provided. Each end of a braced wall line shall intersect perpendicularly with other braced wall lines or their projections.

2006 VIRGINIA CONSTRUCTION CODE (Part I of the Virginia Uniform Statewide Building Code) – Effective May 1, 2008

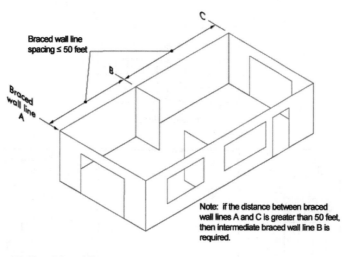

Note: if the distance between braced wall lines A and C is greater than 50 feet, then intermediate braced wall line B is required.

For SI: 1 foot = 305 mm

FIGURE R602.10.1.1
BRACED WALL LINE SPACING

R602.10.1.2 Braced wall panels. Braced wall panels shall be full-height sections of wall constructed along a braced wall line to resist lateral loads in accordance with the intermittent bracing methods specified in Section R602.10.2 or the continuous sheathing methods specified in Section R602.10.3. Mixing of bracing methods shall be permitted as follows:

1. Mixing bracing methods from story to story shall be permitted.

2. Mixing bracing methods from braced wall line to braced wall line within a story shall be permitted, except that continuous sheathing methods shall conform to the additional requirements of Section R602.10.3.

3. Mixing intermittent bracing methods along a braced wall line shall be permitted for single-family dwellings in Seismic Design Categories A, B and C and townhouses in Seismic Design Categories A and B. The required percentage of bracing for the braced wall line with mixed methods shall use the higher bracing percentage, per Table R602.10.1.5, of all methods used.

R602.10.1.3 Braced wall panel location. Braced wall panels shall be located at least every 25 feet (7620 mm) on center and shall begin no more than 12.5 feet (3810 mm) from each end of a braced wall line or its projection as shown in Figure R602.10.1.3(1) and Figure R602.10.4, but not less than the percentages given in Table R602.10.1.5. Braced wall lines with continuous sheathing shall conform to the additional requirements of Section R602.10.3.3.

All braced wall panels shall be permitted to be offset out-of-plane from the designated braced wall line up to 4 feet (1219 mm) provided the total out-to-out offset in any braced wall line is not more than 8 feet (2438 mm) as shown in Figure R602.10.1.3(2).

2006 VIRGINIA CONSTRUCTION CODE (Part I of the Virginia Uniform Statewide Building Code) – Effective May 1, 2008

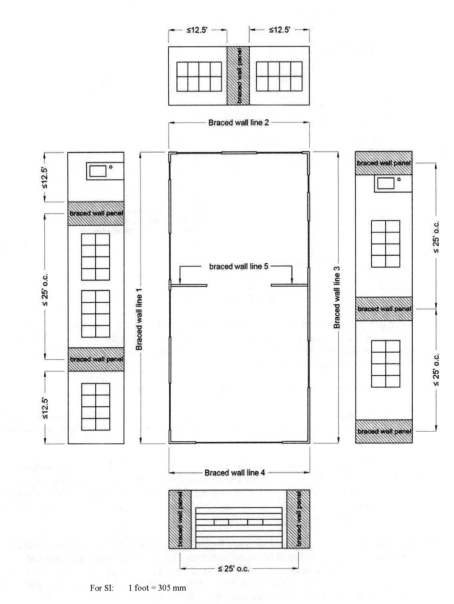

For SI: 1 foot = 305 mm

FIGURE R602.10.1.3(1)
BRACED WALL PANELS AND BRACED WALL LINES

2006 VIRGINIA CONSTRUCTION CODE (Part I of the Virginia Uniform Statewide Building Code) – Effective May 1, 2008

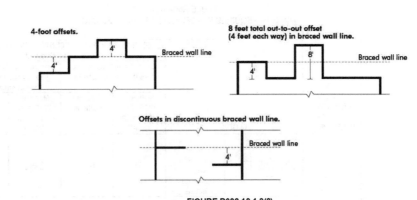

FIGURE R602.10.1.3(2)
OFFSETS PERMITTED FOR BRACED WALL PANELS ALONG A BRACED WALL LINE

R602.10.1.4 Angled walls. The walls of a braced wall line shall be permitted to angle out of plane for a maximum diagonal length of 8 feet (2438 mm). Where the angled wall occurs at a corner, the length of the braced wall line shall be measured from the projected corner as shown in Figure R602.10.1.4. Where the diagonal length is greater than 8 feet (2438 mm), it shall be considered its own braced wall line.

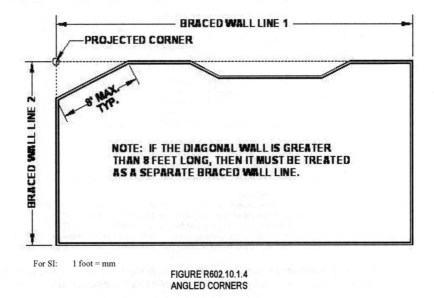

For SI: 1 foot = mm

FIGURE R602.10.1.4
ANGLED CORNERS

R602.10.1.5 Minimum required percentage of bracing. The minimum required percentage of bracing along each braced wall line shall be in accordance with Table R602.10.1.5 and shall be the greater of that required by the Seismic Design Category or the design wind speed.

2006 VIRGINIA CONSTRUCTION CODE (Part I of the Virginia Uniform Statewide Building Code) – Effective May 1, 2008

TABLE R602.10.1.5[a,b,c]
MINIMUM REQUIRED PERCENTAGE OF WALL BRACING

SEISMIC DESIGN CATEGORY (SDC) OR WIND SPEED	FLOOR		MINIMUM REQUIRED PERCENTAGE OF FULL-HEIGHT BRACING PER WALL LINE			
			Braced wall line spacing less than or equal to 35'		Braced wall line spacing greater than 35' and less than or equal to 50'	
			Methods WSP, CS-WSP, CS-G, CS-PF	All other methods[d]	Methods WSP, CS-WSP, CS-G, CS-PF	All other methods[d]
SDC A, B or wind speed ≤100 mph		One-story house or top floor of a two- or three-story house.	16%	16%	23%	23%
		First floor of a two-story or second floor of a three-story house.	16%	25%	23%	36%
		First floor of a three-story house.	25%	35%	36%	50%
SDC C or wind speed <110 mph		One-story house or top floor of a two- or three-story house.	16%	25%	23%	36%
		First floor of a two-story house or second floor of a three-story house.	30%	45%	43%	64%
		First floor of a three-story house.	45%	60%	64%	86%

For SI: 1 foot = 305 mm
a.   Foundation cripple wall panels shall be braced in accordance with Section R602.10.8.
b.   Methods of bracing shall be as described in Sections R602.10.2 and R602.10.3.
c.   The total amount of bracing required for a given braced wall line shall be the product of the minimum required percentage and all the applicable adjustment factors described in Sections R602.10.4, R602.10.7 and R602.10.8.
d.   For Method GB, the percentage required shall be doubled for one-sided applications.

R602.10.2 Intermittent bracing methods. Intermittent braced wall panels shall comply with this section. The location of each panel shall be identified on the construction documents.

R602.10.2.1 Intermittent braced wall panels. Intermittent braced wall panels shall be constructed in accordance with one of the methods listed in Table R602.10.2.1.

2006 VIRGINIA CONSTRUCTION CODE (Part I of the Virginia Uniform Statewide Building Code) – Effective May 1, 2008

TABLE R602.10.2.1
INTERMITTENT BRACING METHODS

METHOD	MATERIAL	MINIMUM THICKNESS	FIGURE	CONNECTION CRITERIA
LIB	Let-in-bracing	1x4 wood or approved metal straps at 45° to 60° angles		Wood: 2-8d nails per stud Metal: per manufacturer
DWB	Diagonal wood board at 24" spacing	⅝"		2-8d (2½" x 0.113") nails or 2 staples, 1¾" per stud
WSP	Wood structural panel	⅜"		6d common (2" x 0.113") nails at 6" spacing (panel edges) and at 12" spacing (intermediate supports) or 16 ga. x 1¾ staples: at 3" spacing (panel edges) at 6" spacing (intermediate supports)
SFB	Structural fiberboard sheathing	½" or ²⁵/₃₂" for 16" stud spacing only		1½ galvanized roofing nails or 8d common 2½" x 0.131") nails at 3" spacing (panel edges) at 6" spacing (intermediate supports)
GB	Gypsum board	½"		Nails at 7" spacing at panel edges including top and bottom plates; for exterior sheathing nail size, see Table R602.3(1); for interior gypsum board nail size, see Table R702.3.5
PBS	Particleboard sheathing	⅜" or ½" for 16" stud spacing only		1½" galvanized roofing nails or 8d common (2½ x 0.131") nails at 3" spacing (panel edges) at 6" spacing (intermediate supports)
PCP	Portland cement plaster	See Section R703.6		1½", 11 gage, ⁷/₁₆" head nails at 16" spacing or ⁷/₁₆", 16 gage staples at 6" spacing
HPS	Hardboard panel siding	7/16"		0.092" dia., 0.225" head nails with length to accommodate 1½" penetration into studs at 4" spacing (panel edges), at 8" spacing (intermediate supports)
ABW	Alternate braced wall	See Figure R602.10.1(1)		See Figure R602.10.2.1(1)
IPF	Intermittent portal frame	See Figure R602.10.2.1(2)		See Figure R602.10.1(2)

For SI: 1 inch = 25.4 mm, 1 foot = 305 mm

2006 VIRGINIA CONSTRUCTION CODE (Part I of the Virginia Uniform Statewide Building Code) – Effective May 1, 2008

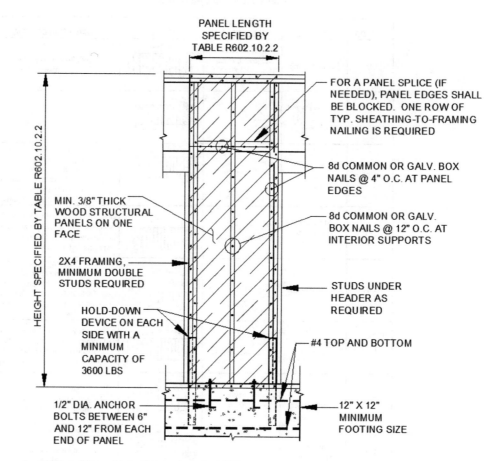

PANEL LENGTH
SPECIFIED BY
TABLE R602.10.2.2

HEIGHT SPECIFIED BY TABLE R602.10.2.2

FOR A PANEL SPLICE (IF NEEDED), PANEL EDGES SHALL BE BLOCKED. ONE ROW OF TYP. SHEATHING-TO-FRAMING NAILING IS REQUIRED

8d COMMON OR GALV. BOX NAILS @ 4" O.C. AT PANEL EDGES

MIN. 3/8" THICK WOOD STRUCTURAL PANELS ON ONE FACE

8d COMMON OR GALV. BOX NAILS @ 12" O.C. AT INTERIOR SUPPORTS

2X4 FRAMING, MINIMUM DOUBLE STUDS REQUIRED

STUDS UNDER HEADER AS REQUIRED

HOLD-DOWN DEVICE ON EACH SIDE WITH A MINIMUM CAPACITY OF 3600 LBS

#4 TOP AND BOTTOM

1/2" DIA. ANCHOR BOLTS BETWEEN 6" AND 12" FROM EACH END OF PANEL

12" X 12" MINIMUM FOOTING SIZE

For SI: 1 foot = 305 mm, 1 inch = 25.4 mm, 1 pound = 4.45 N

FIGURE R602.10.2.1(1)
METHOD ABW: ALTERNATE BRACED WALL PANEL

2006 VIRGINIA CONSTRUCTION CODE (Part I of the Virginia Uniform Statewide Building Code) – Effective May 1, 2008

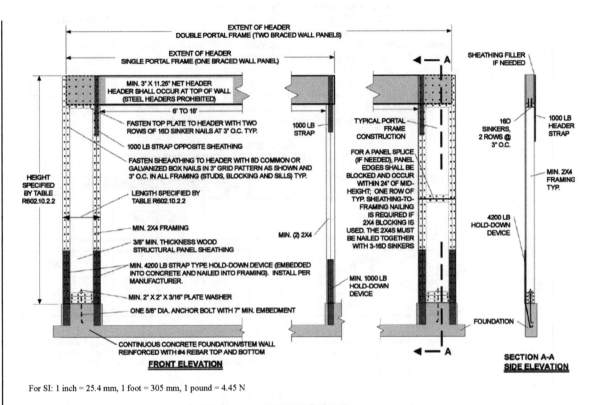

For SI: 1 inch = 25.4 mm, 1 foot = 305 mm, 1 pound = 4.45 N

FIGURE R602.10.2.1(2)
METHOD IPF: INTERMITTENT PORTAL FRAME BRACED WALL PANEL

- 41 -

2006 VIRGINIA CONSTRUCTION CODE (Part I of the Virginia Uniform Statewide Building Code) – Effective May 1, 2008

R602.10.2.2 Minimum length of intermittent braced wall panels. The minimum length of each intermittent braced wall panel shall comply with Table R602.10.2.2. For Methods DWB, WSP, SFB, GB, PBS, PCP and HPS, each panel shall cover at least three studs where studs are spaced 16 inches (406 mm) on center or at least two studs where studs are spaced 24 inches (610 mm) on center. Only those full-height braced wall panels complying with the length requirements of Table R602.10.2.2(1) shall be permitted to contribute towards the minimum required percentage of bracing.

Exception: For Methods DWB, WSP, SFB, PBS, PCP and HPS, panel lengths less than the dimensions shown in Table R602.10.2.2 shall be permitted provided the effective lengths in accordance with Table R602.10.2(2) are used in place of actual lengths when determining compliance with the percentage of bracing required by Table R602.10.1.5.

TABLE R602.10.2.2(1)
MINIMUM LENGTH OF INTERMITTENT BRACED WALL PANELS[a,b]

BRACING METHOD	FLOOR		HEIGHT OF INTERMITTENT BRACED WALL PANEL				
			8'	9'	10'	11'	12'
DWB, WSP, SFB, GB[c], PBS, PCP, HPS	All		48"	48"	48"	53"	58"
ABW	All		28"	32"	34"	38"	42"
IPF		One-story house	16"	16"	16"	18"	20"
		First floor of a two-story house	24"	24"	24"	27"	29"

For SI: 1 foot = 305 mm, 1 inch = 25.4 mm
a.   Interpolation shall be permitted.
b.   When determining compliance with the percentage of bracing required by Table R602.10.1.5, the effective length of Method LIB shall be equivalent to 48" (1219 mm) provided it complies with the Table R602.10.2.1.
c.   Gypsum board applied to both sides of the braced wall panel; where the gypsum board is applied to one side, the required length shall be doubled.

TABLE R602.10.2(2)
EFFECTIVE LENGTHS FOR BRACE WALL PANELS
WHEN DETERMINING PERCENTAGE OF BRACING[a]

ACTUAL LENGTH OF BRACED WALL PANEL	WALL HEIGHT		
	8'	9'	10'
48"	48"	48"	48"
42"	36"	36"	N/A
36"	27"	N/A	N/A

For SI: 1 inch = 25.4 mm
a.   Interpolation shall be permitted.

R602.10.2.3 Adhesive attachment of sheathing in Seismic Design Category C. Adhesive attachment of wall sheathing shall not be permitted in Seismic Design Category C.

R602.10.3 Continuous sheathing methods. Braced wall lines with continuous sheathing constructed in accordance with this section shall be permitted.

R602.10.3.1 Continuous sheathing braced wall panels. Continuous sheathing methods require structural panel sheathing to be used on all sheathable surfaces of a braced wall line including areas above and below openings and gable end walls. Braced wall panels shall be constructed in accordance with one of the methods listed in Table R602.10.3.1.

2006 VIRGINIA CONSTRUCTION CODE (Part I of the Virginia Uniform Statewide Building Code) – Effective May 1, 2008

TABLE R602.10.3.1
CONTINUOUS SHEATHING METHODS

METHOD	MATERIAL	MINIMUM THICKNESS	FIGURE	CONNECTION CRITERIA
CS-WSP	Wood structural panel	⅜"		6d common (2" x 0.113") nails at 6" spacing (panel edges) and at 12" spacing (intermediate supports) or 16 ga. x 1¾ staples: at 3" spacing (panel edges) and 6" spacing (intermediate supports)
CS-G[a]	Wood structural panel supporting roof load only adjacent garage openings	⅜"		See Method CS-WSP
CS-PF[b]	Continuous portal frame	See Figure R602.10.3.1		See Figure R602.10.3.1

For SI: 1 inch = 25.4 mm

a.   Applies to one wall of a garage only.

b.   The number of continuous portal frame panels in a braced wall line shall not exceed four. Continuous portal frame panels shall not be stacked vertically in multi-story buildings.

2006 VIRGINIA CONSTRUCTION CODE (Part I of the Virginia Uniform Statewide Building Code) – Effective May 1, 2008

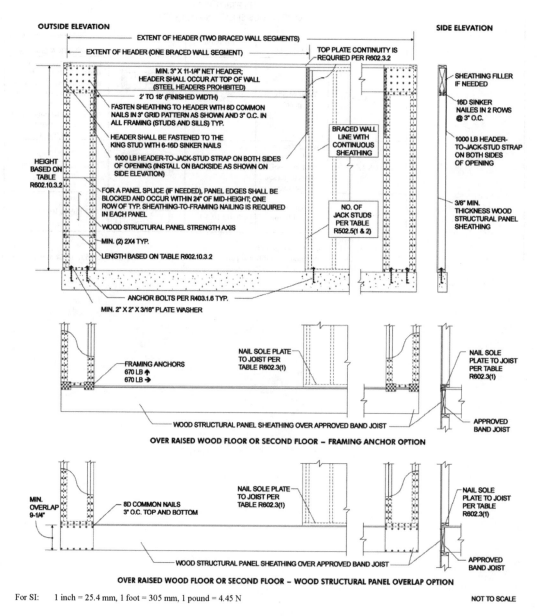

For SI: 1 inch = 25.4 mm, 1 foot = 305 mm, 1 pound = 4.45 N

NOT TO SCALE

FIGURE R602.10.3.1
METHOD CS-PF: CONTINUOUS PORTAL FRAME BRACED WALL PANELS

R602.10.3.2 Length of braced wall panels with continuous sheathing. Braced wall panels along a braced wall line with continuous sheathing shall be full-height with a length based on the adjacent clear opening height in accordance with Table R602.10.3.2. Where a panel has an opening on either side of differing heights, the taller opening shall govern when determining the panel length from Table R602.10.3.2. Only those full-height braced wall panels complying with the length requirements of Table R602.10.3.2 shall be permitted to contribute towards the minimum required percentage of bracing per Table R602.10.1.5. For Method CS-PF, wall height shall be measured from the top of the header to the bottom of the bottom plate as shown in Figure R602.10.4.3.1.

TABLE R602.10.3.2
LENGTH REQUIREMENTS FOR BRACED WALL PANELS
IN A BRACED WALL LINE WITH CONTINUOUS SHEATHING[a]

METHOD	ADJACENT CLEAR OPENING HEIGHT	WALL HEIGHT				
		8'	9'	10'	11'	12'
CS-WSP	64"	24"	27"	30"	33"	36"
	68"	26"	27"	30"	33"	36"
	72"	28"	27"	30"	33"	36"
	76"	29"	30"	30"	33"	36"
	80"	31"	33"	30"	33"	36"
	84"	35"	36"	33"	36"	36"
	88"	39"	39"	36"	38"	36"
	92"	44"	42"	39"	41"	36"
	96"	48"	45"	42"	43"	39"
	100"		48"	45"	47"	42"
	104"		51"	48"	48"	44"
	108"		54"	51"	51"	47"
	112"			54"	53"	50"
	116"			57"	56"	53"
	120"			60"	58"	55"
	124"				61"	58"
	128"				63"	61"
	132"				66"	64"
	136"					66"
	140"					69"
	144"					72"
CS-G	≤120"	24"	27"	30"	33"	36"
CS-PF	≤120"	16"	18"	20"	22"	24"

For SI: 1 inch = 25.4 mm, 1 foot = 305 mm
a.   Interpolation shall be permitted.

R602.10.3.3 Braced wall panel location and corner construction. Full-height wall panels complying with the length requirements of Table R602.10.3.2 shall be located at each end of a braced wall line with continuous sheathing and at least every 25 feet (7620 mm) on center.

A minimum 24 inch (610 mm) wood structural panel corner return shall be provided at both ends of a braced wall line with continuous sheathing in accordance with Figures R602.10.3.3(1) and R602.10.3.3(2). In lieu of the corner return, a hold-down device with a minimum uplift design value of 800 lb (3560 N) shall be fastened to the corner stud and to the foundation or framing below in accordance with Figure R602.10.3.3(3).

Exception: The first braced wall panel shall be permitted to begin 12.5 feet (3810 mm) from each end of the braced wall line provided one of the following is satisfied:

1. A minimum 24 inch (610 mm) long, full-height wood structural panel is provided at both sides of a corner constructed in accordance with Figures R602.10.3.3(1) and R602.10.3.3(4), or

2. The braced wall panel closest to the corner shall have a hold-down device with a minimum uplift design value of 800 lb (3560 N) fastened to the stud at the edge of the braced wall panel closest to the corner and to the foundation or framing below in accordance with Figure R602.10.3.3(5).

2006 VIRGINIA CONSTRUCTION CODE (Part I of the Virginia Uniform Statewide Building Code) – Effective May 1, 2008

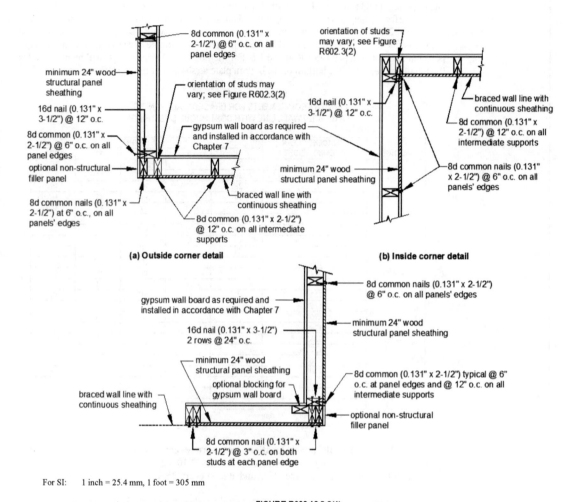

For SI: 1 inch = 25.4 mm, 1 foot = 305 mm

FIGURE R602.10.3.3(1)
TYPICAL EXTERIOR CORNER FRAMING FOR CONTINUOUS SHEATHING

2006 VIRGINIA CONSTRUCTION CODE (Part I of the Virginia Uniform Statewide Building Code) – Effective May 1, 2008

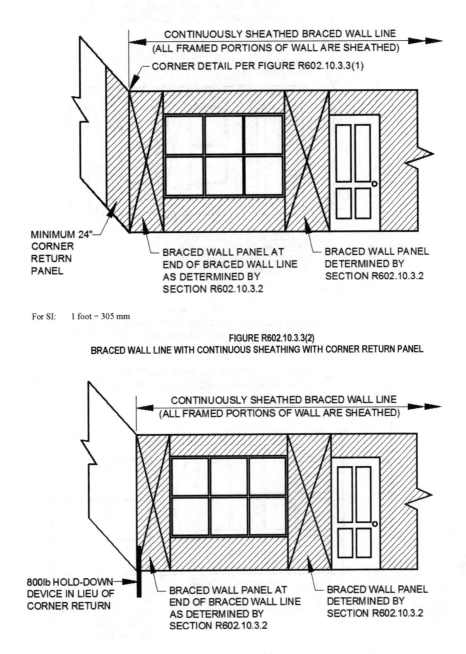

For SI: 1 foot = 305 mm

FIGURE R602.10.3.3(2)
BRACED WALL LINE WITH CONTINUOUS SHEATHING WITH CORNER RETURN PANEL

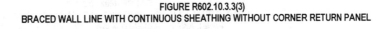

For SI: 1 foot = 305 mm, 1 pound = 4.45 N

FIGURE R602.10.3.3(3)
BRACED WALL LINE WITH CONTINUOUS SHEATHING WITHOUT CORNER RETURN PANEL

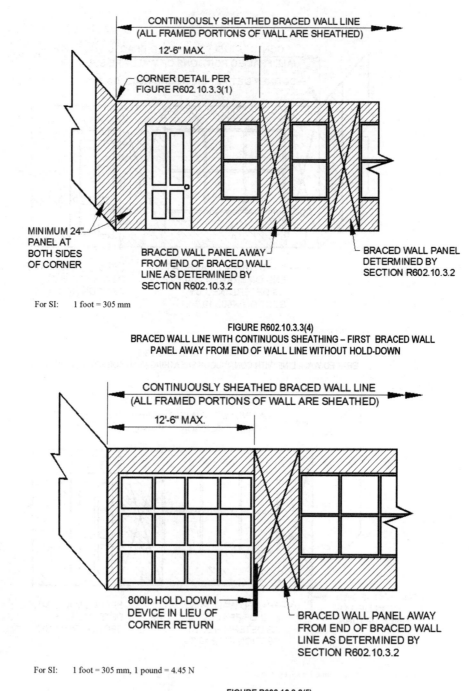

For SI: 1 foot = 305 mm

FIGURE R602.10.3.3(4)
BRACED WALL LINE WITH CONTINUOUS SHEATHING – FIRST BRACED WALL
PANEL AWAY FROM END OF WALL LINE WITHOUT HOLD-DOWN

For SI: 1 foot = 305 mm, 1 pound = 4.45 N

FIGURE R602.10.3.3(5)
BRACED WALL LINE WITH CONTINUOUS SHEATHING – FIRST BRACED WALL
PANEL AWAY FROM END OF WALL LINE WITH HOLD-DOWN

2006 VIRGINIA CONSTRUCTION CODE (Part I of the Virginia Uniform Statewide Building Code) – Effective May 1, 2008

R602.10.4 Braced wall panel finish material. Braced wall panels shall have ½-inch thick gypsum board installed on the side of the wall opposite the bracing material and fastened in accordance with Table R702.3.5.

Exceptions:

1. Braced wall panels that are constructed in accordance with Methods GB, ABW, IPF and CS-PF.

2. When an approved interior finish material with an in-plane shear resistance equivalent to gypsum board is installed.

3. For Methods DWB, WSP, SFB, PBS, PCP, and HPS, interior gypsum board may be partially or entirely omitted provided the minimum required percentage of bracing in Table R602.10.1.5 is multiplied by an adjustment factor of 1.5.

R602.10.5 Braced wall panel connections. Braced wall panels shall be connected to floor/ceiling framing or foundations as follows:

1. Where framing is perpendicular to a braced wall panel above or below, a rim joist or blocking shall be provided along the entire length of the braced wall panel in accordance with Figure R602.10.5(1). Fastening of wall plates to framing, rim joist or blocking shall be in accordance with Table R602.3(1).

2. Where framing is parallel to a braced wall panel above or below, a rim joist, end joist or other parallel framing member shall be provided directly above and below the panel in accordance with Figure R602.10.5(2). Where a parallel framing member cannot be located directly above and below the panel, full-depth blocking at 16 inch (406 mm) spacing shall be provided between the parallel framing members to each side of the braced wall panel in accordance with Figure R602.10.5(2). Fastening of blocking and wall plates shall be in accordance with Table R602.3(1).

3. Connections of braced wall panels to concrete or masonry shall be in accordance with Section R403.1.6.

2006 VIRGINIA CONSTRUCTION CODE (Part I of the Virginia Uniform Statewide Building Code) – Effective May 1, 2008

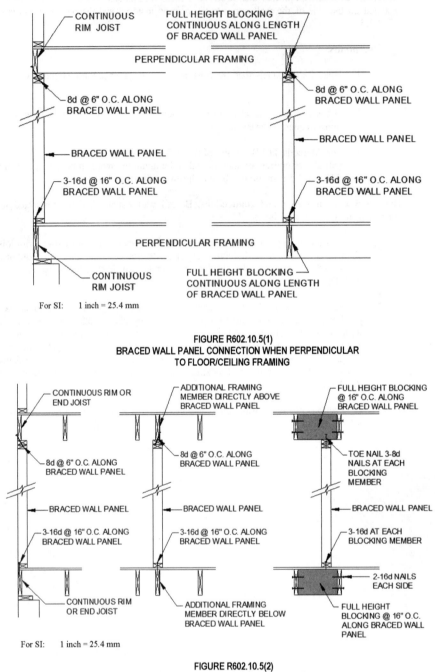

For SI: 1 inch = 25.4 mm

FIGURE R602.10.5(1)
BRACED WALL PANEL CONNECTION WHEN PERPENDICULAR
TO FLOOR/CEILING FRAMING

For SI: 1 inch = 25.4 mm

FIGURE R602.10.5(2)
BRACED WALL PANEL CONNECTION WHEN PARALLEL
TO FLOOR/CEILING FRAMING

2006 VIRGINIA CONSTRUCTION CODE (Part I of the Virginia Uniform Statewide Building Code) – Effective May 1, 2008

R602.10.6 Braced wall panel support. Braced wall panels shall be supported as follows:

1. Braced wall panels shall be permitted to be supported on cantilevered floor joists meeting the cantilever limits of Section R502.3.3 provided joists are blocked at the nearest bearing wall location.

2. Elevated post or pier foundations supporting braced wall panels shall be designed in accordance with accepted engineering practice.

3. Masonry stem walls supporting braced wall panels with a length of 48 inches (1220 mm) or less shall be reinforced in accordance with Figure R602.10.6. Masonry stem walls supporting braced wall panels with a length greater than 48 inches (1220 mm) shall be constructed in accordance with Section R403.1. Braced wall panels constructed in accordance with Methods ABW and IPF shall not be permitted to attach to masonry stem walls.

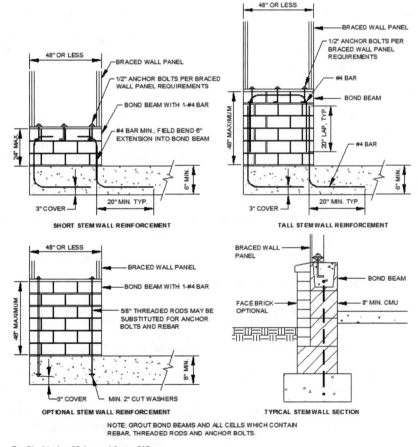

For SI: 1 inch = 25.4 mm, 1 foot = 305 mm

FIGURE R602.10.6
MASONRY STEM WALLS SUPPORTING BRACED WALL PANELS

R602.10.7 Panel joints. All vertical joints of braced wall panel sheathing shall occur over and be fastened to common studs. Horizontal joints in braced wall panels shall occur over and be fastened to common blocking of a minimum 1-½ inch (38 mm) thickness. Panel joints for Method IPF shall be constructed in accordance with Figure R602.10.2.1(2). Panel joints for Method CS-PF shall be constructed in accordance with Figure R602.10.3.1.

> **Exception:** Blocking at horizontal joints shall not be required in braced wall panels constructed using Methods WSP, SFB, GB, PBS or HPS where the percentage of bracing required by Table R602.10.1.5 is multiplied by an adjustment factor of 2.0.

R602.10.8 Cripple wall bracing. Cripple walls shall be braced with a percentage and type of bracing as required for the wall above in accordance with Table R602.10.1.5 with the following modifications for cripple wall bracing:

1. The bracing percentage as determined from Table R602.10.1.5 shall be multiplied by an adjustment factor of 1.15, and

2. The wall panel spacing shall be decreased from 25 feet (7620 mm) to 18 feet (5486 mm).

Cripple walls shall be permitted to be redesignated as the first story walls for purposes of determining wall bracing requirements. If the cripple walls are redesignated, the stories above the redesignated story shall be counted as the second and third stories respectively.

37. Change Section R613.2 to read:

R613.2 Window sills. In dwelling units, where the opening of an operable window is located more than 72 inches (1829 mm) above the finished grade or surface below, the lowest part of the clear opening of the window shall be a minimum of 18 inches (457 mm) above the finished floor of the room in which the window is located. Glazing between the floor and 18 inches (457 mm) shall be fixed or have openings through which a 4-inch-diameter (102 mm) sphere cannot pass.

Exceptions:

1. Windows whose openings will not allow a 4-inch-diameter (102 mm) sphere to pass through the opening when the opening is in its largest opened position.

2. Openings that are provided with window guards that comply with ASTM F 2006 or F 2090.

38. Change Section R806.4 and add Table R806.4 to read:

R806.4 Unvented attic assemblies. Unvented attic assemblies (spaces between the ceiling joists of the top story and the roof rafters) shall be permitted if all the following conditions are met:

1. The unvented attic space is completely contained within the building thermal envelope.

2. No interior vapor retarders are installed on the ceiling side (attic floor) of the unvented attic assembly.

3. Where wood shingles or shakes are used, a minimum ¼ inch (6 mm) vented air space separates the shingles or shakes and the roofing underlayment above the structural sheathing.

4. In climate zones 5, 6, 7 and 8, any air-impermeable insulation shall be a vapor retarder, or shall have a vapor retarder coating or covering in direct contact with the underside of the insulation.

5. Either Items a, b or c shall be met, depending on the air permeability of the insulation directly under the structural roof sheathing.

a. Air-impermeable insulation only. Insulation shall be applied in direct contact to the underside of the structural roof sheathing.

b. Air-permeable insulation only. In addition to the air-permeable installed directly below the structural sheathing, rigid board or sheet insulation shall be installed directly above the structural roof sheathing as specified in Table R806.4 for condensation control.

c. Air-impermeable and air-permeable insulation. The air-impermeable insulation shall be applied in direct contact to the underside of the structural roof sheathing as specified in Table R806.4 for condensation control. The air-permeable insulation shall be installed directly under the air-impermeable insulation.

TABLE R806.4
INSULATION FOR CONDENSATION CONTROL

CLIMATE ZONE	MINIMUM RIGID BOARD OR AIR-IMPERMEABLE INSULATION R-VALUE[a]
2B and 3B tile roof only	0 (none required)
1, 2A, 2B, 3A, 3B, 3C	R-5
4C	R-10
4A, 4B	R-15
5	R-20
6	R-25
7	R-30
8	R-35

a.   Contributes to but does not supersede Chapter 11 energy requirements.

39. Change Section M1502.6 to read:

M1502.6 Duct length. The maximum length of a clothes dryer exhaust duct shall not exceed 35 feet (10 668 mm) from the dryer location to the wall or roof termination. The maximum length of the duct shall be reduced 2.5 feet (762 mm) for each 45-degree (0.8 rad) bend and 5 feet (1524 mm) for each 90-degree (1.6 rad) bend. The maximum length of the exhaust duct does not include the transition duct.

Exceptions:

1. Where the make and model of the clothes dryer to be installed is known and the manufacturer's installation instructions for the dryer are provided to the building official, the maximum length of the exhaust duct, including any transition duct, shall be permitted to be in accordance with the dryer manufacturer's installation instructions.

2. Where large-radius 45-degree (0.8 rad) and 90-degree (1.6 rad) bends are installed, determination of the equivalent length of clothes dryer exhaust duct for each bend by engineering calculation in accordance with the ASHRAE Fundamentals Handbook shall be permitted.

40. Change Section M1701.1 to read as follows and delete the remainder of Chapter 17:

M1701.1 Scope. Solid-fuel-burning appliances shall be provided with combustion air, in accordance with the appliance manufacturer's installation instructions. Oil-fired appliances shall be provided with combustion air in accordance with NFPA 31. The methods of providing combustion air in this chapter do not apply to fireplaces, fireplace stoves and direct-vent appliances. The requirements for combustion and dilution air for gas-fired appliances shall be in accordance with Chapter 24.

41. Add Section M1801.1.1 to read:

M1801.1.1 Equipment changes. Upon the replacement or new installation of any fuel-burning appliances or equipment in existing buildings, an inspection or inspections shall be conducted to ensure that the connected vent or chimney systems comply with the following:

1. Vent or chimney systems are sized in accordance with this code.

2. Vent or chimney systems are clean, free of any obstruction or blockages, defects or deterioration and are in operable condition.

Where not inspected by the local building department, persons performing such changes or installations shall certify to the building official that the requirements of Items 1 and 2 of this section are met.

42. Change Section G2411.1 to read:

G2411.1 Gas pipe bonding. Each above-ground portion of a gas piping system that is likely to become energized shall be electrically continuous and bonded to an effective ground-fault current path. Gas piping shall be considered to be bonded where it is connected to appliances that are connected to the equipment grounding conductor of the circuit supplying that appliance.

CSST gas piping systems shall be bonded to the electrical service grounding electrode system at the point where the gas service piping enters the building. The bonding conductor size shall be not less than #6 AWG copper wire or equivalent.

43. Add Section G2415.17 to read:

404.17 Isolation. Metallic piping and metallic tubing that conveys fuel gas from an LP-gas storage container shall be provided with an approved dielectric fitting to electrically isolate the underground portion of the pipe or tube from the above ground portion that enters a building. Such dielectric fitting shall be installed above ground, outdoors.

44. Add Section G2425.1.1 to read:

G2425.1.1 Equipment changes. Upon the replacement or new installation of any fuel-burning appliances or equipment in existing buildings, an inspection or inspections shall be conducted to ensure that the connected vent or chimney systems comply with the following:

1. Vent or chimney systems are sized in accordance with this code.

2. Vent or chimney systems are clean, free of any obstruction or blockages, defects or deterioration and are in operable condition.

Where not inspected by the local building department, persons performing such changes or installations shall certify to the building official that the requirements of Items 1 and 2 of this section are met.

45. Change Section P2602.1 to read:

P2602.1 General. The water and drainage system of any building or premises where plumbing fixtures are installed shall be connected to a public or private water-supply and a public or private sewer system. As provided for in Section 103.11 of Part I of the Virginia Uniform Statewide Building Code (13 VAC 5-63) for functional design, water supply sources and sewage disposal systems are regulated and approved by the Virginia Department of Health and the Virginia Department of Environmental Quality.

Note: See also the Memorandums of Agreement in the "Related Laws Package" which is available from the Virginia Department of Housing and Community Development.

46. Change Section P2903.5 to read:

P2903.5 Water hammer. The flow velocity of the water distribution system shall be controlled to reduce the possibility of water hammer. A water-hammer arrestor shall be installed where quick-closing valves are utilized, unless otherwise approved. Water hammer arrestors shall be installed in accordance with manufacturer's specifications. Water hammer arrestors shall conform to ASSE 1010.

2006 VIRGINIA CONSTRUCTION CODE (Part I of the Virginia Uniform Statewide Building Code) – Effective May 1, 2008

47. Add Section P3002.2.1 to read:

P3002.2.1 Tracer wire. Nonmetallic sanitary sewer piping that discharges to public systems shall be locatable. An insulated copper tracer wire, 18 AWG minimum in size and suitable for direct burial or an equivalent product, shall be utilized. The wire shall be installed in the same trench as the sewer within 12 inches (305 mm) of the pipe and shall be installed from within five feet of the building wall to the point where the building sewer intersects with the public system. At a minimum, one end of the wire shall terminate above grade in an accessible location that is resistant to physical damage, such as with a cleanout or at the building wall.

48. Replace Section P3007, Sumps and Ejectors, with the following:

SECTION P3007
SUMPS AND EJECTORS

P3007.1 Building subdrains. Building subdrains that cannot be discharged to the sewer by gravity flow shall be discharged into a tightly covered and vented sump from which the liquid shall be lifted and discharged into the building gravity drainage system by automatic pumping equipment or other approved method. In other than existing structures, the sump shall not receive drainage from any piping within the building capable of being discharged by gravity to the building sewer.

P3007.2 Valves required. A check valve and a full open valve located on the discharge side of the check valve shall be installed in the pump or ejector discharge piping between the pump or ejector and the gravity drainage system. Access shall be provided to such valves. Such valves shall be located above the sump cover required by Section P3007.3.2 or, where the discharge pipe from the ejector is below grade, the valves shall be accessibly located outside the sump below grade in an access pit with a removable access cover.

P3007.3 Sump design. The sump pump, pit and discharge piping shall conform to the requirements of Sections P3007.3.1 through P3007.3.5.

> **P3007.3.1 Sump pump.** The sump pump capacity and head shall be appropriate to anticipated use requirements.

> **P3007.3.2 Sump pit.** The sump pit shall be not less than 18 inches (457 mm) in diameter and 24 inches (610 mm) deep, unless otherwise approved. The pit shall be accessible and located such that all drainage flows into the pit by gravity. The sump pit shall be constructed of tile, concrete, steel, plastic or other approved materials. The pit bottom shall be solid and provide permanent support for the pump. The sump pit shall be fitted with a gastight removable cover adequate to support anticipated loads in the area of use. The sump pit shall be vented in accordance with Chapter 31.

> **P3007.3.3 Discharge piping.** Discharge piping shall meet the requirements of Section P3007.2.

> **P3007.3.4 Maximum effluent level.** The effluent level control shall be adjusted and maintained to at all times prevent the effluent in the sump from rising to within 2 inches (51 mm) of the invert of the gravity drain inlet into the sump.

> **P3007.3.5 Ejector connection to the drainage system.** Pumps connected to the drainage system shall connect to the building sewer or shall connect to a wye fitting in the building drain a minimum of 10 feet (3048 mm) from the base of any soil stack, waste stack or fixture drain. Where the discharge line connects into horizontal drainage piping, the connection shall be made through a wye fitting into the top of the drainage piping.

P3007.4 Sewage pumps and sewage ejectors. A sewage pump or sewage ejector shall automatically discharge the contents of the sump to the building drainage system.

P3007.5 Macerating toilet systems. Macerating toilet systems shall comply with CSA B45.9 or ASME A112.3.4 and shall be installed in accordance with the manufacturer's installation instructions.

2006 VIRGINIA CONSTRUCTION CODE (Part I of the Virginia Uniform Statewide Building Code) – Effective May 1, 2008

P3007.6 Capacity. A sewage pump or sewage ejector shall have the capacity and head for the application requirements. Pumps or ejectors that receive the discharge of water closets shall be capable of handling spherical solids with a diameter of up to and including 2 inches (51 mm). Other pumps or ejectors shall be capable of handling spherical solids with a diameter of up to and including 1 inch (25.4 mm). The minimum capacity of a pump or ejector based on the diameter of the discharge pipe shall be in accordance with Table 3007.6.

Exceptions:

1. Grinder pumps or grinder ejectors that receive the discharge of water closets shall have a minimum discharge opening of 1.25 inches (32 mm).

2. Macerating toilet assemblies that serve single water closets shall have a minimum discharge opening of 0.75 inch (19 mm).

TABLE P3007.6
MINIMUM CAPACITY OF SEWAGE PUMP OR SEWAGE EJECTOR

DIAMETER OF DISCHARGE PIPE (inches)	CAPACITY OF PUMP OR EJECTOR
2	21
2½	30
3	46

For SI: 1 inch = 25.4 mm, 1 gallon per minute = 3.785 L/m

49. Change the title of Chapter 32 to read:

CHAPTER 32
TRAPS AND STORM DRAINAGE

50. Add Section P3202, Storm Drainage, to read:

SECTION P3202
STORM DRAINAGE

P3202.1 Scope. The provisions of this section shall govern the materials, design, construction and installation of storm drainage.

P3202.2 Subsoil drains. Subsoil drains shall be open-jointed, horizontally split or perforated pipe conforming to one of the standards listed in Table P3202.2. Such drains shall not be less than 4 inches (102 mm) in diameter. Where the building is subject to backwater, the subsoil drain shall be protected by an accessibly located backwater valve. Subsoil drains shall not be required to have either a gas-tight cover or vent. The sump and pumping system shall comply with Section P3202.3.

TABLE P3202.2
SUBSOIL DRAIN PIPE

MATERIAL	STANDARD
Asbestos-cement pipe	ASTM C 508
Cast-iron pipe	ASTM A 74, ASTM A 888, CISPI 301
Polyethylene (PE) plastic pipe	ASTM F 405, CSA B182.1, CSA B182.6, CSA B182.8
Polyvinyl chloride (PVC) plastic pipe (type sewer pipe, PS25, PS50 or PS100	ASTM D 2729, ASTM F 891, CSA B182.2, CSA B182.4
Stainless steel drainage systems, Type 316L	ASME A112.3.1
Vitrified clay pipe	ASTM C 4, ASTM C 700

P3202.3 Pumping system. The sump pump, pit and discharge piping shall conform to Section P3202.3.1 through P3202.3.4.

P3202.3.1 Pump capacity and head. The sump pump shall be of a capacity and head appropriate to anticipated use requirements.

P3202.3.2 Sump pit. The sump pit shall not be less than 18 inches (457 mm) in diameter and 24 inches (610 mm) deep, unless otherwise approved. The pit shall be accessible and located such that all drainage flows into the pit by gravity. The sump pit shall be constructed of tile, steel, plastic, cast-iron, concrete or other approved material, with a removable cover adequate to support anticipated loads in the area of use. The pit floor shall be solid and provide permanent support for the pump.

P3202.3.3 Electrical. Electrical outlets shall meet the requirements of Chapters 33 through 42.

P3202.3.4 Piping. Discharge piping shall meet the requirements of Sections P3002.1, P3002.2, P3002.3 and P3003. Discharge piping shall include an accessible full flow check valve. Pipe and fittings shall be the same size, or larger than, pump discharge tapping.

51. Add Section E3501.8 to read:

E3501.8 Energizing service equipment. The building official shall give permission to energize the electrical service equipment of a one- or two-family dwelling unit when all of the following requirements have been approved:

1. The service wiring and equipment, including the meter socket enclosure, shall be installed and the service wiring terminated.

2. The grounding electrode system shall be installed and terminated.

3. At least one receptacle outlet on a ground fault protected circuit shall be installed and the circuit wiring terminated.

4. Service equipment covers shall be installed.

5. The building roof covering shall be installed.

6. Temporary electrical service equipment shall be suitable for wet locations unless the interior is dry and protected from the weather.

52. Add the following referenced standards to Chapter 43:

Standard reference number	Title	Referenced in code section number
ASTM C4-03	Specification for Clay Drain Tile and Perforated Clay Drain Tile	P3202.3
ASTM C508-00	Specification for Asbestos-Cement Underdrain Pipe	P3202.3
ASTM D2729-96a	Specification for Poly (Vinyl Chloride) (PVC) Sewer Pipe and Fittings	P3202.3
ASTM E2178-03	Standard Test Method for Air Permeance of Building Materials	R202
ASTM F405-97	Specification for Polyethylene (PE) Tubing and Fittings	P3202.3
CSA B182.1-02	Plastic Drain and Sewer Pipe and Pipe Fittings	P3202.3
CSA B182.6-02	Profile Polyethylene Sewer Pipe and Pipe Fittings	P3202.3
CSA B182.8-02	Profile Polyethylene Storm Sewer and Drainage Pipe and Fittings	P3202.3

CHAPTER 4

SPECIAL DETAILED REQUIREMENTS BASED ON USE AND OCCUPANCY

Add Section 407.8 to the IBC to read:

407.8 Special locking arrangement. Means of egress doors shall be permitted to contain locking devices restricting the means of egress in areas in which the clinical needs of the patients require restraint of movement, where all of the following conditions are met:

1. The locks release upon activation of the fire alarm system or the loss of power.

2. The building is equipped with an approved automatic sprinkler system in accordance with Section 903.3.1.1.

3. A manual release device is provided at a nursing station responsible for the area.

4. A key-operated switch or other manual device is provided adjacent to each door equipped with the locking device. Such switch or other device, when operated, shall result in direct interruption of power to the lock – independent of the control system electronics.

5. All staff shall have keys or other means to unlock the switch or other device or each door provided with the locking device.

Add Section 407.9 to the IBC to read:

407.9 Emergency power systems. Emergency power shall be provided for medical life support equipment, operating, recovery, intensive care, emergency rooms, fire detection and alarm systems in any Group I-2 occupancy licensed by the Virginia Department of Health as a hospital, nursing home or hospice facility.

Change Section 408.2 of the IBC to read:

408.2 Other occupancies. Buildings or portions of buildings in Group I-3 occupancies where security operations necessitate the locking of required means of egress shall be permitted to be classified as a different occupancy. Occupancies classified as other than Group I-3 shall meet the applicable requirements of this code for that occupancy provided provisions are made for the release of occupants at all times. Where the provisions of this code for occupancies other than Group I-3 are more restrictive than the provisions for Group I-3 occupancies, the Group I-3 occupancy provisions shall be permitted to be used.

Means of egress from detention and correctional occupancies that traverse other use areas shall, as a minimum, conform to requirements for detention and correctional occupancies.

Exception: It is permissible to exit through a horizontal exit into other contiguous occupancies that do not conform to detention and correctional occupancy egress provisions but that do comply with requirements set forth in the appropriate occupancy, as long as the occupancy is not a high-hazard use.

Add a new Section 408.3.4 to the IBC to read as follows and renumber existing Sections 408.3.4, 408.3.5 and 408.3.6 to become Sections 408.3.5, 408.3.6 and 408.3.7 respectively:

408.3.4 Ships ladders. Ships ladders in accordance with Section 1009.12 shall be permitted from facility observation or control rooms.

Change Section 408.3.6 of the IBC to read:

408.3.6 Sallyports. A sallyport shall be permitted in a means of egress where there are provisions for continuous and unobstructed passage through the sallyport during an emergency egress condition. A sallyport is a security vestibule with two or more doors where the intended purpose is to prevent continuous and unobstructed passage by allowing the release of only one door at a time.

2006 VIRGINIA CONSTRUCTION CODE (Part I of the Virginia Uniform Statewide Building Code) – Effective May 1, 2008

Add Section 408.3.8 to the IBC to read:

408.3.8 Guard tower doors. A hatch or trap door not less than 16 square feet (.929 m^2) in area through the floor and having minimum dimensions of not less than 2 feet (609.6 mm) in any direction shall be permitted to be used to access guard towers.

Add Section 408.5.1 to the IBC to read:

408.5.1 Noncombustible shaft openings in communicating floor levels. Where vertical openings are permitted without enclosure protection in accordance with Section 408.5, noncombustible shafts such as plumbing chases shall also be permitted without enclosure protection. Where additional stories are located above or below, the shaft shall be permitted to continue with fire and smoke damper protection provided at the fire resistance rated floor/ceiling assembly between the non-communicating stories.

Change Section 408.8 of the IBC to read:

408.8 Windowless buildings. For the purposes of this section, a windowless building or portion of a building is one with nonopenable windows, windows not readily breakable or without windows. Windowless buildings shall be provided with an engineered smoke control system to provide a tenable environment for exiting from the smoke compartment in the area of fire origin in accordance with Section 909 for each windowless smoke compartment.

Add Section 415.1.1 to the IBC to read:

415.1.1 Flammable and combustible liquids. Notwithstanding the provisions of this chapter, the storage, handling, processing, and transporting of flammable and combustible liquids shall be in accordance with the mechanical code and the fire code listed in Chapter 35 of this code. Regulations governing the installation, repair, upgrade, and closure of underground and aboveground storage tanks under the Virginia State Water Control Board regulations 9 VAC 25-91 and 9 VAC 25-580 are adopted and incorporated by reference to be an enforceable part of this code. Where differences occur between the provisions of this code and the incorporated provisions of the State Water Control Board regulations, the provisions of the State Water Control Board regulations shall apply.

Add IBC Section 421 Manufactured Homes and Industrialized Buildings

Add Section 421.1 to the IBC to read:

421.1 General. The provisions of this section shall apply to the installation or erection of manufactured homes subject to the Virginia Manufactured Home Safety Regulations (13 VAC 5-95) and industrialized buildings subject to the Virginia Industrialized Building Safety Regulations (13 VAC 5-91).

Add Section 421.2 to the IBC to read:

421.2 Site work for manufactured homes. The installation of a manufactured home is generally subject to the requirements of the Virginia Manufactured Home Safety Regulations (13 VAC 5-95). Under those regulations, the building official is responsible for assuring that the installation complies with the manufacturer's installation instructions and any special conditions or limitations of use stipulated by the label. To the extent that any aspect of the installation is not provided for in the manufacturer's installation instructions, then the installation shall comply with applicable requirements of this code. In the case where the manufacturer's installation instructions for a manufactured home are not available, the NCSBCS/ANSI A225.1 standard, 1994 edition, may be substituted for the manufacturer's installation instructions. Foundations, stoops, decks, porches, alterations and additions associated with manufactured homes are subject to the requirements of this code and all administrative requirements of this code for permits, inspections and certificates of occupancy are also applicable. The requirements of the IRC shall be permitted to be used for the technical requirements for such construction work. In addition, Appendix E of the IRC entitled, "Manufactured Housing Used As Dwellings," shall be an acceptable alternative to this code for construction work associated with the installation of manufactured homes and for additions, alterations and repairs to manufactured homes.

Add Section 421.3 to the IBC to read:

2006 VIRGINIA CONSTRUCTION CODE (Part I of the Virginia Uniform Statewide Building Code) – Effective May 1, 2008

421.3 Wind load requirements for manufactured homes. Manufactured homes shall be anchored to withstand the wind loads established by the federal regulation for the area in which the manufactured home is installed. For the purpose of this code, Wind Zone II of the federal regulation shall include the cities of Chesapeake, Norfolk, Portsmouth, and Virginia Beach.

Add Section 421.4 to the IBC to read:

421.4 Skirting requirements for manufactured homes. As used in this section, "skirting" means a weather-resistant material used to enclose the space from the bottom of the manufactured home to grade. Manufactured homes installed or relocated shall have skirting installed within 60 days of occupancy of the home. Skirting materials shall be durable, suitable for exterior exposures and installed in accordance with the manufacturer's installation instructions. Skirting shall be secured as necessary to ensure stability, to minimize vibrations, to minimize susceptibility to wind damage and to compensate for possible frost heave. Each manufactured home shall have a minimum of one opening in the skirting providing access to any water supply or sewer drain connections under the home. Such openings shall be a minimum of 18 inches (457 mm) in any dimension and not less than 3 square feet (.28 m²) in area. The access panel or door shall not be fastened in a manner requiring the use of a special tool to open or remove the panel or door. On-site fabrication of the skirting by the owner or installer of the home shall be acceptable, provided that the material meets the requirements of this code.

Add Section 421.5 to the IBC to read:

421.5 Site work for industrialized buildings. Site work for the erection and installation of an industrialized building is generally subject to the requirements of the Virginia Industrialized Building Safety Regulations (13 VAC 5-91) and the building official has certain enforcement responsibilities under those regulations. To the extent that any aspect of the erection or installation of an industrialized building is not covered by those regulations, this code shall be applicable. In addition, all administrative requirements of this code for permits, inspections and certificates of occupancy are also applicable. The requirements of the IRC shall be permitted to be used for any construction work that is subject to this code where the industrialized building would be classified as a Group R-5 building.

Add Section 421.6 to the IBC to read:

421.6 Relocated industrialized buildings; alterations and additions. Industrialized buildings constructed prior to January 1, 1972 shall be subject to Section 117 when relocated. Alterations and additions to existing industrialized buildings shall be subject to pertinent provisions of this code. Building officials shall be permitted to require the submission of plans and specifications for the model to aid in the evaluation of the proposed alteration or addition. Such plans and specifications shall be permitted to be submitted in electronic or other available format acceptable to the building official.

CHAPTER 7

FIRE-RESISTANCE-RATED CONSTRUCTION

Add Section 701.2 to the IBC to read:

701.2 Fire-resistance assembly marking. Concealed fire walls, vertical fire separation assemblies, fire barriers, fire partitions and smoke barriers shall be designated above ceilings and on the inside of all ceiling access doors which provide access to such fire rated assemblies by signage having letters no smaller than 1 inch (25.4 mm) in height. Such signage shall indicate the fire-resistance rating of the assembly and the type of assembly and be provided at horizontal intervals of no more than 8 feet (2438 mm).

Note: An example of suggested formatting for the signage would be "ONE HOUR FIRE PARTITION."

Delete Sections 707.14.1 and 707.14.2 of the IBC, including all subsections of Section 707.14.2.

Add exception 4 to Section 715.4.3 of the IBC to read:

4. Horizontal sliding doors in smoke barriers that comply with Section 408.3 are permitted in smoke barriers in occupancies in Group I-3.

Add an exception to Section 715.5.4 of the IBC to read:

Exception: Security glazing protected on both sides by an automatic sprinkler system shall be permitted in doors and windows in smoke barriers in Group I-3 occupancies. Individual panels of glazing shall not exceed 1,296 square inches (0.84 m²), shall be in a gasketed frame and installed in such a manner that the framing system will deflect without breaking (loading) glazing before the sprinkler system operates. The sprinkler system shall be designed to wet completely the entire surface of the affected glazing when actuated.

Change Section 716.5.3 of the IBC to read:

716.5.3 Shaft enclosures. Shaft enclosures that are permitted to be penetrated by ducts and air transfer openings shall be protected with approved fire and smoke dampers installed in accordance with their listing.

Exceptions:

1. Fire and smoke dampers are not required where steel exhaust subducts are extended at least 22 inches (559 mm) vertically in exhaust shafts , provided there is a continuous airflow upward to the outside.

2. Fire dampers are not required where penetrations are tested in accordance with ASTM E119 as part of the fire-resistance rated assembly.

3. Fire and smoke dampers are not required where ducts are used as part of an approved smoke control system in accordance with Section 909.

4. Fire and smoke dampers are not required where the penetrations are in parking garage exhaust or supply shafts that are separated from other building shafts by not less than 2-hour fire-resistance-rated construction.

5. Smoke dampers are not required where the building is equipped throughout with an automatic sprinkler system in accordance with Section 903.3.1.1.

CHAPTER 9

FIRE PROTECTION SYSTEMS

Add the following definitions to Section 902 of the IBC to read:

EMERGENCY COMMUNICATION EQUIPMENT. Emergency communication equipment includes, but is not limited to, two-way radio communications, signal booster, bi-directional amplifiers, radiating cable systems or internal multiple antenna, or a combination of the foregoing.

EMERGENCY PUBLIC SAFETY PERSONNEL. Emergency public safety personnel includes firefighters, emergency medical personnel, law-enforcement officers and other emergency public safety personnel routinely called upon to provide emergency assistance to members of the public in a wide variety of emergency situations, including, but not limited to, fires, medical emergencies, violent crimes and terrorist attacks.

Change the following definition in Section 902 of the IBC to read:

AUTOMATIC FIRE-EXTINGUISHING SYSTEM. An approved system of devices and equipment which automatically detects a fire and discharges an approved fire-extinguishing agent onto or in the area of a fire and shall include among other systems an automatic sprinkler system, unless otherwise expressly stated.

Change Section 903.2.1.2 of the IBC to read:

2006 VIRGINIA CONSTRUCTION CODE (Part I of the Virginia Uniform Statewide Building Code) – Effective May 1, 2008

903.2.1.2 Group A-2. An automatic sprinkler system shall be provided for Group A-2 occupancies where one of the following conditions exists:

1. The fire area exceeds 5,000 square feet (465 m^2);

2. The fire area has an occupant load of 100 or more in night clubs or 300 or more in other Group A-2 occupancies; or

3. The fire area is located on a floor other than the level of exit discharge.

Change Item 2 of Section 903.2.1.3 of the IBC to read:

2. In Group A-3 occupancies other than churches, the fire area has an occupant load of 300 or more.

Change Section 903.2.7 of the IBC to read:

903.2.7 Group R. An automatic sprinkler system installed in accordance with Section 903.3 shall be provided throughout all buildings with a Group R fire area, except in the following R-2 occupancies when the necessary water pressure or volume, or both, for the system is not available:

Exceptions:

1. Buildings which do not exceed two stories, including basements which are not considered as a story above grade, and with a maximum of 16 dwelling units per fire area. Each dwelling unit shall have at least one door opening to an exterior exit access that leads directly to the exits required to serve that dwelling unit.

2. Buildings where all dwelling units are not more than two stories above the lowest level of exit discharge and not more than one story below the highest level of exit discharge of exits serving the dwelling unit and a two-hour fire barrier is provided between each pair of dwelling units. Each bedroom of a dormitory or boarding house shall be considered a dwelling unit under this exception.

Add Section 903.3.1.2.2 to the IBC to read:

903.3.1.2.2 Attics. Sprinkler protection shall be provided for attics in buildings of Type III, IV or V construction in Group R-2 occupancies that are designed, or developed and marketed to senior citizens, 55 years of age or older and in Group I-1 occupancies in accordance with Section 6.7.2 of NFPA 13R.

Change Section 903.4.2 of the IBC to read:

903.4.2 Alarms. Approved audible devices shall be connected to every automatic sprinkler system. Such sprinkler water-flow alarm devices shall be activated by water flow equivalent to the flow of a single sprinkler of the smallest orifice size installed in the system. Alarm devices shall be provided on the exterior of the building in an approved location. Where a fire alarm system is installed, actuation of the automatic sprinkler system shall actuate the building fire alarm system. Group R-2 occupancies that contain 16 or more dwelling units or sleeping units; or any dwelling unit or sleeping unit two or more stories above the lowest level of exit discharge; or any dwelling unit or sleeping unit more than one story below the highest level of exit discharge of exits serving the dwelling unit or sleeping unit, shall provide a manual fire alarm box at an approved location to activate the suppression system alarm.

Add an exception to Section 905.2 of the IBC to read:

Exception: The residual pressure of 100 psi for 2½ inch hose connection and 65 psi for 1½ inch hose connection is not required in buildings equipped throughout with an automatic sprinkler system in accordance with Section 903.3.1.1 and where the highest floor level is not more than 150 feet above the lowest level of fire department vehicle access.

Change Section 906.1 of the IBC to read:

2006 VIRGINIA CONSTRUCTION CODE (Part I of the Virginia Uniform Statewide Building Code) – Effective May 1, 2008

906.1 General. Portable fire extinguishers shall be provided in occupancies and locations as required by the *International Fire Code*.

Exceptions:

1. Group R-2 occupancies.

2. In Group I-3 occupancies, portable fire extinguishers shall be permitted to be located at staff locations and the access to such extinguishers shall be permitted to be locked.

Change Section 907.2.1.1 of the IBC to read:

907.2.1.1 System initiation in Group A occupancies with an occupant load of 1,000 or more and in certain night clubs. Activation of the fire alarm in Group A occupancies with an occupant load of 1,000 or more and in night clubs with an occupant load of 300 or more shall initiate a signal using an emergency voice/alarm communications system in accordance with NFPA 72.

Exception: Where approved, the prerecorded announcement is allowed to be manually deactivated for a period of time, not to exceed 3 minutes, for the sole purpose of allowing a live voice announcement from an approved, constantly attended location.

Change Section 907.2.9 of the IBC to read:

907.2.9 Group R-2. A manual fire alarm system shall be installed in Group R-2 occupancies.

Exceptions:

1. A fire alarm system is not required in buildings not more than two stories in height where all dwelling units or sleeping rooms and contiguous attic and crawl spaces are separated from each other and public or common areas by at least 1-hour fire partitions and each dwelling unit or sleeping room has an exit directly to a public way, exit court or yard.

2. Manual fire alarm boxes are not required throughout the building when the following conditions are met:

   2.1. The building is equipped throughout with an automatic sprinkler system in accordance with Section 903.3.1.1 or Section 903.3.1.2; and

   2.2. The notification appliances will activate upon sprinkler flow.

Change Section 907.9.2 of the IBC to read:

907.9.2 Audible alarms. Audible alarm notification appliances shall be provided and shall sound a distinctive sound that is not to be used for any purpose other than that of a fire alarm. The audible alarm notification appliances shall provide a sound pressure level of 15 decibels (dBA) above the average ambient sound level or 5 dBA above the maximum sound level having a duration of at least 60 seconds, whichever is greater, in every occupied space within the building. The minimum sound pressure levels shall be: 70 dBA in occupancies in Groups R and I-1; 90 dBA in mechanical equipment rooms and 60 dBA in other occupancies. The maximum sound pressure level for audible alarm notification appliances shall be 120 dBA at the minimum hearing distance from the audible appliance. Where the average ambient noise is greater than 105 dBA, visible alarm notification appliances shall be provided in accordance with NFPA 72 and audible alarm notification appliances shall not be required.

Exceptions:

1. Visible alarm notification appliances shall be allowed in lieu of audible alarm notification appliances in critical-care areas of Group I-2 occupancies.

2. Sound pressure levels in Group I-3 occupancies shall be permitted to be limited to only the notification of occupants in the affected smoke compartment.

Change Section 909.6 of the IBC to read:

909.6 Pressurization method. When approved by the building official, the means of controlling smoke shall be permitted by pressure differences across smoke barriers. Maintenance of a tenable environment is not required in the smoke control zone of fire origin.

Add IBC Section 913 In-Building Emergency Communications Coverage

Add Section 913.1 to the IBC to read:

913.1 General. In-building emergency communication equipment to allow emergency public safety personnel to send and receive emergency communications shall be provided in new buildings and structures in accordance with this section.

> **Exceptions:**
>
> 1. Buildings of Use Groups A-5, I-4, within dwelling units of R-2, R-3, R-4, R-5, and U.
>
> 2. Buildings of Type IV and V construction without basements.
>
> 3. Above grade single story buildings of less than 20,000 square feet.
>
> 4. Buildings or leased spaces occupied by federal, state, or local governments, or the contractors thereof, with security requirements where the building official has approved an alternative method to provide emergency communication equipment for emergency public safety personnel.
>
> 5. Where the owner provides technological documentation from a qualified individual that the structure or portion thereof does not impede emergency communication signals.

Add Sections 913.2, 913.2.1, 913.2.2 and 913.2.3 to the IBC to read:

913.2 Where required. For localities utilizing public safety wireless communications, new buildings and structures shall be equipped throughout with dedicated infrastructure to accommodate and perpetuate continuous emergency communication.

913.2.1 Installation. Radiating cable systems, such as coaxial cable or equivalent shall be installed in dedicated conduits, raceways, plenums, attics, or roofs, compatible for these specific installations as well as other applicable provisions of this code.

913.2.2 Operations. The locality will assume all responsibilities for the installation and maintenance of additional emergency communication equipment. To allow the locality access to and the ability to operate such equipment, sufficient space within the building shall be provided.

913.2.3 Inspection. In accordance with Section 113.3, all installations shall be inspected prior to concealment.

Add Section 913.3 to the IBC to read:

913.3 Acceptance test. Upon completion of installation, after providing reasonable notice to the owner or their representative, emergency public safety personnel shall have the right during normal business hours, or other mutually agreed upon time, to enter onto the property to conduct field tests to verify that the required level of radio coverage is present at no cost to the owner. Any noted deficiencies shall be provided in an inspection report to the owner to the owner or the owner's representative.

CHAPTER 10

MEANS OF EGRESS

2006 VIRGINIA CONSTRUCTION CODE (Part I of the Virginia Uniform Statewide Building Code) – Effective May 1, 2008

Change Section 1004.3 of the IBC to read:

1004.3 Posting of occupant load. Every room or space that is an assembly occupancy and where the occupant load of that room or space is 50 or more shall have the occupant load of the room or space posted in a conspicuous place, near the main exit or exit access doorway from the room or space. Posted signs shall be of an approved legible permanent design and shall be maintained by the owner or authorized agent.

Change Exception 3 of Section 1007.3 of the IBC to read:

3. The clear width of 48 inches (1219 mm) between handrails and the area of refuge is not required at exit stairways in buildings or facilities equipped throughout with an automatic sprinkler system installed in accordance with Section 903.3.1.1 or 903.3.1.2.

Change Section 1007.4 of the IBC to read:

1007.4 Elevators. In order to be considered part of an accessible means of egress, an elevator shall comply with the emergency operation and signaling device requirements of Section 2.27 of ASME A17.1. Standby power shall be provided in accordance with Sections 2702 and 3003. The elevator shall be accessed from either an area of refuge complying with Section 1007.6 or a horizontal exit.

> **Exceptions:**
>
> 1. Elevators are not required to be accessed from an area of refuge or horizontal exit in open parking garages.
>
> 2. Elevators are not required to be accessed from an area of refuge or horizontal exit in buildings and facilities equipped throughout with an automatic sprinkler system installed in accordance with Section 903.3.1.1 or 903.3.1.2.

Change Section 1007.6.2 of the IBC to read:

1007.6.2 Separation. Each area of refuge shall be separated from the remainder of the story by a smoke barrier complying with Section 709 or a horizontal exit complying with Section 1021. Each area of refuge shall be designed to minimize the intrusion of smoke.

> **Exceptions:**
>
> 1. Areas of refuge located within a vertical exit enclosure.
>
> 2. Areas of refuge where the area of refuge and areas served by the area of refuge are equipped throughout with an automatic sprinkler system installed in accordance with Section 903.3.1.1 or 903.3.1.2.

Change Item 2 of Section 1008.1.8.3 of the IBC to read:

2. In buildings in occupancy Groups B, F, M and S, the main exterior door or doors are permitted to be equipped with key-operated locking devices from the egress side provided:

    2.1. The locking device is readily distinguishable as locked,

    2.2. A readily visible durable sign is posted on the egress side on or adjacent to the door stating: THIS DOOR TO REMAIN UNLOCKED WHEN BUILDING IS OCCUPIED. The sign shall be in letters 1 inch (25 mm) high on a contrasting background,

    2.3. The use of the key-operated locking device is revokable by the building official for due cause.

Change Section 1008.1.8.6 of the IBC to read:

1008.1.8.6 Delayed egress locks. Approved, listed, delayed egress locks shall be permitted to be installed on doors serving any occupancy including Group A-3, airport facilities, except Group A, E and H occupancies in buildings which are equipped throughout with an automatic sprinkler system in accordance with Section 903.3.1.1 or an approved automatic smoke or heat detection system installed in accordance with Section 907, provided that the doors unlock in accordance with Items 1 through 6 below. A building occupant shall not be required to pass through more than one door equipped with a delayed egress lock before entering an exit.

1.   The doors unlock upon actuation of the automatic sprinkler system or automatic fire detection system.

2.   The doors unlock upon loss of power controlling the lock or lock mechanism.

3.   The door locks shall have the capability of being unlocked by a signal from the fire command center.

4.   The initiation of an irreversible process which will release the latch in not more than 15 seconds when a force of not more than 15 pounds (67 N) is applied for 1 second to the release device. Initiation of the irreversible process shall activate an audible signal in the vicinity of the door. Once the door lock has been released by the application of force to the releasing device, relocking shall be by manual means only.

     Exception: Where approved, a delay of not more than 30 seconds is permitted.

5.   A sign shall be provided on the door located above and within 12 inches (305 mm) of the release device reading: PUSH UNTIL ALARM SOUNDS. DOOR CAN BE OPENED IN 15 SECONDS.

     Exception: Where approved, such sign shall read: PUSH UNTIL ALARM SOUNDS. DOOR CAN BE OPENED IN 30 SECONDS.

6.   Emergency lighting shall be provided at the door.

Add Section 1008.1.8.8 to the IBC to read:

1008.1.8.8 Locking arrangements in correctional facilities. In occupancies in Groups A-3, A-4, B, E, F, I, M and S within penal facilities, doors in means of egress serving rooms or spaces occupied by persons whose movements must be controlled for security reasons shall be permitted to be locked if equipped with egress control devices which shall unlock manually and by at least one of the following means:

1.   Actuation of an automatic fire suppression system required by Section 903.2.

2.   Actuation of a key-operated manual alarm station required by Section 907.2.

3.   A signal from a central control station.

Add Section 1008.1.10 to the IBC to read:

1008.1.10 Locking certain residential sliding doors. In dwelling units of Group R-2 buildings, exterior sliding doors which are one story or less above grade, or shared by two dwelling units, or are otherwise accessible from the outside, shall be equipped with locks. The mounting screws for the lock case shall be inaccessible from the outside. The lock bolt shall engage the strike in a manner that will prevent it from being disengaged by movement of the door.

Exception: Exterior sliding doors which are equipped with removable metal pins or charlie bars.

Add Section 1008.1.11 to the IBC to read:

1008.1.11 Door viewers in certain residential buildings. Entrance doors to dwelling units of Group R-2 buildings shall be equipped with door viewers with a field of vision of not less than 180 degrees.

Exception: Entrance doors having a vision panel or side vision panels.

2006 VIRGINIA CONSTRUCTION CODE (Part I of the Virginia Uniform Statewide Building Code) – Effective May 1, 2008

Change Exception 4 of Section 1009.3 of the IBC to read:

4. In Group R-3 occupancies; within dwelling units in Group R-2 occupancies; and in Group U occupancies that are accessory to a Group R-3 occupancy or accessory to individual dwelling units in Group R-2 occupancies; the maximum riser height shall be 8.25 inches (210 mm); the minimum tread depth shall be 9 inches (229 mm); the minimum winder tread depth at the walk line shall be 10 inches (254 mm); and the minimum winder tread depth shall be 6 inches (152 mm). A nosing not less than 0.75 inch (19.1 mm) but not more than 1.25 inches (32 mm) shall be provided on stairways with solid risers where the tread depth is less than 11 inches (279 mm).

Add Exception 6 to Section 1009.3 of the IBC to read:

6. Stairways in penal facilities serving guard towers, observation stations and control rooms not more than 250 square feet (23 m²) in area shall be permitted to have risers not exceeding 8 inches (203 mm) in height and treads not less than 9 inches (229 mm) in depth.

Change Exception 2 of Section 1009.3.3 of the IBC to read:

2. Solid risers are not required for occupancies in Group I-3. There are no restrictions on size of the opening in the riser.

Add Section 1009.12 to the IBC to read:

1009.12 Ships ladders. Ships ladders are permitted as an element of a means of egress to and from facility observation or control rooms not more than 250 square feet (23 m²) in area which serves not more than 3 occupants and for access to unoccupied roofs.

Ships ladders shall have a maximum projected tread of 5 inches (127 mm), a minimum tread depth of 8.5 inches (216 mm), a minimum tread width of 15 inches (612 mm) and a maximum riser height of 9.5 inches (241 mm).

Handrails shall be provided on both sides of ships ladders.

Change Exception 4 of Section 1011.1 of the IBC to read:

4. Exit signs are not required in dayrooms, sleeping rooms or dormitory spaces in occupancies in Group I-3.

Add Exception 5 to Item 2 of Section 1014.2 of the IBC to read:

5. A maximum of one exit access is permitted to pass through kitchens, store rooms, closets or spaces used for similar purposes provided such a space is not the only means of exit access.

Change Table 1015.1 of the IBC to read:

TABLE 1015.1
SPACES WITH ONE MEANS OF EGRESS

OCCUPANCY	MAXIMUM OCCUPANT LOAD
A, B, Eᵃ, F, M, U	50
H-1, H-2, H-3	3
H-4, H-5, I-1, I-3, I-4, R	10
S	29

a.   Day care maximum occupant load is 10.

Change Exception 2 of Section 1015.2.1 of the IBC to read:

2. Where a building is equipped throughout with an automatic sprinkler system in accordance with Section 903.3.1.1 or 903.3.1.2, the separation distance of the exit doors or exit access doorways shall not be less than one-fourth of the length of the maximum overall diagonal dimension of the area served.

Change Table 1017.1 of the IBC to read:

TABLE 1017.1
CORRIDOR FIRE-RESISTANCE RATING

OCCUPANTY	OCCUPANT LOAD SERVED BY CORRIDOR	REQUIRED FIRE-RESISTANCE RATING (hours)	
		Without sprinkler system	With sprinkler system[b]
H-1, H-2, H-3	All	1	1
H-4, H-5	Greater than 30	1	1
A, B, E, F, M, S, U	Greater than 30	1	0
R	Greater than 10	1	0.5
I-2[a], I-4	All	Not Permitted	0
I-1, I-3	All	Not Permitted	0

a. For requirements for occupancies in Group I-2, see Section 407.3.
b. Buildings equipped throughout with an automatic sprinkler system in accordance with Section 903.3.1.1 or 903.3.1.2.

CHAPTER 11

ACCESSIBILITY

Add an exception to Section 1101.2 of the IBC to read:

Exception: Wall-mounted visible alarm notification appliances in Group I-3 occupancies shall be permitted to be a maximum of 120 inches (3048 mm) above the floor or ground, measured from the bottom of the appliance. Such appliances shall otherwise comply with all applicable requirements.

Add Section 1106.8 to the IBC to read:

1106.8 Identification of accessible parking spaces. In addition to complying with applicable provisions of this chapter, all accessible parking spaces shall be identified by above grade signs. A sign or symbol painted or otherwise displayed on the pavement of a parking space shall not constitute an above grade sign. All above grade parking space signs shall have the bottom edge of the sign no lower than 4 feet (1219 mm) nor higher than 7 feet (2133 mm) above the parking surface. All disabled parking signs shall include the following language: PENALTY, $100-500 Fine, TOW-AWAY ZONE. Such language may be placed on a separate sign and attached below existing above grade disabled parking signs, provided that the bottom edge of the attached sign is no lower than four feet above the parking surface.

Change Item 1 of Section 1110.1 of the IBC to read:

1. Accessible parking spaces required by Section 1106.1.

CHAPTER 12

INTERIOR ENVIRONMENT

Add the following definitions to Section 1202.1 of the IBC:

DAY-NIGHT AVERAGE SOUND LEVEL (LDN). A 24-hour energy average sound level expressed in dBA, with a 10 decibel penalty applied to noise occurring between 10 p.m. and 7 a.m.

SOUND TRANSMISSION CLASS (STC) RATING. A single number characterizing the sound reduction performance of a material tested in accordance with ASTM E90-90, "Laboratory Measurement of Airborne Sound Transmission Loss of Building Partitions."

Add Section 1203.4.4 to the IBC to read:

1203.4.4 Insect screens in occupancies other than Group R. Every door, window and other outside opening for natural ventilation serving structures classified as other than a residential group containing habitable rooms, food preparation areas, food service areas, or any areas where products to be included or utilized in food for human

2006 VIRGINIA CONSTRUCTION CODE (Part I of the Virginia Uniform Statewide Building Code) – Effective May 1, 2008

consumption are processed, manufactured, packaged, or stored, shall be supplied with approved tightly fitting screens of not less than 16 mesh per inch (16 mesh per 25 mm) and every screen door used for insect control shall have a self-closing device.

Exception: Screen doors shall not be required for out swinging doors or other types of openings which make screening impractical, provided other approved means, such as air curtains or insect repellent fans are provided.

Add Section 1203.4.5 to the IBC to read:

1203.4.5 Insect screens in Group R occupancies. Every door, window and other outside opening required for natural ventilation purposes which serves a structure classified as a residential group shall be supplied with approved tightly fitted screens of not less than 16 mesh per inch (16 mesh per 25 mm) and every screen door used for insect control shall have a self-closing device.

Change Section 1207.1 of the IBC to read:

1207.1 Scope. Sections 1207.2 and 1207.3 shall apply to common interior walls, partitions and floor/ceiling assemblies between adjacent dwelling units or between dwelling units and adjacent public areas such as halls, corridors, stairs or service areas. Section 1207.4 applies to the construction of the exterior envelope of Group R occupancies within airport noise zones and to the exterior envelope of Group A, B, E, I and M occupancies in any locality in whose jurisdiction a United States Master Jet Base is located or any adjacent locality when such requirements are enforced by a locality pursuant to Section 15.2-2295 of the Code of Virginia.

Add Section 1207.4 to the IBC to read:

1207.4 Airport noise attenuation standards. Where the Ldn is determined to be 65 dBA or greater, the minimum STC rating of structure components shall be provided in compliance with Table 1207.4. As an alternative to compliance with Table 1207.4, structures shall be permitted to be designed and constructed so as to limit the interior noise level to no greater than 45 Ldn. Exterior structures, terrain and permanent plantings shall be permitted to be included as part of the alternative design. The alternative design shall be certified by an RDP.

Add Table 1207.4 to the IBC to read:

TABLE 1207.4
AIRPORT NOISE ATTENUATION STANDARDS

LDN	STC OF EXTERIOR WALLS AND ROOF/CEILING ASSEMBLIES	STC OF DOORS AND WINDOWS
65-69	39	25
70-74	44	33
75 or greater	49	38

CHAPTER 14

EXTERIOR WALLS

Change Section 1405.12.2 of the IBC to read:

1405.12.2 Window sills. In Occupancy Groups R-2 and R-3, one- and two-family and multiple-family dwellings, where the opening of the sill portion of an operable window is located more than 72 inches (1829 mm) above the finished grade or other surface below, the lowest part of the clear opening of the window shall be a minimum of 18 inches (457 mm) above the finished floor surface of the room in which the window is located. Glazing between the floor and a height of 18 inches (457 mm) shall be fixed or have openings such that a 4-inch (102 mm) diameter sphere cannot pass through.

Exception: Openings that are provided with window guards that comply with ASTM F 2006 or F 2090.

CHAPTER 16
STRUCTURAL DESIGN

Change Section 1609.3 of the IBC to read:

1609.3 Basic wind speed. The basic wind speed, in mph, for the determination of the wind loads shall be determined by Figure 1609. Wind speeds for localities in special wind regions, near mountainous terrains, and near gorges shall be based on elevation. Areas at 4,000 feet in elevation or higher shall use 110 V mph (48.4 m/s) and areas under 4,000 feet in elevation shall use 90 V mph (39.6 m/s). Gorge areas shall be based on the highest recorded speed per locality or in accordance with local jurisdiction requirements determined in accordance with Section 6.5.4 of ASCE 7.

In nonhurricane-prone regions, when the basic wind speed is estimated from regional climatic data, the basic wind speed shall be not less than the wind speed associated with an annual probability of 0.02 (50-year mean recurrence interval), and the estimate shall be adjusted for equivalence to a 3-second gust wind speed at 33 feet (10 m) above ground in Exposure Category C. The data analysis shall be performed in accordance with Section 6.5.4.2 of ASCE 7.

Add Section 1612.1.1 to the IBC to read:

1612.1.1 Elevation of manufactured homes. New or replacement manufactured homes to be located in any flood hazard zone shall be placed in accordance with the applicable elevation requirements of this code.

Exception: Manufactured homes installed on sites in an existing manufactured home park or subdivision shall be permitted to be placed so that the manufactured home chassis is supported by reinforced piers or other foundation elements of at least equivalent strength that are no less than 36 inches (914 mm) in height above grade in lieu of being elevated at or above the base flood elevation provided no manufactured home at the same site has sustained flood damage exceeding 50% of the market value of the home before the damage occurred.

CHAPTER 17
STRUCTURAL TESTS AND SPECIAL INSPECTIONS

Change Section 1703.1 of the IBC to read:

1703.1 Approved agency. An approved agency responsible for laboratory testing or special inspections, or both, must comply with the qualification, certification and experience requirements of ASTM E 329 or the alternatives listed herein.

Change Section 1703.1.1 of the IBC to read:

1703.1.1 Independent. An approved agency shall be objective and competent. The agency shall also disclose possible conflicts of interest so that objectivity can be confirmed. The special inspector and their agents shall be independent from the person, persons or contractor responsible for the physical construction of the project requiring special inspections.

Change Section 1703.1.3 of the IBC to read:

1703.1.3 Personnel. An approved agency shall employ experienced personnel educated in conducting, supervising and evaluating tests or inspections, or both. Upon request by the building official, documentation shall be provided demonstrating the applicable agency's accreditation as noted in ASTM E 329 and individuals' resumes indicating pertinent training, certifications and other qualifications for special inspection personnel associated with the proposed construction requiring special inspections. The building official may prescribe the manner of qualification documentation and frequency of updating information regarding agency or individual inspector approval.

Firms providing special inspection services or individual inspectors seeking approval of alternative certifications or qualifications, or both, listed in ASTM E 329 may submit documentation demonstrating equivalency. This

2006 VIRGINIA CONSTRUCTION CODE (Part I of the Virginia Uniform Statewide Building Code) – Effective May 1, 2008

documentation may include evidence of meeting other recognized standards or alternative certifications to demonstrate that the minimum qualifications, certification and experience intended by ASTM E 329 have been met. The building official may, if satisfied that equivalency has been demonstrated, approve the credentials of the firm or individual.

Change Section 1704.1 of the IBC to read:

1704.1 General. Where application is made for construction as described in this section, the owner shall employ one or more special inspectors to provide inspections during construction on the types of work listed under Section 1704. All individuals or agents performing special inspection functions shall operate under the direct supervision of an RDP in responsible charge of special inspection activities; also known as the "special inspector." The special inspector shall ensure that the individuals under their charge are performing only those special inspections or laboratory testing that are consistent with their knowledge, training and certification for the specified inspection or laboratory testing.

Exceptions:

1. Special inspections are not required for work of a minor nature or as warranted by conditions in the jurisdiction as approved by the building official.

2. Special inspections are not required for building components unless the design involves the practice of professional engineering or architecture as defined by the laws of this Commonwealth and regulations governing the professional registration and certification of engineers or architects.

3. Unless otherwise required by the building official, special inspections are not required for occupancies in Group R-3, R-4 or R-5 and occupancies in Group U that are accessory to a residential occupancy including, but not limited to, those listed in Section 312.1.

Change Section 1704.1.1 of the IBC to read:

1704.1.1 Statement of special inspections. The permit applicant shall submit a statement of special inspections prepared by the RDP in responsible charge in accordance with Section 111.1. This statement shall be in accordance with Section 1705.

Exceptions:

1. A statement of special inspections is not required for structures designed and constructed in accordance with the conventional construction provisions of Section 2308.

2. The statement of special inspections is permitted to be prepared by a qualified person approved by the building official for construction not designed by a registered design professional.

Change category "11" of Table 1704.4 of the IBC to read:

VERIFICATION AND INSPECTION	CONTINUOUS	PERIODIC	REFERENCED STANDARDª	IBC REFERENCE
11. Inspect formwork for shape, location and dimensions of the concrete member being formed, shoring and reshoring.	–	X	ACI 318: 6.1, 6.2	1906

CHAPTER 18

SOILS AND FOUNDATIONS

Change the exception to Section 1803.5 of the IBC to read:

Exception: Compacted fill material less than 12 inches (305 mm) in depth need not comply with an approved report, provided it is a natural non-organic material that is not susceptible to swelling when exposed to moisture and it has been compacted to a minimum of 90 percent Modified Proctor in accordance with ASTM D 1557. The compaction shall be verified by a qualified inspector approved by the building official. Material other than natural material may be used as fill material when accompanied by a certification from an RDP and approved by the building official.

CHAPTER 27

ELECTRICAL

Change Section 2701.1 of the IBC to read:

2701.1 Scope. This chapter governs the electrical components, equipment and systems used in buildings and structures covered by this code. Electrical components, equipment and systems shall be designed and constructed in accordance with this code and NFPA 70. Any reference in this code to the *ICC Electrical Code* shall be considered to be references to NFPA 70.

Add Section 2701.1.1 to the IBC to read:

2701.1.1 Changes to NFPA 70. The following change shall be made to NFPA 70:

1.   Change Sections 334.10(2) and 334.10(3) of NFPA 70 to read:

   (2)   Multifamily dwellings not exceeding four floors above grade and multifamily dwellings of any height permitted to be of Types III, IV and V construction except in any case as prohibited in 334.12.

   (3)   Other structures not exceeding four floors above grade and other structures of any height permitted to be of Types III, IV and V construction except in any case as prohibited in 334.12. In structures exceeding four floors above grade, cables shall be concealed within walls, floors or ceilings that provide a thermal barrier of material that has at least a 15-minute finish rating as identified in listings of fire-rated assemblies.

       For the purpose of Items 2 and 3 above, the first floor of a building shall be that floor that has 50 percent or more of the exterior wall surface area level with or above finished grade. One additional level that is the first level and not designed for human habitation and used only for vehicle parking, storage or similar use shall be permitted.

Add Section 2701.1.2 to the IBC to read:

2701.1.2 Temporary connection to dwelling units. The building official shall give permission to energize the electrical service equipment of a one- or two-family dwelling unit when all of the following requirements have been approved:

1.   The service wiring and equipment, including the meter socket enclosure, shall be installed and the service wiring terminated.

2.   The grounding electrode system shall be installed and terminated.

3.   At least one receptacle outlet on a ground fault protected circuit shall be installed and the circuit wiring terminated.

4.   Service equipment covers shall be installed.

5.   The building roof covering shall be installed.

6.   Temporary electrical service equipment shall be suitable for wet locations unless the interior is dry and protected from the weather.

Add Section 2701.1.3 to the IBC to read:

2006 VIRGINIA CONSTRUCTION CODE (Part I of the Virginia Uniform Statewide Building Code) – Effective May 1, 2008

2701.1.3 Assisted living facility generator requirements. Generators installed to comply with regulations for assisted living facilities licensed by the Virginia Department of Social Services shall be permitted to be optional standby systems.

Change Section 2702.2.17 of the IBC to read:

2702.2.17 Group I-2 and I-3 occupancies. Emergency power shall be provided in accordance with Section 407.8 for Group I-2 occupancies licensed by the Virginia Department of Health as a hospital, nursing or hospice facility. Emergency power shall be provided for doors in Group I-3 occupancies in accordance with Section 408.4.2.

CHAPTER 28
MECHANICAL SYSTEMS

Change Section 2801.1 of the IBC to read:

2801.1 Scope. Mechanical appliances, equipment and systems shall be constructed and installed in accordance with this chapter, the *International Mechanical Code* and the *International Fuel Gas Code*. Masonry chimneys, fireplaces and barbecues shall comply with the *International Mechanical Code* and Chapter 21 of this code.

Exception: This code shall not govern the construction of water heaters, boilers and pressure vessels to the extent which they are regulated by the Virginia Boiler and Pressure Vessel Regulations (16 VAC 25-50). However, the building official may require the owner of a structure to submit documentation to substantiate compliance with those regulations.

Add IBC Section 2802 Heating Facilities.

Add Section 2802.1 to the IBC to read:

2802.1 Required heating in dwelling units. Heating facilities shall be required in every dwelling unit or portion thereof which is to be rented, leased or let on terms, either expressed or implied, to furnish heat to the occupants thereof. The heating facilities shall be capable of maintaining the room temperature at 65°F (18°C) during the period from October 15 to May 1 during the hours between 6:30 a.m. and 10:30 p.m. of each day and not less than 60°F (16°C) during other hours when measured at a point three feet (914 mm) above the floor and three feet (914 mm) from the exterior walls. The capability of the heating system shall be based on the outside design temperature required for the locality by this code.

Add Section 2802.2 to the IBC to read:

2802.2 Required heating in nonresidential structures. Heating facilities shall be required in every enclosed occupied space in nonresidential structures. The heating facilities shall be capable of producing sufficient heat during the period from October 1 to May 15 to maintain a temperature of not less than 65°F (18°C) during all working hours. The required room temperature shall be measured at a point three feet (914 mm) above the floor and three feet (914 mm) from the exterior walls.

Processing, storage and operation areas that require cooling or special temperature conditions and areas in which persons are primarily engaged in vigorous physical activities are exempt from these requirements.

Add Section 2803, Amendments, to the IBC and add Section 2803.1 to the IBC to read:

2803.1 Changes to the *International Mechanical Code.* The following changes shall be made to the *International Mechanical Code*:

1. Add the following definitions to Section 202 of the *International Mechanical Code*:

BREATHING ZONE. The region within an occupied space between planes 3 and 72 inches (75 and 1800 mm) above the floor and more than 2 feet (600 mm) from the walls of the space or from fixed air-conditioning equipment.

NET OCCUPIABLE FLOOR AREA. The floor area of an occupiable space defined by the inside surfaces of its walls but excluding shafts, column enclosures and other permanently enclosed, inaccessible and unoccupiable areas. Obstructions in the space such as furnishings, display or storage racks and other obstructions, whether temporary or permanent, shall not be deducted from the space area.

OCCUPIABLE SPACE. An enclosed space intended for human activities, excluding those spaces intended primarily for other purposes, such as storage rooms and equipment rooms, that are only intended to be occupied occasionally and for short periods of time.

ZONE. One occupiable space or several occupiable spaces with similar occupancy classification (see Table 403.3), occupant density, zone air distribution effectiveness and zone primary airflow rate per unit area.

2. Replace Section 403 of the *International Mechanical Code* to read:

SECTION 403
MECHANICAL VENTILATION

403.1 Ventilation system. Mechanical ventilation shall be provided by a method of supply air and return or exhaust air. The amount of supply air shall be approximately equal to the amount of return and exhaust air. The system shall not be prohibited from producing negative or positive pressure. The system to convey ventilation air shall be designed and installed in accordance with Chapter 6.

403.2 Outdoor air required. The minimum outdoor airflow rate shall be determined in accordance with Section 403.3. Ventilation supply systems shall be designed to deliver the required rate of outdoor airflow to the breathing zone within each occupiable space.

Exception: Where the registered design professional demonstrates that an engineered ventilation system design will prevent the maximum concentration of contaminants from exceeding that obtainable by the rate of outdoor air ventilation determined in accordance with Section 403.3, the minimum required rate of outdoor air shall be reduced in accordance with such engineered system design.

403.2.1 Recirculation of air. The outdoor air required by Section 403.3 shall not be recirculated. Air in excess of that required by Section 403.3 shall not be prohibited from being recirculated as a component of supply air to building spaces, except that:

1. Ventilation air shall not be recirculated from one dwelling to another or to dissimilar occupancies.

2. Supply air to a swimming pool and associated deck areas shall not be recirculated unless such air is dehumidified to maintain the relative humidity of the area at 60 percent or less. Air from this area shall not be recirculated to other spaces where 10 percent or more of the resulting supply airstream consists of air recirculated from these spaces.

3. Where mechanical exhaust is required by Note b in Table 403.3, recirculation of air from such spaces shall be prohibited. All air supplied to such spaces shall be exhausted, including any air in excess of that required by Table 403.3.

4. Where mechanical exhaust is required by Note h in Table 403.3, mechanical exhaust is required and recirculation is prohibited where 10 percent or more of the resulting supply airstream consists of air recirculated from these spaces.

403.2.2 Transfer air. Except where recirculation from such spaces is prohibited by Table 403.3, air transferred from occupiable spaces is not prohibited from serving as makeup air for required exhaust systems in such spaces as kitchens, baths, toilet rooms, elevators and smoking lounges. The amount of

2006 VIRGINIA CONSTRUCTION CODE (Part I of the Virginia Uniform Statewide Building Code) – Effective May 1, 2008

transfer air and exhaust air shall be sufficient to provide the flow rates as specified in Section 403.3. The required outdoor airflow rates specified in Table 403.3 shall be introduced directly into such spaces or into the occupied spaces from which air is transferred or a combination of both.

403.3 Outdoor airflow rate. Ventilation systems shall be designed to have the capacity to supply the minimum outdoor airflow rate determined in accordance with this section. The occupant load utilized for design of the ventilation system shall not be less than the number determined from the estimated maximum occupant load rate indicated in Table 403.3. Ventilation rates for occupancies not represented in Table 403.3 shall be those for a listed occupancy classification that is most similar in terms of occupant density, activities and building construction; or shall be determined by an approved engineering analysis. The ventilation system shall be designed to supply the required rate of ventilation air continuously during the period the building is occupied, except as otherwise stated in other provisions of the code.

With the exception of smoking lounges, the ventilation rates in Table 403.3 are based on the absence of smoking in occupiable spaces. Where smoking is anticipated in a space other than a smoking lounge, the ventilation system serving the space shall be designed to provide ventilation over and above that required by Table 403.3 in accordance with accepted engineering practice.

Exception: The occupant load is not required to be determined, based on the estimated maximum occupant load rate indicated in Table 403.3 where approved statistical data document the accuracy of an alternate anticipated occupant density.

403.3.1 Zone outdoor airflow. The minimum outdoor airflow required to be supplied to each zone shall be determined as a function of occupancy classification and space air distribution effectiveness in accordance with Sections 403.3.1.1 through 403.3.1.3.

403.3.1.1 Breathing zone outdoor airflow. The outdoor airflow rate required in the breathing zone (V_{bz}) of the occupiable space or spaces in a zone shall be determined in accordance with Equation 4-1.

$$V_{bz} = R_p P_z + R_a A_z \qquad \textbf{(Equation 4-1)}$$

where:
A_z = zone floor area: the net occupiable floor area of the space or spaces in the zone.
P_z = zone population: the number of people in the space or spaces in the zone.
R_p = people outdoor air rate: the outdoor airflow rate required per person from Table 403.3
R_a = area outdoor air rate: the outdoor airflow rate required per unit area from Table 403.3

403.3.1.2 Zone air distribution effectiveness. The zone air distribution effectiveness (E_z) shall be determined using Table 403.3.1.2.

TABLE 403.3.1.2
ZONE AIR DISTRIBUTION EFFECTIVENESS[a,b,c,d,e]

Air Distribution Configuration	E_z
Ceiling or floor supply of cool air	1.0[f]
Ceiling or floor supply of warm air and floor return	1.0
Ceiling supply of warm air and ceiling return	0.8[g]
Floor supply of warm air and ceiling return	0.7
Makeup air drawn in on the opposite side of the room from the exhaust and/or return	0.8
Makeup air drawn in near to the exhaust and/or return location	0.5

For SI: 1 foot = 304.8 mm, 1 foot per minute = 0.00506 m/s, $^0C = [(^0F) - 32]/1.8$.

a.   "Cool air" is air cooler than space temperature.
b.   "Warm air" is air warmer than space temperature.
c.   "Ceiling" includes any point above the breathing zone.
d.   "Floor" includes any point below the breathing zone.
e.   "Makeup air" is air supplied or transferred to a zone to replace air removed from the zone by exhaust or return systems.
f.   Zone air distribution effectiveness of 1.2 shall be permitted for systems with a floor supply of cool air and ceiling return, provided that low-velocity displacement achieves unidirectional flow and thermal stratification.
g.   Zone air distribution effectiveness of 1.0 shall be permitted for systems with a ceiling supply of warm air, provided that supply air temperature is less than 15^0 F above space temperature and provided that the 150 foot-per-minute supply air jet reaches to within 4.5 feet of floor level.

403.3.1.3 Zone outdoor airflow. The zone outdoor airflow rate (V_{oz}), shall be determined in accordance with Equation 4-2.

$$V_{oz} = V_{bz}/E_z \qquad \textbf{(Equation 4.2)}$$

403.3.2 System outdoor airflow. The outdoor air required to be supplied by each ventilation system shall be determined in accordance with Sections 403.3.2.1 through 403.2.3 as a function of system type and zone outdoor airflow rates.

403.3.2.1 Single zone systems. Where one air handler supplies a mixture of outdoor air and recirculated return air to only one zone, the system outdoor air intake flow rate (V_{ot}) shall be determined in accordance with Equation 4-3.

$$V_{ot} = V_{oz} \qquad \textbf{(Equation 4-3)}$$

403.3.2.2 100-percent outdoor air systems. Where one air handler supplies only outdoor air to one or more zones, the system outdoor air intake flow rate (V_{ot}) shall be determined using Equation 4-4.

$$V_{ot} = \Sigma_{\text{all zones}} V_{oz} \qquad \textbf{(Equation 4-4)}$$

403.3.2.3 Multiple zone recirculating systems. Where one air handler supplies a mixture of outdoor air and recirculated return air to more than one zone, the system outdoor air intake flow rate (V_{ot}) shall be determined in accordance with Sections 403.3.2.3.1 through 403.3.2.3.5.

403.3.2.3.1 Primary Outdoor Air Fraction. The primary outdoor air fraction (Z_p) shall be determined for each zone in accordance with Equation 4-5.

$$Z_p = V_{oz}/V_{pz} \qquad \textbf{(Equation 4-5)}$$

where:

V_{pz} = Primary airflow: The airflow rate supplied to the zone from the air-handling unit at which the outdoor air intake is located. It includes outdoor intake air and recirculated air from that air-handling unit but does not include air transferred or air recirculated to the zone by other means. For design purposes, V_{pz} shall be the zone design primary airflow rate, except for zones with variable air volume supply and V_{pz} shall be the lowest expected primary airflow rate to the zone when it is fully occupied.

403.3.2.3.2 System ventilation efficiency. The system ventilation efficiency (E_v) shall be determined using Table 403.3.2.3.2 or Appendix A of ASHRAE 62.1.

TABLE 403.3.2.3.2
SYSTEM VENTILATION EFFICIENCY[a,b]

Max(Z_p)	E_v
0.15	1.0
0.25	0.9
0.35	0.8
0.45	0.7
0.55	0.6
0.65	0.5
0.75	0.4
> 0.75	0.3

a. Max(Z_p) is the largest value of Z_p calculated using Equation 4-5 among all the zones served by the system.
b. Interpolating between table values shall be permitted.

403.3.2.3.3 Uncorrected outdoor air intake. The uncorrected outdoor air intake flow rate (V_{ou}) shall be determined in accordance with Equation 4-7.

$$V_{ou} = D \, \Sigma_{\text{all zones}} R_p P_z + \Sigma_{\text{all zones}} R_a A_z \qquad \textbf{(Equation 4-7)}$$

2006 VIRGINIA CONSTRUCTION CODE (Part I of the Virginia Uniform Statewide Building Code) – Effective May 1, 2008

where:

D = Occupant diversity: the ratio of the system population to the sum of the zone populations, determined in accordance with Equation 4-8.

$$D = P_s / \Sigma_{\text{all zones}} \, P_z$$ **(Equation 4-8)**

where:

P_s = System population: The total number of occupants in the area served by the system. For design purposes, P_s shall be the maximum number of occupants expected to be concurrently in all zones served by the system.

403.3.2.3.4 Outdoor air intake flow rate. The outdoor air intake flow rate (V_{ot}) shall be determined in accordance with Equation 4-9.

$$V_{ot} = V_{ou} / E_v$$ **(Equation 4-9)**

TABLE 403.3
MINIMUM VENTILATION RATES

OCCUPANCY CLASSIFICATION	People Outdoor Airflow Rate in Breathing Zone Cfm/person	Area Outdoor Airflow Rate in Breathing Zone R_a cfm/ft^{2a}	Default Occupant Density #/1000 ft^{2a}	Exhaust Airflow Rate Cfm/ft^{2a}
Correctional Facilities				
Cells				
without plumbing fixtures	5	0.12	25	–
with plumbing fixtures[g]	5	0.12	25	1.0
Dining halls (See Food and Beverage Service)	–	–	–	–
Guard stations	5	0.06	15	–
Day room	5	0.06	30	–
Booking/waiting	7.5	0.06	50	–
Dry cleaners, laundries				
Coin-operated dry cleaner	15	–	20	–
Coin-operated laundries	7.5	0.06	20	–
Commercial dry cleaner	30	–	30	–
Commercial laundry	25	–	10	–
Storage, pick up	7.5	.12	30	–
Education				
Auditoriums	5	0.06	150	–
Corridors (See Public Spaces)	–	–	–	–
Media center	10	0.12	25	–
Sports locker rooms[g]	–	–	–	0.5
Music/theater/dance	10	0.06	35	–
Smoking lounges[g]	60		70	–
Daycare (through age 4)	10	0.18	25	–
Classrooms (ages 5-8)	10	0.12	25	–
Classrooms (age 9 plus)	10	0.12	35	–
Lecture classroom	7.5	0.06	65	–
Lecture hall (fixed seats)	7.5	0.06	150	–
Art classroom[g]	10	0.18	20	0.7
Science laboratories[g]	10	0.18	25	1.0
Wood/metal shops[g]	10	0.18	20	0.5
Computer lab	10	0.12	25	–
Multi-use assembly	7.5	0.06	100	–
Locker/dressing rooms[g]	–	–	–	0.25
Food and beverage service				
Bars, cocktail lounges	7.5	0.18	100	–
Cafeteria, fast food	7.5	0.18	100	–
Dining rooms	7.5	0.18	70	–
Kitchens (cooking)[b]	–	–	–	0.7

2006 VIRGINIA CONSTRUCTION CODE (Part I of the Virginia Uniform Statewide Building Code) – Effective May 1, 2008

OCCUPANCY CLASSIFICATION	People Outdoor Airflow Rate in Breathing Zone Cfm/person	Area Outdoor Airflow Rate in Breathing Zone R_a cfm/ft²ª	Default Occupant Density #/1000 ft²ª	Exhaust Airflow Rate Cfm/ft²ª
Hospitals, nursing and convalescent homes				
Autopsy rooms[b]	–	–	–	0.5
Medical procedure rooms	15	–	20	–
Operating rooms	30	–	20	–
Patient rooms	25	–	10	–
Physical recovery	15	–	20	–
Recovery and ICU	15	–	20	–
Hotels, motels, resorts and dormitories				
Multi-purpose assembly	5	0.06	120	–
Bathrooms/Toilet – private[g]	–	–	–	25/50[f]
Bedroom/living room	5	0.06	10	–
Conference/meeting	5	0.06	50	–
Dormitory sleeping areas	5	0.06	20	–
Gambling casinos	7.5	0.18	120	–
Lobbies/pre-function	7.5	0.06	30	–
Offices				
Conference rooms	5	0.06	50	–
Office spaces	5	0.06	5	–
Reception areas	5	0.06	30	–
Telephone/data entry	5	0.06	60	–
Main entry lobbies	5	0.06	10	–
Private dwellings, single and multiple				
Garages, common for multiple units[b]	–	–	–	0.75
Garages, separate for each dwelling[b]	–	–	–	100 cfm/car
Kitchens[b]	–	–	–	25/100[f]
Living areas[c]	0.35 ACH but not less than 15 cfm/person	–	Based upon number of bedrooms. first bedroom 2; each additional bedroom: 1	–
Toilet rooms and bathrooms[g]	–			20/50[f]
Public spaces				
Corridors	–	0.06	–	–
Elevator car	–	–	–	1.0
Shower room (per shower head)[g]	–	–	–	50/20[f]
Smoking lounges[b]	60	–	70	–
Toilet rooms - public[g]	–	–	–	50/70[e]
Places of religious worship	5	0.06	120	–
Courtrooms	5	0.06	70	–
Legislative chambers	5	0.06	50	–
Libraries	5	0.12	10	–
Museums (children's)	7.5	0.12	40	–
Museums/galleries	7.5	0.06	40	–
Retail stores, sales floors and showroom floors				
Sales (except as below)	7.5	0.12	15	–
Dressing rooms	–	–	–	0.25
Mall common areas	7.5	0.06	40	–
Shipping and receiving	–	0.12	–	–
Smoking lounges[b]	60	–	70	–
Storage rooms	–	0.12	–	–
Warehouses (See Storage)	–	–	–	–
Specialty shops				
Automotive motor-fuel dispensing stations[b]	–	–	–	1.5
Barber	7.5	0.06	25	0.5
Beauty and nail salons[b,h]	20	0.12	25	0.6
Embalming room[b]	–	–	–	2.0
Pet shops (animal areas)[b]	7.5	0.18	10	0.9
Supermarkets	7.5	0.06	8	–
Sports and amusement				
Disco/dance floors	20	0.06	100	–
Bowling alleys (seating areas)	10	0.12	40	–
Game arcades	7.5	0.18	20	–
Ice arenas without combustion engines	–	0.30	–	0.5
Gym, stadium, arena (play area)	–	0.30	–	–
Spectator areas	7.5	0.06	150	–
Swimming pools (pool and deck area)	–	0.48	–	–
Health club/aerobics room	20	0.06	40	–
Health club/weight room	20	0.06	10	–

2006 VIRGINIA CONSTRUCTION CODE – EFFECTIVE MAY 1, 2008

OCCUPANCY CLASSIFICATION	People Outdoor Airflow Rate in Breathing Zone Cfm/person	Area Outdoor Airflow Rate in Breathing Zone R_a cfm/ft^{2a}	Default Occupant Density #/1000 ft^{2a}	Exhaust Airflow Rate Cfm/ft^{2a}
Storage				
Repair garages, enclosed parking garages[b,d]	–	–	–	0.75
Warehouses	–	0.06	–	–
Theaters				
Auditoriums (See Education)	–	–	–	–
Lobbies	5	0.06	150	–
Stages, studios	10	0.06	70	–
Ticket booths	5	0.06	60	–
Transportation				
Platforms	7.5	0.06	100	–
Transportation waiting	7.5	0.06	100	–
Workrooms				
Bank vaults/safe deposit	5	0.06	5	–
Darkrooms	–	–	–	1.0
Copy, printing rooms	5	0.06	4	0.5
Meat processing[c]	15	–	10	–
Pharmacy (prep. area)	5	0.18	10	–
Photo studios	5	0.12	10	–
Computer (without printing)	5	0.06	4	–

For SI: 1 cubic foot per minute = 0.0004719 m^3/s, 1 ton = 908 kg, 1 cubic foot per minute per square foot = 0.00508 m^3/(s m^2), C = [(F) – 32]/1.8, 1 square foot = 0.0929 m^2.

a. Based upon net occupiable floor area
b. Mechanical exhaust required and the recirculation of air from such spaces is prohibited (see Section 403.2.1, Item 3).
c. Spaces unheated or maintained below 50^0 F are not covered by these requirements unless the occupancy is continuous.
d. Ventilation systems in enclosed parking garages shall comply with Section 404.
e. Rates are per water closet or urinal. The higher rate shall be provided where periods of heavy use are expected to occur, such as, toilets in theaters, schools, and sports facilities. The lower rate shall be permitted where periods of heavy use are not expected.
f. Rates are per room unless otherwise indicated. The higher rate shall be provided where the exhaust system is designed to operate intermittently. The lower rate shall be permitted where the exhaust system is designed to operate continuously during normal hours of use.
g. Mechanical exhaust is required and recirculation is prohibited except that recirculation shall be permitted where the resulting supply airstream consists of not more than 10 percent air recirculated from these spaces (see Section 403.2.1, Items 2 and 4).
h. For nail salons, the required exhaust shall include ventilation tables or other systems that capture the contaminants and odors at their source and are capable of exhausting a minimum of 50 cfm per station.

403.4 Exhaust Ventilation. Exhaust airflow rate shall be provided in accordance with the requirements in Table 403.3. Exhaust makeup air shall be permitted to be any combination of outdoor air, recirculated air and transfer air, except as limited in accordance with Section 403.2.

403.5 System operation. The minimum flow rate of outdoor air that the ventilation system must be capable of supplying during its operation shall be permitted to be based on the rate per person indicated in Table 403.3 and the actual number of occupants present.

403.6 Variable air volume system control. Variable air volume air distribution systems, other than those designed to supply only 100-percent outdoor air, shall be provided with controls to regulate the flow of outdoor air. Such control system shall be designed to maintain the flow rate of outdoor air at a rate of not less than that required by Section 403.3 over the entire range of supply air operating rates.

403.7 Balancing. The ventilation air distribution system shall be provided with means to adjust the system to achieve at least the minimum ventilation airflow rate as required by Sections 403.3 and 403.4. Ventilation systems shall be balanced by an approved method. Such balancing shall verify that the ventilation system is capable of supplying and exhausting the airflow rates required by Sections 403.3 and 403.4.

3. Change Section 404.2 of the *International Mechanical Code* to read:

404.2 Minimum ventilation. Automatic operation of the system shall not reduce the ventilation airflow rate below 0.05 cfm per square foot (0.00025 m^3/s·m^2) of the floor area and the system shall be capable of producing a ventilation rate of 0.75 cfm per square foot (0.0035 m^3/s·m^2) of floor area.

4. Change Section 504.6.1 of the *International Mechanical Code* to read:

504.6.1 Maximum length. The maximum length of a clothes dryer exhaust duct shall not exceed 35 feet (10668 mm) from the dryer location to the outlet terminal. The maximum length of the duct shall be reduced 21/2 feet (762 mm) for each 45 degree (0.79 rad) bend and 5 feet (1524 mm) for each 90 degree (1.6 rad) bend. The maximum length of the exhaust duct does not include the transition duct.

2006 VIRGINIA CONSTRUCTION CODE (Part I of the Virginia Uniform Statewide Building Code) – Effective May 1, 2008

Exception: Where the make and model of the clothes dryer to be installed is known and the manufacturer's installation instructions for such dryer are provided to the code official, the maximum length of the exhaust duct, including any transition duct, shall be permitted to be in accordance with the dryer manufacturer's installation instructions.

5. Change Section 507.2.2 of the *International Mechanical Code* to read:

507.2.2. Type II hoods. Type II hoods shall be installed where cooking or dishwashing appliances produce heat, steam, or products of combustion and do not produce grease or smoke, such as steamers, kettles, pasta cookers and dishwashing machines.

Exceptions:

1. Under-counter-type commercial dishwashing machines.

2. A Type II hood is not required for dishwashers and potwashers that are provided with heat and water vapor exhaust systems that are supplied by the appliance manufacturer and are installed in accordance with the manufacturer's instructions.

3. A single light-duty electric convection, bread, retherm, steamer or microwave oven designed for countertop installation. The additional heat and moisture loads generated by such appliances shall be accounted for in the design of the HVAC system.

4. A Type II hood is not required for the following electrically heated appliances: toasters, steam tables, popcorn poppers, hot dog cookers, coffee makers, rice cookers, egg cookers, holding/warming ovens. The additional heat and moisture loads generated by such appliances shall be accounted for in the design of the HVAC system.

6. Change Section 701.1 of the International Mechanical Code to read as follows and delete the remainder of Chapter 7:

701.1 Scope. Solid-fuel-burning appliances shall be provided with combustion air in accordance with the appliance manufacturer's installation instructions. Oil-fired appliances shall be provided with combustion air in accordance with NFPA 31. The methods of providing combustion air in this chapter do not apply to fireplaces, fireplace stoves and direct-vent appliances. The requirements for combustion and dilution air for gas-fired appliances shall be in accordance with the International Fuel Gas Code.

7. Add Section 801.1.1 to the *International Mechanical Code* to read:

801.1.1 Equipment changes. Upon the replacement or new installation of any fuel-burning appliances or equipment in existing buildings, an inspection or inspections shall be conducted to ensure that the connected vent or chimney systems comply with the following:

1. Vent of chimney systems are sized in accordance with this code.

2. Vent or chimney systems are clean, free of any obstructions or blockages, defects or deterioration and are in operable condition.

Where not inspected by the local building department, persons performing such changes or installations shall certify to the building official that the requirements of Items 1 and 2 of this section are met.

Add Section 2804.1 to the IBC to read:

2804.1 Changes to the *International Fuel Gas Code*. The following changes shall be made to the *International Fuel Gas Code*:

1. Change Section 301.1 of the *International Fuel Gas Code* to read:

2006 VIRGINIA CONSTRUCTION CODE (Part I of the Virginia Uniform Statewide Building Code) – Effective May 1, 2008

301.1 Scope. This code shall apply to the installation of fuel gas piping systems, fuel gas utilization equipment, and related accessories as follows:

1. Coverage of piping systems shall extend from the point of delivery to the connections with gas utilization equipment. (See "point of delivery.")

2. Systems with an operating pressure of 125 psig (862 kPa gauge) or less.

   Piping systems for gas-air mixtures within the flammable range with an operating pressure of 10 psig (69 kPa gauge) or less.

   LP-Gas piping systems with an operating pressure of 20 psig (140 kPa gauge) or less.

3. Piping systems requirements shall include design, materials, components, fabrication, assembly, installation, testing and inspection.

4. Requirements for gas utilization equipment and related accessories shall include installation, combustion and ventilation air and venting.

This code shall not apply to the following:

1. Portable LP-Gas equipment of all types that are not connected to a fixed fuel piping system.

2. Installation of farm equipment such as brooders, dehydrators, dryers, and irrigation equipment.

3. Raw material (feedstock) applications except for piping to special atmosphere generators.

4. Oxygen-fuel gas cutting and welding systems.

5. Industrial gas applications using gases such as acetylene and acetylenic compounds, hydrogen, ammonia, carbon monoxide, oxygen, and nitrogen.

6. Petroleum refineries, pipeline compressor or pumping stations, loading terminals, compounding plants, refinery tank farms, and natural gas processing plants.

7. Integrated chemical plants or portions of such plants where flammable or combustible liquids or gases are produced by chemical reactions or used in chemical reactions.

8. LP-Gas installations at utility gas plants.

9. Liquefied natural gas (LNG) installations.

10. Fuel gas piping in power and atomic energy plants.

11. Proprietary items of equipment, apparatus, or instruments such as gas generating sets, compressors, and calorimeters.

12. LP-Gas equipment for vaporization, gas mixing, and gas manufacturing.

13. Temporary LP-Gas piping for buildings under construction or renovation that is not to become part of the permanent piping system.

14. Installation of LP-Gas systems for railroad switch heating.

15. Installation of LP-Gas and compressed natural gas (CNG) systems on vehicles.

2006 VIRGINIA CONSTRUCTION CODE (Part I of the Virginia Uniform Statewide Building Code) – Effective May 1, 2008

16. Except as provided in Section 401.1.1, gas piping, meters, gas pressure regulators, and other appurtenances used by the serving gas supplier in the distribution of gas, other than undiluted LP-Gas.

17. Building design and construction, except as specified herein.

2. Change Section 310.1 of the *International Fuel Gas Code* to read:

310.1 Gas pipe bonding. Each above-ground portion of a gas piping system that is likely to become energized shall be electrically continuous and bonded to an effective ground-fault current path. Gas piping shall be considered to be bonded where it is connected to appliances that are connected to the equipment grounding conductor of the circuit supplying that appliance.

CSST gas piping systems shall be bonded to the electrical service grounding electrode system at the point where the gas service piping enters the building. The bonding conductor size shall be not less than #6 AWG copper wire or equivalent.

3. Add Section 404.8.3 to the *International Fuel Gas Code* to read:

404.8.3 Coating application. Joints in gas piping shall not be coated prior to testing and approval.

4. Add Section 404.17 to the *International Fuel Gas Code* to read:

404.17 Isolation. Metallic piping and metallic tubing that conveys fuel gas from an LP-gas storage container shall be provided with an approved dielectric fitting to electrically isolate the underground portion of the pipe or tube from the above ground portion that enters a building. Such dielectric fitting shall be installed above ground, outdoors.

5. Add Section 505.1.1 to the *International Fuel Gas Code* to read:

501.1.1 Equipment changes. Upon the replacement or new installation of any fuel-burning appliances or equipment in existing buildings, an inspection or inspections shall be conducted to ensure that the connected vent or chimney systems comply with the following:

1. Vent or chimney systems are sized in accordance with this code.

2. Vent or chimney systems are clean, free of any obstruction or blockages, defects or deterioration and are in operable condition.

Where not inspected by the local building department, persons performing such changes or installations shall certify to the building official that the requirements of Items 1 and 2 of this section are met.

CHAPTER 29

PLUMBING SYSTEMS

Change Section 2901.1 of the IBC to read:

2901.1 Scope. The provisions of this chapter and the *International Plumbing Code* shall govern the design and installation of all plumbing systems and equipment, except that as provided for in Section 103.11 for functional design, water supply sources and sewage disposal systems are regulated and approved by the Virginia Department of Health and the Virginia Department of Environmental Quality. The approval of pumping and electrical equipment associated with such water supply sources and sewage disposal systems shall, however, be the responsibility of the building official.

Note: See also the Memorandum of Agreement in the "Related Laws Package" which is available from DHCD.

2006 VIRGINIA CONSTRUCTION CODE (Part I of the Virginia Uniform Statewide Building Code) – Effective May 1, 2008

Add Section 2901.1.1 to the IBC to read;

2901.1.1 Changes to the *International Plumbing Code*. The following changes shall be made to the *International Plumbing Code*:

1. Change Section 310.4 to read:

    310.4 Water closet compartment. Each water closet utilized by the public or employees shall occupy a separate compartment with walls or partitions and a door enclosing the fixtures to ensure privacy.

    Exceptions:

    1. Water closet compartments shall not be required in a single-occupant toilet room with a lockable door.

    2. Toilet rooms located in day care and child-care facilities and containing two or more water closets shall be permitted to have one water closet without an enclosing compartment.

    3. Water closet compartments or partitions shall not be required in toilet facilities for inmates in I-3 occupancies.

2. Delete Sections 311 and 311.1.

3. Change Category 5 of Table 403.1 to read:

NO.	CLASSIFICATION	OCCUPANCY	DESCRIPTION	WATER CLOSETS (URINALS SEE SECTION 419.2)		LAVATORIES		BATHTUBS/ SHOWERS	DRINKING FOUNTAIN (SEE SECTION 410.1)	OTHER
				MALE	FEMALE	MALE	FEMALE			
5	Institutional	I-3	Prisons[b]	1 per cell		1 per cell		1 per 15	1 per 100	
		I-3	Reformitories, detention centers, and correctional centers[b]	1 per 15		1 per 15		1 per 15	1 per 100	
		I-3	Employees	1 per 25		1 per 35		—	1 per 100	—

4. Delete Section 701.9.

5. Add Section 703.6 to read:

    703.6 Nonmetallic building sewer location. Nonmetallic sanitary sewer piping installed and located within six feet (1829 mm) of finished grade that discharges to public systems shall be locatable. An insulated copper tracer wire, 18 AWG minimum in size and suitable for direct burial or an equivalent product, shall be utilized. The wire shall be installed in the same trench as the sewer within 12 inches (305 mm) of the pipe and shall be installed to within 5 feet (1524 mm) of the building wall where the building sewer intersects with the public system. The ends of the wire shall terminate above grade in an accessible location that is not subject to physical damage, such as with a cleanout or at the building wall. Only one accessible location is required to be provided for the wire terminations on either end of each sewer installation.

CHAPTER 30

ELEVATORS AND CONVEYING SYSTEMS

Change Section 3002.4 of the IBC to read:

3002.4 Elevator car to accommodate ambulance stretcher. Where elevators are provided in buildings four or more stories above grade plane or four or more stories below grade plane, at least one elevator shall be provided for fire department emergency access to all floors. The elevator car shall be of such a size and arrangement to accommodate a

2006 VIRGINIA CONSTRUCTION CODE (Part I of the Virginia Uniform Statewide Building Code) – Effective May 1, 2008

24-inch by 84-inch (610 mm by 2134 mm) ambulance stretcher in the horizontal, open position and shall be identified by the international symbol for emergency medical services (star of life). The symbol shall not be less than 3 inches (76 mm) high and shall be placed inside on both sides of the hoistway door frame on the designated and alternate landing floors required to be established by ASME A17.1.

Exception: Elevators in multistory dwelling units or guest rooms.

Add Section 3006.7 to the IBC to read:

3006.7 Machine-room-less designs. Where machine-room-less designs are utilized they shall comply with the provisions of ASME A17.1 and incorporate the following:

1. Where the elevator car-top will be used as a work platform, it shall be equipped with permanently installed guards on all open sides. Guards shall be permitted to be of collapsible design, but otherwise must conform to all applicable requirements of this code for guards.

2. Where the equipment manufacturer's procedures for machinery removal and replacement depend on overhead structural support or lifting points, such supports or lifting points shall be permanently installed at the time of initial equipment installation.

3. Where the structure that the elevator will be located in is required to be fully sprinklered by this code, the hoistway that the elevator machine is located in shall be equipped with a fire suppression system as a machine room in accordance with NFPA 13. Smoke detectors for the automatic initiation of Phase I Emergency Recall Operation, and heat detectors or other approved devices that automatically disconnect the main line power supply to the elevators, shall be installed within the hoistway.

CHAPTER 31

SPECIAL CONSTRUCTION

Change Section 3109 to read:

SECTION 3109
SWIMMING POOLS, SWIMMING POOL ENCLOSURES AND SAFETY DEVICES

Change Section 3109.3 to read:

3109.3 Public swimming pools. Public swimming pools shall be designed and constructed in conformance with ANSI/NSPI-1 or ANSI/NSPI-2, as applicable, and shall be completely enclosed by a fence at least 4 feet (1290 mm) in height or a screen enclosure. Openings in the fence shall not permit the passage of a 4-inch-diameter (102 mm) sphere. The fence or screen enclosure shall be equipped with self-closing and self-latching gates.

CHAPTER 33

SAFEGUARDS DURING CONSTRUCTION

Delete IBC Sections 3305 and 3305.1.

CHAPTER 34

EXISTING STRUCTURES

Change Section 3401.1 of the IBC to read:

2006 VIRGINIA CONSTRUCTION CODE (Part I of the Virginia Uniform Statewide Building Code) – Effective May 1, 2008

3401.1 Scope. The provisions of this chapter and the applicable requirements of Chapter 1 shall control the alteration, repair, addition and change of occupancy of existing structures.

Delete IBC Sections 3401.2 and 3401.3.

Delete IBC Section 3403.

Change Section 3405.1 of the IBC to read:

3405.1 Standards for replacement glass. In accordance with Section 36-99.2 of the Code of Virginia, any replacement glass installed in buildings constructed prior to the first edition of the USBC shall meet the quality and installation standards for glass installed in new buildings as are in effect at the time of installation. In addition, as a requirement of this code, the installation or replacement of glass in buildings constructed under any edition of the USBC shall be as required for new installations.

Delete IBC Section 3406.

Delete IBC Section 3408.

Change Section 3410.2 of the IBC to read:

3410.2 Applicability. When specifically requested by an owner or an owner's agent in structures where there is work involving additions, alterations or changes of occupancy, the provisions in Sections 3410.2.1 through 3410.2.5 shall apply to existing occupancies that will continue to be, or are proposed to be, in Groups A, B, E, F, M, R, S and U. These provisions shall not apply to buildings with occupancies in Group H or I.

Add an exception to Section 3410.2.1 of the IBC to read:

Exception: Plumbing, mechanical and electrical systems in buildings undergoing a change of occupancy shall be subject to any applicable requirements of Section 103.3 of this code.

Add IBC Section 3411 Retrofit Requirements.

Add Section 3411.1 to the IBC to read:

3411.1 Scope. In accordance with Section 103.7 and as setout herein, the following buildings are required to be provided with certain fire protection equipment or systems or other retrofitted components.

Add Section 3411.2 to the IBC to read:

3411.2 Smoke detectors in colleges and universities. In accordance with Section 36-99.3 of the Code of Virginia, college and university buildings containing dormitories for sleeping purposes shall be provided with battery-powered or AC-powered smoke detector devices installed therein in accordance with this code in effect on July 1, 1982. All public and private college and university dormitories shall have installed such detectors regardless of when the building was constructed. The chief administrative office of the college or university shall obtain a certificate of compliance with the provisions of this subsection from the building official of the locality in which the college or university is located or in the case of state-owned buildings, from the Director of the Virginia Department of General Services. The provisions of this section shall not apply to any dormitory at a state-supported military college or university which is patrolled 24 hours a day by military guards.

Add Section 3411.3 to the IBC to read:

3411.3 Smoke detectors in certain juvenile care facilities. In accordance with Section 36-99.4 of the Code of Virginia, battery-powered or AC-powered smoke detectors shall be installed in all local and regional detention homes, group homes, and other residential care facilities for children and juveniles which are operated by or under the auspices of the Virginia Department of Juvenile Justice, regardless of when the building was constructed, by July 1, 1986, in accordance with the provisions of this code that were in effect on July 1, 1984. Administrators of such homes and facilities shall be responsible for the installation of the smoke detector devices.

2006 VIRGINIA CONSTRUCTION CODE (Part I of the Virginia Uniform Statewide Building Code) – Effective May 1, 2008

Add Section 3411.4 to the IBC to read:

3411.4 Smoke detectors for the deaf and hearing-impaired. In accordance with Section 36-99.5 of the Code of Virginia, smoke detectors providing an effective intensity of not less than 100 candela to warn a deaf or hearing-impaired individual shall be provided, upon request by the occupant to the landlord or proprietor, to any deaf or hearing-impaired occupant of any of the following occupancies, regardless of when constructed:

1. All dormitory buildings arranged for the shelter and sleeping accommodations of more than 20 individuals;

2. All multiple-family dwellings having more than two dwelling units, including all dormitories, boarding and lodging houses arranged for shelter and sleeping accommodations of more than five individuals; or

3. All buildings arranged for use of one-family or two-family dwelling units.

A tenant shall be responsible for the maintenance and operation of the smoke detector in the tenant's unit.

A hotel or motel shall have available no fewer than one such smoke detector for each 70 units or portion thereof, except that this requirement shall not apply to any hotel or motel with fewer than 35 units. The proprietor of the hotel or motel shall post in a conspicuous place at the registration desk or counter a permanent sign stating the availability of smoke detectors for the hearing impaired. Visual detectors shall be provided for all meeting rooms for which an advance request has been made.

Add Sections 3411.5, 3411.5.1 and 3411.5.2 to the IBC to read:

3411.5 Assisted living facilities (formerly known as adult care residences or homes for adults). Existing assisted living facilities licensed by the Virginia Department of Social Services shall comply with this section.

3411.5.1. Fire protective signaling system and fire detection system. A fire protective signaling system and an automatic fire detection system meeting the requirements of the USBC, Volume I, 1987 Edition, Third Amendment, shall be installed in assisted living facilities by August 1, 1994.

Exception: Assisted living facilities that are equipped throughout with a fire protective signaling system and an automatic fire detection system.

3411.5.2. Single and multiple station smoke detectors. Battery or AC-powered single and multiple station smoke detectors meeting the requirements of the USBC, Volume I, 1987 Edition, Third Amendment, shall be installed in assisted living facilities by August 1, 1994.

Exception: Assisted living facilities that are equipped throughout with single and multiple station smoke detectors.

Add Section 3411.6 to the IBC to read:

3411.6 Smoke detectors in buildings containing dwelling units. AC-powered smoke detectors with battery backup or an equivalent device shall be required to be installed to replace a defective or inoperative battery-powered smoke detector located in buildings containing one or more dwelling units or rooming houses offering to rent overnight sleeping accommodations, when it is determined by the building official that the responsible party of such building or dwelling unit fails to maintain battery-powered smoke detectors in working condition.

Add Section 3411.7 to the IBC to read:

3411.7 Fire suppression, fire alarm and fire detection systems in nursing homes and facilities. Fire suppression systems as required by the edition of this code in effect on October 1, 1990, shall be installed in all nursing facilities licensed by the Virginia Department of Health by January 1, 1993, regardless of when such facilities or institutions were constructed. Units consisting of certified long-term care beds located on the ground floor of general hospitals shall be exempt from the requirements of this section.

2006 VIRGINIA CONSTRUCTION CODE (Part I of the Virginia Uniform Statewide Building Code) – Effective May 1, 2008

Fire alarm or fire detector systems, or both, as required by the edition of this code in effect on October 1, 1990, shall be installed in all nursing homes and nursing facilities licensed by the Virginia Department of Health by August 1, 1994.

Add Section 3411.8 to the IBC to read:

3411.8 Fire suppression systems in hospitals. Fire suppression systems shall be installed in all hospitals licensed by the Virginia Department of Health as required by the edition of this code in effect on October 1, 1995, regardless of when such facilities were constructed.

Add Section 3411.9 to the IBC to read:

3411.9 Identification of handicapped parking spaces by above grade signs. All parking spaces reserved for the use of handicapped persons shall be identified by above grade signs, regardless of whether identification of such spaces by above grade signs was required when any particular space was reserved for the use of handicapped persons. A sign or symbol painted or otherwise displayed on the pavement of a parking space shall not constitute an above grade sign. Any parking space not identified by an above grade sign shall not be a parking space reserved for the handicapped within the meaning of this section. All above grade handicapped parking space signs shall have the bottom edge of the sign no lower than four feet (1219 mm) nor higher than seven feet (2133 mm) above the parking surface. Such signs shall be designed and constructed in accordance with the provisions of Chapter 11 of this code. All disabled parking signs shall include the following language: PENALTY, $100-500 Fine, TOW-AWAY ZONE. Such language may be placed on a separate sign and attached below existing above grade disabled parking signs, provided that the bottom edge of the attached sign is no lower than four feet above the parking surface.

Add Section 3411.10 to the IBC to read:

3411.10 Smoke detectors in hotels and motels. Smoke detectors shall be installed in hotels and motels as required by the edition of VR 394-01-22, USBC, Volume II, in effect on March 1, 1990, by the dates indicated, regardless of when constructed.

Add Section 3411.11 to the IBC to read:

3411.11 Sprinkler systems in hotel and motels. By September 1, 1997, an automatic sprinkler system shall be installed in hotels and motels as required by the edition of VR 394-01-22, USBC, Volume II, in effect on March 1, 1990, regardless of when constructed.

Add Section 3411.12 to the IBC to read:

3411.12 Fire suppression systems in dormitories. An automatic fire suppression system shall be provided throughout all buildings having a Group R-2 fire area which are more than 75 feet (22 860 mm) or six stories above the lowest level of exit discharge and which are used, in whole or in part, as a dormitory to house students by any public or private institution of higher education, regardless of when such buildings were constructed, in accordance with the edition of this code in effect on August 20, 1997 and the requirements for sprinkler systems under the edition of the NFPA 13 standard referenced by that code. The automatic fire suppression system shall be installed by September 1, 1999. The chief administrative office of the college or university shall obtain a certificate of compliance from the building official of the locality in which the college or university is located or in the case of state-owned buildings, from the Director of the Virginia Department of General Services.

Exceptions:

1. Buildings equipped with an automatic fire suppression system in accordance with Section 903.3.1.1 or the 1983 or later editions of NFPA 13.

2. Any dormitory at a state-supported military college or university which is patrolled 24 hours a day by military guards.

3. Application of the requirements of this section shall be modified in accordance with the following:

2006 VIRGINIA CONSTRUCTION CODE (Part I of the Virginia Uniform Statewide Building Code) – Effective May 1, 2008

3.1. Building systems, equipment or components other than the fire suppression system shall not be required to be added or upgraded except as necessary for the installation of the fire suppression system and shall only be required to be added or upgraded where the installation of the fire suppression system creates an unsafe condition.

3.2. Residential sprinklers shall be used in all sleeping rooms. Other sprinklers shall be quick response or residential unless deemed unsuitable for a space. Standard response sprinklers shall be used in elevator hoist ways and machine rooms.

3.3. Sprinklers shall not be required in wardrobes in sleeping rooms that are considered part of the building construction or in closets in sleeping rooms, when such wardrobes or closets (i) do not exceed 24 square feet (2.23 m²) in area, (ii) have the smallest dimension less than 36 inches (914 mm), and (iii) comply with all of the following:

    3.3.1. A single station smoke detector monitored by the building fire alarm system is installed in the room containing the wardrobe or closet that will activate the general alarm for the building if the single station smoke detector is not cleared within five minutes after activation.

    3.3.2. The minimum number of sprinklers required for calculating the hydraulic demand of the system for the room shall be increased by two and the two additional sprinklers shall be corridor sprinklers where the wardrobe or closet is used to divide the room. Rooms divided by a wardrobe or closet shall be considered one room for the purpose of this requirement.

    3.3.3. The ceiling of the wardrobe, closet or room shall have a fire resistance rating of not less than 1/2 hour.

3.4. Not more than one sprinkler shall be required in bathrooms within sleeping rooms or suites having a floor area between 55 square feet (5.12 m²) and 120 square feet (11.16 m²) provided the sprinkler is located to protect the lavatory area and the plumbing fixtures are of a noncombustible material.

3.5. Existing standpipe residual pressure shall be permitted to be reduced when the standpipe serves as the water supply for the fire suppression system provided the water supply requirements of NFPA 13 - 94 are met.

3.6. Limited service controllers shall be permitted for fire pumps when used in accordance with their listing.

3.7. Where a standby power system is required, a source of power in accordance with Section 701-11 (d) or 701-11 (e) of NFPA 70 - 96 shall be permitted.

Add Section 3411.13 to the IBC to read:

3411.13 Fire extinguishers and smoke detectors in SRCF's. SRCF's shall be provided with at least one approved type ABC portable fire extinguisher with a minimum rating of 2A10BC installed in each kitchen. In addition, SRCF's shall provide at least one approved and properly installed battery operated smoke detector outside of each sleeping area in the vicinity of bedrooms and bedroom hallways and on each additional floor.

Add Section 3411.14 to the IBC to read:

3411.14 Smoke detectors in adult day care centers. Battery-powered or AC-powered smoke detector devices shall be installed in all adult day care centers licensed by the Virginia Department of Social Services, regardless of when the building was constructed. The location and installation of the smoke detectors shall be determined by the provisions of this code in effect on October 1, 1990. The licensee shall obtain a certificate of compliance from the building official of the locality in which the center is located, or in the case of state-owned buildings, from the Director of the Virginia Department of General Services.

Add Section 3411.15 to the IBC to read:

2006 VIRGINIA CONSTRUCTION CODE (Part I of the Virginia Uniform Statewide Building Code) – Effective May 1, 2008

3411.15 Posting of occupant load. Every room or space that is an assembly occupancy and where the occupant load of that room or space is 50 or more, shall have the occupant load of the room or space as determined by the building official posted in a conspicuous place, near the main exit or exit access doorway from the room or space. Posted signs shall be of an approved legible permanent design and shall be maintained by the owner or authorized agent.

CHAPTER 35

REFERENCED STANDARDS

Change the referenced standards in Chapter 35 of the IBC as follows (standards not shown remain the same):

Standard reference number	Title	Referenced in code section number
ANSI/NSPI-1-2003	American National Standard for Public Swimming Pools	3109.3
ANSI/NSPI-2-1999	American National Standard for Public Swimming Pools	3109.3
ASTM E 329-02	Standard Specification for Agencies Engaged in the Testing and/or Inspection of Materials Used in Construction	1703.1, 1703.1.3
NFPA 13-07	Installation of Sprinkler Systems	707.2, 903.3.1.1, 903.3.2, 903.3.5.1.1, 903.3.5.2, 904.11, 905.3.4, 907.8, 3104.5, 3104.9
NFPA 13D-07	Installation of Sprinkler Systems in One- and Two-Family Dwellings and Manufactured Homes	903.3.1.3, 903.3.5.1.1
NFPA 13R-07	Installation of Sprinkler Systems in Residential Occupancies up to and Including Four Stories in Height	903.3.1.2, 903.3.5.1.1, 903.3.5.1.2, 903.4
NFPA 14-07	Installation of Standpipe and Hose Systems	905.2, 905.3.4, 905.4.2, 905.8
NFPA 70-05	National Electrical Code	2701.1
NFPA 72-07	National Fire Alarm Code	901.6, 903.4.1, 904.3.5, 907.2, 907.2.1.1, 907.2.10, 907.2.10.4, 907.2.11.2, 907.2.11.3, 907.2.12.2.3, 907.2.12.3, 907.4, 907.5, 907.9.2, 907.10, 907.14, 907.16, 907.17, 911.1, 3006.5
NFPA 704-07	Identification of the Hazards of Materials for Emergency Response	414.7.2, 415.2

APPENDIX F

RODENT PROOFING

The following provisions of Appendix F of the IBC are part of this code:

F101.2 Foundation wall ventilation openings.

F101.6 Pier and wood construction. (Includes all provisions.)

2006 VIRGINIA CONSTRUCTION CODE (Part I of the Virginia Uniform Statewide Building Code) – Effective May 1, 2008

APPENDIX H

SIGNS

The following provisions of Appendix H of the IBC are part of this code:

H101.2 Signs exempt from permits.

H102 Definitions. (Includes all definitions.)

H103 Location. (Includes Section H103.1.)

H105 through H114. (Includes all provisions.)

APPENDIX I

PATIO COVERS

The following provisions from Appendix I of the IBC are part of this code:

I101 through I104 (Includes all provisions.)

CHAPTER **6**

VIRGINIA
LABOR LAWS

This chapter outlines legal requirements for employers and employee programs covered under Virginia labor laws. Programs such as workers' compensation, unemployment compensation, and work rules for minors are governed by the state. Of particular interest to employers is the Code of Virginia (CoV), particularly Title 65.2—Workers' Compensation, Title 60.2—Unemployment Compensation, and Title 40.1—Labor and Employment, which detail the responsibilities of employers and employees in regards to workers' compensation and unemployment insurance.

WORKERS' COMPENSATION

Workers' compensation insurance is required by Virginia labor law for employers with three or more employees. Workers' compensation offers financial security for employees who are injured on the job and may also provide benefits to dependants of employees who are injured. Employers that are required to carry workers' compensation insurance must have either a certificate of self-insurance issued by the Virginia Workers' Compensation Commission or be a member of a self-insurance association that has been approved by the State Corporation Commission (CoV 65.2-802). Contractors are required to pay for the necessary medical treatment for as long as necessary, regardless of cost.

Determining how many employees a company has differs for each of the business entity types. Sole proprietors, partners, and members of limited liability corporations may choose to be counted as employees and be covered by the insurance, but they are normally considered owners of the business and not counted towards the employee total. Officers of corporations are considered employees and would be counted in the number of employees (CoV 65.2-101 (2) n). Executive officers of corporations may choose to reject coverage for accidents by filing a Notice of Rejection with the insurer (CoV 65.2-300 B). Independent contractors are normally not considered employees of a company.

Contractors should include a provision in their subcontractor's contract that 20 percent of the total cost of the contract will be retained if the subcontractor cannot provide proof of workers' compensation.

All companies that are required to carry workers' compensation must display a copy of Form VWC 1, Notice of Workers' Compensation, in the workplace. A copy can be downloaded from the Virginia Workers' Compensation Commission's Web site at *www.vwc.state.va.us* or contact

Virginia Workers' Compensation Commission
1000 DMV Drive
Richmond, VA 23220
(877) 664-2566

Employers are also required to file an annual report with the Workers' Compensation Commission showing compliance with the code, although, the insurance carrier may do this on behalf of the employer (CoV 65.2-804.A.1). Should a contractor cancel the insurance policy, the contractor must give written notice to the employees 30 days in advance of the cancellation (CoV 65.2-804.A.2).

No employee may be fired for making a workers' compensation claim. Should an employee be fired, they may bring suit in the circuit court (CoV 65.2-308).

Fines for Violating Workers' Compensation Insurance Laws

Failure to notify employees of insurance cancellation is punishable by a fine of $500 to $5,000 (CoV 65.2-805) and will be guilty of a Class 2 misdemeanor (CoV 65.2/806).

UNEMPLOYMENT INSURANCE

Unemployment insurance compensation offers a weekly stipend to employees who have lost their job. The Virginia Employment Commission (VEC) has information regarding job placement and referrals, unemployment insurance, disability insurance, employment and training, labor market information, payroll taxes, and other topics available online at *www.vec.virginia.gov/vecportal/*.

A company is liable to pay unemployment insurance if it has paid more than $1,500 in total gross payroll for a quarter or if it has employed one or more employees who has worked any portion of a day during 20 different weeks in one calendar year (CoV 60.2-210). Any company that meets either of these criteria must register with the Virginia Employment Commission and pay the unemployment tax.

How the Unemployment Insurance Program is Funded

The Unemployment Insurance (UI) program is funded by unemployment taxes paid by employers on employee wages. The UI fund then provides direct payments to the unemployed individual. The payments ensure continuation of essential needs while the former employee searches for a new job. The tax rate varies for each employer depending on the experience rating assigned by the VEC (CoV 60.2-531). As a general guideline, newly formed companies pay the lowest amount while foreign companies pay the maximum amount.

Benefits Paid

The amount of unemployment insurance paid depends on the wages of the employee and is calculated on a review of the previous four calendar quarters. The minimum weekly benefit amount is $50 and the maximum weekly benefit amount is $326. Typically, an unemployed worker's benefits may not exceed 26 weeks

(CoV 60.2-607). Additional information about unemployment insurance may be obtained from

Virginia Employment Commission
Customer Service
Post Office Box 1358
Richmond, Virginia 23218
(804) 786-4359
www.vec.virginia.gov

Reducing Costs for the Employer

Just as with any insurance program, the easiest way to reduce costs is to keep premiums low. The more substantiated claims there are against the employer, the higher the tax rate and the premiums paid. To prevent claims from being filed successfully, employers must ensure that all necessary hiring and firing is handled in the proper way. An employer must keep accurate employment records, follow written company procedures, work with employees to resolve issues, and carefully document the termination process. An employee may be terminated for valid reasons and still collect UI if it can be shown that the termination process was improper or the conditions of employment were unacceptable. An employee may even quit employment voluntarily and still be eligible for UI if it can be demonstrated that they left the company with good cause.

Forms

All companies liable under the unemployment insurance act must file:

- Form VEC-FC-27, Report to Determine Liability for State Unemployment Tax
- Form VEC-FC-20, Employer's Quarterly Report, which identifies wages and taxes paid

Employer Guidance

The VEC has a 26-page *Employer's Handbook* detailing reporting requirements, computing tax rates, and benefits information available for download at *www.vec. virginia.gov/vecportal/employer/vec_forms.cfm.*

WAGE REQUIREMENTS

A **minimum wage** is the lowest possible rate that can be paid to an employee. Virginia wage requirements do not differ from the federal minimum wage requirements of $5.85 per hour and will be increased to $6.55 July 24 2008. The federal Fair Labor Standards Act (FLSA) is detailed in the *Contractor's Business Reference Manual* by Kaplan AEC.

Hiring Minors

Most Virginia employers are governed not only by state child labor laws but by the child labor provisions of the federal Fair Labor Standards Act (FLSA). When federal and state laws both apply, the more restrictive law prevails.

The FLSA sets the basic minimum age at 16 for general employment and 18 for occupations declared particularly hazardous for young workers. Persons younger than 16 are only allowed to work in limited, specified occupations and are prohibited from working in the following industries: baking, manufacturing, processing, construction, warehousing, and transportation.

Virginia law also sets minimum ages and restricts or prohibits employment of specified age groups of minors in specified hazardous occupations. For a complete list of the hazardous occupations, see the Virginia Administrative Code, 16VAC15-50-20, at the end of this chapter.

Summary of Minors' Work Regulations

- State law prohibits employment of children younger than 14 years old (CoV 40.1-78).

- Only children between the ages of 14 and 15 need to obtain a work permit.

- A work permit will be revoked whenever the issuing authority determines the employment is impairing the health or education of the minor.

- Children generally must attend school until age 18 unless they are 16 or older and have graduated from high school or received a state general education diploma.

- Labor laws applicable to adult employees are also generally applicable to minor employees, including workers' compensation insurance requirements.

- The child labor laws do not generally apply to minors who deliver newspapers or work at odd jobs (such as yard work and babysitting) in private homes where the minor is not regularly employed.

Work Hours

- Children ages 14 to 15 may not work more than 3 hours on a school day, 18 hours in a school week, 8 hours a day on a non-school day, and no more than 40 hours during a non-school week.

- Minors may not work before 7:00 a.m. or after 7:00 p.m., except between June 1st and Labor Day, when they may work as late as 9:00 p.m.

- Minors must be given a 30-minute break after five hours of work.

For additional information, contact:

Virginia Department of Labor and Industry
Division of Labor and Employment Law
13 South Thirteenth Street
Richmond, Virginia 23219-4101
(804) 371-2327
www.doli.state.va.us

Fines

Failure to comply with labor laws, whether intentional or not, can be punishable by a $1,000 fine (CoV 40.1-113).

ADDITIONAL WORKPLACE REQUIREMENTS

Deductions from Paychecks

FLSA standards allow employers to deduct cash register shortages and equipment breakages from an employee's paycheck; however, Virginia labor code prohibits these deductions from paychecks unless an employee voluntarily signs a permission statement. The only other permissible paycheck deductions are state and federal taxes and court ordered deductions such as child support or alimony (CoV 40.1-29.c).

Right to Work

Virginia code prohibits places of employment to be a closed shop. This means that no workplace may require all employees to be a member of a union. The code also prohibits denying employment to a person who is not a union member or who is a union member (CoV 40.1-58 to 40.1-69).

Record Retention

The Virginia Employment Commission requires that all payroll records must be maintained for a period of four years (16VAC5-32-10.B).

CODE OF VIRGINIA (COV)
TITLE 65.2 WORKERS' COMPENSATION

§65.2-101. Definitions

As used in this title:

"Average weekly wage" means:

1. a. The earnings of the injured employee in the employment in which he was working at the time of the injury during the period of 52 weeks immediately preceding the date of the injury, divided by 52; but if the injured employee lost more than seven consecutive calendar days during such period, although not in the same week, then the earnings for the remainder of the 52 weeks shall be divided by the number of weeks remaining after the time so lost has been deducted. When the employment prior to the injury extended over a period of less than 52 weeks, the method of dividing the earnings during that period by the number of weeks and parts thereof during which the employee earned wages shall be followed, provided that results fair and just to both parties will be thereby obtained. When, by reason of a shortness of time during which the employee has been in the employment of his employer or the casual nature or terms of his employment, it is impractical to compute the average weekly wages as above defined, regard shall be had to the average weekly amount which during the 52 weeks previous to the injury was being earned by a person of the same grade and character employed in the same class of employment in the same locality or community.

   b. When for exceptional reasons the foregoing would be unfair either to the employer or employee, such other method of computing average weekly wages may be resorted to as will most nearly approximate the amount which the injured employee would be earning were it not for the injury.

2. Whenever allowances of any character made to an employee in lieu of wages are a specified part of the wage contract, they shall be deemed a part of his earnings. For the purpose of this title, the average weekly wage of the members of the Virginia National Guard, the Virginia Naval Militia and the Virginia State Defense Force, registered members on duty or in training of the United States Civil Defense Corps of this Commonwealth, volunteer firefighters engaged in firefighting activities under the supervision and control of the Department of Forestry, and forest wardens shall be deemed to be such amount as will entitle them to the maximum compensation payable under this title; however, any award entered under the provisions of this title on behalf of members of the National Guard, the Virginia Naval Militia or their dependents, or registered members on duty or in training of the United States Civil Defense Corps of this Commonwealth or their dependents, shall be subject to credit for benefits paid them under existing or future federal law on account of injury or occupational disease covered by the provisions of this title.

3. Whenever volunteer firefighters, volunteer lifesaving or volunteer rescue squad members, volunteer law-enforcement chaplains, auxiliary or reserve police, auxiliary or reserve deputy sheriffs, volunteer emergency medical technicians, members of volunteer search and rescue organizations, volunteer members of community emergency response teams, and volunteer members of medical reserve corps are deemed employees under this title, their average weekly wage shall be deemed sufficient to produce the minimum compensation provided by this title for injured workers or their dependents. For the purposes of workers' compensation insurance premium calculations, the monthly payroll

for each volunteer firefighter or volunteer lifesaving or volunteer rescue squad member shall be deemed to be $300.

4. The average weekly wage of persons, other than those covered in subdivision 3 of this definition, who respond to a hazardous materials incident at the request of the Department of Emergency Management shall be based upon the earnings of such persons from their primary employers.

"Award" means the grant or denial of benefits or other relief under this title or any rule adopted pursuant thereto.

"Change in condition" means a change in physical condition of the employee as well as any change in the conditions under which compensation was awarded, suspended, or terminated which would affect the right to, amount of, or duration of compensation.

"Client company" means any person that enters into an agreement for professional employer services with a professional employer organization.

"Coemployee" means an employee performing services pursuant to an agreement for professional employer services between a client company and a professional employer organization.

"Commission" means the Virginia Workers' Compensation Commission as well as its former designation as the Virginia Industrial Commission.

"Employee" means:

1. a. Every person, including aliens and minors, in the service of another under any contract of hire or apprenticeship, written or implied, whether lawfully or unlawfully employed, except (i) one whose employment is not in the usual course of the trade, business, occupation or profession of the employer or (ii) as otherwise provided in subdivision 2 of this definition.

b. Any apprentice, trainee, or retrainee who is regularly employed while receiving training or instruction outside of regular working hours and off the job, so long as the training or instruction is related to his employment and is authorized by his employer.

c. Members of the Virginia National Guard and the Virginia Naval Militia, whether on duty in a paid or unpaid status or when performing voluntary service to their unit in a nonduty status at the request of their commander.

   Income benefits for members of the National Guard or Naval Militia shall be terminated when they are able to return to their customary civilian employment or self-employment. If they are neither employed nor self-employed, those benefits shall terminate when they are able to return to their military duties. If a member of the National Guard or Naval Militia who is fit to return to his customary civilian employment or self-employment remains unable to perform his military duties and thereby suffers loss of military pay which he would otherwise have earned, he shall be entitled to one day of income benefits for each unit training assembly or day of paid training which he is unable to attend.

d. Members of the Virginia State Defense Force.

e. Registered members of the United States Civil Defense Corps of this Commonwealth, whether on duty or in training.

f. Except as provided in subdivision 2 of this definition, all officers and employees of the Commonwealth, including (i) forest wardens; (ii) judges, clerks, deputy clerks, and employees of juvenile and domestic relations district courts and general district courts; and (iii) secretaries and administrative assistants for officers and members of the General Assembly employed pursuant to §30-19.4 and compensated as provided in the general appropriation act, who shall be deemed employees of the Commonwealth.

g. Except as provided in subdivision 2 of this definition, all officers and employees of a municipal corporation or political subdivision of the Commonwealth.

h. Except as provided in subdivision 2 of this definition, (i) every executive officer, including president, vice-president, secretary, treasurer, or other officer, elected or appointed in accordance with the charter and bylaws of a corporation, municipal or otherwise, and (ii) every manager of a limited liability company elected or appointed in accordance with the articles of organization or operating agreement of the limited liability company.

i. Policemen and firefighters, sheriffs and their deputies, town sergeants and their deputies, county and city commissioners of the revenue, county, and city treasurers, attorneys for the Commonwealth, clerks of circuit courts and their deputies, officers, and employees, and electoral board members appointed in accordance with §24.2-106, who shall be deemed employees of the respective cities, counties, and towns in which their services are employed and by whom their salaries are paid or in which their compensation is earnable.

j. Members of the governing body of any county, city, or town in the Commonwealth, whenever coverage under this title is extended to such members by resolution or ordinance duly adopted.

k. Volunteers, officers, and employees of any commission or board of any authority created or controlled by a local governing body, or any local agency or public service corporation owned, operated, or controlled by such local governing body, whenever coverage under this title is authorized by resolution or ordinance duly adopted by the governing board of any county, city, town, or any political subdivision thereof.

l. Except as provided in subdivision 2 of this definition, volunteer firefighters, volunteer lifesaving or rescue squad members, volunteer law-enforcement chaplains, auxiliary or reserve police, auxiliary or reserve deputy sheriffs, volunteer emergency medical technicians, members of volunteer search and rescue organizations, volunteer members of regional hazardous materials emergency response teams, volunteer members of community emergency response teams, and volunteer members of medical reserve corps, who shall be deemed employees of (i) the political subdivision or state institution of higher education in which the principal office of such volunteer fire company, volunteer lifesaving or rescue squad, volunteer law-enforcement chaplains, auxiliary or reserve police force, auxiliary or reserve deputy sheriff force, volunteer emergency medical technicians, volunteer search and rescue organization, regional hazardous materials emergency response team, community emergency response team, or medical reserve corps is located if the governing body of such political subdivision or state institution of higher education has adopted a resolution acknowledging those persons as employees for the purposes of this title or (ii) in the case of volunteer firefighters or volunteer lifesaving or rescue squad members, the companies or squads for which volunteer services are provided whenever such companies or squads elect to be included as an employer under this title.

m.(1) Volunteer firefighters, volunteer lifesaving or rescue squad members, volunteer law-enforcement chaplains, auxiliary or reserve police, auxiliary or reserve deputy sheriffs, volunteer emergency medical technicians, members of volunteer search and rescue organizations, and any other persons who respond to an incident upon request of the Department of Emergency Management, who shall be deemed employees of the Department of Emergency Management for the purposes of this title.

(2) Volunteer firefighters when engaged in firefighting activities under the supervision and control of the Department of Forestry, who shall be deemed employees of the Department of Forestry for the purposes of this title.

n. Any sole proprietor, shareholder of a stock corporation having only one shareholder, member of a limited liability company having only one member, or all partners of a business electing to be included as an employee under the workers' compensation coverage of such business if the insurer is notified of this election. Any sole proprietor, shareholder or member or the partners shall, upon such election, be entitled to employee benefits and be subject to employee responsibilities prescribed in this title.

When any partner or sole shareholder, member, or proprietor is entitled to receive coverage under this title, such person shall be subject to all provisions of this title as if he were an employee; however, the notices required under §§65.2-405 and 65.2-600 of this title shall be given to the insurance carrier, and the panel of physicians required under §65.2-603 shall be selected by the insurance carrier.

o. The independent contractor of any employer subject to this title at the election of such employer provided (i) the independent contractor agrees to such inclusion and (ii) unless the employer is self-insured, the employer's insurer agrees in writing to such inclusion. All or part of the cost of the insurance coverage of the independent contractor may be borne by the independent contractor.

When any independent contractor is entitled to receive coverage under this section, such person shall be subject to all provisions of this title as if he were an employee, provided that the notices required under §§65.2-405 and 65.2-600 are given either to the employer or its insurance carrier.

However, nothing in this title shall be construed to make the employees of any independent contractor the employees of the person or corporation employing or contracting with such independent contractor.

p. The legal representative, dependents, and any other persons to whom compensation may be payable when any person covered as an employee under this title shall be deceased.

q. Jail officers and jail superintendents employed by regional jails or jail farm boards or authorities, whether created pursuant to Article 3.1 (§53.1-95.2 et seq.) or Article 5 (§53.1-105 et seq.) of Chapter 3 of Title 53.1, or an act of assembly.

r. AmeriCorps members who receive stipends in return for volunteering in local, state, and nonprofit agencies in the Commonwealth, who shall be deemed employees of the Commonwealth for the purposes of this title.

s. Food Stamp recipients participating in the work experience component of the Food Stamp Employment and Training Program, who shall be deemed employees of the Commonwealth for the purposes of this title.

t. Temporary Assistance for Needy Families recipients not eligible for Medicaid participating in the work experience component of the Virginia Initiative for Employment Not Welfare Program, who shall be deemed employees of the Commonwealth for the purposes of this title.

2. "Employee" shall not mean:

a. Officers and employees of the Commonwealth who are elected by the General Assembly, or appointed by the Governor, either with or without the confirmation of the Senate. This exception shall not apply to any "state employee" as defined in §51.1-124.3 nor to Supreme Court Justices, judges of the Court of Appeals, judges of the circuit or district courts, members of the Workers' Compensation Commission and the State Corporation Commission, or the Superintendent of State Police.

b. Officers and employees of municipal corporations and political subdivisions of the Commonwealth who are elected by the people or by the governing bodies, and who act in purely administrative capacities and are to serve for a definite term of office.

c. Any person who is a licensed real estate salesperson, or a licensed real estate broker associated with a real estate broker, if (i) substantially all of the salesperson's or associated broker's remuneration is derived from real estate commissions, (ii) the services of the salesperson or associated broker are performed under a written contract specifying that the salesperson is an independent contractor, and (iii) such contract includes a provision that the salesperson or associated broker will not be treated as an employee for federal income tax purposes.

d. Any taxicab or executive sedan driver, provided the Commission is furnished evidence that such individual is excluded from taxation by the Federal Unemployment Tax Act.

e. Casual employees.

f. Domestic servants.

g. Farm and horticultural laborers, unless the employer regularly has in service more than two full-time employees.

h. Employees of any person, firm, or private corporation, including any public service corporation, that has regularly in service less than three employees in the same business within this Commonwealth, unless such employees and their employers voluntarily elect to be bound by this title. However, this exemption shall not apply to the operators of underground coal mines or their employees. An executive officer who is not paid salary or wages on a regular basis at an agreed upon amount and who rejects coverage under this title pursuant to §65.2-300 shall not be included as an employee for purposes of this subdivision.

i. Employees of any common carrier by railroad engaging in commerce between any of the several states or territories or between the District of Columbia and any of the states or territories and any foreign nation or nations, and any person suffering injury or death while he is employed by such carrier in such commerce. This title shall not be construed to lessen the liability of any such common carrier or to diminish or take away in any respect any right that any person so employed, or the personal representative, kindred or relation, or dependent of such person, may have under the act of Congress relating to the liability of common carriers by railroad to their employees in certain cases, approved April 22, 1908, or under §§8.01-57 through 8.01-62 or §56-441.

j. Employees of common carriers by railroad who are engaged in intrastate trade or commerce. However, this title shall not be construed to lessen the liability of such common carriers or take away or diminish any right that any employee or, in case of his death, the personal representative of such employee of such common carrier may have under §§8.01-57 through 8.01-61 or §56-441.

    k. Except as provided in subdivision 1 of this definition, a member of a volunteer firefighting, lifesaving, or rescue squad when engaged in activities related principally to participation as a member of such squad whether or not the volunteer continues to receive compensation from his employer for time away from the job.

    l. Except as otherwise provided in this title, noncompensated employees and noncompensated directors of corporations exempt from taxation pursuant to §501(c)(3) of Title 26 of the United States Code (Internal Revenue Code of 1954).

    m. Any person performing services as a sports official for an entity sponsoring an interscholastic or intercollegiate sports event or any person performing services as a sports official for a public entity or a private, nonprofit organization which sponsors an amateur sports event. For the purposes of this subdivision, "sports official" includes an umpire, referee, judge, scorekeeper, timekeeper, or other person who is a neutral participant in a sports event. This shall not include any person, otherwise employed by an organization or entity sponsoring a sports event, who performs services as a sports official as part of his regular employment.

"Employer" includes (i) any person, the Commonwealth, or any political subdivision thereof and any individual, firm, association, or corporation, or the receiver or trustee of the same, or the legal representative of a deceased employer, using the service of another for pay and (ii) any volunteer fire company or volunteer lifesaving or rescue squad electing to be included and maintaining coverage as an employer under this title. If the employer is insured, it includes his insurer so far as applicable.

"Executive officer" means (i) the president, vice-president, secretary, treasurer, or other officer, elected or appointed in accordance with the charter and bylaws of a corporation, and (ii) the managers elected or appointed in accordance with the articles of organization or operating agreement of a limited liability company. However, such term does not include noncompensated officers of corporations exempt from taxation pursuant to §501(c)(3) of Title 26 of the United States Code (Internal Revenue Code of 1954).

"Filed" means hand delivered to the Commission's office in Richmond or any regional office maintained by the Commission; sent by telegraph, electronic mail, or facsimile transmission; or posted at any post office of the United States Postal Service by certified or registered mail. Filing by first-class mail, telegraph, electronic mail, or facsimile transmission shall be deemed completed only when the application actually reaches a Commission office.

"Injury" means only injury by accident arising out of and in the course of the employment or occupational disease as defined in Chapter 4 (§65.2-400 et seq.) of this title and does not include a disease in any form, except when it results naturally and unavoidably from either of the foregoing causes. Such term shall not include any injury, disease, or condition resulting from an employee's voluntary:

    1. Participation in employer-sponsored off-duty recreational activities which are not part of the employee's duties; or

    2. Use of a motor vehicle that was provided to the employee by a motor vehicle dealer as defined by §46.2-1500 and bears a dealer's license plate as defined by §46.2-1550 for (i) commuting to or from work or (ii) any other nonwork activity.

Such term shall include any injury, disease, or condition:

1. Arising out of and in the course of the employment of (a) an employee of a hospital as defined in §32.1-123; (b) an employee of a health care provider as defined in §8.01-581.1; (c) an employee of the Department of Health or a local department of health; (d) a member of a search and rescue organization; or (e) any person described in clauses (i) through (iv), (vi), and (ix) of subsection A of §65.2-402.1 otherwise subject to the provisions of this title; and

2. Resulting from (a) the administration of vaccinia (smallpox) vaccine, Cidofivir and derivatives thereof, or Vaccinia Immune Globulin as part of federally initiated smallpox countermeasures, or (b) transmission of vaccinia in the course of employment from an employee participating in such countermeasures to a coemployee of the same employer.

"Professional employer organization" means any person that enters into a written agreement with a client company to provide professional employer services.

"Professional employer services" means services provided to a client company pursuant to a written agreement with a professional employer organization whereby the professional employer organization initially employs all or a majority of a client company's workforce and assumes responsibilities as an employer for all coemployees that are assigned, allocated, or shared by the agreement between the professional employer organization and the client company.

"Staffing service" means any person, other than a professional employer organization, that hires its own employees and assigns them to a client to support or supplement the client's workforce. It includes temporary staffing services that supply employees to clients in special work situations such as employee absences, temporary skill shortages, seasonal workloads, and special assignments and projects.

§65.2-300. Presumption of Acceptance of Provisions of Title; Exemptions; Notice and Rejection

A. Every employer and employee, except as herein stated, shall be conclusively presumed to have accepted the provisions of this title respectively to pay and accept compensation for personal injury or death by accident arising out of and in the course of the employment and shall be bound thereby. Except as otherwise provided herein, no contract or agreement, written or implied, and no rule, regulation or other device shall in any manner operate to relieve any employer in whole or in part of any obligation created by this title.

B. An executive officer may reject coverage under this title for injury or death by accident, but not with respect to occupational disease, if prior to such accident, notice is given to the employer and filed with the Commission in the manner described herein.

The notice shall be in substantially the form prescribed by the Commission and shall be given by the executive officer by sending the same in a registered letter, addressed to the employer at his last known address or place of business, or by giving it personally to the employer or any of his agents upon whom a summons in a civil action may be served under the laws of the Commonwealth. A copy of the notice in prescribed form shall also be filed with the Commission. Such notice shall be effective as of the last to occur of (i) the date of the inception of the policy or (ii) the delivery of such notice to the employer as provided in this subsection.

C. An executive officer who rejects coverage under this title shall, in any action to recover damages for personal injury or death brought against an employer accepting the compensation provisions of this title, proceed at common law, and the employer may avail himself of the defenses of contributory negligence, negligence of a fellow servant and assumption of risk, as such defenses exist at common law.

D. An executive officer who has rejected coverage under this title may nevertheless by notice revoke such rejection and thereby accept coverage under the provisions of this title. A notice revoking such rejection shall be given to the employer and a copy filed with the Commission in the manner provided for rejecting such coverage. Coverage under this title shall not be extended to injuries that occur within five days of the giving of such notice.

§65.2-302. Statutory Employer

A. When any person (referred to in this section as "owner") undertakes to perform or execute any work which is a part of his trade, business or occupation and contracts with any other person (referred to in this section as "subcontractor") for the execution or performance by or under such subcontractor of the whole or any part of the work undertaken by such owner, the owner shall be liable to pay to any worker employed in the work any compensation under this title which he would have been liable to pay if the worker had been immediately employed by him.

B. When any person (referred to in this section as "contractor") contracts to perform or execute any work for another person which work or undertaking is not a part of the trade, business or occupation of such other person and contracts with any other person (referred to in this section as "subcontractor") for the execution or performance by or under the subcontractor of the whole or any part of the work undertaken by such contractor, then the contractor shall be liable to pay to any worker employed in the work any compensation under this title which he would have been liable to pay if that worker had been immediately employed by him.

C. When the subcontractor in turn contracts with still another person (also referred to as "subcontractor") for the performance or execution by or under such last subcontractor of the whole or any part of the work undertaken by the first subcontractor, then the liability of the owner or contractor shall be the same as the liability imposed by subsections A and B of this section.

D. 1. Liability for compensation pursuant to this section may not be imposed against any person who, at the time of an injury sustained by a worker engaged in the maintenance or repair of real property managed by such person, and for which injury compensation is sought:
   a. Was engaged in the business of property management on behalf of the owners of such property and was acting merely as an agent of the owner;
   b. Did not engage in and had no employees engaged in the same trade, business or occupation as the worker seeking compensation; and
   c. Did not seek or obtain from such property's owners, or from any other property owners for whom such person rendered property management services, profit from the services performed by individuals engaged in the same trade, business or occupation as the worker seeking compensation.
   2. For purposes of this subsection, "the business of property management" means the oversight, supervision, and care of real property or improvements to real property, on behalf of such property's owners.
   3. For purposes of this subsection, "property owners" or "property's owners" means (i) owners in fee of such property or (ii) persons having legal entitlement to the use or occupation of such property at the time of the injury for which liability is sought to be imposed pursuant to this section.

§65.2-304. Indemnity of Principal from Subcontractor

When the principal contractor is liable to pay compensation under §65.2-302 or §65.2-303, he shall be entitled to indemnity from any person who would have been liable to pay compensation to the worker independently of such sections or from an intermediate contractor and shall have a cause of action therefor.

A principal contractor when sued by a worker of a subcontractor shall have the right to join that subcontractor or any intermediate contractor as a party.

§65.2-305. Voluntary Subjection to Provisions of Title; Effect of Taking Out Insurance or Qualifying as Self-Insurer

A. Those employers not subject to this title may, by complying with the provisions of this title and the applicable rules of the Commission, voluntarily elect to be bound by it as to accidents or occupational diseases or both.

B. Every employer taking out a workers' compensation insurance policy, or qualifying as a self-insurer, shall be subject to all the provisions of this title, regardless of the number of employees or whether he is an employer of farm and horticultural laborers and domestic servants. Such employers not otherwise covered by this title shall be subject to this title only during the period covered by such insurance. Every employee of an employer who has complied with the foregoing requirements shall be subject to all the provisions of this title except that executive officers may reject coverage as provided in §65.2-300.

§65.2-306. When Compensation Not Allowed for Injury or Death; Burden of Proof

A. No compensation shall be awarded to the employee or his dependents for an injury or death caused by:
   1. The employee's willful misconduct or intentional self-inflicted injury;
   2. The employee's attempt to injure another;
   3. The employee's intoxication;
   4. The employee's willful failure or refusal to use a safety appliance or perform a duty required by statute;
   5. The employee's willful breach of any reasonable rule or regulation adopted by the employer and brought, prior to the accident, to the knowledge of the employee; or
   6. The employee's use of a nonprescribed controlled substance identified as such in Chapter 34 (§54.1-3400 et seq.) of Title 54.1.

B. The person or entity asserting any of the defenses in this section shall have the burden of proof with respect thereto. However, if the employer raises as a defense the employee's intoxication or use of a nonprescribed controlled substance identified as such in Chapter 34 of Title 54.1, and there was at the time of the injury an amount of alcohol or nonprescribed controlled substance in the bodily fluids of the employee which (i) is equal to or greater than the standard set forth in §18.2-266, or (ii) in the case of use of a nonprescribed controlled substance, yields a positive test result from a Substance Abuse and Mental Health Services Administration (SAMHSA) certified laboratory, there shall be a rebuttable presumption, which presumption shall not be available if the employee dies as a result of his injuries, that the employee was intoxicated due to the consumption of alcohol or using a nonprescribed controlled substance at the time of his injury. The employee may overcome such a presumption by clear and convincing evidence.

§65.2-308. Discharge of Employee for Exercising Rights Prohibited; Civil Action; Relief

A. No employer or person shall discharge an employee solely because the employee intends to file or has filed a claim under this title or has testified or is about to testify in any proceeding under this title. The discharge of a person who has filed a fraudulent claim is not a violation of this section.

B. The employee may bring an action in a circuit court having jurisdiction over the employer or person who allegedly discharged the employee in violation of this section. The court shall have jurisdiction, for cause shown, to restrain violations and order appropriate relief, including actual damages and attorney's fees to successful claimants and the rehiring or reinstatement of the employee, with back pay plus interest at the judgment rate as provided in §6.1-330.54.

§65.2-802. Requirements for Licensure as Group Self-Insurance Association; Annual Assessment

A. Two or more employers having a common interest may be licensed by the State Corporation Commission as a group self-insurance association and permitted to enter into agreements to pool their liabilities under this title. The members of any such group self-insurance association may also enter into agreements to pool their liabilities for workers' compensation benefits which may arise under the laws of any other jurisdiction and other types of employers' liabilities for the death or disablement of, or injury to, their employees. Benefits payable by any such association for such members' liabilities under the laws of any other jurisdiction shall extend only to employees otherwise eligible for coverage under the provisions of this title.

B. The State Corporation Commission shall not license a group self-insurance association or grant authorization for an employer to become a member of such group unless it receives in such form as it requires satisfactory proof of the solvency of any such employer, the financial ability of each to meet his obligations as a member, and the ability of the group to pay or cause to be paid the compensation in the amount and manner and when due as provided for in this title and as may be agreed upon with respect to other types of employers' liabilities which may be authorized and provided hereunder.

C. Members of a group shall execute a written agreement under which each agrees to jointly and severally assume and discharge any liability under this title of employers party to such agreement. Agreements among the members shall be subject to approval by the State Corporation Commission; however, no such agreement nor membership in a group self-insurance association shall relieve an employer of the liabilities imposed by this title with respect to his employees. In addition to the rights of the association under such agreements, in the event of failure of the association to enforce such rights after reasonable notice to the association, the State Corporation Commission shall have the right independently to enforce on behalf of the association the joint and several liability of its members under this title and the liability of members for any unpaid contributions and assessments. The State Corporation Commission shall be entitled to recover its expenses and attorneys' fees.

D. Any person, firm, or corporation desiring to engage in the business of providing services for a group self-insurance association shall satisfy the State Corporation Commission of its ability to perform the services necessary to fulfill the employer's obligations under this title before it undertakes to provide such services to any group self-insurance association. The State Corporation Commission may from time to time review and alter any decision approving an employer as a member of a group or its approval of a group or of an agency servicing a group. The State Corporation Commission may in its discretion require the deposit of an acceptable security, indemnity, or bond or the purchase of such excess insurance or the ceding of reinsurance on a specific or aggregate excess of loss basis as may be required by the circumstances.

E. The State Corporation Commission may establish reasonable requirements and standards for the approval of a group self-insurance association and the administration of such associations including, without limitation, the quality, amount and accounting of security deposits, bonds, excess insurance and reinsurance, the membership in any group self-insurance association, the amount of advance payments and reserves required of group self-insurance associations, the investment of such funds, the form and content of financial information to be submitted by a group self-insurance association and the frequency of such submissions, and the terms of agreements between members of a group self-insurance association. The State Corporation Commission may, after notice and hearing, embody such requirements and standards and such other requirements as may be reasonably necessary for the purposes of this section in regulations; however, any group self-insurance association entering into a reinsurance transaction pursuant to the provisions of this section shall be deemed an insurer for purposes of such transaction and shall be subject to Article 3.1 (§38.2-1316.1 et seq.) of Chapter 13 of Title 38.2.

F. Notwithstanding any provision of this title to the contrary, each licensed group self-insurance association shall be assessed annually by the State Corporation Commission in like manner and amount to that provided by Chapter 4 (§38.2-400 et seq.) of Title 38.2 and shall pay such assessment in accordance with the aforesaid provisions of law; however, for the purposes of such assessment "direct gross premium income" of a licensed group self-insurance association shall be the aggregate of the amounts determined to be subject to the tax imposed by §65.2-1006 on each employer member of such association.

G. Notwithstanding the provisions of §49-25, neither the State Corporation Commission nor any other entity or person, as obligee under any surety bond required under this section or any regulation adopted hereunder, shall be required to institute suit against an association as a condition precedent to the surety's performance under the bond.

§65.2-804. Evidence of Compliance with Title; Notices of Cancellation of Insurance

A. 1. Each employer subject to this title shall file with the Workers' Compensation Commission, in form prescribed by it, annually or as often as may be necessary, evidence of his compliance with the provisions of §65.2-801 and all others relating thereto; however, any employer who secures his liability under this title pursuant to subdivision A 1 of §65.2-801 may have his insurance carrier make such filing. Evidence of an employer's compliance with the provisions of subdivision A 1 of §65.2-801 shall be deemed to satisfy such provisions if it includes the name and address of the insured, the insured's federal employer identification number, his policy number, dates of insurance coverage, the name and address of his insurer, and the insurer's identification number. Proof of coverage information filed with the Commission by an insurance carrier or rate service organization on behalf of an employer shall in no event be aggregated by the Commission with the proof of coverage information filed by or on behalf of other employers. Every employer who has complied with the foregoing provision and has subsequently cancelled his insurance or his membership in a licensed group self-insurance association shall immediately notify the Workers' Compensation Commission of such cancellation, the date thereof and the reasons therefor. Every insurance carrier or group self-insurance association shall in like manner notify the Workers' Compensation Commission immediately upon the cancellation of any policy issued by it or any membership agreement, whichever is applicable, under the provisions of this title, except that a carrier or group self-insurance association need not set forth its reasons for cancellation unless requested by the Workers' Compensation Commission.

2. Every employer who cancels his insurance or his membership in a licensed group self-insurance association shall, prior to canceling his insurance or his membership, give thirty days' written notice to his employees covered. Every employer who receives the notice required under subsection B of this section shall immediately forward a copy to his employees covered. Where the employer is a mine owner or operator, the notice or copy of notice required to be given by this subsection shall also be given to the Chief Mine Inspector. The provisions of this subsection shall not apply with respect to a cancellation incident to a change of insurance or membership where no lapse of coverage occurs.

B. No policy of insurance hereafter issued under the provisions of this title, nor any membership agreement in a group self-insurance association, shall be cancelled or nonrenewed by the insurer issuing such policy or by the group self-insurance association canceling or nonrenewing such membership, except on thirty days' notice to the employer and the Workers' Compensation Commission, unless the employer has obtained other insurance and the Workers' Compensation Commission is notified of that fact by the insurer assuming the risk, or unless, in the event of cancellation, said cancellation is for nonpayment of premiums; then ten days' notice shall be given the employer and the Workers' Compensation Commission.

§65.2-805. Civil Penalty for Violation of §65.2-804

A. If such employer fails to comply with the provisions of §65.2-804, he shall be assessed a civil penalty of not less than $500 nor more than $5,000, and he shall be liable during continuance of such failure to any employee either for compensation under this title or at law in a suit instituted by the employee against such employer to recover damages for personal injury or death by accident, and in any such suit such employer shall not be permitted to defend upon any of the following grounds:
1. That the employee was negligent;
2. That the injury was caused by the negligence of a fellow employee; or
3. That the employee had assumed the risk of the injury.

B. The civil penalty herein provided may be assessed by the Commission in an open hearing with the right of review and appeal as in other cases. Upon a finding by the Commission of such failure to comply, and after fifteen days' written notice thereof sent by certified mail to the employer, if such failure continues, the Commission may order the employer to cease and desist all business transactions and operations until found by the Commission to be in compliance with the provisions of this chapter.

C. Any civil penalty assessed pursuant to this section shall be paid into the Uninsured Employer's Fund established in Chapter 12 (§65.2-1200 et seq.) of this title.

§65.2-806. Criminal Penalties

In addition to the fine assessed pursuant to §65.2-805, any employer who knowingly and intentionally fails to comply with the provisions of §65.2-804 shall be guilty of a Class 2 misdemeanor.

Venue for the prosecution hereof when there is an injury shall lie in the county or city wherein the injury occurred.

§65.2-807. Cost of Insurance May Not Be Deducted From Wages

It shall not be lawful for any employer to deduct from the wages of any of his employees any part of the cost of insurance as provided for in §65.2-801 to insure liability, or to require or permit any of his employees to contribute in any manner toward such cost of insurance. For any violation of the provisions of this section, an employer shall be subject to a fine not exceeding $100 for each offense and shall refund to the individual employee the amount or amounts deducted or contributed. The fine herein provided may be assessed and the refund ordered by the Workers' Compensation Commission in an open hearing with the right of review and appeal as in other cases.

CODE OF VIRGINIA
TITLE 60.2 UNEMPLOYMENT COMPENSATION

§60.2-114. Records and Reports

A. Each employing unit shall keep true and accurate work records, containing such information as the Commission may prescribe. Such records shall be open to inspection and be subject to being copied by the Commission or its authorized representatives at any reasonable time and as often as may be necessary. The Commission may require from any employing unit any sworn or unsworn reports, with respect to persons employed by it, which the Commission deems necessary for the effective administration of this title. Information thus obtained shall not be published or be open to public inspection, other than to public employees in the performance of their public duties, in any manner revealing the employing unit's identity, except as the Commissioner or his delegates deem appropriate, nor shall such information be used in any judicial or administrative proceeding other than one arising out of the provisions of this title; however, the Commission shall make its records about a claimant available to the Workers' Compensation Commission if it requests such records. However, any claimant at a hearing before an appeal tribunal or the Commission shall be supplied with information from such records to the extent necessary for the proper presentation of his claim. Notwithstanding other provisions of this section, the Commissioner, or his delegate, may, in his discretion, reveal information when such communication is not inconsistent with the proper administration of this title.

B. Notwithstanding the provisions of subsection A, the Commission shall, on a reimbursable basis, furnish wage and unemployment compensation information contained in its records to the Secretary of Health and Human Services and the Division of Child Support Enforcement of the Department of Social Services for their use as necessary for the purposes of the National Directory of New Hires established under §453 (i) of the Social Security Act.

C. Notwithstanding the provisions of subsection A, the Commission shall, upon written request, furnish any agency or political subdivision of the Commonwealth, or its designated agent, such information as it may require for the purpose of collecting fines, penalties, and costs owed to the Commonwealth or its political subdivisions. Such information shall not be published or used in any administrative or judicial proceeding, except in matters arising out of the collection of fines, penalties, and costs owed to the Commonwealth or its political subdivisions.

D. Each employing unit shall report only to the Virginia New Hire Reporting Center the initial employment of any person, as defined in §60.2-212 in compliance with §63.2-1946.

E. Any member or employee of the Commission and any member, employee or agent of any agency or political subdivision of the Commonwealth who violates any provision of this section shall be guilty of a Class 2 misdemeanor.

§60.2-210. Employer

A. The term "employer" means any employing unit which:
1. In any calendar quarter in either the current or preceding calendar year paid for some service in employment wages of $1,500 or more or such other amount as provided by federal law pursuant to 26 U.S.C. §3306; or
2. For some portion of a day in each of twenty different weeks, whether or not such weeks were consecutive, in either the current or the preceding calen-

dar year, has or had in its employment at least one individual, irrespective of whether the same individual was in employment in each such day.

B. The term "employer" shall also mean:

1. Any employing unit which acquired the organization, trade, separate establishment or business or substantially all the assets thereof, of another which at the time of such acquisition was an employer subject to this title;

2. Any employing unit which acquired the organization, trade or business or substantially all the assets thereof, of another employing unit and which, if treated as a single unit with such other employing unit, would be an employer under subsection A of this section;

3. Any employing unit which together with one or more other employing units, is owned or controlled, by legally enforceable means or otherwise, directly or indirectly by the same interests, or which owns or controls one or more other employing units, by legally enforceable means or otherwise, and which if treated as a single unit with such other employing unit, would be an employer under subsection A or B of this section;

4. Any employing unit which having become an employer under subsection A of this section or subdivisions 1, 2, 3, 6, 7 or 8 of this subsection has not, under §60.2-509, ceased to be an employer subject to this title;

5. For the effective period of its election pursuant to §60.2-510, any other employing unit which has elected to become fully subject to this title;

6. Any employing unit not an employer by reason of any other subdivision of this section (i) for which, within either the current or preceding calendar year, service is or was performed with respect to which such employing unit is liable for any federal tax against which credit may be taken for taxes required to be paid into a state unemployment fund; or (ii) which, as a condition for approval of this title for full tax credit against the tax imposed by the Federal Unemployment Tax Act, is required, pursuant to such act, to be an "employer" under this title;

7. Any employing unit for which service in employment, as defined in subdivisions 1 through 3 of subsection A of §60.2-213, is performed;

8. Any employing unit, for which service in employment, as defined in subdivision 4 of subsection A of §60.2-213, is performed;

9. For the purposes of subdivision 2 of subsection A of this section and subdivisions 8 and 10 of this subsection if any week includes both December 31 and January 1, the days of that week up to January 1 shall be deemed one calendar week and the days beginning January 1 another such week;

10. Any employing unit for which agricultural labor in employment as defined in §60.2-214 is performed; or

11. Any employing unit for which domestic service in employment as defined in §60.2-215 is performed.

C. 1. In determining whether an employing unit for which service other than domestic service is also performed is an employer under subsection A or subdivision 10 of subsection B of this section, the wages earned or the employment of an employee performing domestic service shall not be taken into account.

2. In determining whether an employing unit for which service other than agricultural labor is also performed is an employer under subsection A or subdivision 11 of subsection B of this section, the wages earned or the employment of an employee performing service in agricultural labor shall not be taken into account. If an employing unit is determined an employer of agricultural labor, such employing unit shall be determined an employer for the purpose of subsection A of this section.

§60.2-607. Maximum Total Benefit Amounts

The maximum total amount of benefits payable to any individual during any benefit year shall be determined from the "Benefit Table" shown in §60.2-602 but shall not exceed twenty-six times such individual's weekly benefit amount, except when benefits are paid pursuant to the provisions of §60.2-610 or §60.2-611. Such determination shall be based only upon wages paid for insured work during such individual's base period. The Commission shall maintain a separate account for each individual who is paid wages for insured work. After the expiration of each calendar quarter the Commission shall credit each individual's account with the wages paid to him for insured work in such calendar quarter.

VIRGINIA EMPLOYMENT COMMISSION

16VAC5-32-10. Employing Unit Records

A. Each employing unit as defined under §60.2-211 of the Code of Virginia, having services performed for it by one or more individuals in its employ, shall maintain records reasonably protected against damage or loss as hereinafter indicated and shall preserve such records. These records shall include for each worker:

1. A full legal name;
2. A Social Security account number;
3. The state or states in which his services are performed; and if any of such services are performed outside the Commonwealth of Virginia not incidental to the services within the Commonwealth of Virginia, his base of operations with respect to such services (or if there is no base of operations then the place from which such services are directed or controlled), and his residence (by state). Where the services are performed outside the United States, the country in which performed;
4. The date of hire, rehire, or return to work after temporary layoff;
5. The date when work ceased and the reason for such cessation;
6. Scheduled hours (except for workers without a fixed schedule of hours, such as those working outside their employer's establishment in such a manner that the employer has no record or definite knowledge of their working hours);
7. a. Wages earned in any week by a partially employed individual as such individual is defined in 16VAC5-10-10;
    b. Whether any week was in fact a week of less than full-time work;
    c. Time lost, if any, by each such worker, and the reason therefor;
8. Total wages in each pay period, and the total wages payable for all pay periods ending in each quarter, showing separately (i) money wages, including tips and dismissal or severance pay, and (ii) the cash value of other remuneration;
9. Any special payments for service other than those rendered exclusively in a given quarter, such as annual bonuses, gifts, prizes, etc., showing separately (i) money payments, (ii) other remuneration, and (iii) nature of said payments;
10. Amounts paid each worker as advancement, allowance or reimbursement for traveling or other business expenses, dates of payment, and the amounts of expenditures actually incurred and accounted for by such worker;
11. Location in which the worker's services are performed within or outside of the United States and dates such services are performed outside of the United States. For the purposes of this subdivision, "United States" means the 50 states, the District of Columbia, the Commonwealth of Puerto Rico, and the U.S. Virgin Islands.

B. Employers shall provide the Commission upon request all payroll records, federal W2 and 1099 forms, federal and state employment and income tax returns, and any other records that would be relevant to ensuring that wages had been accurately reported and taxes or refunds correctly computed and paid. Records required by this chapter to be maintained by employing units under the Act shall be preserved for four years from the date of payment of the tax based thereon and shall be subject to examination and audit by the Commission.

C. If such records are not maintained, there shall be a presumption in favor of the party making an allegation, and the burden of overcoming such presumption shall rest upon the party failing to maintain the required records.

CODE OF VIRGINIA (COV)
TITLE 40.1 LABOR AND EMPLOYMENT

§40.1-28.1. Employers to Allow Employees At Least One Day of Rest in Each Week

Except in an emergency, every employer shall allow each person employed by him in connection with any business or service at least twenty-four consecutive hours of rest in each calendar week in addition to the regular periods of rest normally allowed or legally required in each working day.

§40.1-29. Time and medium of payment; withholding wages; written statement of earnings; agreement for forfeiture of wages; proceedings to enforce compliance; penalties.

A. 1. All employers operating a business shall establish regular pay periods and rates of pay for employees except executive personnel. All such employers shall pay salaried employees at least once each month and employees paid on an hourly rate at least once every two weeks or twice in each month, except that (i) a student who is currently enrolled in a work-study program or its equivalent administered by any secondary school, institution of higher education or trade school, and (ii) employees whose weekly wages total more than 150 percent of the average weekly wage of the Commonwealth as defined in §65.2-500, upon agreement by each affected employee, may be paid once each month if the institution or employer so chooses. Upon termination of employment an employee shall be paid all wages or salaries due him for work performed prior thereto; such payment shall be made on or before the date on which he would have been paid for such work had his employment not been terminated.

2. Any such employer who knowingly fails to make payment of wages in accordance with this section shall be subject to a civil penalty not to exceed $1,000 for each violation. The Commissioner shall notify any employer who he alleges has violated any provision of this section by certified mail. Such notice shall contain a description of the alleged violation. Within 15 days of receipt of notice of the alleged violation, the employer may request an informal conference regarding such violation with the Commissioner. In determining the amount of any penalty to be imposed, the Commissioner shall consider the size of the business of the employer charged and the gravity of the violation. The decision of the Commissioner shall be final.

B. Payment of wages or salaries shall be (i) in lawful money of the United States, (ii) by check payable at face value upon demand in lawful money of the United States, (iii) by electronic automated fund transfer in lawful money of the United States into an account in the name of the employee at a financial institution designated by the employee, or (iv) by credit to a prepaid debit card or card account from which the employee is able to withdraw or transfer funds with full disclosure by the employer of any applicable fees and affirmative consent thereto by the employee.

Failure of the employee to designate a financial institution or consent to payment by credit to a prepaid debit card or card account under clause (iii) or clause (iv) shall require payment of wages and salaries to be made in accordance with clause (i) or clause (ii) of this subsection. However, payment may be made under clause (iv) to an employee who has not affirmatively consented thereto if (a) payment cannot be made under clause (iii) because the employee has failed to designate a financial institution and (b) the employee is employed at any facility where the operation of amusement devices is authorized pursuant to a certificate of inspection issued under § 36-98.3 and any regulations promulgated thereunder.

C. No employer shall withhold any part of the wages or salaries of any employee except for payroll, wage or withholding taxes or in accordance with law, without the written and signed authorization of the employee. An employer, upon request of his employee, shall furnish the latter a written statement of the gross wages earned by the employee during any pay period and the amount and purpose of any deductions therefrom.

D. No employer shall require any employee, except executive personnel, to sign any contract or agreement which provides for the forfeiture of the employee's wages for time worked as a condition of employment or the continuance therein, except as otherwise provided by law.

E. An employer who willfully and with intent to defraud fails or refuses to pay wages in accordance with this section is guilty of a Class 1 misdemeanor if the value of the wages earned and not paid by the employer is less than $10,000 and is guilty of a Class 6 felony if the value of the wages earned and not paid is $10,000 or more or, regardless of the value of the wages earned and not paid, if the conviction is a second or subsequent conviction under this section. For purposes of this section, the determination as to the "value of the wages earned" shall be made by combining all wages the employer failed or refused to pay pursuant to this section.

F. The Commissioner may require a written complaint of the violation of this section and, with the written and signed consent of an employee, may institute proceedings on behalf of an employee to enforce compliance with this section, and to collect any moneys unlawfully withheld from such employee which shall be paid to the employee entitled thereto. In addition, following the issuance of a final order by the Commissioner or a court, the Commissioner may engage private counsel, approved by the Attorney General, to collect any moneys owed to the employee or the Commonwealth. Upon entry of a final order of the Commissioner, or upon entry of a judgment, against the employer, the Commissioner or the court shall assess attorney's fees of one-third of the amount set forth in the final order or judgment.

G. In addition to being subject to any other penalty provided by the provisions of this section, any employer who fails to make payment of wages in accordance with subsection A shall be liable for the payment of all wages due, plus interest at an annual rate of eight percent accruing from the date the wages were due.

H. Civil penalties owed under this section shall be paid to the Commissioner for deposit into the general fund of the State Treasurer. The Commissioner shall prescribe procedures for the payment of proposed assessments of penalties which are not contested by employers. Such procedures shall include provisions for an employer to consent to abatement of the alleged violation and pay a proposed penalty or a negotiated sum in lieu of such penalty without admission of any civil liability arising from such alleged violation.

Final orders of the Commissioner, the general district courts or the circuit courts may be recorded, enforced and satisfied as orders or decrees of a circuit court upon certification of such orders by the Commissioner or the court as appropriate.

§40.1-51.2:2. Remedy for Discrimination

A. Any employee who believes that he or she has been discharged or otherwise discriminated against by any person in violation of §40.1-51.2:1 may, within sixty days after such violation occurs, file a complaint with the Commissioner alleging such discharge or discrimination. Upon receipt of such complaint, the Commissioner shall cause such investigation to be made as he deems appropriate. If, upon such investigation, he determines that the provisions of §40.1-51.2:1 have been violated, he shall attempt by conciliation to have the violation abated without economic loss to the employee. In the event a voluntary agreement cannot be obtained, the Commissioner shall bring an action in a circuit court having jurisdiction over the person charged with the violation. The court shall have jurisdiction, for cause shown, to restrain violations and order appropriate relief, including rehiring or reinstatement of the employee to his former position with back pay plus interest at a rate not to exceed eight percent per annum.

B. Should the Commissioner, based on the results of his investigation of the complaint, refuse to issue a charge against the person that allegedly discriminated against the employee, the employee may bring action in a circuit court having jurisdiction over the person allegedly discriminating against the employee, for appropriate relief.

§40.1-58. Policy of article.

It is hereby declared to be the public policy of Virginia that the right of persons to work shall not be denied or abridged on account of membership or nonmembership in any labor union or labor organization.

§40.1-58.1. Application of article to public employers and employees.

As used in this article, the words, "person," "persons," "employer," "employees," "union," "labor union," "association," "organization" and "corporation" shall include but not be limited to public employers, public employees and any representative of public employees in this Commonwealth. The application of this article to public employers, public employees and their representatives shall not be construed as modifying in any way the application of §40.1-55 to government employees.

§40.1-59. Agreements or combinations declared unlawful.

Any agreement or combination between any employer and any labor union or labor organization whereby persons not members of such union or organization shall be denied the right to work for the employer, or whereby such membership is made a condition of employment or continuation of employment by such employer, or whereby any such union or organization acquires an employment monopoly in any enterprise, is hereby declared to be against public policy and an illegal combination or conspiracy.

§40.1-60. Employers not to require employees to become or remain members of union.

No person shall be required by an employer to become or remain a member of any labor union or labor organization as a condition of employment or continuation of employment by such employer.

§40.1-61. Employers not to require abstention from membership or officeholding in union.

No person shall be required by an employer to abstain or refrain from membership in, or holding office in, any labor union or labor organization as a condition of employment or continuation of employment.

§40.1-62. Employer not to require payment of union dues, etc.

No employer shall require any person, as a condition of employment or continuation of employment, to pay any dues, fees or other charges of any kind to any labor union or labor organization.

§40.1-63. Recovery by individual unlawfully denied employment.

Any person who may be denied employment or be deprived of continuation of his employment in violation of §§40.1-60, 40.1-61 or § 40.1-62 or of one or more of such sections, shall be entitled to recover from such employer and from any other person, firm, corporation or association acting in concert with him by appropriate action in the courts of this Commonwealth such damages as he may have sustained by reason of such denial or deprivation of employment.

§40.1-64. Application of article to contracts.

The provisions of this article shall not apply to any lawful contract in force on April 30, 1947, but they shall apply in all respects to contracts entered into thereafter and to any renewal or extension of an existing contract.

§40.1-65. Agreement or practice designed to cause employer to violate article declared illegal.

Any agreement, understanding or practice which is designated to cause or require any employer, whether or not a party thereto, to violate any provision of this article is hereby declared to be an illegal agreement, understanding or practice and contrary to public policy.

§40.1-66. Conduct causing violation of article illegal; peaceful solicitation to join union.

Any person, firm, association, corporation, or labor union or organization engaged in lockouts, layoffs, boycotts, picketing, work stoppages or other conduct, a purpose of which is to cause, force, persuade or induce any other person, firm, association, corporation or labor union or organization to violate any provision of this article shall be guilty of illegal conduct contrary to public policy; provided that nothing herein contained shall be construed to prevent or make illegal the peaceful and orderly solicitation and persuasion by union members of others to join a union, unaccompanied by any intimidation, use of force, threat of use of force, reprisal or threat of reprisal, and provided that no such solicitation or persuasion shall be conducted so as to interfere with, or interrupt the work of any employee during working hours.

§40.1-67. Injunctive relief against violation; recovery of damages.

Any employer, person, firm, association, corporation, labor union or organization injured as a result of any violation or threatened violation of any provision of this article or threatened with any such violation shall be entitled to injunctive relief against any and all violators or persons threatening violation, and also to recover from such violator or violators, or person or persons, any and all damages of any character cognizable at common law resulting from such violations or threatened violations. Such remedies shall be independent of and in addition to the penalties and remedies prescribed in other provisions of this article.

§40.1-68. Service of process on clerk of State Corporation Commission as attorney for union.

Any labor union or labor organization doing business in this Commonwealth, all of whose officers and trustees are nonresidents of this Commonwealth, shall by written power of attorney, filed with the Department of Labor and Industry and the State Corporation Commission, appoint the clerk of the State Corporation Commission its attorney or agent upon whom all legal process against the union or organization may be served, and who shall be authorized to enter an appearance on its behalf. The manner of service of process on the clerk of the State Corporation Commission, the mailing thereof to the labor union or organization, the fees therefor, the effect of judgments, decrees and orders, and the procedure in cases where no power of attorney is filed as required, shall be the same as provided for in cases of foreign corporations.

§40.1-69. Violation a misdemeanor.
Any violation of any of the provisions of this article by any person, firm, association, corporation, or labor union or organization shall be a misdemeanor.

§40.1-78. Employment of Children under Fourteen and Sixteen
A. No child under fourteen years of age shall be employed, permitted or suffered to work in, about or in connection with any gainful occupation except as specified in this chapter.

B. No child under sixteen years of age shall be employed, permitted or suffered to work in, about or in connection with any gainful occupation during school hours unless he has reached the age of fourteen and is enrolled in a regular school work-training program and a work-training certificate has been issued for his employment as provided in §40.1-88.

§40.1-113. Child Labor Offenses; Civil Penalties
A. Whoever employs, procures, or, having under his control, permits a child to be employed, or issues an employment certificate in violation of any of the provisions of this chapter other than §§40.1-100.2, 40.1-103 and 40.1-112, shall be subject to a civil penalty not to exceed $1,000 for each violation. In determining the amount of such penalty, the appropriateness of such penalty to the size of the business of the person charged and the gravity of the violation shall be considered. The determination by the Commissioner shall be final, unless within fifteen days after receipt of such notice the person charged with the violation notifies the Commissioner by certified mail that he intends to contest the proposed penalty before the appropriate general district court.

B. Civil penalties owed under this section shall be paid to the Commissioner for deposit into the general fund of the treasury of the Commonwealth. The Commissioner shall prescribe procedures for the payment of proposed penalties which are not contested by employers.

FREQUENTLY ASKED QUESTIONS

Virginia Labor & Employment Law

1. **If an employee believes he has been terminated unfairly, does he have a legal right to challenge the termination?**

   Virginia is an employment-at-will state; this means the employer may terminate any employee at any time, for any reason, or for no reason. As a general rule, therefore, the employee has no right to challenge the termination. There are a few very limited exceptions. For example, an employee may not be discriminated against or terminated because he has filed a safety complaint or exercised his rights under OSHA law. Virginia Code § 40.1-51.2:1. Also, federal law protects employees from discrimination because of age, race, sex, religion, national origin or handicap.

2. **Who handles discrimination questions?**

   If the employee believes he has been discriminated against because of his age, race, sex, religion, national origin or disability, he may be protected by federal discrimination laws, and a complaint may be filed with 1) the Virginia Council on Human Rights, Suite 1202, Washington Building, 1100 Bank Street, Richmond, Virginia 23219, phone (804) 225-2292; or the federal Equal Employment Opportunity Commission, 830 E. Main Street, Suite 600, Richmond, Virginia 23219; phone (804) 771-2200.

3. **Does an employer have to provide employees breaks or a meal period?**

   No, unless the employee is under the age of 16.

4. **Are there any restrictions as to how many hours an employee can be required to work or when he may work?**

   No, not after an employee attains his 16th birthday.

5. **Who handles unemployment compensation questions?**

   The Virginia Employment Commission; contact the closest regional office, or the Richmond Central Office, 703 East Main Street, Richmond, Virginia 23219, phone (804) 786-3004.

6. **Who handles workers' compensation questions?**

   The Virginia Workers' Compensation Commission; contact the closest regional office, or the Richmond Central office, 1000 DMV Drive, Richmond, Virginia 23220, phone (804) 367-8600.

7. **Who handles overtime issues?**

   The United States Department of Labor; Wage and Hour Division, 400 North 8th Street, Richmond, Virginia, 23240, phone (804) 771-2995.

8. **What is the overtime law, and who enforces it?**

   Generally, time-and-a-half must be paid for all hours over 40 hours a week, but there are exceptions. Time-and-a-half for overtime is required not by state law, but by the federal Fair Labor Standards Act, enforced by the United States Department of Labor, Wage and Hour Division. Overtime claims should be made directly to the federal Wage and Hour Division at the closest regional office, or at the Richmond District Office. You may also contact the United States Department of Labor at 1-866-4-US-WAGE.

9. **Must an employer provide or pay for an employee for vacation, holiday, sick, or severance pay?**

   The law does not require any employer to provide fringe benefits of any kind, such as vacation, holiday, sick pay, severance pay, and retirement benefits.

If the employer agrees to provide such benefits, and the employee performs work in reliance on that promise, the employee may be entitled to the benefits as a matter of contract law, and may file a private lawsuit in court to require the employer to give benefits. DOLI cannot assist with these claims.

10. **What deductions can be made from an employee's wages?**
    The only deductions allowed are 1) payroll, wage or withholding taxes, and deductions otherwise authorized by law, and 2) those amounts authorized to be deducted by written and signed authorization of the employee. The authorization must be truly voluntary and not signed as a condition of employment. Virginia Code §40.1-29(C).

11. **Can an employer legally deduct from an employee's wages money to cover damaged equipment or cash register shortages if the employee does not provide a truly voluntary written and signed consent?**
    No. The Code prohibits an employer from requiring an employee to sign any contract or agreement which provides for the forfeiture of the employee's wages. Virginia Code §40.1-29(D).

12. **Can an employer be fined for a violation of the payment of wage law?**
    A civil monetary penalty up to $1,000.00 per violation may be assessed. Each failure to pay properly each employee for each pay period is considered to be a separate violation. A willful violation, or a violation with intent to defraud, constitutes a crime punishable by jail and a fine up to $2,500.00. In addition to being subject to civil monetary penalties and criminal prosecution, any employer who fails to make payment of wages in accordance with the payment of wage law shall be liable for the payment of all wages due plus interest at an annual rate of 8% accruing from the date the wages were due. Virginia Code §40.1-29.

**VIRGINIA ADMINISTRATIVE CODE
AGENCY 15, DEPT. OF LABOR AND INDUSTRY**

16VAC15-50-20. Hazardous Occupations

This section identifies the occupations on farms, in gardens, and in orchards which are particularly hazardous for minors under 16 years of age. No employer shall employ, suffer, or permit a minor under 16 years of age to work in any of the following occupations, deemed to be particularly hazardous, except as provided in 16VAC15-50-30:

1. Operating a tractor of over 20 PTO horsepower, or connecting or disconnecting an implement or any of its parts to or from such a tractor.
2. Operating or assisting to operate (including starting, stopping, adjusting, feeding, or any other activity involving physical contact associated with the operation) any of the following machines:
   a. Corn picker, cotton picker, grain combine, hay mower, forage harvester, hay baler, potato digger, or mobile pea viner;
   b. Feed grinder, crop dryer, forage blower, auger conveyor, or the unloading mechanism of a nongravity-type self-unloading wagon or trailer; or
   c. Power post-hole digger, power post driver, or nonwalking-type rotary tiller.
3. Operating or assisting to operate (including starting, stopping, adjusting, feeding, or any other activity involving physical contact associated with the operation) any of the following machines:
   a. Earthmoving equipment;
   b. Fork lift;
   c. Potato combine; or
   d. Chain saw.
4. Working on a farm in a yard, pen, or stall occupied by:
   a. A bull, boar, or stud horse maintained for breeding purposes; or
   b. A sow with suckling pigs, or cow with newborn calf (with umbilical cord present).
5. Working from a ladder at a height of over 20 feet for purposes such as pruning trees, picking fruit, etc.
6. Driving a bus, truck, or automobile when transporting passengers, or riding on a tractor as a passenger or helper.
7. Working inside:
   a. A fruit, forage, or grain storage designed to retain an oxygen deficient or toxic atmosphere;
   b. An upright silo within two weeks after silage has been added or when a top unloading device is in operating position;
   c. A manure pit; or
   d. A horizontal silo while operating a tractor for packing purposes.
8. Handling or applying (including cleaning or decontaminating equipment, disposal or return of empty containers, or serving as a flagman for aircraft applying) agricultural chemicals classified under the Federal Insecticide, Fungicide, and Rodenticide Act (7 USC §135 et seq.) as Category I of toxicity, identified by the word "poison" and the "skull and crossbones" on the label; or Category II of toxicity, identified by the word "warning" on the label;
9. Handling or using a blasting agent including, but not limited to, dynamite, black powder, sensitized ammonium nitrate, blasting caps, and primer cord; or
10. Transporting, transferring, or applying anhydrous ammonia.

CHAPTER 7

VIRGINIA TAXES

This chapter outlines the responsibilities an employer incurs when paying wages. It also covers each business entity's filing and reporting responsibilities. Any company that pays wages to at least one employee is responsible for payroll taxes and withholding taxes. Corporations, other than subchapter S corporations, pay taxes on income.

Virginia's state taxes include the corporate income tax and the sales and use tax. Virginia's tax structure requires that all companies, both foreign and domestic, pay the same types of taxes. Percentage rates may vary depending on whether a company is domestic or foreign. Sales and use tax are taxed at the state level and not at the local level. Real estate tax, machinery and tools tax, and tangible personal property tax are taxed at the local level.

Virginia differs from most states in that its counties and cities are separate taxing entities. A company pays either county or city taxes depending on its location. If it is located within the corporate limits of a town, it is subject to town taxes in addition to county levies.

Information about Virginia's local taxes can be found in *A Virginia Guide: Local Taxes on Business,* which is available at *www.YesVirginia.org* or at *www.tax.virginia.gov/.* See the Appendix for additional tax information.

PAYROLL TAXES

Payroll taxes are calculated on an employee's earnings and are deducted directly from the employee's paycheck. Tax deductions are made from employee's wages for FICA, Medicare, and personal income taxes. The employer is required to pay Virginia Unemployment Tax (2.92 percent to 6.2 percent of the first $8,000 of earnings) on behalf of the employee and to match deductions made for FICA and Medicare. Virginia accepts electronic filing of tax returns. Payroll tax records must be kept for at least 3 years.

Virginia Income Tax Withholding

Virginia income tax withholding is based on Form VA-4, Virginia Employee's Income Tax Withholding Exemption Certificate. Each employee *must* furnish this certificate at the time of hiring. If a Form W-4 is not available in time for the employee's first wage payment, exemptions are calculated as if the employee were single with no allowances.

An employer who furnishes 250 or more wage statements (W-2s) to the Virginia Department of Taxation is required to submit the W-2s by magnetic media. Employers with 100 or more employees are required to file via magnetic media. Payments of Virginia taxes may be made electronically. Virginia requires employers to file a Form VA-6 by January 31. Form VA-6 is a summary of all taxes withheld by the employer.

A new employer is asked to estimate the amount of tax liability the company will be responsible for each month. If this estimate is less than $100 per month, the Department of Taxation assigns a quarterly payment schedule. If the liability ranges from $101 to $1,000 per month, a monthly filing status is assigned. Companies with more than a $1,000 monthly liability are assigned a semiweekly payment schedule. (See Table 7.1.)

Virginia Unemployment Tax

A Virginia unemployment tax payment is required if a company is liable under federal law. Self-employed individuals and partners in a partnership are exempt from the Virginia unemployment tax. Unemployment tax is charged against the first $8,000 in earnings for each employee each calendar year. The unemployment tax payment is assessed at a variable rate depending on several factors, including:

- the total amount of unemployment paid out;

- the trust fund balance;

- a pool charge to compensate for charges that cannot be assigned to any Virginia employer; and

- a fund building charge when the fund drops below 50 percent of solvency.

New employers are taxed at 2.92 percent (plus any special charges) for at least a 12-month period ending June 30. They are then charged the computed rate starting the following January 1. The computed tax rate may vary from 0 percent to 6.2 percent.

Foreign corporations are typically charged 6.2 percent.

Excerpts from the Virginia Employment Commission (VEC) employer handbook providing more details of this tax and its administration are included in Chapter 7 of the *Contractor's Business Reference Manual* by Kaplan AEC.

Penalties

Failure to make tax deposits or file required information for Virginia taxes incurs penalties. Established penalties are shown in Table 7-2.

TABLE 7.1
Tax Liability Payment Schedule

Monthly Withholding Liability	Payment Schedule
Less than $100	Quarterly
$101 to $1,000	Monthly
Over $1,000	Semi-Weekly

TABLE 7.2

Virginia Tax Penalties

Late Filing Withholding Tax	6% Per Month Past Due
Late Payment of Tax	6% Per Month Past Due
Minimum Penalty	$10
Maximum Penalty	30% of Tax Due

CORPORATE TAXES

Corporate Income Tax

All corporations registered with the State Corporation Commission must file a corporate income tax return with the Virginia Department of Taxation. The corporate income tax rate is 6 percent of a company's federal taxable income. Federal income tax is not deductible in Virginia. Virginia accepts the federal Modified Accelerated Cost Recovery System (MACRS) for depreciation.

If the corporation has multistate activities and its income is taxable by both Virginia and other states, Virginia allows the corporation to allocate and apportion income among Virginia and other states.

TAX CREDITS

Enterprise Zone Tax Credits

Virginia's enterprise zone program offers several special state tax incentives for qualified businesses locating or expanding in an enterprise zone. These tax incentives are the general tax credit and the refundable real property improvement tax credit.

General Tax Credit. New and existing companies investing up to $15 million and creating up to 50 jobs over a 30-month period may receive a ten-year general income tax credit (80 percent the first year and 60 percent in years two through ten). To qualify for this credit, 25 percent of a business' new, full-time employees must meet low-income standards for the area or reside within an enterprise zone. Existing businesses, businesses already located in an enterprise zone when designated, and businesses relocating to a zone must increase full-time employment by at least 10 percent, with 25 percent of the 10 percent increase meeting the low-income standards for the area or living within the locality's zone. For projects investing over $15 million and creating 50 or more jobs over a 30-month period, the amount of credit is negotiable.

Refundable Real Property Improvement Tax Credit. A credit against state income tax equal to 30 percent of qualified enterprise zone improvements is available for rehabilitation projects that invest $50,000 or an amount equal to the current assessed value of the real property, whichever is greater. The minimum investment for new construction projects is $250,000. The maximum cumulative credit is $125,000 in any five-year period. The credit is applied first to tax liability; the remaining balance, if any, is refunded.

Sixty enterprise zones are authorized statewide in Virginia. Currently, 56 zones have been designated. In addition to state incentives, each enterprise zone community offers additional local incentives to qualified businesses. For additional information about Virginia's enterprise program, contact:

Virginia Department of Housing and Community Development
Planning and Development Office
501 North Second Street
Richmond, Virginia 23219-1321
(804) 371-7030
www.dhcd.virginia.gov/

STATE BUSINESS TAXES IMPOSED IN LIEU OF CORPORATE INCOME TAX

Subchapter S Corporations

Subchapter S corporations are required to file a Virginia Small Business Corporation Return of Income even though they are exempt from the Virginia corporate income tax. Individual shareholders report their income on their personal income tax return.

Limited Liability Companies

Limited liability companies are treated as partnerships for federal income tax purposes and for Virginia income tax purposes. Members who hold interest in the company must report any income on their personal income tax returns.

Partnerships

Partnerships are exempt from the Virginia corporate income tax. Individual partners report income on their personal income tax return.

Sole Proprietors

Sole proprietors must report their business income on their personal income tax returns.

For additional information on business tax requirements contact:

Virginia Department of Taxation
Office of Customer Services
Post Office Box 1115
Richmond, Virginia 23218-1115
(804) 367-8031
www.tax.state.va.us

SALES AND USE TAX

The sales and use tax is imposed at the state and local levels in Virginia. The combined rate is 5 percent. A seller is subject to a sales tax imposed on gross receipts derived from retail sales or leases of taxable tangible personal property unless the retail sales or leases are specifically exempt by law. When a seller does not collect the sales tax from the purchaser, the purchaser is required to pay a use tax on the purchase unless the use of the property is exempt.

LOCAL TAXES

All cities, counties, and towns in Virginia have the authority to levy taxes on businesses that operate in their jurisdiction. These taxes include tangible personal property taxes, license taxes, and utility taxes.

Tangible Personal Property Tax

Tangible personal property is taxed at the local level in Virginia. The tax is based on a percentage or percentages of the original cost. Tangible personal property includes, but is not limited to, machinery and equipment, office equipment, furniture and fixtures of nonmanufacturing businesses, trucks, and automobiles. It does not include merchants' capital.

Several categories of tangible personal property are segregated for taxation at assessment ratios and rates that may be below that of other tangible personal property. For example, localities may assess and tax tangible personal property used in a research and development business at a level not to exceed that applicable to machinery and tools.

Heavy Construction Machinery. Localities may establish a separate class of tangible personal property for heavy construction machinery, including but not limited to land movers, bulldozers, front-end loaders, graders, packers, power shovels, cranes, pile drivers, and ditch and other types of diggers, and levy a tax on it at a rate equal to or less than the tax rate levied on other tangible personal property.

Trucks and Automobiles. Localities assess trucks and automobiles of manufacturing and nonmanufacturing companies as tangible personal property.

Automobiles that are registered with the Virginia Division of Motor Vehicles are valued by means of a recognized pricing guide. If the model and year of the vehicle are not listed in the pricing guide, the value is based on a percentage or percentages of original cost. The commissioner of revenue may select another method to establish the fair market value of the automobile if the percentage or percentages of original cost do not accurately reflect the fair market value.

Trucks under two tons that are registered with the Virginia Division of Motor Vehicles may be valued by means of a recognized pricing guide or on the basis of a percentage or percentages of original cost if the model and year of the vehicle are not listed in the pricing guide.

Trucks weighing two tons or more that are registered with the Division of Motor Vehicles are valued by means of either a recognized pricing guide, using the lowest value specified in the guide, or on the basis of a percentage or percentages of original cost.

Tangible Personal Property Tax Exemptions. Localities have the option of exempting or partially exempting the following from personal property tax: certified pollution control facilities and equipment; certified solar energy equipment, facilities, or devices; and certified recycling equipment.

License Tax

Localities may impose a license tax on contractors. The license tax is usually based on gross receipts during the previous tax year; however, it is sometimes imposed either on gross purchases or at a flat rate. If both a town and county impose a license tax, a company located in a town pays the tax only to the town unless the governing body of the town votes to permit the additional collection of a county license tax. Forty-one of the 95 counties in Virginia impose a license tax. All 39 Virginia cities impose this tax.

For more detailed information on license taxes, consult the *Guide to Local Taxes on Business* (*www.YesVirginia.org/pdf/guides/local_taxes2.pdf*).

Utility Tax

All cities, counties, and towns have the authority to levy a tax on the utility bills of business firms, (e.g., electric, gas, water, telephone, and sewer bills). Most of the localities that currently impose the tax have a modest ceiling on the amount of tax that can be collected. If both a town and county charge utility taxes, a company pays the utility tax only to the town.

PERSONAL TAXES

Virginia residents pay individual state income and estate taxes, and local real estate, tangible personal property, utility, and excise taxes. They also pay a combined state and local sales and use tax.

Individual Income Tax

The individual income tax rate is 2 percent on the first $3,000 of Virginia taxable income, 3 percent on the next $2,000, 5 percent on the next $12,000, and 5.75 percent on amounts over $17,000.

Virginia's taxable income tax is based on an individual's federal adjusted gross income with modifications, if applicable, and with subtractions for personal exemptions and standard or itemized deductions. Individuals are allowed either itemized deductions or a standard deduction. If taxpayers itemize deductions on their federal return, they must itemize their state return. If they use standard deductions for federal purposes, they must use standard deductions for state purposes. Virginia allows nearly the same itemized deductions as the federal government. It does not allow a deduction for income taxes imposed by state or local taxing jurisdictions.

In Virginia, the personal exemption is $800. An exemption may be claimed for the taxpayer, for the spouse if married and filing jointly, and for each dependent. The standard deduction for a single person is $3,000. The standard deduction for a married person filing a separate return is $2,500 and the standard deduction for a married couple filing a joint return is $5,000. Virginia also allows a deduction equal to the expense allowed under federal law for child and dependent care services that are necessary for gainful employment.

Individuals are eligible to receive a number of income tax credits, including those under the enterprise zone program and the credit for purchase of machinery and equipment to process recyclable materials.

CHAPTER 8

MECHANICS' LIEN LAWS

This chapter presents Virginia regulations concerning liens, including terms, types of liens, filing dates, and notices. A lien may be filed by a contractor, subcontractor, laborer, or material supplier.

One thing contractors should remember is that there is no forgiveness for missing a filing date in processing a lien. If a filing date is missed, the amount that may be claimed is restricted, or the right to file, called "perfecting the lien," may be forfeited. It is also important to include all of the information listed under each required notice.

There may be numerous subcontractors or suppliers working on a single project, but each one must be given the name of the property owner so they can properly file a notice or lien. This information should be identified and provided prior to beginning the project. All correspondence (letters or notices) should be sent by certified mail.

The lien laws referenced in this chapter are from the Code of Virginia (CoV), Title 43 Mechanics and Certain Other Liens, Chapter 1 Mechanics' and Material-men's Liens. These laws may also be accessed on the Virginia Legislature System Web site at *http://leg1.state.va.us/lis.htm.*

DEFINITIONS

general contractor Any person (contractors, laborers, mechanics, and material providers) who contracts with an owner or a contractor (CoV 43-1).

lien A claim on the property of another as security against the payment of a just debt.

mechanics' lien agent A person designated in writing by the owner who will receive notice of the lien (CoV 43-1 and 43-4.01). The agent must be one of the following:
- A licensed title insurance agent
- A title insurance company authorized to write title insurance in the Commonwealth of Virginia
- An attorney licensed to practice law in the Commonwealth of Virginia
- A financial institution authorized to accept deposits

memorandum of lien A general written statement of the type of labor or the materials furnished and the amount of the claim.

owner The person who holds title to the property (CoV 43-1).

LIENS

A **mechanics' lien** is a lien placed on a property, usually by a contractor, subcontractor, or material supplier, for failure to receive payment. If the lien is left unpaid, the property can be sold to pay off the debts. The lien is intended to help a contractor or subcontractor secure payment of a debt. A lien may be filed by contractors, subcontractors, laborers, or suppliers of materials. Basically, the lien is a legal seizure and sale of the property for nonpayment.

In Virginia, all persons performing labor or furnishing materials valued at $50 or more for construction, removal, repair, or improvement of a building or structure can attach a lien. If the claim is for repairs, then the owner must have ordered or authorized the repair; otherwise, a lien cannot be attached to the property (CoV 43-3, A).

If the work is on a condominium, only the condominium that had the work performed may be attached by a lien. If the work is on several condos, then a single lien may be placed on the several condos. Work on a common area allows a single lien on all units, but work on limited common areas would allow a lien only on the units serving that specific area (CoV 43-3, B).

Work consisting of labor or materials supplied for site development or street improvement for individual lots or a condominium would allow a lien on each individual lot or unit based on a fractional cost of the work (CoV 43-3, B).

A waiver of lien can be granted by the person who is entitled to the lien, such as the contractor, supplier, or laborer (CoV 43-3, C). If a lien waiver is signed, the right of the contractor, laborer, or supplier to place on a lien on the property is forever waived.

A contract on a large project, such as a shopping mall, may contain a provision that the contractor and subcontractors waive their right to a lien. This is a "pass through" provision. On a large project, there will be many subcontractors and the general contractor may draft a contract that states the provisions of the original contract pass through to subcontractors.

The subcontractor may not be aware that the right to file a lien has been waived in the original contract, and the subcontractor will not necessarily be bound by the provision. In Virginia, the subcontractor must be made aware of the waiver and then willingly sign away the right to file.

A waiver for partial payment may be offered to a contractor for a progress payment. It is recommended that the waiver be read carefully to ensure that the offer is specific to releasing only rights for the partial payment and not for the entire amount of the work to be performed. The language of the waiver must be specific that it is only for the payment received, and especially not for all work or materials up to a certain date if the owner is retaining money owed the contractor upon completion.

Perfecting a Lien

The general contractor, or others entitled to file a lien, can file a memorandum any time after the work is started or materials delivered, but not later than 90 days from the last day of the month when work was last performed or materials delivered (CoV 43-4). Suit must be brought within 6 months of filing the memorandum or 60 days after completing the work (CoV 43-17). The lien memorandum must include the following:

- The name of the property owner
- The identity of the claimant (contractor, subcontractor, supplier, or laborer). No memorandum may be submitted for labor or materials more than 150 days prior to completion of supplied labor or furnishing of materials
- The amount of the claim
- The date the amount is due
- A statement of intent to claim the benefit of the lien
- A brief description of the property

A lien must be filed in the clerk's office in the county or city where the building is located. A sample memorandum is supplied in 43.5 of the laws included at the end of this chapter.

Perfection of a Lien by a Subcontractor. The subcontractor must follow the memorandum process of 43-4 and give written notice to the owner of the property, the lien agent, or the general contractor. This provides notice that labor or materials have been supplied and payment must be directed to the person owed (CoV 43-7). The amount of the lien cannot be greater than the amount the owner owes the general contractor.

Posting of Building Permit

A building permit must be posted. For construction of one- or two-family residential dwellings, the permit may include the name, address, and telephone number of a lien agent, but this is not mandatory. If an agent is listed, notification of the lien must be given to the agent within 30 days of the default. If there is no agent listed, no notification is required (CoV 43-4.01).

Lien Recording

A memorandum of lien is entered by the clerk of the county or city into the deed books in the clerk's office and in the general index of deeds (CoV 43-4.1).

Priority of Liens

The order in which liens are considered in the order of priority is (CoV 43-24):

- Laborer
- Materialman
- Subcontractor
- Contractor

The mechanics' lien can have priority over deeds of trust and other liens. The lien exists on the property from the time that labor and materials are provided. When the lien is filed, it covers back to the time when the work or material was started or supplied (CoV 43-21).

CODE OF VIRGINIA (COV)
TITLE 43 MECHANICS AND CERTAIN OTHER LIENS
Chapter 1 Mechanics' and Materialmen's Liens

§43-1. Definitions

As used in this chapter, the term "general contractor" includes contractors, laborers, mechanics, and persons furnishing materials, who contract directly with the owner, and the term "subcontractor" includes all such contractors, laborers, mechanics, and persons furnishing materials, who do not contract with the owner but with the general contractor. As used in this chapter, the term "owner" shall not be construed to mean any person holding bare legal title under an instrument to secure a debt or indemnify a surety. As used in this chapter, the term "mechanics' lien agent" means a person (i) designated in writing by the owner of real estate or a person authorized to act on behalf of the owner of such real estate and (ii) who consents in writing to act, as the owner's designee for purposes of receiving notice pursuant to §43-4.01. Such person shall be an attorney at law licensed to practice in the Commonwealth, a title insurance company authorized to write title insurance in the Commonwealth or one of its subsidiaries or licensed title insurance agents, or a financial institution authorized to accept deposits and to hold itself out to the public as engaged in the banking or savings institution business in the Commonwealth or a service corporation, subsidiary or affiliate of such financial institution. Any such person may perform mechanics' lien agent services as any legal entity. Provided that nothing herein shall be construed to affect pending litigation.

§43-2. Structures, Materials, Etc. Deemed Permanently Annexed to Freehold

For the purpose of this chapter, a well, excavation, sidewalk, driveway, pavement, parking lot, retaining wall, curb and/or gutter, breakwater (either salt or fresh water), underground or field-constructed above-ground storage tank and connected dispensing equipment, water system, drainage structure, filtering system (including septic or waste disposal systems) or swimming pool shall be deemed a structure permanently annexed to the freehold, and all shrubbery, earth, sod, sand, gravel, brick, stone, tile, pipe or other materials, together with the reasonable rental or use value of equipment and any surveying, grading, clearing or earth moving required for the improvement of the grounds upon which such building or structure is situated shall be deemed to be materials furnished for the improvement of such building or structure and permanently annexed to the freehold.

§43-3. Lien for Work Done and Materials Furnished; Waiver of Right to File or Enforce Lien

A. All persons performing labor or furnishing materials of the value of $50 or more, including the reasonable rental or use value of equipment, for the construction, removal, repair or improvement of any building or structure permanently annexed to the freehold, and all persons performing any labor or furnishing materials of like value for the construction of any railroad, shall have a lien, if perfected as hereinafter provided, upon such building or structure, and so much land therewith as shall be necessary for the convenient use and enjoyment thereof, and upon such railroad and franchises for the work done and materials furnished, subject to the provisions of §43-20. But when the claim is for repairs or improvements to existing structures only, no lien shall attach to the property repaired or improved unless such repairs or improvements were ordered or authorized by the owner, or his agent.

If the building or structure being constructed, removed or repaired is part of a condominium as defined in §55-79.41 or under the Horizontal Property Act (§§55-79.1 through 55-79.38), any person providing labor or furnishing material to one or more units or limited common elements within the condominium pursuant to a single contract may perfect a single lien encumbering the one or more units which are the subject of the contract or to which those limited common elements pertain, and for which payment has not been made. All persons providing labor or furnishing materials for the common elements pertaining to all the units may perfect a single lien encumbering all such condominium units. Whenever a lien has been or may be perfected encumbering two or more units, the proportionate amount of the indebtedness attributable to each unit shall be the ratio that the percentage liability for common expenses appertaining to that unit computed pursuant to subsection D of §55-79.83 bears to the total percentage liabilities for all units which are encumbered by the lien. The lien claimant shall release from a perfected lien an encumbered unit upon request of the unit owner as provided in subsection B of §55-79.46 upon receipt of payment equal to that portion of the indebtedness evidenced by the lien attributable to such unit determined as herein provided. In the event the lien is not perfected, the lien claimant shall upon request of any interested party execute lien releases for one or more units upon receipt of payment equal to that portion of the indebtedness attributable to such unit or units determined as herein provided but no such release shall preclude the lien claimant from perfecting a single lien against the unreleased unit or units for the remaining portion of the indebtedness.

B. Any person providing labor or materials for site development improvements or for streets, stormwater facilities, sanitary sewers or water lines for the purpose of providing access or service to the individual lots in a development or condominium units as defined in §55-79.41 or under the Horizontal Property Act (§§55-79.1 through 55-79.38) shall have a lien on each individual lot in the development for that fractional part of the total cost of such labor or materials as is obtained by using "one" as the numerator and the number of lots as the denominator and in the case of a condominium on each individual unit in an amount computed by reference to the liability of that unit for common expenses appertaining to that condominium pursuant to subsection D of §55-79.83; provided, however, no such lien shall be valid as to any lot or condominium unit unless the person providing such labor or materials shall, prior to the sale of such lot or condominium unit, file with the clerk of the circuit court of the jurisdiction in which such land lies a document setting forth a full disclosure of the nature of the lien to be claimed, the amount claimed against each lot or condominium unit and a description of the development or condominium, and shall, thereafter, comply with all other applicable provisions of this chapter. "Site development improvements" means improvements which are provided for the development, such as project site grading, rather than for an individual lot.

Nothing contained herein shall be construed to prevent the filing of a mechanic's lien under the provisions of subsection A.

C. Any right to file or enforce any mechanic's lien granted hereunder may be waived in whole or in part at any time by any person entitled to such lien.

§43-4. Perfection of Lien by General Contractor; Recordation and Notice

A general contractor, or any other lien claimant under §§43-7 and 43-9, in order to perfect the lien given by §43-3, provided such lien has not been barred by §43-4.01 C, shall file a memorandum of lien at any time after the work is commenced or material furnished, but not later than 90 days from the last day of the month in which he last performs labor or furnishes material, and in no event later than 90 days from the time such building, structure, or railroad is completed, or the work thereon otherwise terminated. The memorandum shall be filed in the clerk's office in the county or city in which the building, structure or railroad, or any part thereof is located. The memorandum shall show the names of the owner of the property sought to be charged, and of the claimant of the lien, the amount and consideration of his claim, and the time or times when the same is or will be due and payable, verified by the oath of the claimant, or his agent, including a statement declaring his intention to claim the benefit of the lien, and giving a brief description of the property on which he claims a lien. It shall be the duty of the clerk in whose office the memorandum is filed to record and index the same as provided in §43-4.1, in the name of the claimant of the lien and of the owner of the property. From the time of such recording and indexing all persons shall be deemed to have notice thereof. A lien claimant who is a general contractor also shall file along with the memorandum of lien, a certification of mailing of a copy of the memorandum of lien on the owner of the property at the owner's last known address. The cost of recording the memorandum shall be taxed against the person found liable in any judgment or decree enforcing such lien. The lien claimant may file any number of memoranda but no memorandum filed pursuant to this chapter shall include sums due for labor or materials furnished more than 150 days prior to the last day on which labor was performed or material furnished to the job preceding the filing of such memorandum. However, any memorandum may include (i) sums withheld as retainages with respect to labor performed or materials furnished at any time before it is filed, but not to exceed 10 percent of the total contract price and (ii) sums which are not yet due because the party with whom the lien claimant contracted has not yet received such funds from the owner or another third party. The time limitations set forth herein shall apply to all labor performed or materials furnished on construction commenced on or after July 1, 1980.

§43-4.01. Posting of Building Permit; Identification of Mechanics' Lien Agent in Building Permit; Notice to Mechanics' Lien Agent; Effect of Notice

A. The building permit for any one- or two-family residential dwelling unit issued pursuant to the Uniform Statewide Building Code shall be conspicuously and continuously posted on the property for which the permit is issued until all work is completed on the property. The permit shall be posted on the property before any labor is performed or any material furnished on the property for which the building permit is issued.

B. If, at the time of issuance, the building permit contains the name, mailing address, and telephone number of the mechanics' lien agent as defined in §43-1, any person entitled to claim a lien under this title may notify the mechanics' lien agent that he seeks payment for labor performed or material furnished by registered or certified mail or by physical delivery. Such notice shall contain (i) the name, mailing address, and telephone number of the person sending such notice, (ii) the building permit number on the building permit, (iii) a description of the property as shown on the building permit, and (iv) a statement that the person filing such notice seeks payment for labor performed or material furnished. A return receipt or other receipt showing delivery of the notice to the addressee or written evidence that such notice was delivered by the postal service or other carrier to but not accepted by the addressee shall be prima facie evidence of receipt. An inaccuracy in the notice as to the description of the property shall not bar a person from claiming a lien under this title or filing a memorandum or otherwise perfecting or enforcing a lien as provided in subsection C if the property can otherwise be reasonably identified from the description.

In the event that the mechanics' lien agent dies, resigns, or otherwise becomes unable or unwilling to serve during the construction period, the owner or the general contractor shall immediately appoint a successor mechanics' lien agent with all the rights, duties, and obligations of the predecessor mechanics' lien agent. The permit shall be displayed as provided in subsection A. Until such time as the successor is named and displayed as provided, notice given hereunder to the predecessor mechanics' lien agent at the address shown shall be deemed good notice, notwithstanding the fact that the agent may have died, resigned or become otherwise unable or unwilling to serve.

C. Except as provided otherwise in this subsection, no person other than a person claiming a lien under subsection B of §43-3 may claim a lien under this title or file a memorandum or otherwise perfect and enforce a lien under this title with respect to a one or two family residential dwelling unit if such person fails to notify any mechanics' lien agent identified on the building permit in accordance with subsection B above (i) within thirty days of the first date that he performs labor or furnishes material to or for the building or structure or (ii) within thirty days of the date such a permit is issued, if such labor or materials are first performed or furnished by such person prior to the issuance of a building permit. However, the failure to give any such notices within the appropriate thirty-day period as required by the previous sentence shall not bar a person from claiming a lien under this title or from filing a memorandum or otherwise perfecting and enforcing a lien under this title, provided that such lien is limited to labor performed or materials furnished on or after the date a notice is given by such person to the mechanics' lien agent in accordance with subsection B above. A person performing labor or furnishing materials with respect to a one or two family residential dwelling unit on which a building permit is not posted at the time he first performs his labor or first furnishes his material shall determine from appropriate authorities whether a permit of the type described in subsection B above has been issued and the date on which it is issued. The issuing authority shall maintain the mechanics' lien agent information in the same manner and in the same location in which it maintains its record of building permits issued.

No person shall be required to comply with this subsection as to any memorandum of lien which is recorded prior to the issuance of a building permit nor shall any person be required to comply with this subsection when the building permit does not designate a mechanics' lien agent.

D. Unless otherwise agreed in writing, the only duties of the mechanics' lien agent shall be to receive notices delivered to him pursuant to subsection B and to provide any notice upon request to a settlement agent, as defined in §6.1-2.10, involved in a transaction relating to the residential dwelling unit.

E. Mechanics' lien agents are authorized to enter into written agreements with third parties with regard to funds to be advanced to them for disbursement, and the transfer, disbursement, return and other handling of such funds shall be governed by the terms of such written agreements.

F. A mechanics' lien agent as defined in §43-1 may charge a reasonable fee for services rendered in connection with administration of notice authorized herein and the disbursement of funds for payment of labor and materials for the construction or repair of improvements on real estate.

§43-4.1. Liens to be Recorded in Deed Books and Indexed in General Index of Deeds

Notwithstanding the provision of any other section of this title, or any other provision of law requiring documents to be recorded in the miscellaneous lien book or the deed books in the clerk's office of any court, on and after July 1, 1964, all memoranda or notices of liens, in the discretion of the clerk, shall be recorded in the deed books in such clerk's office, and shall be indexed in the general index of deeds, and such general index shall show the type of such lien.

§43-5. Sufficiency of Memorandum and Affidavit Required by §43-4

The memorandum and affidavit required by §43-4 shall be sufficient if substantially in form and effect as follows:

Memorandum for Mechanic's Lien Claimed by General Contractor

Name of owner: . . . .

Address of owner: . . . .

Name of claimant: . . . .

Address of claimant: . . . .

1. Type of materials or services furnished: . . . .

. . . .

2. Amount claimed: $ . . . .

3. Type of structure on which work done or materials furnished: . . . .

. . . .

4. Brief description and location of real property: . . . .

. . . .

5. Date from which interest on the above amount is claimed:

It is the intent of the claimant to claim the benefit of a lien. The undersigned hereby certifies that he has mailed a copy of this memorandum of lien to the owner of the property at the owner's last known address: . . . .

(address), on . . . . (date of mailing).

. . . . (Name of claimant).

Affidavit.

State of Virginia,

County (or city) of . . . . to wit:

I, ... (notary or other officer)

for the county (or city) aforesaid, do certify that . . . .

claimant, or . . . . agent for claimant, this day made oath

before me in my county (or city) aforesaid that . . . .

(the owner) is justly indebted to claimant in the sum of . . . .

dollars for the consideration stated in the foregoing memorandum, and that the same is payable as therein stated.

Given under my hand this the . . . . day of . . . . 20 . . . .

. . . . (Notary Public or Magistrate, et cetera.)

§43-7. Perfection of Lien by Subcontractor; Extent of Lien; Affirmative Defense; Provisions Relating to Time-Share Estates

A. Any subcontractor, in order to perfect the lien given him by §43-3 shall comply with §43-4, and in addition give notice in writing to the owner of the property or his agent of the amount and character of his claim. But the amount for which a subcontractor may perfect a lien under this section shall not exceed the amount in which the owner is indebted to the general contractor at the time the notice is given, or shall thereafter become indebted to the general contractor upon his contract with the general contractor for such structure or building or railroad. It shall be an affirmative defense or affirmative partial defense, as the case may be, to a suit to perfect a lien of a subcontractor that the owner is not indebted to the general contractor or is indebted to the general contractor for less than the amount of the lien sought to be perfected.

B. Where the property referred to in subsection A hereof is a time-share unit, as defined by §55-362, the word "agent," as used in subsection A, shall be deemed to include the developer, during the developer control period, or the time-share estate owners' association, after the developer control period.

Within ten days of receipt of the notice, the developer or the time-share estate owners' association shall mail by first class mail a copy of the notice to all time-share estate owners whose interests are affected by the subcontractor's lien on the time-share unit. Failure on the part of the developer or time-share estate owners' association to so notify the appropriate time-share estate owners within the time period set forth above shall result in the developer's or the association's being liable for the full amount of the subcontractor's claim, but such failure shall not affect the validity of any lien perfected under this section. Assessments levied by the estate owners' association to pay the liability hereby imposed shall be made only against the time-share estate owners of record in the time-share estate project at the time the liability was incurred.

C. Where the property referred to in subsection A hereof is a time-share unit, as defined by §55-362, the memorandum required to be filed pursuant to §43-4 need show only the name of the developer during the developer control period, or the time-share estate owners' association, after the developer control period.

§43-8. Sufficiency of Memorandum, Affidavit, and Notice Required by §43-7

The memorandum, affidavit and notice required by §43-7 shall be sufficient if substantially in form and effect as follows:

Memorandum for Mechanic's Lien Claimed by Subcontractor

Name of owner: . . . .

Address of owner: . . . .

Name of general contractor (if any): . . . .

Name of claimant: . . . .

Address of claimant: . . . .

1. Type of materials or services furnished: . . . .

. . . .

2. Amount claimed: $ . . . .

3. Type of structure on which work done or materials furnished: . . . .

. . . .

4. Brief description and location of real property: . . . .

. . . .

5. Date from which interest on the above amount is claimed:

Date: . . . .

. . . . (Name of claimant).

Affidavit.

State of Virginia,

County (or city) of . . . . to wit:

I, ... (notary or other officer)
for the county (or city) aforesaid, do certify that . . . .
claimant, or . . . . agent for claimant, this day made oath
before me in my county (or city) aforesaid that. . . . .
(the owner) is justly indebted to claimant in the sum of . . . .
dollars for the consideration stated in the foregoing memorandum, and that the
same is payable as therein stated.

Given under my hand this the . . . . day of . . . . 20 . . . .

. . . . (Notary Public or Magistrate, et cetera.)

Notice.

To . . . . (owner).

You are hereby notified that (general contractor) is indebted to me in the sum of
. . . . dollars ($ . . . .) with interest thereon from the . . . . .
day of . . . . , 20 . . . . . for work done (or materials furnished, as the
case may be,) in and about the construction (or removal, etc.) of a . . . .

(describe structure, whether dwelling, store, etc.) that the general contractor named
above contracted to construct (or remove, etc.) for you or on property owned by
you in the county (or city) of . . . . , and that I have duly recorded a
mechanic's lien for the same.

Given under my hand this the . . . . day of . . . . , 20 . . . . .

. . . . (Subcontractor).

§43-9. Perfection of Lien By Person Performing Labor or Furnishing Materials for a Subcontractor; Extent of Lien

Any person performing labor or furnishing materials for a subcontractor, in order to
perfect the lien given him by §43-3, shall comply with the provisions of §43-4, and in
addition thereto give notice in writing to the owner of the property, or his agent, and to
the general contractor, or his agent, of the amount and character of his claim. But the
amount for which a lien may be perfected by such person shall not exceed the amount
for which such subcontractor could himself claim a lien under §43-7.

§43-10. Sufficiency of Memorandum, Affidavit, and Notice Required by §43-9

The memorandum, affidavit and notice required by §43-9 shall be sufficient if substantially in form and effect as follows:

Memorandum for Mechanic's Lien Claimed by Sub-subcontractor

Name of owner: . . . .

Address of owner: . . . .

Name of general contractor (if any) and subcontractor: . . . .
. . . .
Name of claimant: . . . .
Address of claimant: . . . .
1. Type of materials or services furnished: . . . .
. . . .
2. Amount claimed: $ . . . .
3. Type of structure on which work done or materials furnished: . . . .
. . . .
4. Brief description and location of real property:. . . . .
. . . .
5. Date from which interest on the above amount is claimed:
Date: . . . .
. . . . (Name of claimant).
. . . .(Signature of claimant or agent for claimant).
Affidavit.
State of Virginia,
County (or city) of . . . . to wit:

I, ... (notary or other officer)
for the county (or city) aforesaid, do certify that . . . .
claimant, or . . . . agent for claimant, this day made oath
before me in my county (or city) aforesaid that. . . . .
(the owner) is justly indebted to claimant in the sum of . . . .
dollars for the consideration stated in the foregoing memorandum, and that the
same is payable as therein stated.
Given under my hand this the . . . . day of . . . . 20 . . . .
. . . . (Notary Public or Magistrate, et cetera.)
Notice.
To . . . . (owner).
To . . . . (owner) and . . . .
(general contractor):
You are hereby notified that . . . ., a subcontractor
under you, said . . . . (general contractor) for the
construction (or removal, etc.,) of a . . . . (describe
structure) for you, or on property owned by you, said (owner) is indebted to me
in the sum of . . . . dollars ($ . . . .
interest thereon from the . . . . day of . . . ., 20 . . . . .
(for work done or materials furnished) in and about the construction (or removal,
etc.,) of said (naming structure), situated in the county (or city) of . . . .
Virginia, and that I have duly recorded a mechanic's lien for the same.
Given under my hand this the . . . . day of. . . . . , 20. . . . .
. . . . (Sub-subcontractor).

§43-11. How Owner or General Contractor Made Personally Liable to Subcontractor, Laborer, or Materialman

1. Any subcontractor or person furnishing labor or material to the general contractor or subcontractor, may give a preliminary notice in writing to the owner or his agent or the general contractor, stating the nature and character of his contract and the probable amount of his claim.

2. Additionally, if such subcontractor, or person furnishing labor or material shall at any time after the work is done or material furnished by him and before the expiration of thirty days from the time such building or structure is completed or the work thereon otherwise terminated furnish the owner thereof or his agent and also the general contractor, or the general contractor alone in case he is the only one notified, with a second notice stating a correct account, verified by affidavit, of his actual claim against the general contractor or subcontractor, for work done or materials furnished and of the amount due, then the owner, or the general contractor, if he alone was notified, shall be personally liable to the claimant for the actual amount due to the subcontractor or persons furnishing labor or material by the general contractor or subcontractor, provided the same does not exceed the sum in which the owner is indebted to the general contractor at the time the second notice is given or may thereafter become indebted by virtue of his contract with the general contractor, or in case the general contractor alone is notified the sum in which he is indebted to the subcontractor at the time the second notice is given or may thereafter become indebted by virtue of his contract with the general contractor. But the amount which a person supplying labor or material to a subcontractor can claim shall not exceed the amount for which such subcontractor could file his claim.

3. Any bona fide agreement for deductions by the owner because of the failure or refusal of the general contractor to comply with his contract shall be binding upon such subcontractor, laborer or materialman.

4. The provisions of this section are subject to the qualification that before any such personal liability of the owner or general contractor herein provided for shall be binding the two notices herein required, with such returns thereon as is sufficient under §8.01-325, shall be recorded and indexed as provided in §43-4.1 in the appropriate clerk's office; or the two notices herein required shall be mailed by registered or certified mail to and received by the owner or general contractor upon whom personal liability is sought to be imposed, and a return receipt therefor showing delivery to the addressee shall be prima facie evidence of receipt.

§43-13. Funds Paid to General Contractor or Subcontractor Must Be Used to Pay Persons Performing Labor or Furnishing Material

Any contractor or subcontractor or any officer, director or employee of such contractor or subcontractor who shall, with intent to defraud, retain or use the funds, or any part thereof, paid by the owner or his agent, the contractor or lender to such contractor or by the owner or his agent, the contractor or lender to a subcontractor under any contract for the construction, removal, repair or improvement of any building or structure permanently annexed to the freehold, for any other purpose than to pay persons performing labor upon or furnishing material for such construction, repair, removal or improvement, shall be guilty of larceny in appropriating such funds for any other use while any amount for which the contractor or subcontractor may be liable or become liable under his contract for such labor or materials remains unpaid, and may be prosecuted upon complaint of any person or persons who have not been fully paid any amount due them.

The use by any such contractor or subcontractor or any officer, director or employee of such contractor or subcontractor of any moneys paid under the contract, before paying all amounts due or to become due for labor performed or material furnished for such building or structure, for any other purpose than paying such amounts, shall be prima facie evidence of intent to defraud.

§43-13.1. Use of Lien Waiver Form; Forgery or Signing Without Authority

Any person who knowingly presents a waiver of lien form to an owner, his agent, contractor, lender, or title company for the purpose of obtaining funds or title insurance and who forges or signs without authority the name of any person listed thereon shall be guilty of a felony and punished as provided in §18.2-172. (Class 5 felony, jail from 1 to 10 years, and a $2,500 fine.)

§43-13.2. When an Affidavit or a Signed Statement of Payment is Required of Owner Prior to Sale

A person who is both the owner of a one- or two-family residential dwelling unit and either a developer of such property, a contractor in connection with the development or improvement of such property or a contractor or subcontractor furnishing labor or material in connection with the development or improvement of such property shall, at the time of settlement on the sale of such property, provide the purchaser with an affidavit or a signed statement attested to by a witness stating either (i) that all persons performing labor or furnishing materials in connection with the improvements on such property and with whom such owner is in privity of contract have been paid in full or (ii) the name, address and amount payable or claimed to be payable to any person so performing labor or furnishing materials and with whom such owner is in privity of contract. Willful failure to provide such statement or any willful material misrepresentation with respect to such a statement which causes a monetary loss to a financial institution, title company, contractor, subcontractor, supplier, owner, mechanics' lien agent or any other person or institution shall be punishable as a Class 5 felony.

§43-13.3. An Affidavit or a Signed Statement of Payment Required of Owner Prior to Sale or Refinance; Penalty

Any person who is the owner of a one- or two-family residential dwelling unit not included within the scope of §43-13.2 shall, at the time of settlement on the sale of such property, provide the purchaser, or lender in the case of a permanent loan or refinance, with an affidavit or a signed statement attested to by a witness stating either (i) that all persons performing labor or furnishing materials in connection with any improvements on such property within 120 days prior to the date of settlement and with whom such owner is in privity of contract have been paid in full, or (ii) the name, address and amount payable or claimed to be payable to any person so performing labor or furnishing materials and with whom such owner is in privity of contract. Any willful material misrepresentation in the affidavit or signed statement attested to by a witness which causes a monetary loss to any financial institution, title company, or purchaser shall be punishable as a Class 3 misdemeanor.

§43-14.1. Service of Notices

Any notice authorized or required by this chapter, except the notice required by §43-11, may be served by any sheriff or constable who shall make return of the time and manner of service; or any such notice may be served by certified or registered mail and a return receipt therefor shall be prima facie evidence of receipt.

§43-15. Inaccuracies in Memorandum or Description Not Affecting Lien

No inaccuracy in the memorandum filed, or in the description of the property to be covered by the lien, shall invalidate the lien, if the property can be reasonably identified by the description given and the memorandum conforms substantially to the requirements of §§43-5, 43-8 and 43-10, respectively, and is not willfully false.

§43-16. What Owner May Do When Contractor Fails or Refuses to Complete Building

If the owner is compelled to complete his building, structure, or railroad, or any part thereof undertaken by a general contractor in consequence of the failure or refusal of the general contractor to do so, the amount expended by the owner for such completion shall have priority over all mechanics' liens which have been or may be placed on such building, structure, or railroad by such general contractor, a subcontractor under him, or any person furnishing labor or materials to either of them.

§43-17. Limitation on Suit to Enforce Lien

No suit to enforce any lien perfected under §§43-4, 43-5 and 43-7 to 43-10 shall be brought after six months from the time when the memorandum of lien was recorded or after sixty days from the time the building, structure or railroad was completed or the work thereon otherwise terminated, whichever time shall last occur; provided, however, that the filing of a petition to enforce any such lien in any suit wherein such petition may be properly filed shall be regarded as the institution of a suit under this section; and, provided further, that nothing herein shall extend the time within which such lien may be perfected.

§43-17.1. Hearing on Validity of Lien

Any party, having an interest in real property against which a lien has been filed, may, upon a showing of good cause, petition the court of equity having jurisdiction wherein the building, structure, other property, or railroad is located to hold a hearing to determine the validity of any perfected lien on the property. After reasonable notice to the lien claimant and any party to whom the benefit of the lien would inure and who has given notice as provided in §43-18 of the Code of Virginia, the court shall hold a hearing and determine the validity of the lien. If the court finds that the lien is invalid, it shall forthwith order that the memorandum or notice of lien be removed from record.

§43-18. Lien of General Contractor to Inure to Benefit of Subcontractor

The perfected lien of a general contractor on any building or structure shall inure to the benefit of any subcontractor, and of any person performing labor or furnishing materials to a subcontractor who has not perfected a lien on such building or structure, provided such subcontractor, or person performing labor or furnishing materials shall give written notice of his claim against the general contractor, or subcontractor, as the case may be, to the owner or his agent before the amount of such lien is actually paid off or discharged.

§43-19. Validity and Priority of Lien Not Affected By Assignments

Every assignment or transfer by a general contractor, in whole or in part, of his contract with the owner or of any money or consideration coming to him under such contract, or by a subcontractor of his contract with the general contractor, in whole or in part, or of any money or consideration coming to him under his contract with the general contractor, and every writ of fieri facias, attachment or other process against the general contractor or subcontractor to subject or encumber his interest arising under such contract, shall be subject to the liens given by this chapter to laborers, mechanics, and materialmen. No such assignment or transfer shall in any way affect the validity or the priority of satisfaction of liens given by this chapter.

§43-20. Extent of Lien Where Owner Has Less Than Fee in Land

Subject to the provisions of §43-3, if the person who shall cause a building or structure to be erected or repaired owns less than a fee simple estate in the land, then only his interest therein shall be subject to liens created under this chapter. When the vendee under a contract for the sale of real estate causes a building or structure to be erected or repaired on the land which is the subject of the contract and the owner has actual knowledge of such erection or repairs, the interest of the owner in the land shall be subject to liens created under this chapter; and for the purposes of §43-21, the interest of such an owner in the land, to the extent of the unpaid purchase price, shall be deemed to be a recorded purchase money deed of trust lien created at the time the contract of sale was fully executed. As used in this section, "a contract for the sale of real estate" shall not include a lease of real estate containing an option to purchase the leased real estate or an option to purchase real estate unless the option is enforceable against the optionee.

§43-21. Priorities Between Mechanics' and Other Liens

No lien or encumbrance upon the land created before the work was commenced or materials furnished shall operate upon the building or structure erected thereon, or materials furnished for and used in the same, until the lien in favor of the person doing the work or furnishing the materials shall have been satisfied; nor shall any lien or encumbrance upon the land created after the work was commenced or materials furnished operate on the land, or such building or structure, until the lien in favor of the person doing the work or furnishing the materials shall have been satisfied.

Unless otherwise provided in the subordination agreement, if the holder of the prior recorded lien of a purchase money deed of trust subordinates to the lien of a construction money deed of trust, such subordination shall be limited to the construction money deed of trust and said prior lien shall not be subordinate to mechanics' and materialmen's liens to the extent of the value of the land by virtue of such agreement.

In the enforcement of the liens acquired under the previous sections of this chapter, any lien or encumbrance created on the land before the work was commenced or materials furnished shall be preferred in the distribution of the proceeds of sale only to the extent of the value of the land estimated, exclusive of the buildings or structures, at the time of sale, and the residue of the proceeds of sale shall be applied to the satisfaction of the liens provided for in the previous sections of this chapter. Provided that liens filed for performing labor or furnishing materials for the repair or improvement of any building or structure shall be subject to any encumbrance against such land and building or structure of record prior to the commencement of the improvements or repairs or the furnishing of materials or supplies therefor. Nothing contained in the foregoing proviso shall apply to liens that may be filed for the construction or removal of any building or structure.

§43-22. How Liens Are Enforced

The liens created and perfected under this chapter may be enforced in a court of equity by a bill filed in the county or city wherein the building, structure, or railroad, or some part thereof is situated, or wherein the owner, or if there be more than one, any of them, resides. The plaintiff shall file with his bill an itemized statement of his account, showing the amount and character of the work done or materials furnished, the prices charged therefor, the payments made, if any, the balance due, and the time from which interest is claimed thereon, the correctness of which account shall be verified by the affidavit of himself, or his agent. When suit is brought for the enforcement of any such lien against the property bound thereby, all parties entitled to such liens upon the property or any portion thereof may file petitions in such suit asking for the enforcement of their respective liens to have the same effect as if an independent suit were brought by each claimant.

§43-23. Priority Among Liens Perfected Under This Chapter

There shall be no priority among the liens created and perfected under this chapter, except that the lien of a subcontractor shall be preferred to that of his general contractor; the lien of persons performing labor or furnishing materials for a subcontractor, shall be preferred to that of such subcontractor; and liens filed by persons performing manual labor shall have priority over materialmen to the extent of the labor performed during the thirty days immediately preceding the date of the performance of the last labor.

§43-23.1. Forfeiture of Lien

Any person who shall, with intent to mislead, include in his memorandum of lien work not performed upon, or materials not furnished for, the property described in his memorandum shall thereby forfeit any right to a lien under this chapter.

§43-23.2. Remedies Cumulative

The remedies afforded by this chapter shall be deemed cumulative in nature and not be construed to be in lieu of any other legal or equitable remedies.

CHAPTER 9

VIRGINIA OSHA REGULATIONS

T he Virginia Department of Labor and Industry, Virginia Occupational Safety and Health (VOSH) Compliance is the agency responsible for enforcing the Virginia Occupational Safety and Health program in accordance with Virginia code and regulations. The VOSH compliance program conducts workplace inspections based on injury and illness reports and worker complaints to ensure that workplace conditions are safe and healthful. The VOSH Consultation Service provides educational material for workplace safety. For more information regarding VOSH, the consultation service, Illness and Injury Prevention Program, and workplace posters, refer to the VOSH Web site at *www.doli.virginia.gov.*

VIRGINIA OSHA LAWS AND REGULATIONS

It is the responsibility of every employer and employee to comply with health and safety standards, rules, and regulations. The regulations applicable to OSHA can be found in the Virginia Administrative Code (VAC) 16VAC25-60, which is included at the end of this chapter. These regulations are also available on line at *http://leg1.state.va.us/lis.htm.*

The VOSH Web site also includes the regulations that are unique to Virginia at *http://www.dli.state.va.us/.* The sections that differ from the federal OSHA standards are the Virginia Confined Space Standards for the Construction Industry (16VAC25-140, 16VAC25-150, 16VAC25-160, and 16VAC25-170).

Basic Standards

Regardless of a contractor's specialty, OSHA requires that all employers follow some basic guidelines in regards to maintaining a safe and healthful work environment. The basic guidelines include the following:

■ The Job Safety and Health Protection poster must be posted in a conspicuous place at each location that employees report to work. This poster can be downloaded from the VOSH Web site. (A copy of the poster is also included in the Appendix.)

- All notices received from the Commissioner of Labor and Industry must be posted in a prominent place (16VAC25-60-40).
- Any VOSH citations must be displayed at or near the place of violation for three days or until the problem is corrected (16VAC25-60-40 2).
- All records required to be kept under the federal OSHA regulations must be maintained for five years (OSHA 1904.33(a)).

Employee Rights

Any employee has the right to file a complaint with a VOSH office if the employee believes the workplace environment is unsafe. Complaints are classified as formal (written complaints made by employees) and nonformal (complaints made by authorized representatives or unsigned written complaints by employees). Nonformal complaints are handled by a letter from VOSH to the employer. In the case of formal complaints, it is the responsibility of the VOSH office to determine if there are reasonable grounds to believe there is the existence of an unsafe or hazardous condition and to conduct an investigation as soon as possible after notification (16VAC25-60-100).

Employees may not be fired, threatened to be fired, or discriminated against for making a valid complaint with a VOSH office. If an employee believes that they have been fired or discriminated against for filing a complaint or testifying against their employer related to a violation, the employee has 60 days to file a complaint with the commissioner. The Commissioner will then investigate the claim and if the situation warrants will reinstate the employee with back pay and interest (CoV 40.1-51.2:2).

Permits

Any building permits required are covered in Chapter 5, Virginia Uniform Statewide Building Code. As a general guideline, any constructing, demolishing, altering, or renovating of a building requires a permit. Permits can be obtained by the owner, the owner's representative, the contractor, or a licensed engineer.

Variances

Any employer may submit a written application to the commission requesting a temporary or permanent variance from OSHA standards or regulations (16VAC 25-60-190).

Temporary Variance.   Temporary variances are usually used for situations in which a company needs a longer period of time to come into compliance. A temporary variance of up to one year may be granted if the contractor can demonstrate cause (16VAC25-60-200).

Permanent Variance.   A contractor can apply for a permanent variance from a Virginia occupational safety standard if there is an equivalent method employed to provide a place of employment that is as safe as the one provided by the OSHA standard (16VAC25-60-210).

VIRGINIA VOLUNTARY PROTECTION PROGRAM

The VOSH program offers a voluntary protection program (VPP) in which both employers and employees can agree to participate. The purpose of the program is to help promote a safety and health management program that exceeds minimum safety standards. The program works to improve employee morale and reduce workers' compensation costs.

To participate in this program, an employer must first fill out a self-assessment checklist to determine if their current safety program meets the standards of VPP. The next step is to fill out and submit an application to the VPP. VOSH will then conduct an on-site review of the workplace to verify the information listed in the application. A VPP representative is available to answer questions about joining the VPP. For more information, visit the Virginia Department of Labor and Industry Web site at *www.doli.state.va.us/*.

REPORTING AND RECORD KEEPING REQUIREMENTS

The VOSH program closely follows the federal OSHA reporting and record keeping requirements. Records required under OSHA must be maintained for a period of five years. Federal OSHA requirements can be found in the *Contractor's Business Reference Manual* by Kaplan AEC.

OSHA Penalties

The following is a list of some of the common fines for violating OSHA regulations. This list is by no means inclusive of all penalties.

- Serious or Non-serious Violations—Any employer who has received a citation for a violation of a safety or health provision of the Code of Virginia Title 40.1, Labor and Employment, or a standard, rule, or regulation relating to OSHA requirements for serious or nonserious violations may be subject to a penalty of up to $7,000 for each such violation (CoV 40.1-49.4 H).

- Failure to Correct a Problem—If an employer receives a citation, but fails to correct the violation, the employer may be fined up to $7,000 for each day the violation continues (CoV 40.1-49.4 I).

Asbestos Removal

Written notification of any asbestos project of ten linear feet or more or 10 square feet or more needs to be made to the Department of Labor and Industry 20 days before beginning the project. Notice must include the license number of the asbestos contractor (16 VAC25-20-30 A). An asbestos contractor's license is an authorization issued by the Department of Professional and Occupational Regulation that permits a person to enter into contracts to perform asbestos abatement projects.

VIRGINIA ADMINISTRATIVE CODE (VAC)
TITLE 16

16VAC25-60-40. Notification and Posting Requirements

Every employer shall post and keep posted any notice or notices, as required by the commissioner, including the Job Safety and Health Protection Poster which shall be available from the department. Such notices shall inform employees of their rights and obligations under the safety and health provisions of Title 40.1 of the Code of Virginia and this chapter. Violations of notification or posting requirements are subject to citation and penalty.

1. Such notice or notices, including all citations, petitions for variances or extensions of abatement periods, orders, and other documents of which employees are required to be informed by the employer under statute or by this chapter, shall be delivered by the employer to any authorized employee representative, and shall be posted at a conspicuous place where notices to employees are routinely posted and shall be kept in good repair and in unobstructed view. The document must remain posted for 10 working days unless a different period is prescribed elsewhere in Title 40.1 of the Code of Virginia or this chapter.

2. A citation issued to an employer, or a copy of it, shall remain posted in a conspicuous place and in unobstructed view at or near each place of alleged violation for three working days or until the violation has been abated, whichever is longer.

3. A copy of any written notice of contest shall remain posted until all proceedings concerning the contest have been completed.

4. Upon receipt of a subpoena, the employer shall use the methods set forth in this section to further notify his employees and any authorized employee representative of their rights to party status. This written notification shall include both the date, time and place set for court hearing, and any subsequent changes to hearing arrangements. The notification shall remain posted until commencement of the hearing or until an earlier disposition.

16VAC25-60-80. Access to Employee Medical and Exposure Records

A. An employee and his authorized representative shall have access to his exposure and medical records required to be maintained by the employer.

B. When required by a standard, a health care professional under contract to the employer or employed by the employer shall have access to the exposure and medical records of an employee only to the extent necessary to comply with the requirements of the standard and shall not disclose or report without the employee's express written consent to any person within or outside the workplace except as required by the standard.

C. Under certain circumstances it may be necessary for the commissioner to obtain access to employee exposure and medical records to carry out statutory and regulatory functions. However, due to the substantial personal privacy interests involved, the commissioner shall seek to gain access to such records only after a careful determination of the need for such information and only with appropriate safeguards described at 29 CFR 1913.10(i) in order to protect individual privacy. In the event that the employer requests the commissioner to wait 24 hours for the presence of medical personnel to review the records, the commissioner will do so on presentation of an affidavit that the employer has not and will not modify or change any of the records. The commissioner's examination and use of this information shall not exceed that which is necessary to accomplish the purpose for access. Personally identifiable medical information shall be retained only for so long as is needed to carry out the function for which it was sought. Personally identifiable information shall be kept secure while it is being used and shall not be released to other agencies or to the public except under certain narrowly defined circumstances outlined at 29 CFR 1913.10(m).

D. In order to implement the policies described in subsection C of this section, the rules and procedures of 29 CFR Part 1913.10, Rules of Agency Practice and Procedure Concerning Access to Employee and Medical Records, are hereby expressly incorporated by reference. When these rules and procedures are applied to the commissioner the following federal terms should be considered to read as below:

FEDERAL TERM	VOSH EQUIVALENT
Agency	Virginia Department of Labor and Industry
OSHA	VOSH
Assistant Secretary	Commissioner
Office of the Solicitor of Labor	Office of the Attorney General
Department of Justice	Office of the Attorney General
Privacy Act	§§2.2-3800 to 2.2-3809 of the Code of Virginia

16VAC25-60-100. Complaints

A. Any person who believes that a safety or health hazard exists in a workplace may request an inspection by giving notice to the commissioner. Written complaints signed by an employee or an authorized representative will be treated as formal complaints. Complaints by persons other than employees and authorized representatives and unsigned complaints by employees or authorized representatives shall be treated as nonformal complaints. Nonformal complaints will generally be handled by letter and formal complaints will generally result in an inspection.

B. For purposes of this section and §40.1-51.2(b) of the Code of Virginia, the representative(s) that will be recognized as authorized by employees for such action shall be:
    1. A representative of the employee bargaining unit;
    2. Any member of the employee's immediate family acting on behalf of the employee; or
    3. A lawyer or physician retained by the employee.

C. A written complaint may be preceded by an oral complaint at which time the commissioner will either give instructions for filing the written complaint or provide forms for that purpose. Section 40.1-51.2(b) of the Code of Virginia stipulates that the written complaint follow an oral complaint by no more than two working days. However, if an oral complaint gives the commissioner reasonable grounds to believe that a serious condition or imminent danger situation exists, the commissioner may cause an inspection to be conducted as soon as possible without waiting for a written complaint.

VAC
Title 16

D. A complaint should allege that a violation of safety and health laws, standards, rules, or regulations has taken place. The violation or hazard should be described with reasonable particularity.

E. A complaint will be classified as formal or nonformal and be evaluated to determine whether there are reasonable grounds to believe that the violation or hazard complained of exists.

   1. If the commissioner determines that there are no reasonable grounds for believing that the violation or hazard exists, the employer and the complainant shall be informed in writing of the reasons for this determination.

   2. An employee or authorized representative may obtain review of the commissioner's determination that no reasonable grounds for believing that the violation or hazard exists by submitting a written statement of his position with regard to the issue. Upon receipt of such written statement a further review of the matter will be made which may include a requested written statement of position from the employer, further discussions with the complainant or an informal conference with complainant or employer if requested by either party. After review of the matter, the commissioner shall affirm, modify or reverse the original determination and furnish the complainant and the employer written notification of his decision.

F. If the commissioner determines that the complaint is formal and offers reasonable grounds to believe that a hazard or violation exists, then an inspection will be conducted as soon as possible. Valid nonformal complaints may be resolved by letter or may result in an inspection if the commissioner determines that such complaint establishes probable cause to conduct an inspection.

G. If there are several complaints to be investigated, the commissioner may prioritize them by considering such factors as the gravity of the danger alleged and the number of exposed employees.

H. At the beginning of the inspection the employer shall be provided with a copy of the written complaint. The complainant's name shall be deleted and any other information which would identify the complainant shall be reworded or deleted so as to protect the complainant's identity.

I. An inspection pursuant to a complaint may cover the entire operation of the employer, particularly if it appears to the commissioner that a full inspection is warranted. However, if there has been a recent inspection of the worksite or if there is reason to believe that the alleged violation or hazard concerns only a limited area or aspect of the employer's operation, the inspection may be limited accordingly.

J. After an inspection based on a complaint, the commissioner shall inform the complainant in writing whether a citation has been issued and briefly set forth the reasons if not. The commissioner shall provide the complainant with a copy of any resulting citation issued to the employer.

16VAC25-60-110. Discrimination; Discharge or Retaliation; Remedy for Retaliation

A. In carrying out his duties under §40.1-51.2:2 of the Code of Virginia, the commissioner shall consider case law, regulations, and formal policies of federal OSHA. An employee's engagement in activities protected by Title 40.1 does not automatically render him immune from discharge or discipline for legitimate reasons. Termination or other disciplinary action may be taken for a combination of reasons, involving both discriminatory and nondiscriminatory motivations. In such a case, a violation of §40.1-51.2:1 of the Code of Virginia has occurred if the protected activity was a substantial reason for the action, or if the discharge or other adverse action would not have taken place "but for" engagement in protected activity.

Employee activities protected by §40.1-51.2:1 of the Code of Virginia include, but are not limited to:

1. Making any complaint to his employer or any other person under or related to the safety and health provisions of Title 40.1 of the Code of Virginia;
2. Instituting or causing to be instituted any proceeding under or related to the safety and health provisions of Title 40.1 of the Code of Virginia;
3. Testifying or intending to testify in any proceeding under or related to the safety and health provisions of Title 40.1 of the Code of Virginia;
4. Cooperating with or providing information to the commissioner during a worksite inspection; or
5. Exercising on his own behalf or on behalf of any other employee any right afforded by the safety and health provisions of Title 40.1 of the Code of Virginia.

Discharge or discipline of an employee who has refused to complete an assigned task because of a reasonable fear of injury or death will be considered retaliatory only if the employee has sought abatement of the hazard from the employer and the statutory procedures for securing abatement would not have provided timely protection. The condition causing the employee's apprehension of death or injury must be of such a nature that a reasonable person, under the circumstances then confronting the employee, would conclude that there is a real danger of death or serious injury and that there is insufficient time, due to the urgency of the situation, to eliminate the danger through resort to regular statutory enforcement. In addition, in such circumstances, the employee, where possible, must also have sought from his employer, and been unable to obtain, an abatement of the dangerous condition.

Disciplinary measures taken by employers solely in response to employee refusal to comply with appropriate safety rules and regulations shall not be regarded as retaliatory action prohibited by §40.1-51.2:1 of the Code of Virginia.

B. A complaint pursuant to §40.1-51.2:2 of the Code of Virginia may be filed by the employee himself or anyone authorized to act in his behalf.

The investigation of the commissioner shall include an opportunity for the employer to furnish the commissioner with any information relevant to the complaint.

An attempt by an employee to withdraw a previously filed complaint shall not automatically terminate the investigation of the commissioner. Although a voluntary and uncoerced request from the employee that his complaint be withdrawn shall receive due consideration, it shall be the decision of the commissioner whether further action is necessary to enforce the statute.

The filing of a retaliation complaint with the commissioner shall not preclude the pursuit of a remedy through other channels. Where appropriate, the commissioner may postpone his investigation or defer to the outcome of other proceedings.

16VAC25-60-190. General Provisions

A. Any employer or group of employers desiring a permanent or temporary variance from a standard or regulation pertaining to occupational safety and health may file with the commissioner a written application which shall be subject to the following policies:

1. A request for a variance shall not preclude or stay a citation or bill of complaint for violation of a safety or health standard;

2. No variances on record keeping requirements required by the U.S. Department of Labor shall be granted by the commissioner;

3. An employer, or group of employers, who has applied for a variance from the U.S. Department of Labor, and whose application has been denied on its merits, shall not be granted a variance by the commissioner unless there is a showing of changed circumstances significantly affecting the basis upon which the variance was originally denied;

4. An employer to whom the U.S. Secretary of Labor has granted a variance under OSHA provisions shall document this variance to the commissioner. In such cases, unless compelling local circumstances dictate otherwise, the variance shall be honored by the commissioner without the necessity of following the formal requirements which would otherwise be applicable. In addition, the commissioner will not withdraw a citation for violation of a standard for which the Secretary of Labor has granted a variance unless the commissioner previously received notice of and decided to honor the variance; and

5. Incomplete applications will be returned within 30 days to the applicant with a statement indicating the reason or reasons that the application was found to be incomplete.

B. In addition to the information specified in 16VAC25-60-200 A and 16VAC25-60-210 A, every variance application shall contain the following:

1. A statement that the applicant has informed affected employees of the application by delivering a copy of the application to their authorized representative, if there is one, as well as having posted, in accordance with 16VAC25-60-40, a summary of the application which indicates where a full copy of the application may be examined;

2. A statement indicating that the applicant has posted, with the summary of the application described above, the following notice: "Affected employees or their representatives have the right to petition the Commissioner of Labor and Industry for an opportunity to present their views, data, or arguments on the requested variance, or they may submit their comments to the commissioner in writing. Petitions for a hearing or written comments should be addressed to the Commissioner of Labor and Industry, Powers-Taylor Building, 13 South Thirteenth Street, Richmond, VA 23219. Such petitions will be accepted if they are received within 30 days from the posting of this notice or within 30 days from the date of publication of the commissioner's notice that public comments concerning this matter will be accepted, whichever is later.";

3. A statement indicating whether an application for a variance from the same standard or rule has been made to any federal agency or to an agency of another state. If such an application has been made, the name and address of each agency contacted shall be included.

C. Upon receipt of a complete application for a variance, the commissioner shall publish a notice of the request in a newspaper of statewide circulation within 30 days after receipt, advising that public comments will be accepted for 30 days and that an informal hearing may be requested in conformance with subsection D of this section. Further, the commissioner may initiate an inspection of the establishment in regard to the variance request.

D. If within 30 days of the publication of notice the commissioner receives a request to be heard on the variance from the employer, affected employees, the employee representative, or other employers affected by the same standard or regulation, the commissioner will schedule a hearing with the party or parties wishing to be heard and the employer requesting the variance. The commissioner may also schedule a hearing upon his own motion. The hearing will be held within a reasonable time and will be conducted informally in accordance with §§2.2-4019 and 2.2-4021 of the Code of Virginia unless the commissioner finds that there is a substantial reason to proceed under the formal provisions of §2.2-4020 of the Code of Virginia.

E. If the commissioner has not been petitioned for a hearing on the variance application, a decision on the application may be made promptly after the close of the period for public comments. This decision will be based upon the information contained in the application, the report of any variance inspection made concerning the application, any other pertinent staff reports, federal OSHA comments or public records, and any written data and views submitted by employees, employee representatives, other employers, or the public.

F. The commissioner will grant a variance request only if it is found that the employer has met by a preponderance of the evidence, the requirements of either 16VAC25-60-200 B 4 or 16VAC25-60-210 B 4.

　　1. The commissioner shall advise the employer in writing of the decision and shall send a copy to the employee representative if applicable. If the variance is granted, a notice of the decision will be published in a newspaper of statewide circulation.

　　2. The employer shall post a copy of the commissioner's decision in accordance with 16VAC25-60-40.

G. Any party may within 15 days of the commissioner's decision file a notice of appeal to the board. Such appeal shall be in writing, addressed to the board, and include a statement of how other affected parties have been notified of the appeal. Upon notice of a proper appeal, the commissioner shall advise the board of the appeal and arrange a date for the board to consider the appeal. The commissioner shall advise the employer and employee representative of the time and place that the board will consider the appeal. Any party that submitted written or oral views or participated in the hearing concerning the original application for the variance shall be invited to attend the appeal hearing. If there is no employee representative, a copy of the commissioner's letter to the employer shall be posted by the employer in accordance with the requirements of 16VAC25-60-40.

H. The board shall sustain, reverse, or modify the commissioner's decision based upon consideration of the evidence in the record upon which the commissioner's decision was made and the views and arguments presented as provided above. The burden shall be on the party filing the appeal to designate and demonstrate any error by the commissioner which would justify reversal or modification of the decision. The issues to be considered by the board shall be those issues that could be considered by a court reviewing agency action in accordance with §2.2-4027 of the Code of Virginia. All parties involved shall be advised of the board's decision within 10 working days after the hearing of the appeal.

16VAC25-60-200. Temporary Variances

A. The commissioner shall give consideration to an application for a temporary variance from a standard or regulation only if the employer or group of employers is unable to comply with that standard or regulation by its effective date for good cause and files an application which meets the requirements set forth in this section. No temporary variance shall be granted for longer than the time needed to come into compliance with the standard or one year, whichever is shorter.

B. A letter of application for a temporary variance shall be in writing and contain the following information:
   1. Name and address of the applicant;
   2. Address of the place or places of employment involved;
   3. Identification of the standard or part of it from which a temporary variance is sought; and
   4. Evidence to establish that:
      a. The applicant is unable to comply with a standard by its effective date because professional or technical personnel or materials and equipment needed to come into compliance with the standard are unavailable, or because necessary construction or alteration of facilities cannot be completed by the effective date;
      b. The applicant is taking effective steps to safeguard his employees against the hazards covered by the standard; and
      c. The applicant has an effective program for coming into compliance with the standard as quickly as practicable.

C. A temporary variance may be renewed if the application for renewal is filed at least 90 days prior to the expiration date and if the requirements of subsection A of this section are met. A temporary variance may not be renewed more than twice.

16VAC25-60-210. Permanent Variances

A. Applications filed with the commissioner for a permanent variance from a standard or regulation shall be subject to the requirements of 16VAC25-60-190 and the following additional requirements.

B. A letter of application for a permanent variance shall be submitted in writing by an employer or group of employers and shall contain the following information:
   1. Name and address of the applicant;
   2. Address of the place or places of employment involved;
   3. Identification of the standard, or part thereof for which a permanent variance is sought; and
   4. A description of the conditions, practices, means, methods, operations, or processes used and evidence that these would provide employment and a place of employment as safe and healthful as would be provided by the standard from which a variance is sought.

C. A permanent variance may be modified or revoked upon application by an employer, employees, or by the commissioner in the manner prescribed for its issuance at any time except that the burden shall be upon the party seeking the change to show altered circumstances justifying a modification or revocation.

16VAC25-60-260. Issuance of Citation and Proposed Penalty

A. Each citation shall be in writing and describe with particularity the nature of the violation or violations, including a reference to the appropriate safety or health provision of Title 40.1 of the Code of Virginia or the appropriate rule, regulation, or standard. In addition, the citation must fix a reasonable time for abatement of the violation. The citation will contain substantially the following: "NOTICE: This citation will become a final order of the commissioner unless contested within fifteen working days from the date of receipt by the employer." The citation may be delivered to the employer or his agent by the commissioner or may be sent by certified mail or by personal service to an officer or agent of the employer or to the registered agent if the employer is a corporation.

B. A citation issued under subsection A to an employer who violates any VOSH law, standard, rule or regulation shall be vacated if such employer demonstrates that:
   1. Employees of such employer have been provided with the proper training and equipment to prevent such a violation;
   2. Work rules designed to prevent such a violation have been established and adequately communicated to employees by such employer and have been effectively enforced when such a violation has been discovered;
   3. The failure of employees to observe work rules led to the violation; and
   4. Reasonable steps have been taken by such employer to discover any such violation.

C. For the purposes of subsection B only, the term "employee" shall not include any officer, management official or supervisor having direction, management control or custody of any place of employment which was the subject of the violative condition cited.

D. The penalties as set forth in §40.1-49.4 of the Code of Virginia shall also apply to violations relating to the requirements for record keeping, reports or other documents filed or required to be maintained and to posting requirements.

E. In determining the amount of the proposed penalty for a violation the commissioner will ordinarily be guided by the system of penalty adjustment set forth in the VOSH Field Operations Manual. In any event the commissioner shall consider the gravity of the violation, the size of the business, the good faith of the employer, and the employer's history of previous violations.

16VAC25-20-30. Notification and Permit Fee for Asbestos

A. Written notification of any asbestos project of 10 linear feet or more or 10 square feet or more shall be made to the department on a department form. Such notification shall be sent by facsimile transmission as set out in 16VAC25-20-30 J, certified mail, or hand-delivered to the department. Notification shall be postmarked or made 20 days before the beginning of any asbestos project.

B. The department form shall include the following information:
   1. Name, address, telephone number, and Virginia asbestos contractor's license number of persons intending to engage in an asbestos project;
   2. Name, address, and telephone number of facility owner or operator;
   3. Type of notification; amended, emergency, renovation, or demolition;
   4. Description of building, structure, facility, installation, vehicle, or vessel to be demolished or renovated including present use, prior use or uses, age, and address;
   5. Estimate of amount of friable asbestos and method of estimation;
   6. Amount of the asbestos project fee submitted;
   7. Schedule set-up date, removal date, and completion date of asbestos abatement work and times of removal;
   8. Name and Virginia asbestos supervisor's license number of the project supervisor on site;
   9. Name, address, telephone number, contact person, and landfill permit number of the waste disposal site where the asbestos containing material will be disposed;
   10. Detailed description of the demolition or removal methods to be used;

11. Procedures and equipment to control emissions and protect public health during removal, transit, loading, and unloading. Including the monitoring plan;

12. Credit card number, expiration date, and signature of cardholder if a facsimile transmission is to be made pursuant to 16VAC25-20-30 J; and

13. Any other information requested on the department form.

C. An asbestos project permit fee shall be submitted with the completed project notification. The fee shall be in accordance with the following schedule unless a blanket notification is granted under subsection D of this section:

1. $50 for each project equal to or greater than 10 linear feet or 10 square feet up to and including 260 linear feet or 160 square feet;

2. $160 for each project of more than 260 linear feet or 160 square feet up to and including 2600 linear feet or 1600 square feet;

3. $470 for each project of more than 2600 linear feet or 1600 square feet; and

4. If the amount of asbestos is reported in both linear feet and square feet the amounts will be added and treated as if the total were all in square feet for the purposes of this subsection.

D. A blanket notification, valid for a period of one year, may be granted to a contractor who enters into a contract for asbestos removal or encapsulation on a specific site which is expected to last for one year or longer.

1. The contractor shall submit the notification required in 16VAC25-20-30 A to the department 20 days prior to the start of the requested blanket notification period. The notification submitted shall contain the following additional information:

   a. The dates of work required by subdivision B 7 of this section shall be every workday during the blanket notification period excluding weekends or state holidays;

   b. The estimate of asbestos to be removed required under subdivision B 5 of this section shall be signed by the owner and the owner's signature authenticated by a notary; and

   c. A copy of the contract shall be submitted with the notification.

2. The asbestos project permit fee shall be 0.5% of the contract price or $470 whichever is greater. For contracts which require payments per square or linear foot of asbestos removed or encapsulated the contract price shall be the amount of asbestos estimated pursuant to subdivision B 5 of this section times the per foot charge in the contract;

3. The contractor shall submit an amended notification at least one day prior to each time the contractor will not be on site. The fee for each amended notification shall be $15;

4. A contractor shall submit an amended notification whenever the actual amount of asbestos removed or encapsulated exceeds the original estimate. If the contract was for a fixed cost regardless of the amount of asbestos the amendment fee shall be $15. If the contract was based on a price per square or linear foot the amendment fee shall be the difference between the actual amount removed and the estimated amount times the contract price per foot times 0.5% plus $15; and

5. Cancellation of a blanket notification may be made at any time by submitting a notarized notice of cancellation signed by the owner. The notice of cancellation must include the actual amount of asbestos removed and the actual amount of payments made under the contract. The refund shall be the difference between the original asbestos permit fee paid and either the actual amount of payments made under the contract times 0.5% or $470 whichever is greater.

E. Notification of less than 20 days may be allowed in case of an emergency involving protection of life, health, or property, including but not limited to: leaking or ruptured pipes; accidentally damaged or fallen asbestos that could expose nonasbestos workers or the public; unplanned mechanical outages or repairs essential to a work process that require asbestos removal and could only be removed safely during the mechanical outage. Notification and asbestos permit fee shall be submitted within five working days after the start of the emergency abatement. A description of the emergency situation shall be included when filing an emergency notification.

F. No notification shall be effective if an incomplete form is submitted, or if the proper permit fee is not enclosed with the completed form or if the credit card payment required for facsimile transmission in 16VAC25-20-30 J is not approved.

G. On the basis of the information submitted in the asbestos notification, the department shall issue a permit to the contractor within seven working days of the receipt of a completed notification form and permit fee.
   1. The permit shall be effective for the dates entered on the notification.
   2. The permit or a copy of the permit shall be kept on site during work on the project.

H. Amended notifications may be submitted for modification of 16VAC25-20-30 B 3 through 11. No amendments to 16VAC25-20-30 B 1 or 2 shall be allowed. A copy of the original notification form with the amended items circled and the permit number entered shall be submitted at any time prior to the removal date on the original notification.
   1. No amended notification shall be effective if any incomplete form is submitted or if the proper permit amendment fee is not enclosed with the completed notification.
   2. A permit amendment fee shall be submitted with the amended notification form. The fee shall be in accordance with the following schedule:
      a. For modification to 16VAC25-20-30 B 3, 16VAC25-20-30 B 4, and 16VAC25-20-30 B 6 through 16VAC25-20-30 B 10 - $15;
      b. For modifications to 16VAC25-20-30 B 5:
         (1) the difference between the permit fee in 16VAC25-20-30 C for the amended amount of asbestos and the original permit fee submitted; plus
         (2) $15.
   3. Modifications to the completion date may be made at any time up to the completion date on the original notification.
   4. If the amended notification is complete and the required fee is included, the department will issue an amended permit if necessary.

I. The department must be notified prior to any cancellation. A copy of the original notification form marked cancelled must be received no later than the scheduled removal date. Cancellation of a project may also be done by facsimile transmission. Refunds of the asbestos project permit fee will be made for timely cancellations when a notarized notice of cancellation signed by the owner is submitted. Fifteen dollars for processing for the original notification, $15 for each amendment filed and $15 for processing the refund payment will be deducted from the refund payment.

J. Notification for any project, emergency notification, or amendment to notification may be done by facsimile transmission if the required fees are paid by credit card.

VAC
Title 16

16VAC25-80-10. Access to Employee Exposure and Medical Records; In General (29 CFR 1910.20)

Note: The following standard is unique for the enforcement of occupational safety and health within the Commonwealth of Virginia under the jurisdiction of the VOSH Program. The federal OSHA standard counterpart listed at 1910.1020 does not apply; it does not carry the force of law and is not printed in this volume.

(a) Purpose. The purpose of this chapter is to provide employees and their designated representatives a right of access to relevant exposure and medical records, and to provide representatives of the commissioner a right of access to these records in order to fulfill responsibilities under the Occupational Safety and Health Act. Access by employees, their representatives, and the commissioner is necessary to yield both direct and indirect improvements in the detection, treatment and prevention of occupational disease. Each employer is responsible for assuring compliance with this chapter, but the activities involved in complying with the access to medical records provisions can be carried out, on behalf of the employer, by the physician or other health care personnel in charge of employee medical records. Except as expressly provided, nothing in this chapter is intended to affect existing legal and ethical obligations concerning the maintenance and confidentiality of employee medical information, the duty to disclose information to a patient/employee or any other aspect of the medical-care relationship, or affect existing legal obligations concerning the protection of trade secret information.

[45 F.R. 54333, August 15, 1980.]

(b) Scope and application.
   (1) This chapter applies to each general industry, maritime, and construction employer who makes, maintains, contracts for, or has access to employee exposure or medical records, or analyses thereof, pertaining to employees exposed to toxic substances or harmful physical agents.
   (2) This chapter applies to all employee exposure and medical records, and analyses thereof, of employees exposed to toxic substances or harmful physical agents, whether or not the records are related to specific occupational safety and health standards.
   (3) This chapter applies to all employee exposure and medical records, and analyses thereof, made or maintained in any manner, including on an in-house or contractual (e.g., fee-for-service) basis. Each employer shall assure that the preservation and access requirements of this section are complied with regardless of the manner in which records are made or maintained.

(c) Definitions.
   (1) "Access" means the right and opportunity to examine and copy.
   (2) "Analysis using exposure or medical records" means any compilation of data, or any research, statistical or other study based at least in part on information collected from individual employee exposure or medical records or information collected from health insurance claims records, provided that either the analysis has been reported to the employer or no further work is currently being done by the person responsible for preparing the analysis.
   (3) "Designated representative" means any individual or organization to whom an employee gives written authorization to exercise a right of access. For the purposes of access to employee exposure records and analyses using exposure or medical records, a recognized or certified collective bargaining agent shall be treated automatically as a designated representative without regard to written employee authorization.

(4) "Employee" means a current employee, a former employee, or an employee being assigned or transferred to work where there will be exposure to toxic substances or harmful physical agents. In the case of a deceased or legally incapacitated employee, the employee's legal representative may directly exercise all the employee's rights under this chapter.

(5) "Employee exposure record" means a record containing any of the following kinds of information concerning employee exposure to toxic substances or harmful physical agents:

(i) environmental (workplace) monitoring or measuring, including personal, area, grab, wipe, or other form of sampling, as well as related collection and analytical methodologies, calculations, and other background data relevant to interpretation of the results obtained;

(ii) biological monitoring results which directly assess the absorption of a substance or agent by body systems (e.g., the level of a chemical in the blood, urine, breath, hair, fingernails, etc.) but not including results which assess the biological effect of a substance or agent;

(iii) material safety data sheets; or

(iv) in the absence of the above, any other record which reveals the identity (e.g., chemical, common, or trade name) of a toxic substance or harmful physical agent.

(6) (i) "Employee medical record" means a record concerning the health status of an employee which is made or maintained by a physician, nurse, or other health care personnel, or technician, including:

(A) medical and employment questionnaires or histories (including job description and occupational exposures),

(B) the results of medical examinations (pre-employment, pre-assignment, periodic, or episodic) and laboratory tests (including X-ray examinations and all biological monitoring),

(C) medical opinions, diagnoses, progress notes, and recommendations,

(D) descriptions of treatments and prescriptions, and

(E) employee medical complaints.

(ii) "Employee medical record" does not include the following:

(A) physical specimens (e.g., blood or urine samples which are routinely discarded as a part of normal medical practice, and are not required to be maintained by other legal requirements,

(B) records concerning health insurance claims if maintained separately from the employer's medical program and its records, and not accessible to the employer by employee name or other direct personal identifier (e.g., Social Security number, payroll number, etc.), or

(C) records concerning voluntary employee assistance programs (alcohol, drug abuse, or personal counseling programs) if maintained separately from the employer's medical program and its records.

(7) "Employer" means a current employer, a former employer, or a successor employer.

(8) "Exposure" or "exposed" means that an employee is subjected to a toxic substance or harmful physical agent in the course of employment through any route of entry (inhalation, ingestion, skin contact or absorption, etc.), and includes past exposure and potential (e.g., accidental or possible) exposure, but does not include situations where the employer can demonstrate that the toxic substance or harmful physical agent is not used, handled, stored, generated, or present in the workplace in any manner different from typical non-occupational situations.

VAC
Title 16

(9) "Record" means any item, collection, or grouping of information regardless of the form or process by which it is maintained (e.g., paper document, microfiche, microfilm, X-ray film, or automated data processing).

(10) "Specific written consent"

    (i) Means a written authorization containing the following:

        (A) the name and signature of the employee authorizing the release of medical information,

        (B) the date of the written authorization,

        (C) the name of the individual or organization that is authorized to release the medical information,

        (D) the name of the designated representative (individual or organization) that is authorized to receive the released information,

        (E) a general description of the medical information that is authorized to be released,

        (F) a general description of the purpose for the release of the medical information, and

        (G) a date or condition upon which the written authorization will expire (if less than one year).

    (ii) A written authorization does not operate to authorize the release of medical information not in existence on the date of written authorization, unless this is expressly authorized, and does not operate for more than one year from the date of written authorization.

    (iii) A written authorization may be revoked in writing prospectively at any time.

(11) "Toxic substance or harmful physical agent" means any chemical substance, biological agent (bacteria, virus, fungus, etc.), or physical stress (noise, heat, cold, vibration, repetitive motion, ionizing and non-ionizing radiation, hypo- or hyperbaric pressure, etc.) which:

    (i) is regulated by a Federal law or rule due to a hazard to health,

    (ii) is listed in the latest printed edition of the National Institute for Occupational Safety and Health (NIOSH) Registry of Toxic Effects of Chemical Substances (RTECS) (See Appendix B),

    (iii) has yielded positive evidence of an acute or chronic health hazard in human, animal, or other biological testing conducted by, or known to, the employer, or

    (iv) has a material safety data sheet available to the employer indicating that the material may pose a hazard to human health.

(d) Preservation of records.

    (1) Unless a specific occupational safety and health standard provides a different period of time, each employer shall assure the preservation and retention of records as follows:

        (i) Employee medical records. Each employee medical record shall be preserved and maintained for at least the duration of employment plus 30 years, except that health insurance claims records maintained separately from the employer's medical program and its records need not be retained for any specified period;

        (ii) Employee exposure records. Each employee exposure record shall be preserved and maintained for at least 30 years, except that:

            (A) background date to environmental (workplace) monitoring or measuring, such as laboratory reports and worksheets, need only be retained for one year so long as the sampling results, the collection methodology (sampling plan), a description of the analytical and mathematical methods used, and a summary of other background data relevant to interpretation of the results obtained, are retained for at least 30 years; and

(B) material safety data sheets and (c)(5)(iv) records concerning the identity of a substance or agent need not be retained for any specified period as long as some record of the identity (chemical name if known) of the substance or agent, where it was used, and when it was used is retained for at least 30 years; and

(iii) Analyses using exposure of medical records. Each analysis using exposure or medical records shall be preserved and maintained for at least 30 years.

(2) Nothing in this chapter is intended to mandate the form, manner, or process by which an employer preserves a record so long as the information contained in the record is preserved and retrievable, except that X-ray films shall be preserved in their original state.

(e) Access to records.

(1) General.

(i) Whenever an employee or designated representative requests access to a record, the employer shall assure that access is provided in a reasonable time, place, and manner, but in no event later than 15 days after the request for access is made.

(ii) Whenever an employee or designated representative requests a copy of a record, the employer shall, within the period of time previously specified, assure that either:

(A) a copy of the record is provided without cost to the employee or representative,

(B) the necessary mechanical copying facilities (e.g., photocopying) are made available without cost to the employee or representative for copying the record, or

(C) the record is loaned to the employee or representative for a reasonable time to enable a copy to be made.

(iii) Whenever a record has been previously provided without cost to an employee or designated representative, the employer may charge reasonable, non-discriminatory administrative costs (i.e., search and copying expenses but not including overhead expenses) for a request by the employee or designated representative for additional copies of the record, except that

(A) an employer shall not charge for an initial request for a copy of new information that has been added to a record which was previously provided; and

(B) an employer shall not charge for an initial request by a recognized or certified collective bargaining agent for a copy of an employee exposure record or an analysis using exposure or medical records.

(iv) Nothing in this chapter is intended to preclude employees and collective bargaining agents from collectively bargaining to obtain access to information in addition to that available under this chapter.

(2) Employee and designated representative access.

(i) Employee exposure records. Each employer shall, upon request, assure the access of each employee and designated representative to employee exposure records relevant to the employee. For the purpose of this chapter, exposure records relevant to the employee consist of:

(A) records of the employee's past or present exposure to toxic substances or harmful physical agents,

(B) exposure records of other employees with past or present job duties or working conditions related to or similar to those of the employee,

(C) records containing exposure information concerning the employee's workplace or working conditions, and

(D) Exposure records pertaining to workplaces or working conditions to which the employee is being assigned or transferred.

(ii) Employee medical records.

(A) Each employer shall, upon request, assure the access of each employee to employee medical records of which the employee is the subject, except as provided in subsection (e)(2)(ii)(D) below.

(B) Each employer shall, upon request, assure the access of each designated representative to the employee medical records of any employee who has given the designated representative specific written consent. Appendix A to this chapter contains a sample form which may be used to establish specific written consent for access to employee medical records.

(C) Whenever access to employee medical records is requested, a physician representing the employer may recommend that the employee or designated representative:

(1) consult with the physician for the purposes of reviewing and discussing the records requested,

(2) accept a summary of material facts and opinions in lieu of the records requested, or

(3) accept release of the requested records only to a physician or other designated representative.

(D) Whenever an employee requests access to his or her employee medical records, and a physician representing the employer believes that direct employee access to information contained in the records regarding a specific diagnosis of a terminal illness or a psychiatric condition could be detrimental to the employee's health, the employer may inform the employee that access will only be provided to a designated representative of the employee having specific written consent, and deny the employee's request for direct access to this information only. Where a designated representative with specific written consent requests access to information so withheld, the employer shall assure the access of the designated representative to this information, even when it is known that the designated representative will give the information to the employee.

(E) Nothing in this chapter precludes a physician, nurse, or other responsible health care personnel maintaining employee medical records from deleting from requested medical records the identity of a family member, personal friend, or fellow employee who has provided confidential information concerning an employee's health status.

(iii) Analyses using exposure or medical records.

(A) Each employer shall, upon request, assure the access of each employee and designated representative to each analysis using exposure or medical records concerning the employee's working conditions or workplace.

(B) Whenever access is requested to an analysis which reports the contents of employee medical records by either direct identifier (name, address, social security number, payroll number, etc.) or by information which could reasonably be used under the circumstances indirectly to identify specific employees (exact age, height, weight, race, sex, date of initial employment, job title, etc.), the employer shall assure that personal identifiers are removed before access is provided. If the employer can demonstrate that removal of personal identifiers from an analysis is not feasible, access to the personally identifiable portions of the analysis need not be provided.

(3) OSHA access.

(i) Each employer shall, upon request, assure the immediate access of representatives of the Commissioner of the Department of Labor and Industry to employee exposure and medical records and to analyses using exposure or medical records. Rules of agency practice and procedure governing OSHA access to employee medical records are contained in 29 CFR 1913.10.

(ii) Whenever VOSH seeks access to personally identifiable employee medical information by presenting to the employer a written access order pursuant to 29 CFR 1913.10(d), the employer shall prominently post a copy of the written access order and its accompanying cover letter for at least 15 working days.

(f) Trade secrets.

(1) Except as provided in paragraph (f)(2) of this section, nothing in this section precludes an employer from deleting from records requested by an employee or designated representative any trade secret data which discloses manufacturing processes, or discloses the percentage of a chemical substance in a mixture, as long as the employee or designated representative is notified that information has been deleted. Whenever deletion of trade secret information substantially impairs evaluation of the place where or the time when exposure to a toxic substance or harmful physical agent occurred, the employer shall provide alternative information which is sufficient to permit the employee to identify where and when exposure occurred.

(2) Notwithstanding any trade secret claims, whenever access to records is requested, the employer shall provide access to chemical or physical agent identities including chemical names, levels of exposure, and employee health status data contained in the requested records.

(3) Whenever trade secret information is provided to an employee or designated representative, the employer may require, as a condition of access, that the employee or designated representative agree in writing not to use the trade secret information for the purpose of commercial gain and not to permit misuse of the trade secret information by a competitor or potential competitor of the employer.

(g) Employee information.

(1) Upon an employee's first entering into employment, and at least annually thereafter, each employer shall inform employees exposed to toxic substances of harmful physical agents of the following:

(i) the existence, location, and availability of any records covered by this section;

(ii) the person responsible for maintaining and providing access to records; and

(iii) each employee's rights of access to these records.

(2) Each employer shall make readily available to employees a copy of this chapter and its appendices, and shall distribute to employees any informational materials concerning this chapter which are made available to the employer by the Commissioner of the Department of Labor and Industry.

(h) Transfer of records.

(1) Whenever an employer is ceasing to do business, the employer shall transfer all records to this section to the successor employer. The successor employer shall receive and maintain these records.

(2) Whenever an employer is ceasing to do business and there is no successor employer to receive and maintain the records subject to this chapter, the employer shall notify affected employees of their rights of access to records at least 3 months prior to the cessation of the employer's business.

(3) Whenever an employer either is ceasing to do business and there is no successor employer to receive and maintain the records, or intends to dispose of any records required to be preserved for at least 30 years, the employer shall:

(i) transfer the records to the Director of the National Institute for Occupational Safety and Health (NIOSH) if so required by a specific occupational safety and health standard; or

(ii) notify the Director of NIOSH in writing of the impending disposal of records at least 3 months prior to the disposal of the records.

(4) Where an employer regularly disposes of records required to be preserved for at least 30 years, the employer may, with at least 3 months notice, notify the Director of NIOSH on an annual basis of the records intended to be disposed of in the coming year.

(i) Appendices. The information contained in the Appendices to this chapter is not intended, by itself, to create any additional obligations not otherwise imposed by this chapter nor detract from any existing obligation.

(j) Effective date. This section shall become effective on August 21, 1980. All obligations of this chapter commence on the effective date except that the employer shall provide the information required under paragraph (g)(1) of this section to all current employees within 60 days after the effective date.

16VAC25-160-10. Construction industry sanitation standard; in general (29 CFR 1926.51).

Note: The following standard is unique for the enforcement of occupational safety and health within the Commonwealth of Virginia under the jurisdiction of the VOSH Program. The existing federal OSHA standard does not apply; it does not carry the force of law and is not printed in this volume.

(a) Water supply.

(1) Potable drinking water.

(i) Potable water shall be provided and placed in locations readily accessible to all employees.

(ii) The water shall be suitably cool and in sufficient amounts, taking into account the air temperature, humidity and the nature of the work performed to meet the needs of all employees.

(iii) The water shall be dispensed in single-use drinking cups or by fountains. The use of the common drinking cup is prohibited.

(2) Portable containers used to dispense drinking water shall be capable of being tightly closed, and equipped with a tap. Water shall not be dipped from containers.

(3) Any container used to distribute drinking water shall be clearly marked as to the nature of its contents and not used for any other purpose. Water shall not be dipped from containers.

(4) Where single service cups (to be used but once) are supplied, both a sanitary container for the unused cups and a receptacle for disposing of the cups shall be provided.

(5) Maintenance. Potable drinking water, toilet and handwashing facilities shall be maintained in accordance with appropriate public health sanitation practices, and shall include the following:

　(i) Drinking water containers shall be constructed of materials that maintain water quality;

　(ii) Drinking water containers shall be refilled daily and shall be covered; and

　(iii) Drinking water containers shall be regularly cleaned.

(b) Nonpotable water.

(1) Outlets for nonpotable water, such as water for industrial or firefighting purposes only, shall be identified by signs meeting the requirements of Subpart G of this part (16VAC25-175-1926.200 et seq.), to indicate clearly that the water is unsafe and is not to be used for drinking, washing, or cooking purposes.

(2) There shall be no cross-connection, open or potential, between a system furnishing potable water and a system furnishing nonpotable water.

(c) Toilet and handwashing facilities.

(1) One toilet and one handwashing facility shall be provided for each 20 employees or fraction thereof.

(2) Toilet facilities shall be adequately ventilated, appropriately screened, have self-closing doors that can be closed and latched from inside and shall be constructed to insure privacy.

(3) Toilet and handwashing facilities shall be readily accessible to all employees, accessibly located and in close proximity to each other.

(4) Toilet facilities shall be operational and maintained in a clean and sanitary condition.

(5) The requirements of this paragraph for sanitation facilities shall not apply to mobile crews having transportation readily available to nearby toilet facilities.

(d) NOTE: Rescinded as being inconsistent with the more stringent Virginia Standard.

(e) NOTE: Rescinded as being inconsistent with the more stringent Virginia Standard.

(f) Washing facilities. Hand washing facilities shall be refilled with potable water as necessary to ensure an adequate supply of potable water, soap and single use towels.

(g) Revoked

(h) Waste disposal. (1) Disposal of wastes from facilities shall not cause unsanitary conditions.

(i) Definitions.

(1) "Handwashing" facility means a facility providing either a basin, container or outlet with an adequate supply of potable water, soap and single use towels.

(2) "Potable water" means water that meets the standards for drinking purposes of the state or local authority having jurisdiction or water that meets the quality

standards prescribed by the U. S. Environmental Protection Agency's Interim Primary Drinking Water Regulations, published in 40 CFR Part 141.

(3) "Toilet facility" means a fixed or portable facility designed for the containment of the products of both defecation and urination which is supplied with toilet paper adequate to meet employee needs. Toilet facilities include biological, chemical, flush and combustion toilets and sanitary privies.

16VAC25-160-20. General industry standards applicable to construction sanitation (29 CFR 1910.141).

The following requirements from 29 CFR Part 1910 (General Industry) have been identified as applicable to construction (29 CFR 1926.51, Sanitation), in accordance with their respective scope and definitions.

§1910.141 Sanitation

(a) (1) Scope. This section applies to all permanent places of employment.

(2) NOTE: Virginia does not adopt 29 CFR 1910.141(a)(2)(i)-(xi), which sets out definitions applicable to 29 CFR 1910.141. 29 CFR 1910.141(a)(2)(v) has been rescinded.

(v) NOTE: Rescinded as being inconsistent with the more stringent Virginia Standard for potable water (16VAC25-160-10).

NOTE: Virginia does not adopt 29 CFR 1910.141(a)(3) and (4).

(5) Vermin control. Every enclosed workplace shall be so constructed, equipped, and maintained, so far as reasonably practicable, as to prevent the entrance or harborage of rodents, insects, and other vermin. A continuing and effective extermination program shall be instituted where their presence is detected.

NOTE: Virginia does not adopt 29 CFR 1910.141(b) through (g)(1).

(g) (2) Eating and drinking areas. No employee shall be allowed to consume food or beverages in a toilet room nor in any area exposed to a toxic material.

NOTE: Virginia does not adopt 29 CFR 1910.141(g)(3) and (g)(4).

(h) NOTE: Rescinded as being inconsistent with the more stringent Virginia Standard.

16VAC25-160-30. Medical services and first aid (29 CFR 1910.151).

NOTE: Virginia does not adopt 29 CFR 1910.151(a) and (b).

(c) Where the eyes or body of any person may be exposed to injurious corrosive materials, suitable facilities for quick drenching or flushing of the eyes and body shall be provided within the work area for immediate emergency use.

FEDERAL OSHA 1904.33(A)

Basic Requirement

You must save the OSHA 300 Log, the privacy case list (if one exists), the annual summary, and the OSHA 301 Incident Report forms for five (5) years following the end of the calendar year that these records cover.

CODE OF VIRGINIA (COV)
TITLE 40.1 LABOR AND EMPLOYMENT

40.1-49.4. Enforcement of This Title and Standards, Rules or Regulations for Safety and Health; Orders of Commissioner; Proceedings in Circuit Court; Injunctions; Penalties

A. 1. If the Commissioner has reasonable cause to believe that an employer has violated any safety or health provision of Title 40.1 or any standard, rule or regulation adopted pursuant thereto, he shall with reasonable promptness issue a citation to the employer. Each citation shall be in writing and shall describe with particularity the nature of the violation or violations, including a reference to the provision of this title or the appropriate standards, rules or regulations adopted pursuant thereto, and shall include an order of abatement fixing a reasonable time for abatement of each violation.

  2. The Commissioner may prescribe procedures for calling to the employer's attention de minimis violations which have no direct or immediate relationship to safety and health.

  3. No citation may be issued under this section after the expiration of six months following the occurrence of any alleged violation.

  4. (a) The Commissioner shall have the authority to propose civil penalties for cited violations in accordance with subsections G, H, I, and J of this section. In determining the amount of any proposed penalty he shall give due consideration to the appropriateness of the penalty with respect to the size of the business of the employer being charged, the gravity of the violation, the good faith of the employer, and the history of previous violations. In addition, the Commissioner shall have authority to assess interest on all past-due penalties and administrative costs incurred in the collection of penalties for such violations consistent with §2.2-4805.

  (b) After, or concurrent with, the issuance of a citation and order of abatement, and within a reasonable time after the termination of an inspection or investigation, the Commissioner shall notify the employer by certified mail or by personal service of the proposed penalty or that no penalty is being proposed. The proposed penalty shall be deemed to be the final order of the Commissioner and not subject to review by any court or agency unless, within fifteen working days from the date of receipt of such notice, the employer notifies the Commissioner in writing that he intends to contest the citation, order of abatement or the proposed penalty or the employee or representative of employees has filed a notice in accordance with subsection B of this section and any such notice of proposed penalty, citation or order of abatement shall so state.

B. Any employee or representative of employees of an employer to whom a citation and order of abatement has been issued may, within fifteen working days from the time of the receipt of the citation and order of abatement by the employer, notify the Commissioner, in writing, that they wish to contest the abatement time before the circuit court.

C. If the Commissioner has reasonable cause to believe that an employer has failed to abate a violation for which a citation has been issued within the time period permitted for its abatement, which time shall not begin to run until the entry of a final order in the case of any contest as provided in subsection E of this section initiated by the employer in good faith and not solely for delay or avoidance of penalties, a citation for failure to abate will be issued to the employer in the same manner as prescribed by subsection A of this section. In addition, the Commissioner shall notify the employer by certified mail or by personal service of such failure and of the penalty proposed to be assessed by reason of such failure. If, within fifteen working days from the date of receipt of the notice of the proposed penalty, the employer fails to notify the Commissioner that he intends to contest the citation or proposed assessment of penalty, the citation and assessment as proposed shall be deemed a final order of the Commissioner and not subject to review by any court or agency.

D. Civil penalties owed under this section shall be paid to the Commissioner for deposit into the general fund of the Treasurer of the Commonwealth. The Commissioner shall prescribe procedures for the payment of proposed assessments of penalties which are not contested by employers. Such procedures shall include provisions for an employer to consent to abatement of the alleged violation and pay a proposed penalty or a negotiated sum in lieu of such penalty without admission of any civil liability arising from such alleged violation.

Final orders of the Commissioner or the circuit courts may be recorded, enforced and satisfied as orders or decrees of a circuit court upon certification of such orders by the Commissioner or the court as appropriate.

E. Upon receipt of a notice of contest of a citation, proposed penalty, order of abatement or abatement time pursuant to subdivision A 4 (b), subsection B or C of this section, the Commissioner shall immediately notify the attorney for the Commonwealth for the jurisdiction wherein the violation is alleged to have occurred and shall file with the circuit court a bill of complaint. Upon issuance and service of a subpoena in chancery, the circuit court shall promptly set the matter for hearing without a jury. The circuit court shall thereafter issue a written order, based on findings of fact and conclusions of law, affirming, modifying or vacating the Commissioner's citation or proposed penalty, or directing other appropriate relief, and such order shall become final twenty-one days after its issuance. The circuit court shall provide affected employees or their representatives and employers an opportunity to participate as parties to hearings under this subsection.

F. 1. In addition to the remedies set forth above, the Commissioner may file a bill of complaint with the clerk of the circuit court having equity jurisdiction over the employer or the place of employment involved asking the court to temporarily or permanently enjoin any conditions or practices in any place of employment which are such that a danger exists which could reasonably be expected to cause death or serious physical harm immediately or before the imminence of such danger can be eliminated through the enforcement procedures otherwise provided by this title. Any order issued under this section may require such steps to be taken as may be necessary to avoid, correct or remove such imminent danger and prohibit the employment or presence of any individual in locations or under conditions where such imminent danger exists, except individuals whose presence is necessary to avoid, correct or remove such imminent danger or to maintain the capacity of a continuous process operation to resume normal operations without a complete cessation of operations, or where a cessation of operations is necessary, to permit such to be accomplished in a safe and orderly manner. No order issued without prior notice to the employer shall be effective for more than five working days. Whenever and as soon as the Commissioner concludes that conditions or practices described in this subsection exist in any place of employment and that judicial relief shall be sought, he shall immediately inform the affected employer and employees of such proposed course of action.

2. Any court described in this section shall also have jurisdiction, upon petition of the Commissioner or his authorized representative, to enjoin any violations of this title or the standards, rules or regulations promulgated thereunder.

3. If the Commissioner arbitrarily or capriciously fails to seek relief under subdivision 1 of this subsection, any employee who may be injured by reason of such failure, or the representative of such employee, may bring an action against the Commissioner in a circuit court of competent jurisdiction for a writ of mandamus to compel the Commissioner to seek such an order and for such further relief as may be appropriate.

G. Any employer who has received a citation for a violation of any safety or health provision of this title or any standard, rule or regulation promulgated pursuant thereto and such violation is specifically determined not to be of a serious nature may be assessed a civil penalty of up to $7,000 for each such violation.

H. Any employer who has received a citation for a violation of any safety or health provision of this title or any standard, rule or regulation promulgated pursuant thereto and such violation is determined to be a serious violation shall be assessed a civil penalty of up to $7,000 for each such violation.

I. Any employer who fails to abate a violation for which a citation has been issued within the period permitted for its abatement (which period shall not begin to run until the entry of the final order of the circuit court) may be assessed a civil penalty of not more than $7,000 for each day during which such violation continues.

J. Any employer who willfully or repeatedly violates any safety or health provision of this title or any standard, rule or regulation promulgated pursuant thereto may be assessed a civil penalty of not more than $70,000 for each such violation.

K. Any employer who willfully violates any safety or health provisions of this title or standards, rules or regulations adopted pursuant thereto, and that violation causes death to any employee, shall, upon conviction, be punished by a fine of not more than $70,000 or by imprisonment for not more than six months, or by both such fine and imprisonment. If the conviction is for a violation committed after a first conviction of such person, punishment shall be a fine of not more than $140,000 or by imprisonment for not more than one year, or by both such fine and imprisonment.

L. In any proceeding before a judge of a circuit court parties may obtain discovery by the methods provided for in the Rules of the Supreme Court of Virginia.

M. No fees or costs shall be charged the Commonwealth by a court or any officer for or in connection with the filing of the complaint, pleadings, or other papers in any action authorized by this section or §40.1-49.5.

N. Every official act of the circuit court shall be entered of record and all hearings and records shall be open to the public, except any information subject to protection under the provisions of §40.1-51.4:1.

O. The provisions of Chapter 30 (§59.1-406 et seq.) of Title 59.1 shall be considered safety and health standards of the Commonwealth and enforced as to employers pursuant to this section by the Commissioner of Labor and Industry.

UNDERGROUND UTILITIES

Thischapter details the requirements that a contractor must follow before excavating near underground utilities and the procedures to follow after the utilities have been marked. A contractor should become familiar with the phone numbers to call for marking, learn how to verify that the marking has been completed, and be able to determine the type of equipment that may be used within the marked area. The underground utility program is administered by the state corporation commission (*www.scc.virginia.gov*).

MARKING UNDERGROUND UTILITIES

Any time a contractor is going to perform digging operations, the utilities must be marked so that workers know when they are working near utilities and they can take precautions to avoid damaging the utilities. Many underground utilities are not readily apparent without markings. Although most utility companies, such as the telephone company and the power company, install metal signs warning that there are cables underneath, these signs can disappear, erode, or shift over time. The amount of ground cover over the utility may be surprisingly little. This author, using a hand shovel, "discovered" a power line that was only six inches below grade. Over time and after various agricultural and road maintenance operations, several feet of dirt, as well as the marking tape used to cover the cable, had been removed.

Virginia has set up a very user-friendly operation for obtaining utility marking and verifying that the marking is complete so that excavation can begin. To request marking of the area to be excavated contractors can call a statewide toll-free number, 811. The contractor is required to stake or flag the proposed excavation so the utility contractor can mark the appropriate area. To check the status of the marking a contractor can call (800) 552-3120. The utility company will also fax the status if a fax number is supplied. It is a positive response notification system in that the contractor cannot dig until notification has been received that all utilities have been marked.

Once the contractor has verified that the marking is complete, excavation can begin with caution. No power excavating equipment is allowed to be used within two feet on either side of the marked area.

Penalties

If an excavator does not call for marking and damages an underground utility, penalties of up to three times the cost to repair the damage may be assessed, as well as a $10,000 fine. It is also a violation of the State Board for Contractor regulations to dig without calling for marking.

CODE OF VIRGINIA (COV)
TITLE 56 CHAPTER 10.3
UNDERGROUND UTILITY DAMAGE PREVENTION ACT

§56-265.15. Definitions; Calculation of Time Periods

A. As used in this chapter:

"Abandoned" means no longer in service and physically disconnected from a portion of the underground utility line that is in use for storage or conveyance of service.

"Commission" means the State Corporation Commission.

"Contract locator" means any person contracted by an operator specifically to determine the approximate horizontal location of the operator's utility lines that may exist within the area specified by a notice served on a notification center.

"Damage" means any impact upon or removal of support from an underground facility as a result of excavation or demolition which according to the operating practices of the operator would necessitate the repair of such facility.

"Demolish" or "demolition" means any operation by which a structure or mass of material is wrecked, razed, rendered, moved, or removed by means of any tools, equipment, or discharge of explosives which could damage underground utility lines.

"Designer" means any licensed professional designated by the project owner who designs government projects, commercial projects, residential projects consisting of twenty-five or more units, or industrial projects, which projects require the approval of governmental or regulatory authorities having jurisdiction over the project area.

"Emergency" means a sudden or unexpected occurrence involving a clear and imminent danger, demanding immediate action to prevent or mitigate loss of, or damage to, life, health, property, or essential public services.

"Excavate" or "excavation" means any operation in which earth, rock, or other material in the ground is moved, removed, or otherwise displaced by means of any tools, equipment, or explosives and includes, without limitation, grading, trenching, digging, ditching, dredging, drilling, augering, tunneling, scraping, cable or pipe plowing and driving, wrecking, razing, rendering, moving, or removing any structure or mass of material.

"Extraordinary circumstances" means floods, snow, ice storms, tornadoes, earthquakes, or other natural disasters.

"Hand digging" means any excavation involving nonmechanized tools or equipment. Hand digging includes, but is not limited to, digging with shovels, picks, and manual post hole diggers, vacuum excavation or soft digging.

"Notification center" means an organization whose membership is open to all operators of underground facilities located within the notification center's designated service area, which maintains a data base, provided by its member operators, that includes the geographic areas in which its member operators desire transmissions of notices of proposed excavation, and which has the capability to transmit, within one hour of receipt, notices of proposed excavation to member operators by teletype, telecopy, personal computer, or telephone.

"Notify," "notice" or "notification" means the completed delivery of information to the person to be notified, and the receipt of same by such person in accordance with this chapter. The delivery of information includes, but is not limited to, the use of any electronic or technological means of data transfer.

"Operator" means any person who owns, furnishes or transports materials or services by means of a utility line.

"Person" means any individual, operator, firm, joint venture, partnership, corporation, association, municipality, or other political subdivision, governmental unit, department or agency, and includes any trustee, receiver, assignee, or personal representative thereof.

"Soft digging" means any excavation using tools or equipment that utilize air or water pressure as the direct means to break up soil or earth for removal by vacuum excavation.

"Special project notice" means a valid notice to the notification center by an excavator covering a specific, unique or long-term project.

"Utility line" means any item of public or private property which is buried or placed below ground or submerged for use in connection with the storage or conveyance of water, sewage, telecommunications, electric energy, cable television, oil, petroleum products, gas, or other substances, and includes but is not limited to pipes, sewers, combination storm/sanitary sewer systems, conduits, cables, valves, lines, wires, manholes, attachments, and those portions of poles below ground. The term "sewage" as used herein does not include any gravity storm drainage systems. Except for any publicly owned gravity sewer system within a county which has adopted the urban county executive form of government, the term "utility line" does not include any gravity sewer system or any combination gravity storm/sanitary sewer system within any counties, cities, towns or political subdivisions constructed or replaced prior to January 1, 1995. No excavator shall be held liable for the cost to repair damage to any such systems constructed or replaced prior to January 1, 1995, unless such systems are located in accordance with §56-265.19.

"Willful" means an act done intentionally, knowingly, and purposely, without justifiable excuse, as distinguished from an act done carelessly, thoughtlessly, heedlessly or inadvertently.

"Working day" means every day, except Saturdays, Sundays, and legal state and national holidays.

B.   Unless otherwise specified, all time periods used in this chapter shall be calculated from the time of the original notification to the notification center as provided in §56-265.17. In addition, all time periods exclude Saturdays, Sundays, and legal state and national holidays.

§56-265.15:1. Exemptions; Routine Maintenance
Nothing in this chapter shall apply to:
1. Any hand digging performed by an owner or occupant of a property.
2. The tilling of soil for agricultural purposes.
3. Any excavation done by a railroad when the excavation is made entirely on the land which the railroad owns and on which the railroad operates, provided there is no encroachment on any operator's rights-of-way or easements.
4. An excavation or demolition during an emergency, as defined in §56-265.15, provided all reasonable precaution has been taken to protect the underground utility lines.

    In the case of the state highway systems or streets and roads maintained by political subdivisions, officials of the Department of Transportation or the political subdivision where the use of such highways, roads, streets or other public way is impaired by an unforeseen occurrence shall determine the necessity of repair beginning immediately after the occurrence.

5. Any excavation for routine pavement maintenance, including patch type paving or the milling of pavement surfaces, upon the paved portion of any street, road, or highway of the Commonwealth provided that any such excavation does not exceed a depth of twelve inches (0.3 meter).

6. Any excavation for the purpose of mining pursuant to and in accordance with the requirements of a permit issued by the Department of Mines, Minerals and Energy.

7. Any hand digging performed by an operator to locate the operator's utility lines in response to a notice of excavation from the notification center, provided all reasonable precaution has been taken to protect the underground utility lines.

§56-265.16:1. Operators to Join Notification Centers; Certification

A. Every operator, including counties, cities and towns, but excluding the Department of Transportation, having the right to bury underground utility lines shall join the notification center for the area.

B. Every notification center shall be certified by the Commission. The Commission shall determine the optimum number of notification centers in the Commonwealth. If the Commission determines that there shall be more than one notification center in the Commonwealth, it shall define the geographic area to be served by each notification center.

C. Any corporation desiring to serve as the notification center for an area of the Commonwealth may apply to the Commission to be certified as the notification center for that area. The Commission shall have authority to grant, amend, or revoke certificates under regulations promulgated relating to certification. An application for certification shall include such information as the Commission may reasonably require addressing the applicant's operational plan for the notification center.

D. Every Commission action regarding the optimum number of notification centers, the geographic area to be served by each notification center, the promulgation of notification center certification regulations, and the grant, amendment, or revocation of notification center certifications shall be made in furtherance of the purpose of preventing or mitigating loss of, or damage to, life, health, property or essential public services resulting from damage to underground utility lines. Any action by the Commission to approve or revoke any notification center certification shall:

1. Ensure protection for the public from the hazards that this chapter is intended to prevent or mitigate;

2. Ensure that all persons served by the notification center receive an acceptable level of performance, which level shall be maintained throughout the period of the notification center's certification; and

3. Require the notification center and its agents to demonstrate financial responsibility for any damages that may result from their violation of any provision of this chapter. Such requirement may be met by purchasing and maintaining liability insurance on such terms and in such amount as the Commission deems appropriate.

E. A notification center shall maintain an excavator-operator information exchange system in accordance with notification center certification regulations promulgated by the Commission. The members of a notification center shall be responsible for developing and implementing a public awareness program to ensure that all parties affected by this chapter shall be aware of their responsibilities. There shall be only one notification center certified for each geographic area defined by the Commission.

§56-265.17. Notification Required Prior to Excavation or Demolition; Waiting Periods; Marking of Proposed Site

A. Except as provided in subsection G, no person, including operators, shall make or begin any excavation or demolition without first notifying the notification center for that area. Notice to the notification center shall be deemed to be notice to each operator who is a member of the notification center. The notification center shall provide the excavator with the identity of utilities that will be notified of the proposed excavation or demolition. Except for counties, cities, and towns, an excavator who willfully fails to notify the notification center of proposed excavation or demolition shall be liable to the operator whose facilities are damaged by that excavator, for three times the cost to repair the damaged property, provided the operator is a member of the notification center. The total amount of punitive damages awarded under this section, as distinguished from actual damages, shall not exceed $10,000 in any single cause of action.

B. Except in the case of an emergency as defined in §56-265.15, the excavator may commence work under one of the following conditions:
    1. After waiting forty-eight hours, beginning 7:00 A.M. the next working day following notice to the notification center;
    2. At any time, if the excavator confirms that all applicable operators have either marked their underground utility lines or reported that no lines are present in the vicinity of the excavation or demolition. The confirmation shall be obtained by contacting or receiving information from the notification center's excavator-operator information exchange system; or
    3. If informed by the notification center that no operators are to be notified.
        If any operator fails to respond to the excavator-operator information exchange system as required by this chapter, the notification center shall renotify any operator of its failure. This renotification shall not constitute an exemption from the duties of the operator set forth in §56-265.19.

C. The excavator shall exercise due care at all times to protect underground utility lines. If, upon arrival at the site of a proposed excavation, the excavator observes clear evidence of the presence of an unmarked utility line in the area of the proposed excavation, the excavator shall not begin excavating until three hours after an additional call is made to the notification center for the area. The operator of any unmarked utility line shall respond within three hours of the excavator's call to the notification center.

D. The excavator's notification shall be valid for fifteen working days from 7:00 A.M. on the next working day following notice to the notification center. Three working days before the end of the fifteen-working-day period, or at any time when line-location markings on the ground become illegible, the excavator intending to excavate shall contact the notification center and request the re-marking of lines. The operator shall re-mark the lines as soon as possible; however, the re-marking of the lines shall be completed within forty-eight hours from 7:00 A.M. on the next working day following the request for the re-mark. Such re-marking shall be valid for an additional fifteen working days from 7:00 A.M. on the next working day following notice to the notification center.

E. In the event a specific location of the excavation cannot be given as required by subdivision 2 of §56-265.18, prior to notifying the notification center pursuant to subsection A of this section, the person proposing to excavate or demolish shall mark the route or boundary of the site of the proposed excavation or demolition by means of white paint, if practical.

F. The extent of the excavator's proposed work shall be a work area that can be excavated within fifteen working days from 7:00 A.M. on the next working day following notice to the notification center. The area covered under each notice shall not exceed one mile.

G. An excavator may request a special project notice from the notification center for the purpose of notifying the operators of the excavator's desire to enter into an agreement for locating and protecting the operator's underground utility lines for a specific, unique or long-term project. An excavator using a special project notice shall have complete control over all activities within the project area. The terms and conditions of such agreements must be agreed upon, in writing, by the excavator and the operator before excavation commences. Such agreement and compliance with the terms of the agreement shall constitute an exemption from the requirements of subsections A, B, C, D and E of this section.

§56-265.17:1. Notification and Procedures for Designers

A. Each designer, who prepares drawings and plans for projects requiring excavation or demolition work, may notify the notification center and provide the center with the information required by §56-265.18 and the designer's professional license number.

B. If a designer notifies the notification center to receive underground utility line information in accordance with §56-265.17:3, the designer shall:
   1. Indicate on the construction drawings, the type of underground utility lines, the horizontal location of these lines as provided by the operators, and the names of the operators of these lines;
   2. Consider, when designing a project and preparing drawings therefor, the location of existing underground lines so as to minimize damage or interference with the existing facilities;
   3. Indicate, on the construction plans or drawings, the designer ticket number and the notification center's toll-free number; and
   4. Request only one designer ticket per project through the notification center at no cost.

§56-265.17:2. Procedures for Project Owners

The project owner shall provide copies of those portions of the drawings that affect the respective operator with underground utility lines in the project area who have responded in accordance with §56-265.17:3.

§56-265.17:3. Procedures for Operators in Response to a Designer Notice

An operator, upon notification by a designer in accordance with §56-265.17:1, shall:
   1. Respond to the designer's request for underground utility line information within fifteen working days in accordance with subdivisions 2, 3, and 4 of this section;
   2. Provide designers with the operator's name, the type of underground utility line, and the approximate horizontal location of the utility line. The foregoing information may be provided to the designer through the means that include, but are not limited to, field locates, maps, surveys, installation records or

other means. If the designer requests field locates, the operator shall provide field locates in accordance with the accuracy set forth in subsection A of §56-265.19. Marking shall be done by both paint and flags whenever possible;

3. Provide such information about the location of the utility lines to designers for informational purposes only. Operators will not be liable for any incorrect information provided or for the subsequent use of this information, nor will they be subject to civil penalties for the accuracy of the information or marks provided. Any concerns about the accuracy of information or marks should be directed to the appropriate operator; and

4. Respond to the operator-excavator information exchange system by no later than 7:00 A.M. on the sixteenth working day following the designer's notice to the notification center.

§56-265.18. Notification Requirements

Every notice served by any person on a notification center shall contain the following information:

1. The name of the individual serving such notice.
2. The specific location of the proposed work. In the event a specific description of the location of the excavation cannot be given, the person proposing to excavate or demolish shall comply with subsection E of §56-265.17.
3. The name, address, telephone number, and telefacsimile number if available, of the excavator or demolisher, to whom notification can be given.
4. The excavator's or demolisher's field telephone number, if one is available.
5. The type and extent of the proposed work.
6. The name of the person for whom the proposed work is being performed.

§56-265.19. Duties of Operator; Regulations

A. If a proposed excavation or demolition is planned in such proximity to the underground utility line that the utility line may be destroyed, damaged, dislocated, or disturbed, the operator shall mark the approximate horizontal location of the underground utility line on the ground to within two feet of either side of the underground utility line by means of stakes, paint, flags, or a combination thereof. The operator shall mark the underground utility line and report the marking status to the excavator-operator information exchange system by no later than 7:00 A.M. on the third working day following the excavator's notice to the notification center, unless the operator is unable to do so due to extraordinary circumstances. If the operator is unable to mark the location within the time allowed under this section due to extraordinary circumstances, the operator shall notify directly the person who proposes to excavate or demolish and shall, in addition, notify the person of the date and time when the location will be marked. The deferral to mark for extraordinary circumstances shall be no longer than ninety-six hours from 7:00 A.M. on the next working day following notice to the notification center, unless a longer time is otherwise agreed upon by the operator and excavator. The operator shall also inform the notification center of any deferral.

B. If a proposed excavation or demolition is not planned in such proximity to the operator's underground utility lines that the utility line may be damaged, the operator shall so report to the notification center's excavator-operator information exchange system no later than 7:00 A.M. on the third working day following the excavator's notice to the notification center.

C. An operator shall participate in all preplanning and preconstruction meetings originated by state, county or municipal authorities relating to proposed construction projects which may affect the operator's existing or future utility lines and shall cooperate in implementing decisions reached in such preplanning and precon-struction meetings.

D. Any contract locator acting on behalf of an operator and failing to perform the duties imposed by this chapter shall be subject to the liabilities in §56-265.25 and the civil penalties in §56-265.32.

E. Locators shall be trained in applicable locating industry standards and practices no less stringent than the National Utility Locating Contractors Association's loca-tor training standards and practices. Each locator's training shall be documented. Such documents shall be maintained by the operator or contract locator.

F. The Commission shall be authorized to adopt regulations designating: (i) letters for each operator to be used in conjunction with marking of underground utility lines, and (ii) symbols for marking of underground utility lines, in compliance with subsection B of §56-265.17:3. Such letter designation and marking symbols shall be in accordance with industry standards.

G. For underground utility lines abandoned after July 1, 2002, operators shall make a reasonable attempt to keep records of these abandoned utility lines, excluding service lines connected to a single-family dwelling unit. Operators may provide a response to the excavator-operator information exchange system when an operator has knowledge that the operator's abandoned utility lines may be present within the area of the proposed excavation.

H. An operator shall respond to an emergency notice as soon as possible but no later than three hours from the excavator's call to the notification center.

§56-265.20:1. Locating Nonmetallic Underground Utility Lines

Notwithstanding the provisions of §56-257.1, any plastic or other nonmetallic utility lines installed underground on and after July 1, 2002, shall be installed in such a man-ner as to be locatable by the operator for the purposes of this chapter.

§56-265.21. Marking by Color

In marking the approximate location of underground utility lines or proposed excava-tion if required pursuant to subsection E of §56-265.17 the American Public Works Association color codes shall be used.

UTILITY AND TYPE	IDENTITY OF PRODUCT COLOR OR EQUIVALENT
Electric Power Distribution & Transmission	Safety Red
Municipal Electric Systems	Safety Red
Gas Distribution & Transmission	High Visibility Safety Yellow
Oil & Petroleum Products Distribution & Transmission	High Visibility Safety Yellow
Dangerous Materials, Product Lines, Steam Lines	High Visibility Safety Yellow
Telecommunications Systems	Safety Alert Orange
Police & Fire Communications	Safety Alert Orange
Cable Television	Safety Alert Orange

Water Systems	Safety Precaution Blue
Slurry Systems	Safety Precaution Blue
Sewer Systems	Safety Green
Proposed Excavation	White

§56-265.22. Duties of Notification Center Upon Notification by Person Intending to Excavate; Record of Notification Made by Telephone Required

A. The notification center shall, upon receiving notice by a person, notify all member operators whose underground lines are located in the area of the proposed project, excavation or demolition. The notification center shall also indicate the names of those operators being notified to the person providing notice.

B. If the notification required by this chapter is made by telephone, a record of such notification shall be maintained by the operators or notification center notified to document compliance with the requirements of this chapter, and such records shall be maintained in compliance with the applicable statute of limitations.

C. The notification center shall notify excavators, within the time frame allowed by the law to mark underground utility lines, of any responses placed on the excavator-operator information exchange system by a locator. Such notification shall occur by facsimile or other mutually acceptable means of automatically transmitting and receiving this information.

If the excavator cannot provide the notification center with a facsimile number or other mutually acceptable means of automatically transmitting and receiving this information, it shall be the excavator's responsibility to contact the excavator-operator information exchange system after the period allowed by law to mark underground facilities and prior to commencing excavation in order to determine if any responses to the notice have been recorded.

§56-265.22:1. Meetings between Excavators and Operators

A. Any person planning excavation or demolition in such proximity to the underground utility lines that the utility lines may be destroyed, damaged, dislocated, or disturbed may request a meeting with the operator whose underground utility lines are located in the area of the proposed excavation or demolition to discuss the marking of such lines. The project requiring excavation shall be of sufficient complexity to require a pre-marking meeting. The meeting notice shall include all information required by §56-265.18 and a specific time and location for the meeting.

B. The notification center shall, upon receiving a meeting notice, notify all member operators whose underground utility lines are located in the area of the proposed excavation or demolition. The notification center shall provide to the excavator the names of those operators being notified of the meeting.

C. The operators notified by the notification center shall meet with the excavator by 7:00 A.M. on the third working day following the excavator's meeting notice. If an operator does not agree to the excavator's suggested time and location, the operator shall set up a mutually agreeable time and location to meet no later than 7:00 A.M. on the third working day following the meeting notice.

D. The excavator's meeting notice shall not be the notice to excavate required under §56-265.17. The notice to excavate required under §56-265.17 for the project shall not be submitted to the notification center until after the meeting referenced in subsection A of this section has occurred, or after 7:00 A.M. on the third working day following the meeting notice.

§56-265.23. Exemption for Roadway Maintenance Operations by the Virginia Department of Transportation and Certain Counties, Cities, and Towns

Employees of the Virginia Department of Transportation acting within the scope of their employment, and certain employees of those counties, cities, and towns which maintain their streets or roads in accordance with §33.1-23.5:1 or §33.1-41.1 performing street or roadway maintenance operations and acting within the scope of their employment, excavating entirely within the right-of-way of a public road, street or highway of the Commonwealth shall not be required to comply with the provisions of this chapter if reasonable care is taken to protect the utility lines placed in the right-of-way by permit and if they:

1. Excavate within the limits of the original excavation; on the traveled way, shoulders or drainage features of a public road, street, or highway and any excavation does not exceed eighteen inches (0.45 meter) in depth below the grade existing prior to such excavation; or
2. Are replacing previously existing structures in their previous locations.

§56-265.24. Duties of Excavator

A. Any person excavating within two feet on either side of the staked or marked location of an operator's underground utility line or demolishing in such proximity to an underground utility line that the utility line may be destroyed, damaged, dislocated or disturbed shall take all reasonable steps necessary to properly protect, support and backfill underground utility lines. For excavations not parallel to an existing underground utility line, such steps shall include, but may not be limited to:

1. Exposing the underground utility line to its extremities by hand digging;
2. Not utilizing mechanized equipment within two feet of the extremities of all exposed utility lines; and
3. Protecting the exposed utility lines from damage.

    In addition, for excavations parallel to an existing utility line, such steps shall include, but may not be limited to, hand digging at reasonable distances along the line of excavation. The excavator shall exercise due care at all times to protect underground utility lines when exposing these lines by hand digging.

B. If the markings locating the underground lines become illegible due to time, weather, construction, or any other cause, the person performing the excavation or demolition shall so notify the notification center for the area. Such notification shall constitute an extension under subsection D of §56-265.17.

C. If, upon arrival at the site of a proposed excavation, the excavator observes clear evidence of the presence of an unmarked utility line in the area of the proposed excavation, the excavator shall not begin excavating until an additional call is made to the notification center for the area pursuant to subsection B of §56-265.17.

D. In the event of any damage to, or dislocation, or disturbance of any underground utility line including its appurtenances, covering, and coating, in connection with any excavation or demolition, the person responsible for the excavation or demolition operations shall immediately notify the operator of the underground utility line and shall not backfill around the underground utility line until the operator has repaired the damage or has given clearance to backfill. The operator shall either commence repair of the damage or give clearance to backfill within twenty-four hours, and upon his failure to commence or prosecute with diligence such repair or give clearance, the giving of clearance shall be presumed.

E. If the damage, dislocation, or disturbance of the underground utility line creates an emergency, the person responsible for the excavation or demolition shall, in addition to complying with subsection D of this section, take immediate steps reasonably calculated to safeguard life, health and property.

F. With the exception of designers requesting marking of a site, in accordance with §56-265.17, no person, including operators, shall request marking of a site through a notification center unless excavation shall commence within thirty working days from the date of the original notification to the notification center. Except for counties, cities, and towns, any person who willfully fails to comply with this subsection shall be liable to the operator for three times the cost of marking its utility line, not to exceed $1,000.

G. Any person performing excavation or demolition shall provide to the operator of the underground utility line in the area of excavation or to the appropriate regulatory authority having jurisdiction, the number issued by the notification center for that excavation site in response to the excavator's notice, within one hour of a request for the number issued by the notification center.

H. If an excavator discovers an unmarked line, the excavator shall protect this line pursuant to subsection C of this section. An excavator shall not remove an abandoned line without first receiving authorization to do so by the operator.

§56-265.25. Liability of Operator and Excavator; Penalties

A. 1. If any underground utility line is damaged as a proximate result of a person's failure to comply with any provision of this chapter, that person shall be liable to the operator of the underground utility line for the total cost to repair the damaged facilities as that cost is normally computed by the operator, provided the operator is a member of the notification center covering the area in which the damage to the utility line takes place. The liability of such a person for such damage shall not be limited by reason of this chapter.

2. Any person who willfully fails to notify the notification center of proposed excavation or demolition shall be liable to the operator as provided in subsection A of §56-265.17.

3. If, after receiving proper notice, an operator fails to discharge a duty imposed by any provision of this chapter and an underground utility line of such operator is damaged, as a proximate result of the operator's failure to discharge such duty, by any person who has complied with all of the provisions of this chapter, such person shall not be so liable.

B. If an underground utility line of an operator is damaged, as the proximate result of the operator's failure to comply with any provision of this chapter, by any person who has complied with the provisions of this chapter, the operator shall be liable to such person for the total cost to repair any damage to the equipment or facilities of such person resulting from such damage to the operator's underground utility line.

C. Except as specifically set forth herein, the provisions of this chapter shall not be construed to either abrogate any rights, duties, or remedies existing under law or create any rights, duties, defenses, or remedies in addition to any rights, duties, or remedies existing under law.

§56-265.26:1. Utility Line Depth Requirement

Every operator having the right to install underground utility lines shall install such underground utility lines at depths required by accepted industry standards. Such standards shall include, as applicable, standards established by the National Electrical Safety Code, Bellcore Blue Book-Manual of Contractor's Procedures, the Commission's pipeline safety regulations, the Department of Health's waterworks regulations, and the depth standards of the Virginia Cable Telecommunications Association, which shall be established in consultation with the State Corporation Commission no later than July 1, 2002.

§56-265.27

Not set out.

§56-265.28. Sovereign Immunity

Nothing in this chapter shall be construed to abrogate the immunity from suit accruing to the Commonwealth, her political subdivisions, agencies, officers or employees, or the officers or employees of her political subdivisions and agencies, as exists prior to July 1, 1980.

§56-265.29. Other Similar Laws

Compliance with the provisions of this chapter shall not exempt any operator or person from the operation of any other applicable laws, ordinances, regulations, or rules of governmental and regulatory authorities having jurisdiction, unless exempted by such other laws, ordinances, regulations, or rules as a result of such compliance.

§56-265.30. Authority of the State Corporation Commission

A. The Commission shall enforce the provisions of the Underground Utility Damage Prevention Act as set out in this chapter. The Commission may promulgate any rules or regulations necessary to implement the Commission's authority to enforce this chapter.

B. Nothing in this chapter shall be construed to authorize the Commission to promulgate any rules or regulations pursuant to its authority to enforce this chapter that require any person, other than jurisdictional gas or hazardous liquid operators, to report to the Commission any probable violation of this chapter or any incident involving damage, dislocation or disturbance of any utility line.

§56-265.31. Commission to Establish Advisory Committee

A. The Commission shall establish an advisory committee consisting of representatives of the following entities: Commission staff, utility operator, notification center, excavator, municipality, Virginia Department of Transportation, Board for Contractors, and underground line locator. Persons appointed to the advisory committee by the Commission shall have expertise with the operation of the Underground Utility Damage Prevention Act. The advisory committee shall perform duties which may be assigned by the Commission, including the review of reports of violations of the chapter, and make recommendations to the Commission.

B. The members of the advisory committee shall be immune, individually and jointly, from civil liability for any act or omission done or made in performance of their duties while serving as members of such advisory committee, but only in the absence of willful misconduct.

§56-265.32. Commission to Impose Civil Penalties for Certain Violations; Establishment of Underground Utility Damage Prevention Special Fund

A. The Commission may, by judgment entered after a hearing on notice duly served on any person not less than thirty days before the date of the hearing, impose a civil penalty not exceeding $2,500 for each violation, if it is proved that the person violated any of the provisions of this chapter as a result of a failure to exercise reasonable care. Any proceeding or civil penalty undertaken pursuant to this section shall not prevent nor preempt the right of any party to obtain civil damages for personal injury or property damage in private causes of action. This subsection shall not authorize the Commission to impose civil penalties on any county, city or town. However, the Commission shall inform the counties, cities and towns of reports of alleged violations involving the locality and, at the request of the locality, suggest corrective action.

B. The Underground Utility Damage Prevention Special Fund (hereinafter referred to as "Special Fund") is hereby established as a revolving fund to be used by the Commission for administering the regulatory program authorized by this chapter. The Special Fund shall be composed entirely of funds generated by the enforcement of this chapter. Excess funds shall be used to support any one or more of the following: (i) public awareness programs established by a notification center pursuant to subsection B of §56-265.16:1; (ii) training and education programs for excavators, operators, line locators, and other persons; and (iii) programs providing incentives for excavators, operators, line locators, and other persons to reduce the number and severity of violations of the Act. The Commission shall determine the appropriate allocation of any excess funds among such programs, and shall establish required elements for any program established under clause (ii) or (iii).

C. All civil penalties collected pursuant to this section shall be deposited into the Underground Utility Damage Prevention Special Fund. Interest earned on the fund shall be credited to the Special Fund. The Special Fund shall be established on the books of the Commission comptroller and any funds remaining in the Underground Utility Damage Prevention Special Fund at the end of the fiscal year shall not revert to the general fund, but shall remain in the Special Fund.

APPENDIX

CERTIFICATE OF ASSUMED OR FICTITIOUS NAME

This is to certify that the below named person, partnership, limited liability company, or corporation intends to conduct or transact business in the [ ] City [] County of ------- under an assumed or fictitious name. 1. The ASSUMED OR FICTITIOUS NAME of business:

NAME:

2. The above business is owned by the following entity type [ ] SOLE PROPRIETORSHIP (Complete A below) [ ] PARTNERSHIP (Complete B below) [ ] LIMITED LIABILITY COMPANY [ ] CORPORATION (Complete C below).

A. NAME OF OWNER:

RESIDENCE ADDRESS:

POST OFFICE ADDRESS:

B. NAME OF PARTNERSHIP:

OFFICE ADDRESS:..

POST OFFICE ADDRESS:...

(1) Is this a general partnership? [ ] NO [ ] YES. If YES, complete the Statement of Partners on reverse side

(2) Is this a domestic limited partnership? [ ] NO [ ] YES. If YES, a certified copy of this certificate must be filed with the State Corporation Commission. § 59.1-70.

(3) Is this a foreign limited partnership? [ ] NO [ ] YES. If YES, indicate the date of the certificate of registration to transact business in the Commonwealth of Virginia issued by the State Corporation Commission..

A certified copy of this certificate must be filed with the State Corporation Commission §59.1-70. C. NAME OF [ ] CORPORATION [ ] LIMITED LIABILITY COMPANY:

....

OFFICE ADDRESS:...

POST OFFICE ADDRESS:.. (1)

A corporation or limited liability company must file a certified copy of this certificate with the State Corporation Commission. § 59.1-70. (2) Is this a foreign corporation or a foreign limited liability company? [ ] NO [ ] YES. If YES, indicate the date of the certificate of authority/registration to transact business in the Commonwealth of Virginia issued by the State Corporation Commission:...

ACKNOWLEDGMENT

I certify that the foregoing is true and correct to the best of my knowledge and belief. A. Sole Proprietorship: _____
NAME OF OWNER   SIGNATURE OF OWNER

B. Partnership .... _____ NAME
OF GENERAL PARTNER SIGNATURE OF GENERAL PARTNER

C. Corporation .... _____ NAME
OF PRESIDENT SIGNATURE OF PRESIDENT

D. Limited Liability Company ....
_____ NAME OF MEMBER/MANAGER SIGNATURE OF MEMBER/MANAGER

[ ] City [ ] County of ....

Acknowledged, subscribed and sworn to before me this........................ day of ...., 2005.
My commission expires................................. _____
[ ] CLERK/DEPUTY CLERK [ ] NOTARY PUBLIC

CLERK'S OFFICE
Filed in the Clerks' Office of the ....Circuit Court on..
DATE
...., Clerk by _____Deputy Clerk

FORM CC-1417 (MASTER, PAGE ONE OF ONE)
REVISED 5/05 VA. CODE § 59.1-69

Highlight Fields Print for Submission to Court Clear All Data

STATEMENT OF PARTNERS This is to certify that the below named persons intend to carry on business as partners in the [ ] City of [ ] County of .... under an assumed or fictitious name, and that the following is a list of every person owning the GENERAL PARTNERSHIP set forth on the front of this certificate.

.... _____

PRINTED NAME (LAST, FIRST, MIDDLE) SIGNATURE

....

.... RESIDENCE ADDRESS Commonwealth of Virginia County/City of

....:

Subscribed and acknowledged before me by ...., this .... day of ...., 20.............. My commission expires...

_____ [ ] NOTARY PUBLIC [ ] CLERK/DEPUTY CLERK

.... _____

PRINTED NAME (LAST, FIRST, MIDDLE) SIGNATURE

....

.... RESIDENCE ADDRESS Commonwealth of Virginia County/City of

....:

Subscribed and acknowledged before me by ...., this .... day of ...., 20.............. My commission expires...

_____ [ ] NOTARY PUBLIC [ ] CLERK/DEPUTY CLERK

.... _____

PRINTED NAME (LAST, FIRST, MIDDLE) SIGNATURE

....

.... RESIDENCE ADDRESS Commonwealth of Virginia County/City of

....:

Subscribed and acknowledged before me by ...., this .... day of ...., 20.............. My commission expires...

_____ [ ] NOTARY PUBLIC [ ] CLERK/DEPUTY CLERK

.... _____

PRINTED NAME (LAST, FIRST, MIDDLE) SIGNATURE

....

.... RESIDENCE ADDRESS Commonwealth of Virginia County/City of

....:

Subscribed and acknowledged before me by ...., this .... day of ...., 20.............. My commission expires...

_____ [ ] NOTARY PUBLIC [ ] CLERK/DEPUTY CLERK FORM

CC-1417 (MASTER, PAGE TWO OF TWO) REVISED 5/05
VA. CODE § 59.1-69

Job Safety and Health Protection

THE VIRGINIA OCCUPATIONAL SAFETY AND HEALTH (VOSH) LAW, BY AUTHORITY OF TITLE 40.1 OF THE LABOR LAWS OF VIRGINIA, PROVIDES JOB SAFETY AND HEALTH PROTECTION FOR WORKERS. THE PURPOSE OF THE LAW IS TO ASSURE SAFE AND HEALTHFUL WORKING CONDITIONS THROUGHOUT THE STATE. THE VIRGINIA SAFETY AND HEALTH CODES BOARD PROMULGATES AND ADOPTS JOB SAFETY AND HEALTH STANDARDS, AND EMPLOYERS AND EMPLOYEES ARE REQUIRED TO COMPLY WITH THESE STANDARDS.

Employers

Each employer shall furnish to each of his employees employment and a place of employment free from recognized hazards that are causing or are likely to cause death or serious harm to his employees, and shall comply with occupational safety and health standards issued under the Law.

Employees

Each employee shall comply with all occupational safety and health standards, rules, regulations and orders issued under the Law that apply to his own actions and conduct on the job.

Inspection

The Law requires that a representative of the employer and a representative authorized by the employees be given an opportunity to accompany the VOSH inspector for the purpose of aiding the inspection.

Where there is no authorized employee representative, the VOSH inspector must consult with a reasonable number of employees concerning safety and health conditions in the workplace.

Citation

If upon inspection VOSH believes an employer has violated the Law, a citation alleging such violations will be issued to the employer. Each citation will specify a time period within which the alleged violation must be corrected.

The VOSH citation must be prominently displayed at or near the place of alleged violation for three days or until the violation is corrected, whichever is later, to warn employees of dangers that may exist there.

Proposed Penalty

The Law provides for mandatory penalties against private sector employers of up to $7,000 for each serious violation and for optional penalties of up to $7,000 for each other—than—serious violation. Penalties of up to $7,000 per day may be proposed for failure to correct violations within the proposed time period. Also, any employer who willfully or repeatedly violates the Law may be assessed penalties of up to $70,000 for each such violation.

Public Sector employers, all departments, agencies, institutions or other political subdivisions of the Commonwealth, are exempt from the penalty provisions of this Law.

Criminal penalties are also provided for in the Law. Any willful violation resulting in the death of an employee is punishable, upon conviction, by a fine of not more than $70,000 or by imprisonment for not more than six months, or by both. Subsequent conviction of an employer after a first conviction doubles these maximum penalties.

Complaint

Employees or their representatives have the right to file a complaint with the nearest VOSH office requesting an inspection if they believe unsafe or unhealthy conditions exist in their workplace. VOSH will withhold, on request, names of employees filing complaints. Complaints may be made at the Department of Labor and Industry addresses shown below.

Discrimination

The Law provides that employees may not be discharged or discriminated against in any way for filing safety and health complaints or otherwise exercising their rights under the Law.

An employee who believes he has been discriminated against for exercising their rights under the Law, may file a complaint with the Commissioner of the Virginia Department of Labor and Industry within 60 days of the alleged discrimination.

CASPA

Complaints Against State Plan Administration: Any person may complain to the Regional Administrator of OSHA (address below) concerning the Administration of the State Safety and Health Program.

State Coverage

The VOSH program shall apply to all public and private sector businesses in the State except for Federal agencies, businesses under the Atomic Energy Act, railroad rolling stock and tracks, certain Federal enclaves, and businesses covered by the Federal Maritime jurisdiction.

Voluntary Activity

Voluntary efforts by the employer to assure his workplace is in compliance with the Law are encouraged. Voluntary Safety and Health Consultation and Training Programs exist to assist employers. These services may be obtained by contacting the Department of Labor and Industry addresses shown below.

Recordkeeping

Employers now have a new system for tracking workplace injuries and illnesses. OSHA's new recordkeeping log is simplier to understand and use. Using a question and answer format, the revised recordkeeping rule provides answers to record occupational injuries and illnesses, and explains how to classify specific cases. Flowcharts and checklists make the recordkeeping requirements easier to follow. Not all industries are required to do a recordkeeping log. To see if your industry is exempt, visit the OSHA Web site at www.osha.gov/recordkeeping/pub3169text.html.

Fatalities

Any fatality or injuries to three (3) or more employees involving inpatient hospitalization from a workplace incident, must be reported to the nearest VOSH office within eight (8) hours. Failure to report may result in a $5,000 fine.

VIRGINIA DEPARTMENT OF LABOR AND INDUSTRY

Powers-Taylor Building
13 South Thirteenth Street
Richmond, VA 23219
VOICE (804) 371-2327
TDD   (804) 786-2376
FAX   (804) 371-6524

WEB http://www.doli.virginia.gov

U.S. Department of Labor
OSHA Regional Administrator
The Curtis Center, STE 740 West
170 South Independence Mall West
Philadelphia, PA 19106-3309
(215) 861-4900

OCCUPATIONAL SAFETY AND HEALTH OFFICE LOCATIONS

Headquarters
Powers-Taylor Building
13 South Thirteenth Street
Richmond, VA 23219
(804) 371-2327

Central Virginia/
Richmond
Northrun Office Park
1570 East Parham Road
Richmond, VA 23228
(804) 371-3104

Northern Virginia/
Manassas
10515 Battleview Parkway
Manassas, VA 20109
(703) 392-0900

Tidewater/Norfolk
6363 Center Drive
Building 6, Suite 101
Norfolk, VA 2350
(757) 455-0891

Southwest/Roanoke
Brammer Village
3013 Peters Creek Road
Roanoke, VA 24019
(540) 562-3580

Abingdon
Brooksfield Square
Suite 4
966 West Main Street
Abingdon VA 24210
(276) 676-5465

Lynchburg
3704 Old Forest Road
Suite B
Lynchburg, VA 24501
(434) 385-0806

Verona
201 Lee Highway
Verona, VA 24482
(540) 248-9280

VIRGINIA DEPARTMENT OF
LABOR AND INDUSTRY

C. Ray Davenport
Commissioner

VIRGINIA SAFETY AND
HEALTH CODES BOARD

Anna E. Jolly
Chairperson

EMPLOYERS: THIS POSTER MUST BE DISPLAYED IN A PROMINENT PLACE IN THE ESTABLISHMENT TO WHICH YOUR EMPLOYEES NORMALLY REPORT TO WORK.

August 2004

COMMONWEALTH OF VIRGINIA

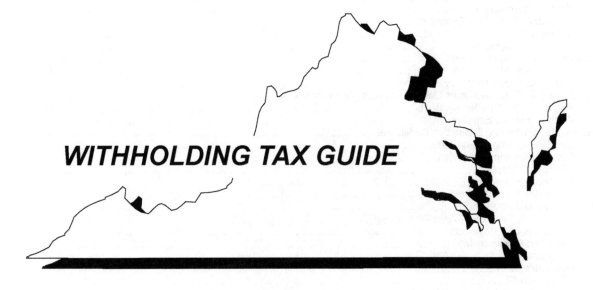

WITHHOLDING TAX GUIDE

www.tax.virginia.gov

VIRGINIA DEPARTMENT OF TAXATION

2614086
Revised 11/07

Table of Contents

USE iFILE OR EFT TO FILE YOUR WITHHOLDING TAXES

GO PAPERLESS!!

iFile is a convenient and fast way to pay taxes. After you enter the tax information, simply click your mouse and your tax return is filed. This service is available 24 hours a day and you will instantly receive a unique confirmation number for your filing.

iFile offers advance scheduling of your payment. You pick a time that is convenient for you to file and pay withholding, sales and use, and corporate income taxes.

iFile provides 12 months of payment history for withholding and sales and use taxes. Best of all the on-line history section alerts you of any unfiled or unpaid months.

Find out more.
Visit our website for details.
Business iFile
www.tax.virginia.gov

FREE INTERNET FILING

FAST. EASY. SECURE.

ELECTRONIC FUNDS TRANSFER
EFT

Although Virginia law requires certain taxpayers to submit payments using **EFT** (see page 7), the Virginia Department of Taxation encourages all businesses to submit tax payments voluntarily by **EFT**. **EFT** is a safe and secure method of ensuring tax payments are received by the Department in a timely and efficient manner.

Payment by **EFT** is available for withholding, sales and use, and corporate income taxes.

You can download the complete **EFT** guide from our website at **www.tax.virginia.gov** or call to request a copy at (804) 440-2541 or write to us at **P. O. Box 1317, Richmond, VA 23218-1317**.

Introduction

This publication contains general information regarding withholding of Virginia income tax from wages. You should use this booklet as a reference guide, not as a substitute for the complete tax law provided by the *Code of Virginia* or the regulations promulgated by the Department of Taxation.

What's New

Monthly Filing Date Change - Effective January 1, 2008, employers who must file withholding tax returns on a monthly basis are required to file those returns on or before the 25th of the following month. This includes months that follow the close of a calendar quarter. Under prior law, monthly filers were required to file the return on or before the last day of the following month for months that close a calendar quarter. For months that did not close a calendar quarter, the return was due on the 20th day of the following month.

Seasonal filers should also submit returns on or before the 25th of the following month for each month that the business has employees.

Withholding Tax for Pass-Through Entities - Beginning January 1, 2008, pass-through entities doing business in the Commonwealth and having taxable income derived from Virginia sources will be required to pay a withholding tax equal to five percent of the nonresident owners' share of income from Virginia sources. Each nonresident owner is allowed a credit for that owner's share of the tax withheld by the pass-through entity.

The Pass-Through Entity Withholding Tax will NOT be reported on these forms.

Filing Threshold and Personal Exemption Amounts for Individual Income Tax - Legislation passed in 2007 increases the individual income tax filing threshold for single individuals and married individuals who file separately from $7,000 to $11,250 for taxable years 2008 and 2009, $11,650 for taxable years 2010 and 2011 and $11,950 for taxable year 2012 and beyond. The filing threshold for married couples increases from $14,000 to $22,500 for taxable years 2008 and 2009, $23,300 for taxable years 2010 and 2011, and $23,900 for taxable year 2012 and beyond.

The legislation also increases the personal exemption amount from $900 to $930 effective for taxable year 2008.

Where To Get Forms And Assistance

Visit Our Website At: www.tax.virginia.gov and use your computer to:
- download forms and instructions
- iReg – register your new business
- review answers to frequently asked questions
- get filing information
- iFile – file withholding and sales and use tax on-line
- e-mail us your questions

Order Forms By Telephone
Call the Forms Request Unit at 804-440-2541. You can place orders 24 hours a day.

Submit A Written Request
Send your inquiry to: **Customer Service, P.O. Box 1115, Richmond, VA 23218-1115.**

Please do not send returns or payments to this address.

Call or Visit Our Offices
Call or visit our Central Office or Norfolk District Office. The addresses and telephone numbers are listed below. Customer service hours are from 8:30 a.m. to 4:30 p.m., Monday through Friday.

Main Office .... **(804) 367-8037**
3600 West Broad Street, Richmond, VA 23230

Norfolk District Office .... **(757) 455-3810**
7 Koger Center, Suite 101, Norfolk, VA 23502

Tenemos servicios disponible en Español

Registering For A Withholding Tax Account

Who Must Register

You must have a Virginia withholding account if you have an employee earning income while in Virginia. This includes a person or business that pays wages or salaries for services performed in Virginia or pays pensions or annuities to Virginia residents.

Visit our website at **www.tax.virginia.gov** to register your business. You may also register with the Virginia Employment Commission (VEC) at the same time you register your business on-line with the Department of Taxation.

Registering on-line has many advantages. It is fast, easy, secure, and most of all reduces errors. You also have the ability to save your registration and complete it at a later time.

Business iReg
www.tax.virginia.gov

Or

Manually complete Form R-1 (Combined Registration Application). For quicker processing, provide all the requested information and mail your completed application to:

Department of Taxation
Registration Unit
P.O. Box 1114
Richmond, VA 23218-1114.

When To Register

Register your business before withholding begins. If you have not registered by the date your first tax payment is due, you may send the payment with your Form R-1 and a letter explaining what period the payment covers. You will be sent preprinted withholding tax returns after processing of your Form R-1 is complete. If you do not register in time to receive preprinted returns, you are still **required** to make your tax payments on time.

Filing Status

If your estimated total withholding is:	You are required to file:
$300 or less per quarter	quarterly
$301 to $2,999 per quarter	monthly
$3,000 or more per quarter	semiweekly

After you have registered, your account will be reviewed each year and your filing period adjusted accordingly. If your filing frequency changes, you will receive a letter of notification and returns for the appropriate filing frequency will be mailed to you. Filing status changes are effective on January 1 of each year and remain in effect until the following January 1.

For businesses operating on a seasonal basis or paying wages or salaries only during certain months of the year, complete the "Seasonal Business" section when registering using iReg or on Form R-1. Your business will be assigned a seasonal filing status and you will be sent returns only for the months selected.

Your Virginia Account Number

The Virginia account number assigned by the Department of Taxation will serve as the identification number for your withholding tax account and for your other major business tax accounts. Please use your account number on any returns, checks, or correspondence you send to us.

Because your registration information also includes your Federal Employer's Identification Number (FEIN), it is helpful if you also include that number on forms and correspondence. If the Internal Revenue Service assigns a new FEIN to your business because of a reorganization, change in business type, or change of ownership, you must file Form R-1 and obtain a new Virginia account number.

You should have only one Virginia account number. If you have more than one account number and do not know which one is correct, please contact us at **(804) 367-8037**. If you acquire another employer's business, do not use that employer's account number. Instead, complete Form R-1 and file it with a statement explaining the change in ownership.

Registration Changes

Use Form R-3, Registration Change Request, to notify the Department of Taxation when:

> ➢ your business name or address changes;
> ➢ you no longer have employees; or
> ➢ you close your business.

Do not use Form R-3 to report a name change that results from a change in ownership. Instead, file Form R-3 to close the former owner's account and file Form R-1 to obtain a Virginia account number for the new owner. In the case of a corporate merger, a copy of the merger statement should be attached to Form R-3.

Virginia Withholding Tax Forms And Due Dates

Form	Title	Description/Due Date
		Employer Forms
iReg	On-line Registration	Used to register your business on-line at our website.
R-1	Combined Registration Application	Used to register you business for withholding tax. You may also register your business on-line by visiting the website at www.tax. virginia.gov and using the iREg process.
R-3	Registration Change Request	Used to report a change of name or address, or to notify the department that an employer is no longer liable for withholding. File before the effective date of the change. If you do not have Form R-3, send a letter.
VA-5	Employer's Return of Virginia Income Tax Withheld	Used by quarterly, monthly and seasonal filers. Quarterly returns are due on April 30, July 31, October 31, and January 31. Monthly returns are due by the 25th day of the following month. Seasonal returns are due on the same dates as monthly returns, for each month that the business has employees.
VA-15	Employer's Payment of Virginia Income Tax Withheld	Used by semi-weekly filers. Payments are due within three banking days of any federal cutoff date (generally Tuesdays and Fridays) if the accumulated tax liability exceeds $500. If the due date falls within three days of the due date for Form VA-16, the payment must be made on Form VA-16.
VA-16	Employer's Payments Quarterly Reconciliation and Return of Virginia Income Tax Withheld	Used by semi-weekly filers to reconcile payments for each calendar quarter. Form VA-16 is due on April 30, July 31, October 31 and January 31.
VA-6	Employer's Annual Reconciliation of Virginia Income Tax Withheld	Annual or final summary of payments for the year. Form VA-6 is due by February 28 each year, or within 30 days after the last payment of wages, with copies of any federal Form W-2, W-2G, 1099, or 1099-R showing Virginia tax withheld attached. Employers with 250 or more annual employee W-2 forms are required to file via magnetic media. See instructions for filing magnetic media on our web site, www.tax.virginia.gov.
		Employee Forms
VA-4	Virginia Employee's Withholding Exemption Certificate	Used to report the number of exemptions an employee is entitled to claim. Obtain from each employee on the date employment begins.
VA-4P	Withholding Exemption Certificate for Recipients of Pension and Annuity Payments	Used to report the number of exemptions that a pension or annuity recipient is entitled to claim. Obtain from each recipient before payments begin.

For timely filing, your return must be postmarked or received on or before the due date. Use iFile instead of mailing to avoid late filing penalties and interest . iFile tax filings are received instantaneously and you can schedule your payment early in the month so you will never be late.

Visit our website, **www.tax.virginia.gov**, to learn more.

Who Must Withhold Virginia Income Tax

Who Is An Employer

As a general rule, any person or entity that meets the definition of "employer" below, must withhold Virginia income tax. An employer is generally a person or entity that pays wages to employees for services performed in Virginia or makes pension or annuity payments to residents of Virginia.

The term "employer" includes the following:

- ➢ An individual, fiduciary, partnership, association, joint enterprise, or corporation for whom an employee performs services;
- ➢ The Commonwealth of Virginia, or any political subdivision thereof, or any agency or instrumentality thereof;
- ➢ The United States or any agency or instrumentality thereof; and
- ➢ Payors of pensions or annuities to residents of Virginia, except that financial institutions are not considered employers with respect to payments from Individual Retirement Accounts (IRA) or simplified employee pension funds (SEP).

An employer is generally subject to the Virginia withholding requirements if the employer is:

- ➢ A resident of Virginia; or
- ➢ Doing business in Virginia; or
- ➢ Domesticated under the laws of Virginia relating to the domestication of foreign corporations; or
- ➢ Making payments of wages or salaries to employees for services performed in Virginia; or
- ➢ Making pension or annuity payments to residents of Virginia.

Conformity To Federal Definitions

The determination of whether an employer-employee relationship exists for purposes of Virginia withholding requirements is made under federal law (U.S. Treasury Reg. §31.3401(c)-1). Anyone classified as an employer for federal purposes is also an employer for Virginia purposes.

Courtesy Filers

An employer who is not otherwise subject to the Virginia withholding requirements, but wishes to withhold Virginia income tax as a courtesy to employees who reside here, may register for an account number. Once registered, the employer will be subject to the same filing requirements as all other Virginia employers.

Who Is An Employee

The term "employee" includes:

- ➢ An individual (resident or nonresident) who performs or performed services in Virginia for wages;
- ➢ A resident of Virginia who performs or performed services outside Virginia for wages;
- ➢ An officer, employee, or elected official of the United States, or any other state or territory, or any political subdivision thereof, or the District of Columbia, or any instrumentality or agency of the governments listed;
- ➢ An officer of a corporation;
- ➢ A resident of Virginia who receives pension or annuity payments.

An employee is generally subject to Virginia income tax withholding if any of the following conditions are met:

- ➢ The individual receives taxable wages for services performed in Virginia and is not eligible for an exemption from withholding;
- ➢ The individual is a resident of Virginia who receives taxable wages for services performed outside Virginia and does not qualify for an exemption from withholding;
- ➢ The individual is a resident of Virginia and receives pension or annuity payments or both from which federal income tax has been withheld (except IRA and SEP payments) and is not eligible for an exemption from withholding.

See "How to compute the Withholding Tax" for additional information.

Taxable And Exempt Payments

Payments Subject To Withholding

Virginia law conforms to the federal definition of income subject to withholding. Virginia withholding is generally required on any payment for which federal withholding is required.

This includes most wages, pensions and annuities, gambling winnings, vacation pay, bonuses, and certain expense reimbursements.

Payments Exempt From Withholding

Payments that are exempt from federal withholding are also exempt from Virginia withholding. In addition, the following payments are exempt from Virginia withholding:

- ➢ Payments made for acting in or serving as a crew member for movies, television series, commercials, or promotional films that are filmed totally or partially in Virginia by an employer that conducts business in Virginia for less than 90 days and that edits, processes, and markets the completed project outside Virginia.
- ➢ Payments made from an Individual Retirement Account (IRA) or simplified employee pension plan (SEP).
- ➢ Payments made to nonresident employees of rail carriers, motor carriers, and water carriers.
- ➢ Payments made to resident and nonresident merchant seamen.

Payments To Nonresidents Under Reciprocity Agreements

When you make wage or salary payments to a nonresident for services performed in this state, you must usually withhold Virginia income tax in the same manner as you would for a resident.

Virginia has entered into reciprocity agreements with other states for individuals who earn income in states other than their states of residence. The agreements allow those individuals to be taxed only by their state of residence on earned or business income, provided that certain conditions are met. The terms of the agreements eliminate a nonresidents liability for Virginia income tax, as well as the requirement for withholding from payments made for services performed in Virginia.

Current reciprocity agreements affect Virginia withholding requirements for residents of the following states: Kentucky, the District of Columbia, Maryland, West Virginia and Pennsylvania. Withholding provisions for residents of these states who work in Virginia are described below.

Kentucky and the District of Columbia:

Wage and salary payments to residents of these states are not subject to Virginia withholding if the employees commute daily to a place of employment in Virginia.

Maryland, West Virginia, and Pennsylvania:

Wage and salary payments made to residents of these states are not subject to Virginia withholding if the employees meet the following conditions:

➤ The employee maintains a legal domicile in another state and lives in Virginia less than 183 days of the taxable year (or does not live in Virginia at all)

➤ The only Virginia source income received during the year was from salaries or wages; and

➤ The Virginia source income is subject to taxation by the individual's state of residence.

Any nonresident who is exempt from Virginia withholding under a reciprocity agreement must indicate this on the Form VA-4, Employee's Exemption Certificate, filed with his or her employer.

Payments To Other Nonresidents

Payments to the following nonresidents for services performed in Virginia are subject to withholding.

➤ Residents of non-reciprocity states. This includes residents of neighboring states (Tennessee and North Carolina) for which Virginia has no reciprocity agreement in place, as well as residents of other states who are working in Virginia on a temporary basis.

➤ Residents of Kentucky, the District of Columbia, Maryland, West Virginia, and Pennsylvania who do not meet the conditions for exemption under Virginia's reciprocity agreements with those states.

Partially Exempt Employment

If an employee performs both taxable and nontaxable services for an employer - for example, services performed both in and outside Virginia - the entire payment for those services is subject to Virginia withholding if at least one-half of the services are taxable. If less than one-half of the employee's time is spent in services not subject to withholding, the entire payment is exempt.

Employee Withholding Exemption Certificates

Use Of Exemption Certificates

To compute Virginia withholding tax for payments made to an employee, you need to know the number of personal exemptions the employee can claim. The employee gives you this information on Form VA-4, Virginia Employee's Income Tax Withholding Exemption Certificate. An employee would also use Form VA-4 to tell an employer that he or she is exempt from Virginia withholding. Recipients of pension and annuity payments use a different certificate, Form VA-4P, to report their exemption information to their payors.

Keep exemption certificates in your records to support your computation of Virginia withholding tax for each employee. Do not send the certificates to the Department of Taxation.

You must use the Virginia exemption certificates for computing Virginia withholding. Federal certificates (Forms W-4 or W-4P) may not be substituted.

Filing Exemption Certificates

Employees must file Form VA-4 with you when their employment begins. Form VA-4P should be filed before pension or annuity distributions begin. If no Form VA-4 or VA-4P is filed, withhold Virginia income tax as if no exemptions had been claimed. A new Form VA-4 or Form VA-4P must be filed if the employee's allowable number of exemptions changes or if an employee previously exempt from Virginia income tax becomes subject to the tax. The form should be filed within ten days of the employee's change in status.

Claiming Exemptions

The employee must complete the Personal Exemption Worksheet to determine the allowable number of exemptions for withholding purposes. An employee may not claim more than the number of personal exemptions that he or she is entitled to claim for purposes of filing an individual income tax return, unless the Department has authorized additional exemptions in writing.

In cases where an employee will be claiming a large amount of itemized deductions on his or her income tax return, basing the withholding computation on the usual number of allowable exemptions may result in withholding too much tax. If an employee can show that such withholding has resulted in a refund of $300 or more for the preceding tax year, he or she may write to the **Department of Taxation, P.O. Box 1115, Richmond, VA 23218-1115** to request permission to claim additional withholding exemptions. The letter should include the employee's name, social security number, estimated Virginia taxable income for the year, gross wages per pay period, and number of pay periods.

If you believe that an employee has claimed too many exemptions, please send a copy of the employee's Form VA-4 to the **Department of Taxation, P.O. Box 1115, Richmond, VA 23218-1115**, and request a review of the information. We will notify you in writing whether you may accept the Form VA-4 as filed or whether the employee must file a new Form VA-4.

Additional Withholding

If an employee wants to have an additional amount of tax withheld from each paycheck, and you agree to do so, the employee must indicate the additional amount on Form VA-4 or Form VA-4P. If you do not agree to withhold additional tax, the employee may need to make estimated tax payments.

Exemption From Withholding

An employee is exempt from Virginia withholding if he or she meets any of the conditions listed on Form VA-4 or VA-4P. The employee must file a new certificate each year to certify the exemption. Be sure to keep copies of any certificate claiming exemption from withholding.

How To File And Pay The Tax

Payment By Electronic Funds Transfer (EFT)

Electronic funds transfer (EFT) is a convenient alternative for making your withholding tax payments. By using EFT, you can transfer funds from your bank account to ours without having to write a check. If you are interested in making EFT payments for your withholding or other business tax accounts, you can download an Electronic Funds Transfer (EFT) Guide from our website at **www.tax.virginia.gov** or you may request a copy by contacting our Forms Request Unit at (804) 440-2541, faxing us at (804) 236-2779, or writing to **P.O. Box 1317, Richmond, VA 23218-1317**.

Mandatory EFT Payments

Any business with a monthly tax liability that exceeds $20,000 for withholding, sales, use, or corporate income taxes must pay their state taxes by EFT. The $ 20,000 threshold amount applies to each tax separately. If you are required to pay by EFT, you will receive a notice from the Department with instructions for setting up your EFT account.

Taxpayers who are required to pay by EFT but fail to do so will be subject to penalties.

Filing And Paying By Mail

Your coupon booklet contains mailing labels for filing your withholding tax returns. If you are using blank or replacement returns, or you are using software to generate your withholding forms, mail your return and payment to the applicable address below.

Quarterly filers mail the documents to **Department of Taxation, P.O. Box 26644, Richmond, VA 23261-6644**.

Monthly, Semi-Weekly and Seasonal filers mail the return and payment to Department of Taxation, P.O. Box 27264, Richmond, VA 23261-7264.

Filing Instructions

After registering, we will provide you with a coupon booklet containing your necessary returns. The booklet will also include line item instructions for completing the returns. In addition, withholding returns and instructions are also available on our website at **www.tax.virginia.gov**.

How Often To File

Your filing status is determined by the average amount of income tax that you withhold each month. When you register your business for withholding tax, you are asked to estimate this figure so the Department can assign a filing status. Based on that information, we assign a quarterly, monthly, semiweekly, or seasonal filing status. In addition, all employers must file an annual summary. You are not responsible for monitoring your monthly tax liability to see if a status change is needed. The Department reviews each account annually and makes any necessary changes. Notices of change in filing status are usually mailed during December of each year and become effective on January 1.

Liability For Filing - After you register for a withholding tax account, you must file a return for every period during which the account remains open, even if there is no tax due. If you do not expect to pay wages for an extended period of time, you may want to close the account until you begin paying wages again.

Extensions Of Time For Filing And Payment - The Department will grant a reasonable extension of time for filing and/or payment when good cause exists. You must apply for an extension in writing before the due date of the applicable return. If the time for payment is extended, we will assess interest on the tax due from the original due date through the date of payment.

Semiweekly Filing

If your average monthly liability is $1,000 or more, we will assign a semiweekly filing status to your account.

If the Virginia income tax withheld as of the close of any federal period is more than $500, a payment must be made within three banking days. Federal cutoff days for withholding deposits are generally Tuesday and Friday of each week. Semiweekly payments are usually made on Form VA-15 or by EFT.

At the end of each calendar quarter, you are required to file a reconciliation on Form VA-16, along with payment of any remaining tax due for the quarter. In addition, if the due date for Form VA-16 falls within three days of the due date of a current month's semiweekly payment, the current payment is included on Form VA-16.

Special Rule For Semiweekly Filers - Semiweekly filers are required to file a summary for each calendar quarter on Form VA-16. The total payments made for the quarter are subtracted from the actual tax withheld, and any remaining balance due is paid with the return. If the balance of tax due is more than 10% of the total tax liability for the quarter, a late payment penalty will be assessed on the amount over 10%.

Monthly Filing

If your average monthly withholding tax liability is over $100 but less than $1,000, a monthly filing status will be assigned.

File Form VA-5 or pay by EFT by the twenty-fifth day of the following month. A list of the due dates for monthly returns is shown below.

Month	Due Date	Month	Due Date
January	February 25	July	August 25
February	March 25	August	September 25
March	April 25	September	October 25
April	May 25	October	November 25
May	June 25	November	December 25
June	July 25	December	January 25

Any tax due must be paid at the time you file Form VA-5. You must file a return for each month even if there is no tax due. When using iFile, you can submit your return at any time before the due date and schedule payment for any date up to the due date.

Quarterly Filing

If the average monthly withholding tax liability is $100 or less, we will assign a quarterly filing status to your account. Quarterly returns must be filed on Form VA-5, with full payment for the tax due, or EFT payments for the tax due must be made on the last day of the month following the close of the quarter.

A list of the return due dates is given below.

Quarter Ended	Due Date
March 31	April 30
June 30	July 31
September 30	October 31
December 31	January 31

You must file a return for each quarter even if there is no tax due.

Seasonal Filing

As a seasonal filer, you are required to file returns for the months you designated when you registered, even if there is no tax due. Seasonal returns are filed on Form VA-5 and are due on the 25th of the following month for each month that the business has an employee. To change the designated months, write to the **Registration Unit, P.O. Box 1114, Richmond, VA 23218-1114**.

Annual Summary, Form VA-6

Every employer must file an annual summary on Form VA-6 or file using iFile at **www.tax.virginia.gov**.

Form VA-6 is due on February 28. If you close your account before the end of the year, you must file Form VA-6 within thirty days of the last month in which you pay wages. When filing Form VA-6, you must attach copies of any federal income statement form from the W-2 or 1099 series that reflects Virginia income tax withheld. The federal forms usually required are Forms W-2, W-2G and 1099-R.

Employers who furnish 250 or more employee wage statements (W-2 forms) must submit the W-2s by magnetic media.

Magnetic Media Reporting - The Department of Taxation accepts cartridge, CD and diskette filing of W-2 information only. See Virginia Magnetic Media Specifications for additional information. Download the Virginia Magnetic Media Specifications at **www.tax.virginia.gov**.

When filing by magnetic media, send your submission with Form VA-6 or iFile VA-6 confirmation and a copy of the Virginia Transmittal Form to: **Department of Taxation, W-2 Processing, P.O. Box 1278, Richmond, VA 23218-1278**.

NOTE: Submitting W-2 information to the Department of Taxation does not take the place of filing state employment data. That information must be transmitted separately to the Virginia Employment Commission.

Form 1099 Requirements - You are required to file copies of Form 1099 with the Department when the forms show Virginia income tax withheld. If you participate in the combined Federal / State Filing Program (CF/SF) for 1099-R, you do not need to file the form with Virginia, however, you must notify the Department by letter at least two weeks before the VA-6 is due (i.e. on or before February 15), of your intent to participate in the program. The letter should be mailed to: **Virginia Department of Taxation, W-2 Processing, P. O. Box 1278, Richmond, Virginia 23218-1278**. See Federal Publication 1220 for information on how to participate. The filing of all other information returns with the IRS is adequate for purposes of complying with Virginia filing requirements.

Adjustments To Returns

If you overpay your withholding tax, you may claim a credit on your return for the next period or request a refund. Refund requests should be mailed to **Department of Taxation, P.O. Box 1115, Richmond, VA 23218-1115**. The Department will allow a refund only if the tax in question was not actually withheld from an employee's wages. Claims for credit or refund must be filed within three years from the due date of the return for the period in which the overpayment occurred. If you underpay your tax, report the underpayment on your next return and attach a detailed explanation. If the underpayment is not discovered until the end of the calendar year, you should pay the tax with your annual summary, Form VA-6.

Late Filing Penalty

The penalty for filing a withholding return after the due date is 6% of the tax due for every month or part of a month that the return is late. The maximum penalty is 30% of the tax due. The minimum penalty is $10.00. The minimum penalty applies even if there is no tax due.

Late Payment Penalty

The penalty for late payment of withholding tax is the same as the late filing penalty (6% per month), and the same minimum and maximum amounts apply. However, the late payment penalty does not apply to any month for which the late filing penalty has already been assessed. Therefore, the total combined penalties for late filing and late payment cannot exceed 30% of the tax due, and the minimum penalty of $10.00 can be assessed only once.

Interest

If tax is paid after the due date, even with an approved extension, interest is accrued on the tax due from the due date through the date of payment. The interest rate is the federal underpayment rate established under Internal Revenue Code Section 6621, plus 2%.

Record Keeping Requirements

Your withholding tax records should include:

> The amounts and dates of wage payments made to each employee;

> The amounts and dates of all Virginia income tax withheld from each employee;

> The name, address, social security number, and period of employment for each employee;

> An exemption certificate (Form VA-4 or Form VA-4P) for each employee;

> Your account number and the amounts and dates of all tax payments made to the Department of Taxation; and

> A list of employees claiming exemption from withholding, including social security numbers.

Keep all records for at least three years after the due date to which they relate or the date the tax was paid, whichever is later.

How To Compute The Tax

Tax Tables And Formula

Tables for computing the tax, based on weekly, biweekly, semimonthly, monthly, and daily or miscellaneous pay periods are provided starting on page 11. To use a table, select the appropriate wage bracket in the left-hand column, then the number of exemptions from the top of the table to arrive at the amount of tax to be withheld. The tax amounts listed in the tables are rounded to the nearest dollar. To compute the exact amount of tax to be withheld, use the formula shown on page 10.

Determining The Payroll Period

For purposes of computing withholding, "payroll period" means the period of service (weekly, monthly, etc.) for which you normally pay wages. You should use the same period that you use for federal withholding tax purposes. If you have a regular payroll period, use that period for computing the tax, even if your employee does not work for the entire period. If you do not have a regular payroll period in place, compute the tax using the Daily or Miscellaneous Payroll Period withholding table. Special instructions for using that table are given below.

For a period of less than one week, you may compute the tax using a weekly payroll period, provided the employee signs a statement certifying that he or she has not worked for any other employer for wages subject to withholding in that calendar week.

Using The Daily Or Miscellaneous Withholding Table

To compute the tax using the Daily or Miscellaneous Payroll Period withholding tax table:

(a) Count the number of days in the period covered by the payment, including Saturdays, Sundays, and holidays. If the wages are not related to a specific period of time (for example, commissions paid upon completion of a sale), count the number of days back from the payment date to the latest of the following dates:

1. the last wage payment made to that employee in the same calendar year;

2. the date employment began, if that date falls in the same calendar year; or

3. January 1 of the year in which you are making the payment.

(b) Divide the wage payment by the number of days computed under (a). This amount is the average daily wage.

(c) Locate the average daily wage amount in the left column of the Daily or Miscellaneous table, then compute the daily tax by selecting the appropriate number of exemptions from the top of the table.

(d) Multiply the daily tax by the number of days computed under (a) to compute the tax for the pay period.

Nonperiodic Payments

Pension And Annuity Payments - If the payment is subject to mandatory federal withholding of 20% or 28% or if payments are not made on a regular basis, withhold Virginia tax at a rate of 4%.

Vacation Pay And Bonuses - If vacation pay or bonuses are included with a regular wage payment, add those amounts to the gross wages for the period and withhold tax on the entire total using the withholding tax tables or formula. If the payments are not included with regular wage payments, compute the tax as described under "Supplemental Wage Payments."

Supplemental Wage Payments - Add supplemental payments (such as commissions, overtime, back pay, and certain reimbursements) that are included with a regular wage payment to the gross wages and withhold tax on the entire total, using the withholding tax tables or formula.

9

If the supplemental wage payment is made separately, compute the tax as follows:

(a) Add the supplemental payment to the regular wages for the current payroll period or to the wages for the last regular payroll period in the same calendar year.

(b) Compute the tax on the total from (a) using the withholding tax tables or formula.

(c) Compute the tax on the regular wages alone.

(d) Subtract the tax computed in (c) from the tax computed in (b). This is the amount that should be withheld from the supplemental payment.

If, however, supplemental wages are paid and tax has been withheld from the employee's regular wages, the employer may determine the tax to be withheld by using a flat percentage rate of 5.75%, without allowance for exemption and without reference to any regular payment of wages.

Other Methods For Computing The Tax

Virginia law allows the Tax Commissioner to approve the use of computation methods other than the formula and tables provided in this booklet. To apply for permission to use an alternative method, write to the **Tax Commissioner, Virginia Department of Taxation, P.O. Box 2475, Richmond, VA 23218-2475**. The requested method must result in substantially the same amount of tax withheld as you would compute using the tables or formula.

Because of several differences between Virginia and federal income tax laws, it is not possible to correctly compute the Virginia tax to be withheld by using a method comparable to the federal "percentage method" or by using a set percentage of the federal tax withheld to determine the Virginia tax amount.

Formula For Computing Tax To Be Withheld

Legend

G = Gross pay for pay period
P = Number of pay periods per year
A = Annualized gross pay (G x P)
E1 = Personal and Dependent Exemptions
E2 = Age 65 and Over & Blind Exemptions
T = Annualized taxable income
W = Annualized tax to be withheld
W/H = Tax to be withheld for pay period

Formula (Effective January 1, 2008)

1. $(G)P - [\$3,000 + (E1 \times \$930) + (E2 \times \$800)] = T$

2. If **T** is:

If T is:		W is:
Not over $3,000		2% of T
Over	But not Over	Then
$3,000	$5,000	$60 + (3% of excess over $3,000)
$5,000	$17,000	$120 + (5% of excess over $5,000)
$17,000		$720 + (5.75% of excess over $17,000)

3. $W \div P = W/H$

Example

John claims exemptions for himself, his wife, and their three children for withholding tax purposes. He is paid on a semimonthly basis, and his gross wages for this pay period were $725.

1. $(G)P - [3,000 + (930)E1] = T$
   $(725)24 - [3,000 + (930)5] = T$
   $17,400 - 7,650 = 9,750$

2. T is over $5,000, but not over $17,000
   $\$120 + 5\%$ of $\$4,750 = W$
   $\$120 + \$237.50 = \$357.50$

3. $W \div P = W/H$
   $\$357.50 \div 24 = \$14.90$

The tax to be withheld for the current period is $14.90.

Pay Period Conversion Table (P)

Annual	=	1	Semimonthly =	24
Semiannual	=	2	Biweekly =	26
Quarterly	=	4	Weekly =	52
Monthly	=	12	Daily =	300

10

Withholding Tables for
Wages Paid
on or After
January 1, 2008

All the tables on pages 12 through 21 have been updated.

Daily Payroll Period
Virginia Income Tax Withholding Table
For Wages Paid After December 31, 2007

IF WAGES ARE-		AND THE TOTAL NUMBER OF PERSONAL EXEMPTIONS CLAIMED ON FORM VA-4 OR VA-4P IS-										
At Least	But Less Than	0	1	2	3	4	5	6	7	8	9	10 and over
		THE AMOUNT OF STATE INCOME TAX TO BE WITHHELD SHALL BE-										
0	$11	0.02	0.00	0.00	0.00	0.00	0.00	0.00	0.00	0.00	0.00	0.00
11	12	0.04	0.00	0.00	0.00	0.00	0.00	0.00	0.00	0.00	0.00	0.00
12	13	0.06	0.00	0.00	0.00	0.00	0.00	0.00	0.00	0.00	0.00	0.00
13	14	0.08	0.02	0.00	0.00	0.00	0.00	0.00	0.00	0.00	0.00	0.00
14	15	0.10	0.04	0.00	0.00	0.00	0.00	0.00	0.00	0.00	0.00	0.00
15	16	0.12	0.06	0.00	0.00	0.00	0.00	0.00	0.00	0.00	0.00	0.00
16	17	0.14	0.08	0.02	0.00	0.00	0.00	0.00	0.00	0.00	0.00	0.00
17	18	0.16	0.10	0.04	0.00	0.00	0.00	0.00	0.00	0.00	0.00	0.00
18	19	0.18	0.12	0.06	0.00	0.00	0.00	0.00	0.00	0.00	0.00	0.00
19	20	0.20	0.14	0.08	0.01	0.00	0.00	0.00	0.00	0.00	0.00	0.00
20	21	0.23	0.16	0.10	0.03	0.00	0.00	0.00	0.00	0.00	0.00	0.00
21	22	0.26	0.18	0.12	0.05	0.00	0.00	0.00	0.00	0.00	0.00	0.00
22	23	0.29	0.20	0.14	0.07	0.01	0.00	0.00	0.00	0.00	0.00	0.00
23	24	0.32	0.23	0.16	0.09	0.03	0.00	0.00	0.00	0.00	0.00	0.00
24	25	0.35	0.26	0.18	0.11	0.05	0.00	0.00	0.00	0.00	0.00	0.00
25	26	0.38	0.29	0.20	0.13	0.07	0.01	0.00	0.00	0.00	0.00	0.00
26	27	0.42	0.32	0.22	0.15	0.09	0.03	0.00	0.00	0.00	0.00	0.00
27	28	0.47	0.35	0.25	0.17	0.11	0.05	0.00	0.00	0.00	0.00	0.00
28	29	0.52	0.38	0.28	0.19	0.13	0.07	0.01	0.00	0.00	0.00	0.00
29	30	0.57	0.41	0.31	0.22	0.15	0.09	0.03	0.00	0.00	0.00	0.00
30	32	0.67	0.51	0.37	0.28	0.19	0.13	0.07	0.01	0.00	0.00	0.00
32	34	0.77	0.61	0.46	0.34	0.25	0.17	0.11	0.05	0.00	0.00	0.00
34	36	0.87	0.71	0.56	0.40	0.31	0.22	0.15	0.09	0.02	0.00	0.00
36	38	0.97	0.81	0.66	0.50	0.37	0.28	0.19	0.13	0.06	0.00	0.00
38	40	1.07	0.91	0.76	0.60	0.45	0.34	0.24	0.17	0.10	0.04	0.00
40	42	1.17	1.01	0.86	0.70	0.55	0.40	0.30	0.21	0.14	0.08	0.02
42	44	1.27	1.11	0.96	0.80	0.65	0.49	0.36	0.27	0.18	0.12	0.06
44	46	1.37	1.21	1.06	0.90	0.75	0.59	0.44	0.33	0.24	0.16	0.10
46	48	1.47	1.31	1.16	1.00	0.85	0.69	0.54	0.39	0.30	0.20	0.14
48	50	1.57	1.41	1.26	1.10	0.95	0.79	0.64	0.48	0.36	0.26	0.18
50	52	1.67	1.51	1.36	1.20	1.05	0.89	0.74	0.58	0.43	0.32	0.23
52	54	1.77	1.61	1.46	1.30	1.15	0.99	0.84	0.68	0.53	0.38	0.29
54	56	1.87	1.71	1.56	1.40	1.25	1.09	0.94	0.78	0.63	0.47	0.35
56	58	1.97	1.81	1.66	1.50	1.35	1.19	1.04	0.88	0.73	0.57	0.42
58	60	2.07	1.91	1.76	1.60	1.45	1.29	1.14	0.98	0.83	0.67	0.52
60	62	2.17	2.01	1.86	1.70	1.55	1.39	1.24	1.08	0.93	0.77	0.62
62	64	2.27	2.11	1.96	1.80	1.65	1.49	1.34	1.18	1.03	0.87	0.72
64	66	2.37	2.21	2.06	1.90	1.75	1.59	1.44	1.28	1.13	0.97	0.82
66	68	2.48	2.31	2.16	2.00	1.85	1.69	1.54	1.38	1.23	1.07	0.92
68	70	2.59	2.41	2.26	2.10	1.95	1.79	1.64	1.48	1.33	1.17	1.02
70	72	2.71	2.53	2.36	2.20	2.05	1.89	1.74	1.58	1.43	1.27	1.12
72	74	2.82	2.64	2.47	2.30	2.15	1.99	1.84	1.68	1.53	1.37	1.22
74	76	2.94	2.76	2.58	2.40	2.25	2.09	1.94	1.78	1.63	1.47	1.32
76	78	3.05	2.87	2.70	2.52	2.35	2.19	2.04	1.88	1.73	1.57	1.42
78	80	3.17	2.99	2.81	2.63	2.45	2.29	2.14	1.98	1.83	1.67	1.52
80	82	3.28	3.10	2.93	2.75	2.57	2.39	2.24	2.08	1.93	1.77	1.62
82	84	3.40	3.22	3.04	2.86	2.68	2.51	2.34	2.18	2.03	1.87	1.72
84	86	3.51	3.33	3.16	2.98	2.80	2.62	2.44	2.28	2.13	1.97	1.82
86	88	3.63	3.45	3.27	3.09	2.91	2.74	2.56	2.38	2.23	2.07	1.92
88	90	3.74	3.56	3.39	3.21	3.03	2.85	2.67	2.49	2.33	2.17	2.02
90	92	3.86	3.68	3.50	3.32	3.14	2.97	2.79	2.61	2.43	2.27	2.12
92	94	3.97	3.79	3.62	3.44	3.26	3.08	2.90	2.72	2.55	2.37	2.22
94	96	4.09	3.91	3.73	3.55	3.37	3.20	3.02	2.84	2.66	2.48	2.32
96	98	4.20	4.02	3.85	3.67	3.49	3.31	3.13	2.95	2.78	2.60	2.42
98	100	4.32	4.14	3.96	3.78	3.60	3.43	3.25	3.07	2.89	2.71	2.53
100	102	4.43	4.25	4.08	3.90	3.72	3.54	3.36	3.18	3.01	2.83	2.65
102	104	4.55	4.37	4.19	4.01	3.83	3.66	3.48	3.30	3.12	2.94	2.76
104	106	4.66	4.48	4.31	4.13	3.95	3.77	3.59	3.41	3.24	3.06	2.88
106	108	4.78	4.60	4.42	4.24	4.06	3.89	3.71	3.53	3.35	3.17	2.99
108	110	4.89	4.71	4.54	4.36	4.18	4.00	3.82	3.64	3.47	3.29	3.11
110	112	5.01	4.83	4.65	4.47	4.29	4.12	3.94	3.76	3.58	3.40	3.22

12

Daily Payroll Period
Virginia Income Tax Withholding Table
For Wages Paid After December 31, 2007

At Least	But Less Than	0	1	2	3	4	5	6	7	8	9	10 and over
		THE AMOUNT OF STATE INCOME TAX TO BE WITHHELD SHALL BE-										
112	114	5.12	4.94	4.77	4.59	4.41	4.23	4.05	3.87	3.70	3.52	3.34
114	116	5.24	5.06	4.88	4.70	4.52	4.35	4.17	3.99	3.81	3.63	3.45
116	118	5.35	5.17	5.00	4.82	4.64	4.46	4.28	4.10	3.93	3.75	3.57
118	120	5.47	5.29	5.11	4.93	4.75	4.58	4.40	4.22	4.04	3.86	3.68
120	122	5.58	5.40	5.23	5.05	4.87	4.69	4.51	4.33	4.16	3.98	3.80
122	124	5.70	5.52	5.34	5.16	4.98	4.81	4.63	4.45	4.27	4.09	3.91
124	126	5.81	5.63	5.46	5.28	5.10	4.92	4.74	4.56	4.39	4.21	4.03
126	128	5.93	5.75	5.57	5.39	5.21	5.04	4.86	4.68	4.50	4.32	4.14
128	130	6.04	5.86	5.69	5.51	5.33	5.15	4.97	4.79	4.62	4.44	4.26
130	132	6.16	5.98	5.80	5.62	5.44	5.27	5.09	4.91	4.73	4.55	4.37
132	134	6.27	6.09	5.92	5.74	5.56	5.38	5.20	5.02	4.85	4.67	4.49
134	136	6.39	6.21	6.03	5.85	5.67	5.50	5.32	5.14	4.96	4.78	4.60
136	138	6.50	6.32	6.15	5.97	5.79	5.61	5.43	5.25	5.08	4.90	4.72
138	140	6.62	6.44	6.26	6.08	5.90	5.73	5.55	5.37	5.19	5.01	4.83
140	142	6.73	6.55	6.38	6.20	6.02	5.84	5.66	5.48	5.31	5.13	4.95
142	144	6.85	6.67	6.49	6.31	6.13	5.96	5.78	5.60	5.42	5.24	5.06
144	146	6.96	6.78	6.61	6.43	6.25	6.07	5.89	5.71	5.54	5.36	5.18
146	148	7.08	6.90	6.72	6.54	6.36	6.19	6.01	5.83	5.65	5.47	5.29
148	150	7.19	7.01	6.84	6.66	6.48	6.30	6.12	5.94	5.77	5.59	5.41
150	152	7.31	7.13	6.95	6.77	6.59	6.42	6.24	6.06	5.88	5.70	5.52
152	154	7.42	7.24	7.07	6.89	6.71	6.53	6.35	6.17	6.00	5.82	5.64
154	156	7.54	7.36	7.18	7.00	6.82	6.65	6.47	6.29	6.11	5.93	5.75
156	158	7.65	7.47	7.30	7.12	6.94	6.76	6.58	6.40	6.23	6.05	5.87
158	160	7.77	7.59	7.41	7.23	7.05	6.88	6.70	6.52	6.34	6.16	5.98
160	162	7.88	7.70	7.53	7.35	7.17	6.99	6.81	6.63	6.46	6.28	6.10
162	164	8.00	7.82	7.64	7.46	7.28	7.11	6.93	6.75	6.57	6.39	6.21
164	166	8.11	7.93	7.76	7.58	7.40	7.22	7.04	6.86	6.69	6.51	6.33
166	168	8.23	8.05	7.87	7.69	7.51	7.34	7.16	6.98	6.80	6.62	6.44
168	170	8.34	8.16	7.99	7.81	7.63	7.45	7.27	7.09	6.92	6.74	6.56
170	172	8.46	8.28	8.10	7.92	7.74	7.57	7.39	7.21	7.03	6.85	6.67
172	174	8.57	8.39	8.22	8.04	7.86	7.68	7.50	7.32	7.15	6.97	6.79
174	176	8.69	8.51	8.33	8.15	7.97	7.80	7.62	7.44	7.26	7.08	6.90
176	178	8.80	8.62	8.45	8.27	8.09	7.91	7.73	7.55	7.38	7.20	7.02
178	180	8.92	8.74	8.56	8.38	8.20	8.03	7.85	7.67	7.49	7.31	7.13
180	182	9.03	8.85	8.68	8.50	8.32	8.14	7.96	7.78	7.61	7.43	7.25
182	184	9.15	8.97	8.79	8.61	8.43	8.26	8.08	7.90	7.72	7.54	7.36
184	186	9.26	9.08	8.91	8.73	8.55	8.37	8.19	8.01	7.84	7.66	7.48
186	188	9.38	9.20	9.02	8.84	8.66	8.49	8.31	8.13	7.95	7.77	7.59
188	190	9.49	9.31	9.14	8.96	8.78	8.60	8.42	8.24	8.07	7.89	7.71
190	192	9.61	9.43	9.25	9.07	8.89	8.72	8.54	8.36	8.18	8.00	7.82
192	194	9.72	9.54	9.37	9.19	9.01	8.83	8.65	8.47	8.30	8.12	7.94
194	196	9.84	9.66	9.48	9.30	9.12	8.95	8.77	8.59	8.41	8.23	8.05
196	198	9.95	9.77	9.60	9.42	9.24	9.06	8.88	8.70	8.53	8.35	8.17
198	200	10.07	9.89	9.71	9.53	9.35	9.18	9.00	8.82	8.64	8.46	8.28
200	202	10.18	10.00	9.83	9.65	9.47	9.29	9.11	8.93	8.76	8.58	8.40
202	204	10.30	10.12	9.94	9.76	9.58	9.41	9.23	9.05	8.87	8.69	8.51
204	206	10.41	10.23	10.06	9.88	9.70	9.52	9.34	9.16	8.99	8.81	8.63
206	208	10.53	10.35	10.17	9.99	9.81	9.64	9.46	9.28	9.10	8.92	8.74
208	210	10.64	10.46	10.29	10.11	9.93	9.75	9.57	9.39	9.22	9.04	8.86
210	212	10.76	10.58	10.40	10.22	10.04	9.87	9.69	9.51	9.33	9.15	8.97
212	214	10.87	10.69	10.52	10.34	10.16	9.98	9.80	9.62	9.45	9.27	9.09
214	216	10.99	10.81	10.63	10.45	10.27	10.10	9.92	9.74	9.56	9.38	9.20
216	218	11.10	10.92	10.75	10.57	10.39	10.21	10.03	9.85	9.68	9.50	9.32
218	220	11.22	11.04	10.86	10.68	10.50	10.33	10.15	9.97	9.79	9.61	9.43
220	222	11.33	11.15	10.98	10.80	10.62	10.44	10.26	10.08	9.91	9.73	9.55
222	224	11.45	11.27	11.09	10.91	10.73	10.56	10.38	10.20	10.02	9.84	9.66
224	226	11.56	11.38	11.21	11.03	10.85	10.67	10.49	10.31	10.14	9.96	9.78
226	228	11.68	11.50	11.32	11.14	10.96	10.79	10.61	10.43	10.25	10.07	9.89
228	230	11.79	11.61	11.44	11.26	11.08	10.90	10.72	10.54	10.37	10.19	10.01

If wages are in excess of the maximum amount shown above,
compute 5.75% of such excess and add to the last amount in the applicable column.

13

Weekly Payroll Period
Virginia Income Tax Withholding Table
For Wages Paid After December 31, 2007

IF WAGES ARE-		AND THE TOTAL NUMBER OF PERSONAL EXEMPTIONS CLAIMED ON FORM VA-4 OR VA-4P IS-										
At Least	But Less Than	0	1	2	3	4	5	6	7	8	9	10 and over
		THE AMOUNT OF STATE INCOME TAX TO BE WITHHELD SHALL BE-										
$0	$98	1	0	0	0	0	0	0	0	0	0	0
98	100	1	0	0	0	0	0	0	0	0	0	0
100	105	1	1	0	0	0	0	0	0	0	0	0
105	110	1	1	0	0	0	0	0	0	0	0	0
110	115	1	1	0	0	0	0	0	0	0	0	0
115	120	1	1	1	0	0	0	0	0	0	0	0
120	125	1	1	1	0	0	0	0	0	0	0	0
125	130	2	1	1	0	0	0	0	0	0	0	0
130	135	2	1	1	0	0	0	0	0	0	0	0
135	140	2	1	1	1	0	0	0	0	0	0	0
140	145	2	2	1	1	0	0	0	0	0	0	0
145	150	2	2	1	1	0	0	0	0	0	0	0
150	155	2	2	1	1	1	0	0	0	0	0	0
155	160	3	2	1	1	1	0	0	0	0	0	0
160	165	3	2	2	1	1	0	0	0	0	0	0
165	170	3	2	2	1	1	0	0	0	0	0	0
170	175	3	2	2	1	1	1	0	0	0	0	0
175	180	4	3	2	1	1	1	0	0	0	0	0
180	185	4	3	2	2	1	1	0	0	0	0	0
185	190	4	3	2	2	1	1	1	0	0	0	0
190	195	4	3	3	2	1	1	1	0	0	0	0
195	200	5	4	3	2	2	1	1	0	0	0	0
200	210	5	4	3	2	2	1	1	1	0	0	0
210	220	6	5	4	3	2	2	1	1	0	0	0
220	230	6	5	4	3	3	2	1	1	1	0	0
230	240	7	6	5	4	3	2	2	1	1	0	0
240	250	7	6	5	4	4	3	2	1	1	1	0
250	260	8	7	6	5	4	3	2	2	1	1	0
260	270	8	7	6	5	5	4	3	2	2	1	1
270	280	9	8	7	6	5	4	3	2	2	1	1
280	290	9	8	7	6	6	5	4	3	2	2	1
290	300	10	9	8	7	6	5	4	3	2	2	1
300	310	10	9	8	7	7	6	5	4	3	2	2
310	320	11	10	9	8	7	6	5	4	3	3	2
320	330	11	10	9	8	8	7	6	5	4	3	2
330	340	12	11	10	9	8	7	6	5	4	4	3
340	350	12	11	10	9	9	8	7	6	5	4	3
350	360	13	12	11	10	9	8	7	6	5	5	4
360	370	13	12	11	10	10	9	8	7	6	5	4
370	380	14	13	12	11	10	9	8	7	6	6	5
380	390	14	13	12	11	11	10	9	8	7	6	5
390	400	15	14	13	12	11	10	9	8	7	7	6
400	410	15	14	13	12	12	11	10	9	8	7	6
410	420	16	15	14	13	12	11	10	9	8	8	7
420	430	16	15	14	13	13	12	11	10	9	8	7
430	440	17	16	15	14	13	12	11	10	9	9	8
440	450	18	17	16	15	14	13	12	11	10	9	8
450	460	18	17	16	15	14	13	12	11	10	10	9
460	470	19	18	17	16	15	14	13	12	11	10	9
470	480	19	18	17	16	15	14	13	12	11	11	10
480	490	20	19	18	17	16	15	14	13	12	11	10
490	500	20	19	18	17	16	15	14	13	12	12	11
500	510	21	20	19	18	17	16	15	14	13	12	11
510	520	22	21	20	19	18	16	15	14	13	13	12
520	530	22	21	20	19	18	17	16	15	14	13	12
530	540	23	22	21	20	19	18	17	16	15	14	13
540	550	23	22	21	20	19	18	17	16	15	14	13
550	560	24	23	22	21	20	19	18	17	16	15	14
560	570	25	23	22	21	20	19	18	17	16	15	14
570	580	25	24	23	22	21	20	19	18	17	16	15
580	590	26	25	24	23	22	21	19	18	17	16	15
590	600	26	25	24	23	22	21	20	19	18	17	16
600	610	27	26	25	24	23	22	21	20	19	18	17
610	620	27	26	25	24	23	22	21	20	19	18	17

14

Weekly Payroll Period
Virginia Income Tax Withholding Table
For Wages Paid After December 31, 2007

At Least	But Less Than	0	1	2	3	4	5	6	7	8	9	10 and over
		— IF WAGES ARE- AND THE TOTAL NUMBER OF PERSONAL EXEMPTIONS CLAIMED ON FORM VA-4 OR VA-4P IS- / THE AMOUNT OF STATE INCOME TAX TO BE WITHHELD SHALL BE-										
620	630	28	27	26	25	24	23	22	21	20	19	18
630	640	29	28	26	25	24	23	22	21	20	19	18
640	650	29	28	27	26	25	24	23	22	21	20	19
650	660	30	29	28	27	26	25	24	22	21	20	19
660	670	30	29	28	27	26	25	24	23	22	21	20
670	680	31	30	29	28	27	26	25	24	23	22	21
680	690	31	30	29	28	27	26	25	24	23	22	21
690	700	32	31	30	29	28	27	26	25	24	23	22
700	710	33	32	30	29	28	27	26	25	24	23	22
710	720	33	32	31	30	29	28	27	26	25	24	23
720	730	34	33	32	31	30	29	28	27	25	24	23
730	740	34	33	32	31	30	29	28	27	26	25	24
740	750	35	34	33	32	31	30	29	28	27	26	25
750	760	35	34	33	32	31	30	29	28	27	26	25
760	770	36	35	34	33	32	31	30	29	28	27	26
770	780	37	36	35	33	32	31	30	29	28	27	26
780	790	37	36	35	34	33	32	31	30	29	28	27
790	800	38	37	36	35	34	33	32	31	30	28	27
800	810	38	37	36	35	34	33	32	31	30	29	28
810	820	39	38	37	36	35	34	33	32	31	30	29
820	830	39	38	37	36	35	34	33	32	31	30	29
830	840	40	39	38	37	36	35	34	33	32	31	30
840	850	41	40	39	38	36	35	34	33	32	31	30
850	860	41	40	39	38	37	36	35	34	33	32	31
860	870	42	41	40	39	38	37	36	35	34	33	31
870	880	42	41	40	39	38	37	36	35	34	33	32
880	890	43	42	41	40	39	38	37	36	35	34	33
890	900	43	42	41	40	39	38	37	36	35	34	33
900	910	44	43	42	41	40	39	38	37	36	35	34
910	920	45	44	43	42	41	39	38	37	36	35	34
920	930	45	44	43	42	41	40	39	38	37	36	35
930	940	46	45	44	43	42	41	40	39	38	37	35
940	950	46	45	44	43	42	41	40	39	38	37	36
950	960	47	46	45	44	43	42	41	40	39	38	37
960	970	48	46	45	44	43	42	41	40	39	38	37
970	980	48	47	46	45	44	43	42	41	40	39	38
980	990	49	48	47	46	45	44	42	41	40	39	38
990	1000	49	48	47	46	45	44	43	42	41	40	39
1000	1010	50	49	48	47	46	45	44	43	42	41	40
1010	1020	50	49	48	47	46	45	44	43	42	41	40
1020	1030	51	50	49	48	47	46	45	44	43	42	41
1030	1040	52	51	49	48	47	46	45	44	43	42	41
1040	1050	52	51	50	49	48	47	46	45	44	43	42
1050	1060	53	52	51	50	49	48	47	45	44	43	42
1060	1070	53	52	51	50	49	48	47	46	45	44	43
1070	1080	54	53	52	51	50	49	48	47	46	45	44
1080	1090	54	53	52	51	50	49	48	47	46	45	44
1090	1100	55	54	53	52	51	50	49	48	47	46	45
1100	1110	56	55	53	52	51	50	49	48	47	46	45
1110	1120	56	55	54	53	52	51	50	49	48	47	46
1120	1130	57	56	55	54	53	52	51	50	48	47	46
1130	1140	57	56	55	54	53	52	51	50	49	48	47
1140	1150	58	57	56	55	54	53	52	51	50	49	48
1150	1160	58	57	56	55	54	53	52	51	50	49	48
1160	1170	59	58	57	56	55	54	53	52	51	50	49
1170	1180	60	59	58	56	55	54	53	52	51	50	49

If wages are in excess of the maximum amount shown above,

compute 5.75% of such excess and add to the last amount in the applicable column.

15

Semi-Monthly Payroll Period
Virginia Income Tax Withholding Table
For Wages Paid After December 31, 2007

IF WAGES ARE-		AND THE TOTAL NUMBER OF PERSONAL EXEMPTIONS CLAIMED ON FORM VA-4 OR VA-4P IS-										
At Least	But Less Than	0	1	2	3	4	5	6	7	8	9	10 and over
		THE AMOUNT OF STATE INCOME TAX TO BE WITHHELD SHALL BE-										
$0	$150	1	0	0	0	0	0	0	0	0	0	0
150	160	1	0	0	0	0	0	0	0	0	0	0
160	170	1	0	0	0	0	0	0	0	0	0	0
170	180	1	0	0	0	0	0	0	0	0	0	0
180	190	1	1	0	0	0	0	0	0	0	0	0
190	200	2	1	0	0	0	0	0	0	0	0	0
200	210	2	1	0	0	0	0	0	0	0	0	0
210	220	2	1	0	0	0	0	0	0	0	0	0
220	230	2	1	1	0	0	0	0	0	0	0	0
230	240	2	2	1	0	0	0	0	0	0	0	0
240	250	3	2	1	0	0	0	0	0	0	0	0
250	260	3	2	1	0	0	0	0	0	0	0	0
260	270	3	2	1	1	0	0	0	0	0	0	0
270	280	3	2	2	1	0	0	0	0	0	0	0
280	290	4	3	2	1	0	0	0	0	0	0	0
290	300	4	3	2	1	0	0	0	0	0	0	0
300	310	4	3	2	1	1	0	0	0	0	0	0
310	320	5	3	2	2	1	0	0	0	0	0	0
320	330	5	4	3	2	1	0	0	0	0	0	0
330	340	5	4	3	2	1	0	0	0	0	0	0
340	350	6	4	3	2	1	1	0	0	0	0	0
350	360	6	5	3	2	2	1	0	0	0	0	0
360	370	7	5	4	3	2	1	0	0	0	0	0
370	380	7	5	4	3	2	1	0	0	0	0	0
380	390	8	6	4	3	2	1	1	0	0	0	0
390	400	8	6	5	4	2	2	1	0	0	0	0
400	410	9	7	5	4	3	2	1	0	0	0	0
410	420	9	7	5	4	3	2	1	0	0	0	0
420	430	10	8	6	4	3	2	1	1	0	0	0
430	440	10	8	6	5	4	2	2	1	0	0	0
440	450	11	9	7	5	4	3	2	1	0	0	0
450	460	11	9	7	6	4	3	2	1	1	0	0
460	470	12	10	8	6	4	3	2	1	1	0	0
470	480	12	10	8	7	5	4	2	2	1	0	0
480	490	13	11	9	7	5	4	3	2	1	0	0
490	500	13	11	9	8	6	4	3	2	1	1	0
500	510	14	12	10	8	6	4	3	2	2	1	0
510	520	14	12	10	9	7	5	4	2	2	1	0
520	530	15	13	11	9	7	5	4	3	2	1	0
530	540	15	13	11	10	8	6	4	3	2	1	1
540	550	16	14	12	10	8	6	5	3	2	2	1
550	560	16	14	12	11	9	7	5	4	3	2	1
560	570	17	15	13	11	9	7	5	4	3	2	1
570	580	17	15	13	12	10	8	6	4	3	2	1
580	590	18	16	14	12	10	8	6	5	3	2	2
590	600	18	16	14	13	11	9	7	5	4	3	2
600	615	19	17	15	13	11	9	7	6	4	3	2
615	630	20	18	16	14	12	10	8	6	5	3	2
630	645	21	19	17	15	13	11	9	7	5	4	3
645	660	21	19	17	16	14	12	10	8	6	4	3
660	675	22	20	18	16	14	12	10	9	7	5	4
675	690	23	21	19	17	15	13	11	9	7	5	4
690	705	24	22	20	18	16	14	12	10	8	6	5
705	720	24	22	20	19	17	15	13	11	9	7	5
720	735	25	23	21	19	17	15	13	12	10	8	6
735	750	26	24	22	20	18	16	14	12	10	8	6
750	765	27	25	23	21	19	17	15	13	11	9	7
765	780	27	25	23	22	20	18	16	14	12	10	8
780	795	28	26	24	22	20	18	16	15	13	11	9
795	810	29	27	25	23	21	19	17	15	13	11	9
810	825	30	28	26	24	22	20	18	16	14	12	10
825	840	30	28	26	25	23	21	19	17	15	13	11

Semi-Monthly Payroll Period
Virginia Income Tax Withholding Table
For Wages Paid After December 31, 2007

At Least	But Less Than	0	1	2	3	4	5	6	7	8	9	10 and over
		IF WAGES ARE- AND THE TOTAL NUMBER OF PERSONAL EXEMPTIONS CLAIMED ON FORM VA-4 OR VA-4P IS-										

At Least	But Less Than	0	1	2	3	4	5	6	7	8	9	10 and over
840	855	31	29	27	25	23	21	19	18	16	14	12
855	870	32	30	28	26	24	22	20	18	16	14	12
870	885	33	31	29	27	25	23	21	19	17	15	13
885	900	34	32	29	28	26	24	22	20	18	16	14
900	915	35	32	30	28	26	24	22	21	19	17	15
915	930	36	33	31	29	27	25	23	21	19	17	15
930	945	36	34	32	30	28	26	24	22	20	18	16
945	960	37	35	33	31	29	27	25	23	21	19	17
960	975	38	36	34	31	29	27	25	24	22	20	18
975	990	39	37	35	32	30	28	26	24	22	20	18
990	1005	40	38	35	33	31	29	27	25	23	21	19
1005	1020	41	39	36	34	32	30	28	26	24	22	20
1020	1035	42	39	37	35	33	30	28	27	25	23	21
1035	1050	42	40	38	36	34	31	29	27	25	23	21
1050	1065	43	41	39	37	34	32	30	28	26	24	22
1065	1080	44	42	40	37	35	33	31	29	27	25	23
1080	1095	45	43	41	38	36	34	32	30	28	26	24
1095	1110	46	44	41	39	37	35	33	30	28	26	24
1110	1125	47	45	42	40	38	36	33	31	29	27	25
1125	1140	48	45	43	41	39	36	34	32	30	28	26
1140	1155	48	46	44	42	40	37	35	33	31	29	27
1155	1170	49	47	45	43	40	38	36	34	32	29	27
1170	1185	50	48	46	44	41	39	37	35	32	30	28
1185	1200	51	49	47	44	42	40	38	35	33	31	29
1200	1215	52	50	47	45	43	41	39	36	34	32	30
1215	1230	53	51	48	46	44	42	39	37	35	33	31
1230	1245	54	51	49	47	45	43	40	38	36	34	31
1245	1260	55	52	50	48	46	43	41	39	37	34	32
1260	1275	55	53	51	49	46	44	42	40	38	35	33
1275	1290	56	54	52	50	47	45	43	41	38	36	34
1290	1305	57	55	53	50	48	46	44	42	39	37	35
1305	1320	58	56	54	51	49	47	45	42	40	38	36
1320	1335	59	57	54	52	50	48	45	43	41	39	37
1335	1350	60	57	55	53	51	49	46	44	42	40	37
1350	1365	61	58	56	54	52	49	47	45	43	41	38
1365	1380	61	59	57	55	53	50	48	46	44	41	39
1380	1395	62	60	58	56	53	51	49	47	44	42	40
1395	1410	63	61	59	56	54	52	50	48	45	43	41
1410	1425	64	62	60	57	55	53	51	48	46	44	42
1425	1440	65	63	60	58	56	54	52	49	47	45	43
1440	1455	66	64	61	59	57	55	52	50	48	46	43
1455	1470	67	64	62	60	58	55	53	51	49	47	44
1470	1485	67	65	63	61	59	56	54	52	50	47	45
1485	1500	68	66	64	62	59	57	55	53	51	48	46
1500	1515	69	67	65	63	60	58	56	54	51	49	47
1515	1530	70	68	66	63	61	59	57	54	52	50	48
1530	1545	71	69	66	64	62	60	58	55	53	51	49
1545	1560	72	70	67	65	63	61	58	56	54	52	50
1560	1575	73	70	68	66	64	62	59	57	55	53	50
1575	1590	74	71	69	67	65	62	60	58	56	53	51
1590	1605	74	72	70	68	65	63	61	59	57	54	52
1605	1620	75	73	71	69	66	64	62	60	57	55	53
1620	1635	76	74	72	69	67	65	63	60	58	56	54
1635	1650	77	75	73	70	68	66	64	61	59	57	55
1650	1665	78	76	73	71	69	67	64	62	60	58	56
1665	1680	79	76	74	72	70	68	65	63	61	59	56
1680	1695	80	77	75	73	71	68	66	64	62	59	57
1695	1710	80	78	76	74	71	69	67	65	63	60	58

If wages are in excess of the maximum amount shown above,
compute 5.75% of such excess and add to the last amount in the applicable column.

17

Biweekly Payroll Period
Virginia Income Tax Withholding Table
For Wages Paid After December 31, 2007

At Least	But Less Than	IF WAGES ARE- AND THE TOTAL NUMBER OF PERSONAL EXEMPTIONS CLAIMED ON FORM VA-4 OR VA-4P IS-										10 and over
		0	1	2	3	4	5	6	7	8	9	
		THE AMOUNT OF STATE INCOME TAX TO BE WITHHELD SHALL BE-										
$0	$140	0	0	0	0	0	0	0	0	0	0	0
140	150	1	0	0	0	0	0	0	0	0	0	0
150	160	1	0	0	0	0	0	0	0	0	0	0
160	170	1	0	0	0	0	0	0	0	0	0	0
170	180	1	1	0	0	0	0	0	0	0	0	0
180	190	1	1	0	0	0	0	0	0	0	0	0
190	200	2	1	0	0	0	0	0	0	0	0	0
200	210	2	1	0	0	0	0	0	0	0	0	0
210	220	2	1	1	0	0	0	0	0	0	0	0
220	230	2	2	1	0	0	0	0	0	0	0	0
230	240	3	2	1	0	0	0	0	0	0	0	0
240	250	3	2	1	1	0	0	0	0	0	0	0
250	260	3	2	1	1	0	0	0	0	0	0	0
260	270	3	2	2	1	0	0	0	0	0	0	0
270	280	4	3	2	1	0	0	0	0	0	0	0
280	290	4	3	2	1	1	0	0	0	0	0	0
290	300	4	3	2	2	1	0	0	0	0	0	0
300	310	5	4	3	2	1	0	0	0	0	0	0
310	320	5	4	3	2	1	1	0	0	0	0	0
320	330	6	4	3	2	1	1	0	0	0	0	0
330	340	6	5	3	2	2	1	0	0	0	0	0
340	350	7	5	4	3	2	1	0	0	0	0	0
350	360	7	5	4	3	2	1	1	0	0	0	0
360	370	8	6	4	3	2	2	1	0	0	0	0
370	380	8	6	5	4	2	2	1	0	0	0	0
380	390	9	7	5	4	3	2	1	0	0	0	0
390	400	9	7	6	4	3	2	1	1	0	0	0
400	410	10	8	6	4	3	2	2	1	0	0	0
410	420	10	8	7	5	4	3	2	1	0	0	0
420	430	11	9	7	5	4	3	2	1	1	0	0
430	440	11	9	8	6	4	3	2	1	1	0	0
440	450	12	10	8	6	5	4	2	2	1	0	0
450	460	12	10	9	7	5	4	3	2	1	0	0
460	470	13	11	9	7	6	4	3	2	1	1	0
470	480	13	11	10	8	6	4	3	2	2	1	0
480	490	14	12	10	8	7	5	4	3	2	1	0
490	500	14	12	11	9	7	5	4	3	2	1	1
500	510	15	13	11	9	8	6	4	3	2	1	1
510	520	15	13	12	10	8	6	5	3	2	2	1
520	530	16	14	12	10	9	7	5	4	3	2	1
530	540	16	14	13	11	9	7	6	4	3	2	1
540	550	17	15	13	11	10	8	6	4	3	2	2
550	560	17	15	14	12	10	8	7	5	4	3	2
560	570	18	16	14	12	11	9	7	5	4	3	2
570	580	18	16	15	13	11	9	8	6	4	3	2
580	590	19	17	15	13	12	10	8	6	5	3	2
590	600	19	17	16	14	12	10	9	7	5	4	3
600	610	20	18	16	14	13	11	9	7	5	4	3
610	620	20	18	17	15	13	11	10	8	6	4	3
620	630	21	19	17	15	14	12	10	8	6	5	4
630	640	21	19	18	16	14	12	11	9	7	5	4
640	650	22	20	18	16	15	13	11	9	7	6	4
650	660	22	20	19	17	15	13	12	10	8	6	4
660	670	23	21	19	17	16	14	12	10	8	7	5
670	680	23	21	20	18	16	14	13	11	9	7	5
680	690	24	22	20	18	17	15	13	11	9	8	6
690	700	24	22	21	19	17	15	14	12	10	8	6
700	710	25	23	21	19	18	16	14	12	10	9	7
710	720	25	23	22	20	18	16	15	13	11	9	7
720	730	26	24	22	20	19	17	15	13	11	10	8
730	740	26	24	23	21	19	17	16	14	12	10	8
740	750	27	25	23	21	20	18	16	14	12	11	9
750	760	27	25	24	22	20	18	17	15	13	11	9
760	770	28	26	24	22	21	19	17	15	13	12	10

Biweekly Payroll Period
Virginia Income Tax Withholding Table
For Wages Paid After December 31, 2007

At Least	But Less Than	0	1	2	3	4	5	6	7	8	9	10 and over
770	780	28	26	25	23	21	19	18	16	14	12	10
780	790	29	27	25	23	22	20	18	16	14	13	11
790	800	29	27	26	24	22	20	19	17	15	13	11
800	810	30	28	26	24	23	21	19	17	15	14	12
810	820	31	29	27	25	23	21	20	18	16	14	12
820	830	31	29	27	25	24	22	20	18	16	15	13
830	840	32	30	28	26	24	22	21	19	17	15	13
840	850	32	30	28	26	25	23	21	19	17	16	14
850	860	33	31	29	27	25	23	22	20	18	16	14
860	870	33	31	29	27	26	24	22	20	18	17	15
870	880	34	32	30	28	26	24	23	21	19	17	15
880	890	35	33	31	28	27	25	23	21	19	18	16
890	900	35	33	31	29	27	25	24	22	20	18	16
900	910	36	34	32	30	28	26	24	22	20	19	17
910	920	36	34	32	30	28	26	25	23	21	19	17
920	930	37	35	33	31	29	27	25	23	21	20	18
930	940	38	35	33	31	29	27	26	24	22	20	18
940	950	38	36	34	32	30	28	26	24	22	21	19
950	960	39	37	35	32	30	28	27	25	23	21	19
960	970	39	37	35	33	31	29	27	25	23	22	20
970	980	40	38	36	34	32	30	28	26	24	22	20
980	990	40	38	36	34	32	30	28	26	24	23	21
990	1000	41	39	37	35	33	31	29	27	25	23	21
1000	1010	42	39	37	35	33	31	29	27	25	24	22
1010	1020	42	40	38	36	34	32	30	28	26	24	22
1020	1030	43	41	39	37	34	32	30	28	26	25	23
1030	1040	43	41	39	37	35	33	31	29	27	25	23
1040	1050	44	42	40	38	36	34	31	29	27	26	24
1050	1060	44	42	40	38	36	34	32	30	28	26	24
1060	1070	45	43	41	39	37	35	33	31	29	27	25
1070	1080	46	44	41	39	37	35	33	31	29	27	25
1080	1090	46	44	42	40	38	36	34	32	30	28	26
1090	1100	47	45	43	41	38	36	34	32	30	28	26
1100	1110	47	45	43	41	39	37	35	33	31	29	27
1110	1120	48	46	44	42	40	38	36	33	31	29	27
1120	1130	48	46	44	42	40	38	36	34	32	30	28
1130	1140	49	47	45	43	41	39	37	35	33	31	28
1140	1150	50	48	45	43	41	39	37	35	33	31	29
1150	1160	50	48	46	44	42	40	38	36	34	32	30
1160	1170	51	49	47	45	43	40	38	36	34	32	30
1170	1180	51	49	47	45	43	41	39	37	35	33	31
1180	1190	52	50	48	46	44	42	40	37	35	33	31
1190	1200	52	50	48	46	44	42	40	38	36	34	32
1200	1210	53	51	49	47	45	43	41	39	37	35	32
1210	1220	54	52	49	47	45	43	41	39	37	35	33
1220	1230	54	52	50	48	46	44	42	40	38	36	34
1230	1240	55	53	51	49	47	44	42	40	38	36	34
1240	1250	55	53	51	49	47	45	43	41	39	37	35
1250	1260	56	54	52	50	48	46	44	42	39	37	35
1260	1270	56	54	52	50	48	46	44	42	40	38	36
1270	1280	57	55	53	51	49	47	45	43	41	39	36
1280	1290	58	56	54	51	49	47	45	43	41	39	37
1290	1300	58	56	54	52	50	48	46	44	42	40	38
1300	1310	59	57	55	53	51	49	46	44	42	40	38
1310	1320	59	57	55	53	51	49	47	45	43	41	39
1320	1330	60	58	56	54	52	50	48	46	43	41	39

If wages are in excess of the maximum amount shown above,
compute 5.75% of such excess and add to the last amount in the applicable column.

Monthly Payroll Period
Virginia Income Tax Withholding Table
For Wages Paid After December 31, 2007

IF WAGES ARE-		AND THE TOTAL NUMBER OF PERSONAL EXEMPTIONS CLAIMED ON FORM VA-4 OR VA-4P IS-										
At Least	But Less Than	0	1	2	3	4	5	6	7	8	9	10 and over
		THE AMOUNT OF STATE INCOME TAX TO BE WITHHELD SHALL BE-										
$0	$260	0	0	0	0	0	0	0	0	0	0	0
260	280	1	0	0	0	0	0	0	0	0	0	0
280	300	1	0	0	0	0	0	0	0	0	0	0
300	320	1	0	0	0	0	0	0	0	0	0	0
320	340	2	0	0	0	0	0	0	0	0	0	0
340	360	2	1	0	0	0	0	0	0	0	0	0
360	380	3	1	0	0	0	0	0	0	0	0	0
380	400	3	1	0	0	0	0	0	0	0	0	0
400	420	3	2	0	0	0	0	0	0	0	0	0
420	440	4	2	1	0	0	0	0	0	0	0	0
440	460	4	3	1	0	0	0	0	0	0	0	0
460	450	4	2	1	0	0	0	0	0	0	0	0
450	500	5	3	2	0	0	0	0	0	0	0	0
500	520	6	4	2	1	0	0	0	0	0	0	0
520	540	6	4	3	1	0	0	0	0	0	0	0
540	560	7	5	3	2	0	0	0	0	0	0	0
560	580	7	5	4	2	0	0	0	0	0	0	0
580	600	8	6	4	2	1	0	0	0	0	0	0
600	620	9	6	4	3	1	0	0	0	0	0	0
620	640	9	7	5	3	2	0	0	0	0	0	0
640	660	10	7	5	4	2	0	0	0	0	0	0
660	680	11	8	6	4	2	1	0	0	0	0	0
680	700	12	9	6	4	3	1	0	0	0	0	0
700	725	13	9	7	5	3	2	0	0	0	0	0
725	750	14	10	8	6	4	2	1	0	0	0	0
750	775	15	12	9	6	4	3	1	0	0	0	0
775	800	17	13	9	7	5	3	2	0	0	0	0
800	825	18	14	10	8	5	4	2	1	0	0	0
825	850	19	15	11	9	6	4	3	1	0	0	0
850	875	20	17	13	9	7	5	3	2	0	0	0
875	900	22	18	14	10	8	5	4	2	1	0	0
900	925	23	19	15	11	8	6	4	3	1	0	0
925	950	24	20	16	13	9	7	5	3	2	0	0
950	975	25	22	18	14	10	8	5	4	2	1	0
975	1000	27	23	19	15	11	8	6	4	3	1	0
1000	1025	28	24	20	16	12	9	7	5	3	2	0
1025	1050	29	25	21	18	14	10	8	5	4	2	1
1050	1075	30	27	23	19	15	11	8	6	4	3	1
1075	1100	32	28	24	20	16	12	9	7	5	3	2
1100	1125	33	29	25	21	17	14	10	7	5	4	2
1125	1150	34	30	26	23	19	15	11	8	6	4	3
1150	1175	35	32	28	24	20	16	12	9	7	5	3
1175	1200	37	33	29	25	21	17	13	10	7	5	4
1200	1225	38	34	30	26	22	19	15	11	8	6	4
1225	1250	39	35	31	28	24	20	16	12	9	7	5
1250	1275	40	37	33	29	25	21	17	13	10	7	5
1275	1300	42	38	34	30	26	22	18	15	11	8	6
1300	1325	43	39	35	31	27	24	20	16	12	9	7
1325	1350	44	40	36	33	29	25	21	17	13	10	7
1350	1375	45	42	38	34	30	26	22	18	14	11	8
1375	1400	47	43	39	35	31	27	23	20	16	12	9
1400	1425	48	44	40	36	32	29	25	21	17	13	10
1425	1450	49	45	41	38	34	30	26	22	18	14	10
1450	1475	50	47	43	39	35	31	27	23	19	16	12
1475	1500	52	48	44	40	36	32	28	25	21	17	13
1500	1525	53	49	45	41	37	34	30	26	22	18	14
1525	1550	54	50	46	43	39	35	31	27	23	19	15
1550	1575	55	52	48	44	40	36	32	28	24	21	17
1575	1600	57	53	49	45	41	37	33	30	26	22	18
1600	1625	58	54	50	46	42	39	35	31	27	23	19
1625	1650	59	55	51	48	44	40	36	32	28	24	20
1650	1675	60	57	53	49	45	41	37	33	29	26	22

Monthly Payroll Period
Virginia Income Tax Withholding Table
For Wages Paid After December 31, 2007

At Least	But Less Than	IF WAGES ARE- AND THE TOTAL NUMBER OF PERSONAL EXEMPTIONS CLAIMED ON FORM VA-4 OR VA-4P IS-										10 and over
		0	1	2	3	4	5	6	7	8	9	
		THE AMOUNT OF STATE INCOME TAX TO BE WITHHELD SHALL BE-										
1675	1700	62	58	54	50	46	42	38	35	31	27	23
1700	1725	63	59	55	51	47`	44	40	36	32	28	24
1725	1750	65	60	56	53	49	45	41	37	33	29	25
1750	1775	66	62	58	54	50	46	42	38	34	31	27
1775	1800	68	63	59	55	51	47	43	40	36	32	28
1800	1825	69	65	60	56	52	49	45	41	37	33	29
1825	1850	71	66	62	58	54	50	46	42	38	34	30
1850	1875	72	68	63	59	55	51	47	43	39	36	32
1875	1900	73	69	65	60	56	52	48	45	41	37	33
1900	1925	75	70	66	61	57	54	50	46	42	38	34
1925	1950	76	72	67	63	59	55	51	47	43	39	35
1950	1975	78	73	69	64	60	56	52	48	44	41	37
1975	2000	79	75	70	66	61	57	53	50	46	42	38
2000	2025	81	76	72	67	63	59	55	51	47	43	39
2025	2075	83	79	75	70	66	61	57	53	49	46	42
2075	2100	85	80	76	72	67	63	58	55	51	47	43
2100	2125	86	82	77	73	69	64	60	56	52	48	44
2125	2150	88	83	79	74	70	66	61	57	53	49	45
2150	2175	89	85	80	76	71	67	62	58	54	51	47
2175	2200	91	86	82	77	73	68	64	60	56	52	48
2200	2225	92	88	83	79	74	70	65	61	57	53	49
2225	2250	94	89	85	80	76	71	67	62	58	54	50
2250	2275	95	91	86	82	77	73	68	64	59	56	52
2275	2300	96	92	88	83	79	74	70	65	61	57	53
2300	2325	98	93	89	84	80	76	71	67	62	58	54
2325	2350	99	95	90	86	81	77	73	68	64	59	55
2350	2375	101	96	92	87	83	78	74	70	65	61	57
2375	2400	102	98	93	89	84	80	75	71	67	62	58
2400	2425	104	99	95	90	86	81	77	72	68	63	59
2425	2450	105	101	96	92	87	83	78	74	69	65	60
2450	2475	106	102	98	93	89	84	80	75	71	66	62
2475	2500	108	103	99	95	90	86	81	77	72	68	63
2500	2525	109	105	100	96	92	87	83	78	74	69	65
2525	2550	111	106	102	97	93	89	84	80	75	71	66
2550	2575	112	108	103	99	94	90	85	81	77	72	68
2575	2600	114	109	105	100	96	91	87	82	78	74	69
2600	2625	115	111	106	102	97	93	88	84	79	75	71
2625	2650	117	112	108	103	99	94	90	85	81	76	72
2650	2675	118	114	109	105	100	96	91	87	82	78	73
2675	2700	119	115	111	106	102	97	93	88	84	79	75
2700	2725	121	116	112	107	103	99	94	90	85	81	76
2725	2750	122	118	113	109	104	100	96	91	87	82	78
2750	2775	124	119	115	110	106	101	97	93	88	84	79
2775	2800	125	121	116	112	107	103	98	94	90	85	81
2800	2825	127	122	118	113	109	104	100	95	91	86	82
2825	2850	128	124	119	115	110	106	101	97	92	88	83
2850	2875	129	125	121	116	112	107	103	98	94	89	85
2875	2900	131	126	122	118	113	109	104	100	95	91	86
2900	2925	132	128	123	119	115	110	106	101	97	92	88
2925	2950	134	129	125	120	116	112	107	103	98	94	89
2950	2975	135	131	126	122	117	113	108	104	100	95	91
2975	3000	137	132	128	123	119	114	110	105	101	97	92
3000	3025	138	134	129	125	120	116	111	107	102	98	94
3025	3050	140	135	131	126	122	117	113	108	104	99	95
3050	3075	141	137	132	128	123	119	114	110	105	101	96
3075	3100	142	138	134	129	125	120	116	111	107	102	98
3100	3125	144	139	135	130	126	122	117	113	108	104	99
3125	3150	145	141	136	132	127	123	119	114	110	105	101

If wages are in excess of the maximum amount shown above,
compute 5.75% of such excess and add to the last amount in the applicable column.

Withholding Formula and Tables for Wages Paid On or After January 1, 2008

Virginia Employee State Income Tax Withholding

For pay periods beginning on or after January 1, 2008, the Virginia withholding formula is:

Key

G = Gross Pay for Pay Period
A = Annualized gross pay
T = Annualized taxable income
W/H = Tax to be withheld for pay period

P = Pay periods per year
E1 = Personal and Dependent Exemptions
E2 = Age 65 and Over & Blind Exemptions
W = Annualized tax to be withheld

Formula

1. $(G) P - [\$3{,}000 + (E1 \times \$900) + (E2 \times 800)] = T$

2. **If T is:**

Not over $3,000		2% of T	
Over	**But not Over**	**Then**	
$ 3,000	$ 5,000	$ 60 + (3% of excess over $3,000)	
$ 5,000	$17,000	$120 + (5% of excess over $5,000)	
$17,000		$720 + (5.75% of excess over $17,000)	

W is:

3. $W \div P = W/H$

Employer's Return of Virginia Income Tax Withheld Instructions

General: An employer who pays wages to one or more employees is required to deduct and withhold state income tax from those wages. Virginia law substantially conforms to the federal definition of "wages." Therefore, Virginia withholding is generally required on any payment for which federal withholding is required, except amounts paid pursuant to individual retirement accounts and simplified employee pension plans as defined in Sections 7701(a) (37) and 408(c) of the Internal Revenue Code.

Filing and Payment Procedure: An employer's filing status is determined by the average amount of income tax withheld each month. When registering a business, an employer is asked to estimate this figure so the Department can assign a filing status. Based on that information, the Department assigns a quarterly, monthly, semi-weekly, or seasonal filing status. In addition, all employers must file an annual summary. Employers are not responsible for monitoring their monthly tax liabilities to see if a status change is needed. The Department reviews each account annually and makes any necessary changes. Notices of change in filing status are usually mailed during December of each year and become effective on January 1.

Payments may be made by check or by Electronic Funds Transfer (EFT). Payments returned by the bank will be subject to a returned payment fee in addition to any other penalties that may be incurred.

Paying by EFT eliminates your requirement to submit Form VA-5, however payments must be made by the same dates that the Form VA-5 would have been due. When no payment is due because the tax liability is zero, you must report a ZERO liability to the Department. This can be done by reporting a zero payment on your EFT transaction. For additional information regarding EFT, please refer to the Department's *Electronic Funds Transfer (EFT) Guide.* A Guide may be obtained from the Department's web site, **www.tax.virginia. gov,** or Forms Request Unit at (804) 440-2541.

- Quarterly Filing: If an employer's average monthly withholding tax liability is less than $100, the account will be assigned a quarterly filing status. Form VA-5, with full payment for the tax, or your EFT payment is due on the last day of the month following the close of the quarter. **A return or EFT zero transaction payment must be filed for each quarter even if there is no tax due.**

- Monthly Filing: If the average monthly withholding tax liability is at least $100, but less than $1,000, a monthly filing status will be assigned. File Form VA-5 or make your EFT payment by the 25th day of the following month. **A return or EFT zero transaction payment must be filed for each month, even if there is no tax due.**

- Seasonal Filing: Seasonal filers, those employers who have employees only during certain months of the year, are required to file returns for the months designated at the time they register for an account, even if there is no tax due. Seasonal returns are filed on Form VA-5 and are due at the normal monthly filing dates.

Mail **quarterly** returns and payments to the **Virginia Department of Taxation, P.O. Box 26644, Richmond, Virginia 23261-6644.**

Mail **monthly and seasonal** returns and payments to the **Virginia Department of Taxation, P.O. Box 27264, Richmond, Virginia 23261-7264.**

Change of Ownership: If there has been a change of ownership, do not use the return with the name and account number of the former owner. Send the return with notice of change to the **Virginia Department of Taxation, P.O. Box 1114, Richmond, Virginia 23218-1114.** You can register a new dealer and/or locations, by either completing a Form R-1, Business Registration Application, or electronically using iReg on the Department's web site, **www.tax. virginia.gov.** The Form R-1 can be obtained from the Department's web site or by calling the Department's Forms Request Unit at (804) 440-2541.

Change of Address/Out-of-Business: If you change your business mailing address or discontinue your business, either send a completed Form R-3, Registration Change Request or a letter to the **Virginia Department of Taxation, P.O. Box 1114, Richmond, Virginia 23218-1114.** The Form R-3 is included in your coupon booklet. A Form R-3 can also be obtained from the Department's web site, **www.tax.virginia.gov,** or by calling the Department's Forms Request Unit at (804) 440-2541.

Questions: If you have any questions about this return, please call (804) 367-8037 or write the **Virginia Department of Taxation, P.O. Box 1115, Richmond, Virginia 23218-1115.**

Preparation of Return

Line 1: Enter amount of income tax withholding liability for the period for which the return is being filed.

Line 2: Enter overpayment or underpayment from a prior period and attach a detailed explanation to the return. Please indicate an underpayment as a negative figure with brackets around the amount.

Line 3: Subtract overpayment (Line 2) from Line 1 or add underpayment (Line 2) to Line 1 and enter the amount. (Line 1 ± Line 2 = Line 3).

Line 4: Enter penalty, if applicable. If you file the return and/or pay the tax after the due date, a penalty is assessed. The penalty is 6% of the tax due for each month or fraction of a month, not to exceed 30%. In no case will the penalty be less than $10, **even if no tax is due.**

Line 5: Enter interest, if applicable. Interest on any tax due will be added at the daily interest rate established in accordance with Section 58.1-15 of the *Code of Virginia* from the date the unpaid tax (or unpaid balance) became due until it is paid. The interest rate is 2% over the underpayment rate established by Section 6621 of the Internal Revenue Code.

Line 6: Enter the total of Lines 3, 4 and 5.

Declaration and Signature: Be sure to sign, date and enter your phone number on the reverse side of the return in the space indicated.

Detach at dotted line below. DO NOT SEND ENTIRE PAGE.

Form VA-5
(Doc ID 355) M

Employer's Return of Virginia Income Tax Withheld

For assistance, call (804)367-8037.

PERIOD	DUE DATE

`000000000000000 3558888 00000`

ACCT NO.	FEIN
NAME	
ADDRESS	
CITY	STATE ZIP

I declare that this return (including accompanying schedules and statements) has been examined by me and to the best of my knowledge and belief is true, correct and complete.

Signature   Date   Phone Number

Va. Dept. of Taxation VA-5 AR W REV 7/07

1. VA Income Tax Withheld
2. Previous Period(s) Adjustments (See Instructions)
3. Adjustment Total
4. Penalty (See Instructions)
5. Interest (See Instructions)
6. Total Amount Due

Employer's Annual or Final Summary of Virginia Income Tax Withheld Return Instructions

General: Form VA-6 must be filed by all employers registered or required to withhold Virginia income tax from wages paid to employees. **The Form VA-6 must be accompanied by a Wage and Tax Statement** (Form W-2 and 1099, State copy) for EACH employee (including those for which no taxes were withheld) the employer had during the year. If magnetic tape, diskette or CD is used to provide the W-2 information, the Form VA-6 must accompany it.

Filing Procedure: Form VA-6 and Form W-2, State copy, must be filed by February 28 of the year following the calendar year in which taxes were withheld from employees or if the employer's business is terminated during the year, within 30 days after the last month in which wages were paid. Mail Form VA-6 with your payment to the **Virginia Department of Taxation, P.O. Box 1278, Richmond, Virginia 23218-1278. A return must be filed even if no tax is due.** Payments returned by the bank will be subject to a returned payment fee in addition to any other penalties that may be incurred.

Change of Address/Out-of-Business: If you change your business mailing address or discontinue your business, either send a completed Form R-3, Registration Change Request, or a letter to the **Virginia Department of Taxation, P.O. Box 1114, Richmond, Virginia 23218-1114.** A Form R-3 can be obtained from the Department's web site, **www.tax.virginia.gov,** or by calling the Department's Forms Request Unit at (804) 440-2541.

Questions: If you have any questions about this return, please call (804) 367-8037 or write the **Virginia Department of Taxation, P.O. Box 1115, Richmond, Virginia 23218-1115.**

Preparation of Return

Lines 1 thru 12:
- *Monthly Filers* - Enter amount of Virginia income tax paid each month, excluding penalty and interest.
- *Quarterly Filers* - Enter amount paid each quarter on Lines 3, 6, 9, and 12, excluding penalty and interest.
- *Semi-Weekly Filers* - Enter amount of Virginia income tax withheld each quarter as shown on Form VA-16, excluding penalty and interest.
- *Seasonal Filers* - Enter amount of Virginia income tax paid each month, excluding penalty and interest.

Line 13: Enter the total of Lines 1 thru 12.

Line 14: Enter the total of Virginia income tax withheld as shown on accompanying Form W-2 and 1099, State copy. Include an adding machine tape or some type of listing showing how this total was obtained.

Line 15: If Line 13 is less than Line 14, enter the difference. If Line 13 is larger than Line 14, attach an explanation of the overpayment to your return.

Line 16: Enter the total number of W-2 and 1099 statements (State copy) sent with this return.

Declaration and Signature: Be sure to sign, date and enter your phone number on the reverse side of the return in the space indicated.

Work Sheet For Employer's Annual or Final Summary of Virginia Income Tax Withheld

Complete this work sheet and transfer line information to the corresponding line numbers on Employer's Annual or Final Summary of Virginia Income Tax Withheld (VA-6) below. See instructions for additional information. **Retain the work sheet for you records.**

1. **January** Virginia Income Tax Paid			9. **September** Virginia Income Tax Paid	
2. **February** Virginia Income Tax Paid			10. **October** Virginia Income Tax Paid	
3. **March** Virginia Income Tax Paid			11. **November** Virginia Income Tax Paid	
4. **April** Virginia Income Tax Paid			12. **December** Virginia Income Tax Paid	
5. **May** Virginia Income Tax Paid			13. **Total Payments** (Add Lines 1 through 12)	
6. **June** Virginia Income Tax Paid			14. **Total Virginia Income Tax Withheld** Enter the total Virginia Tax withheld on W-2 and 1099 Statements	
7. **July** Virginia Income Tax Paid			15. **Additional Payment** Line 13 less Line 14*	
8. **August** Virginia Income Tax Paid			16. **Total Number of Statements** Enter total number of W-2 and 1099 Statements mailed with this return	

* If Line 13 is larger than Line 14, please attach an explanation of the Overpayment to your return.

Detach at dotted line below. DO NOT SEND ENTIRE PAGE.

- -

Employer's Annual or Final Summary of Virginia Income Tax Withheld Return

Form VA-6
(DOC ID 306)
For assistance, call (804)367-8037.

1. Jan		5. May		9. Sep	
2. Feb		6. Jun		10. Oct	
3. Mar		7. Jul		11 Nov	
4. Apr		8. Aug		12. Dec	

Calendar Year   **Due Date**

0000000000000000 3068888 000000

Account Number   **FEIN**

Name

Address

City   **State**   **Zip**

I declare that this return (including accompanying schedules and statements) has been examined by me and to the best of my knowledge and belief is true, correct and complete.

Signature   **Date**   **Phone Number**

Va. Dept. of Taxation VA-6 AR W REV 5/06   Do not write in the space to the right. ➡

13. Total Payments
Add Lines 1 thru 12

14. Total VA Tax Withheld

15. Additional Payment
Lines 13 thru 14
☐ Check if paid by EFT.

16. Total Number of Statements
Number of W-2 and 1099 statements sent with this return.

Employer's Voucher for Payment of Virginia Income Tax Withheld (Semi-Weekly) Coupon Instructions

General: An employer who pays wages to one or more employees is required to deduct and withhold state income tax from those wages. Virginia law substantially conforms to the federal definition of "wages." Therefore, Virginia withholding is generally required on any payment for which federal withholding is required, except amounts paid pursuant to individual retirement accounts and simplified employee pension plans as defined in Sections 7701(a) (37) and 408(c) of the Internal Revenue Code.

Filing Procedure: An employer's filing status is determined by the average amount of income tax withheld each month. When registering a business, an employer is asked to estimate this figure so the Department can assign a filing status. Based on that information, the Department assigns a quarterly, monthly, semi-weekly, or seasonal filing status. In addition, all employers must file an annual summary. Employers are not responsible for monitoring their monthly tax liabilities to see if a status change is needed. The Department reviews each account annually and makes any necessary changes. Notices of change in filing status are usually mailed during December of each year and become effective on January 1.

Payments may be made by check or by Electronic Funds Transfer (EFT). Payments returned by the bank will be subject to a returned payment fee in addition to any other penalties that may be incurred.

Paying by EFT eliminates your requirement to submit Form VA-15, however payments must be made by the same dates that the Form VA-15 would have been due. When no payment is due because the tax liability is zero, you must report a ZERO liability to the Department. This can be done by reporting a zero payment on your EFT transaction. For additional information regarding EFT, please refer to the Department's *Electronic Funds Transfer (EFT) Guide*. A guide may be obtained from the Department's Web-site: **www.tax.virginia.gov,** or Forms Request Unit at (804) 440-2541.

Semi-Weekly Filing: If an employer's average monthly withholding tax liability is $1,000 or more, semi-weekly filing status will be assigned. If the Virginia income tax withheld as of the close of any federal period is more than $500, a payment must be made within three banking days. Federal cut-off days for withholding deposits are generally Tuesday and Friday of each week. Semi-weekly payments are usually made with Form VA-15, or by EFT. At the end of each calendar quarter, a reconciliation must be filed on Form VA-16, along with payment of any remaining tax due for the quarter.

Mail Form VA-15 and payment to: **Virginia Department of Taxation**
P.O. Box 27264
Richmond, VA 23261-7264.

Change of Ownership: If there has been a change of ownership, do not use the return with the name and account number of the former owner. Send the return with notice of change to the **Virginia Department of Taxation, P.O. Box 1114, Richmond, Virginia 23218-1114**. You can register a new dealer and/or locations, by either completing a Form R-1, Business Registration Application, or electronically using iReg on the Department's Web-site: **www.tax.virginia.gov**. A Form R-1 can be obtained from the Department's web site or by calling the Department's Forms Request Unit at (804) 440-2541.

Change of Address/Out-of-Business: If you change your business mailing address or discontinue your business, either send a completed Form R-3, Registration Change Request, or a letter to the **Virginia Department of Taxation, P.O. Box 1114, Richmond, Virginia 23218-1114**. A Form R-3 can be obtained from the Department's Web-site: **www.tax.virginia.gov**, or by calling the Department's Forms Request Unit at (804) 440-2541.

Questions: If you have any questions about this voucher, please call (804) 367-8037 or write the **Virginia Department of Taxation, P.O. Box 1115, Richmond, Virginia 23218-1115**.

Declaration and Signature: Be sure to sign, date and enter your phone number on the voucher in the space indicated.

Detach at dotted line below. DO NOT SEND ENTIRE PAGE.

Form VA-15   Employer's Voucher For Payment of Virginia Income Tax Withheld (Semi-Weekly)
(DOC ID 315)

For assistance, call (804)367-8037.

For Period Ending*

000000000000000 3158888 000000

Account Number		FEIN	
Name			
Address			
City		State	Zip

Declaration and Signature
I declare that this voucher (including accompanying schedules and statements) has been examined by me and to the best of my knowledge and belief is true, correct and complete.

Signature

Date   Phone Number

Total Amount Due

* Please note that this VA-15 form reflects the ending month of the quarterly period in which it is due.

Va. Dept. of Taxation   VA-15 AR W   REV 6/06

Please do not write in the area below.

Employer's Quarterly Reconciliation and Return of Virginia Income Tax Withheld Instructions

General: An employer who pays wages to one or more employees is required to deduct and withhold state income tax from those wages. Virginia law substantially conforms to the federal definition of "wages." Therefore, Virginia withholding is generally required on any payment for which federal withholding is required, except amounts paid pursuant to individual retirement accounts and simplified employee pension plans as defined in Sections 7701(a) (37) and 408(c) of the Internal Revenue Code.

Filing Procedure: This form is used by semi-weekly filers to reconcile payments for each calendar quarter. Form VA-16 is due on April 30, July 31, October 31 and January 31.

Mail Form VA-16 with your payment to: **Virginia Dept. of Taxation**
P.O. Box 27264
Richmond, VA 23261-7264

A return must be filed for each reporting period even if no tax is due. Payments returned by the bank will be subject to a returned payment fee in addition to any other penalties that may be incurred.

Change of Ownership: If there has been a change of ownership, do not use the return with the name and account number of the former owner. Send the return with notice of change to the **Virginia Department of Taxation, P.O. Box 1114, Richmond, Virginia 23218-1114.** You can register a new dealer and/or locations, by either completing a Form R-1, Business Registration Application, or electronically using iReg on the Department's Web-site: **www.tax.virginia.gov.** A Form R-1 can be obtained from the Department's web site or by calling the Department's Forms Request Unit at (804) 440-2541.

Change of Address/Out-of-Business: If you change your business mailing address or discontinue your business, either send a completed Form R-3, Registration Change Request, or a letter to the **Virginia Department of Taxation, P.O. Box 1114, Richmond, Virginia 23218-1114.** A Form R-3 can be obtained from the Department's Web-site: **www.tax.virginia.gov,** or by calling the Department's Forms Request Unit at (804) 440-2541.

Questions: If you have any questions about this return, please call (804) 367-8037 or write the **Virginia Department of Taxation, P.O. Box 1115, Richmond, Virginia 23218-1115.**

Preparation of Return

Line 1: Enter amount of income tax withholding liability for the quarter for which the return is being filed.

Line 2: Enter overpayment or underpayment from a prior period. Attach a detailed explanation of the overpayment or underpayment to the return.

Line 3: Subtract overpayment (Line 2) from Line 1 or add underpayment (Line 2) to Line 1 and enter the amount. (Line 1 ± Line 2 = Line 3).

Line 4: Enter all payments made for the quarter.

Line 5: Subtract Line 4 from Line 3 and enter tax due. If the amount due is more than 10% of Line 3, and Line 3 exceeds $500, compute penalty (Line 6) and interest (Line 7). (Line 3 - Line 4 = Line 5)

Line 6: Enter penalty, if applicable. Semi-weekly filers are also subject to a penalty if at least 90% of the total liability for each calendar quarter has not been paid within 3 days of the close of a quarter. The amount subject to penalty is determined by subtracting 10% of the amount reported on Line 3 from the balance due on Line 5 of the return. If Form VA-16 is filed on time with full payment that exceeds $500, the penalty is 6% of the amount computed above (Line 6). If Form VA-16 is filed or paid late, the penalty will accrue on the unpaid balance at a rate of 6% for each month or fraction of a month, not to exceed 30%. In no case will the penalty be less than $10, **even if no tax is due.**

Line 7: Enter interest, if applicable. If this return is filed after the due date or the tax on Line 5 is more than 10% of Line 3, and Line 3 exceeds $500, interest must be computed at a rate equal to the rate of interest established under Section 6621 of the Internal Revenue Code, plus 2%. Multiply the amount on Line 5 by the interest rate.

Line 8: Enter any Form VA-15 payments that are required to be filed within 3 days from the end of the quarter. For example, if filing a return (Lines 1-7, Form VA-16) for January through March, use Line 8 to make any required payments of employer withholding tax that are due from April 27th through April 30th.

Line 9: Enter the total of Lines 5, 6, 7 and 8. This amount must be paid at the time the return is filed.

Declaration and Signature: Be sure to sign, date and enter your phone number on the reverse side of the return in the space indicated.

This paper is perforated. Detach at dotted line below. DO NOT SEND ENTIRE PAGE.

- -

Form VA-16 Employer's Quarterly Reconciliation and
(Doc ID 316)   Return of Virginia Income Tax Withheld

For assistance, call (804)367-8037.

Period	Due Date

```
000000000000000  3168888  000000
```

Account Number	FEIN
Name	
Address	
City	State	Zip

I declare that this return (including accompanying schedules and statements) has been examined by me and to the best of my knowledge and belief is true, correct and complete.

Signature ____ Date ____ Phone Number ____

Va. Dept. of Taxation   VA-16 AR W   REV 5/06

1. VA Income Tax Withheld

2. Previous Period(s) Adjustments (See Instructions)

3. Adjusted Total

4. Payments Made During This Period

5. Balance of Tax Due This Quarter

6. Penalty (See Instructions)

7. Interest (See Instructions)

8. Payment for Month Following This Period

9. Total Amount Due

☐ **Check if paid by EFT.**

GLOSSARY

A

accelerated depreciation Depreciation method in which a greater amount of depreciation or expense is taken in the early years and less in the later years.

accounts payable Money owed by the business.

accounts receivable Money owed to the business.

accrual method Accounting method that records income and expenses when they are earned or incurred, even though no payment is made.

accumulated depreciation The total amount of depreciation accumulated over several years and charged against appropriate fixed assets.

acid-test ratio Similar to the current ratio, but it is a more severe test for businesses that carry a large amount of inventory.

action level The limit of employee exposure, without regard to the use of respirators, to an airborne concentration of lead of 30 micrograms per cubic meter of air [30 ug/m(3)] calculated as an eight-hour time-weighted average (TWA).

addenda Changes, additions, or clarifications developed after the project has been released for bid.

agent of the principal The person signing for the company; who must be identified as acting as an agent of the company (agent of the principal) and must be acting solely in the interests of the company.

allowances Funds for unique items or skilled work in the project.

Americans with Disabilities Act (ADA) Prohibits job discrimination based on disability. The Americans with Disabilities Act applies to all employers with 15 or more employees.

Articles of Incorporation The corporate by-laws that control what a corporation does, how it is organized, and its financial activities.

asbestos A fibrous mineral with thin fibers.

asset Anything of value belonging to the business. Assets include accounts receivable, cash, land, prepaid bills, equipment, buildings, furniture, and fixtures.

asset management ratio A measure of how well a company is managing its assets.

at-will employment When an employee is hired for an indefinite period of time without an employment contract.

automobile (vehicle) insurance Insurance that covers cars, trucks, trailers, or other self-propelled or towed vehicles used for the business.

average collection period (ACP) An indication of the average number of days required to collect receivables. It is a measure of the company's ability to collect debts (receivables).

B

balance sheet Form that shows the financial condition of the company on a given day.

bid An offer to furnish labor, equipment, and materials in a specified manner and time and for a certain price.

bid bond A guarantee that the successful bidder will enter into a project contract for the agreed-upon price.

bid rigging When a contractor conspires with other bidders to ensure the award of a bid, with the result of a certain bid.

bid sheet A form that must be used to submit a formal bid proposal.

bid shopping Revealing a subcontractor's bid information to a competitor.

bill   A document that 1) changes the current law, 2) adds a new law, or 3) deletes an existing law. The idea for a bill may come from general assembly members, their constituents, lobbyists, the governor, or heads of state agencies charged with administering the law.

board of directors   Act as the representatives of the corporation in overseeing the operation of the corporation.

bond   A surety that guarantees completion of a project or recovery of a loss.

bond rating   The measure of risk of a bond going into default.

builder's risk insurance   Insurance that protects the contractor against any loss or damage to the project structure and materials or equipment purchased for the project while it is under construction.

burglary insurance   Insurance against burglary, robbery, and theft by persons other than employees.

business plan   An organized summary of a business.

C

cash budget   A comparison of expected receipts and planned expenses, disregarding all non-cash assets. A cash budget is intended to ensure that there is enough money for payroll, accounts payable, and other short-term obligations.

cash discount   A discount in the purchase price of supplies or a deduction off the invoice in exchange for prompt payment.

cash flow   Money that has been received and spent. Cash flow is based on cash receipts minus cash disbursements from a given operation over a given period.

cash flow schedule   Reflects the costs of each portion of the project and the anticipated revenues from each progress payment.

cash flow statement   Statement that shows revenue receipts and expenses for a particular reporting period.

cash method   Accounting method that records transactions only when money exchanges hands, that is, when a check is written or a deposit is made.

Circular E   An IRS publication that explains the federal tax responsibilities of an employer.

Civil Rights Act of 1964   Act that prohibits employment discrimination based on race, color, religion, sex, or national origin.

claim   A written statement of disagreement with the purpose of putting a disagreement in writing.

completed contract method   Accounting method that recognizes profit only when the job is completed.

completion-capitalized cost method   Accounting method in which a certain percentage of the project cost and revenue is identified and income and expenses are calculated by that percentage in the current year. The balance is deferred until the project is completed in the next year.

comprehensive general liability (CGL)   A blanket insurance policy that provides broad overage for personal injuries or property damage caused to others who are not employed by the contractor.

Consolidated Omnibus Budget Reconciliation Act (COBRA)   Act that provides for continuing health care benefits for individuals who have lost coverage because of termination of employment or death or divorce of a spouse who had the coverage.

contingency   A percentage added to an estimate to cover any unexpected costs.

contract   A binding agreement between two or more persons.

contract bond (performance bond)   A guarantee that the successful bidder will complete the project in accordance with the plans and specifications and in a timely manner.

contractor   Any person who, for monetary consideration, performs or manages the construction, removal, repair, or improvement of any building or structure.

contractual employment   A contract is signed for a specified period and the employment can be terminated only for cause.

Contract Work Hours and Safety Standards Act   Act that applies to contractors or subcontractors who have service or construction contracts with the federal government over $100,000.

corporation A legally unique entity, separate from its partners (called shareholders). The main benefit to the shareholders is limited liability.

cost control Monitoring costs as the project progresses.

cost of goods sold The sum of the costs of materials sold to a customer.

cost plus contract A contract that charges for materials plus a fee for the contractor.

cost plus fee contract A contract in which a fixed dollar amount is paid to the contractor for their services.

cost plus percentage contract A contract similar to a cost plus fee contract, except that the fee is a percentage of the costs.

critical task A task that depends on one task before another is started.

critical task analysis The process of looking at an entire project, identifying each task, and determining how long each task will take.

current asset Cash or any asset that can be converted to cash within one year or one operating cycle. Such assets may include accounts receivable, inventory, and prepaid expenses.

current liability Any money owed by the contracting company that must be paid within one year. Current liabilities may include loan payments due, accounts payable, wages, and taxes.

current ratio A measure of the ability of a company to pay bills promptly.

D

daily log Log completed every day to create a complete record of everything that happens at the construction site.

Davis-Bacon Act Act that requires that prevailing wage rates and fringe benefits be paid to all employees involved with federal construction projects valued in excess of $2,000.

debt to equity ratio A measure of the investment of creditors and contractors.

depreciation A method of spreading out the cost of equipment or property (asset) over its life span rather than entering the full cost in the first year.

design/build contract A contract in which a prime (or general) contractor takes responsibility for the architectural, engineering, bidding, contracting, construction (building) inspection, and final approval of the project.

detailed survey estimate Estimate based on a takeoff from the drawings and specifications and applies unit costs to all required materials and labor.

direct costs Costs that relate to the actual productive activities of the business.

direct labor cost The basic hourly rate for building, installing, or modifying a work item (unit).

director's and officer's (D & O) liability insurance A type of professional liability insurance that protects the company's senior management for reasonable, proper, and legal acts that occur in carrying out their role as officers of the company.

disbursements journal A journal that tracks how monies are paid out and in what amounts.

doing business as (DBA) A term used to describe a company that uses a name other than the owner's birth name.

drawings Detail the architectural, electrical, mechanical, and plumbing portions of the project.

duration 1. The legal life or existence of the company. 2. The time required to complete each task expressed in hours, shifts, or days.

E

emergency action plan A plan that details what to do in case of an emergency, such as a fire, and what the responsibilities of employees and the employer are, for example, who is responsible for calling 911.

Employee Polygraph Protection Act Act that prohibits most private employers from using any type of lie detector test either for pre-employment screening of job applicants or for testing current employees during the course of employment.

Employee Retirement Income Security Act (ERISA) Act that regulates the minimum standards for employers who maintain pension plans; however, ERISA does not require that employers have pension plans.

Equal Pay Act   Act that requires that men and women be paid equal pay for equal work in an establishment.

equipment costs   All expenses associated with any equipment used for the job.

equipment leasing   Rental of equipment using long-term contracts lasting one year or more.

equipment rental   Rental of equipment to meet short-term equipment needs.

estimate   A projection of job costs.

ethics   Practicing a standard of honesty in all business dealings.

executive summary   A description of the business.

exempt employees   Employees, administrators, and professionals that are exempt from overtime pay requirement and minimum wage provisions because they are salaried employees.

expediter   Orders materials and sets delivery schedules, monitors the ordering process, and reports the delivery status to the site superintendent.

F

Fair Labor Standards Act (FLSA)   Act that sets minimum wage and overtime requirements, including child labor standards.

Family and Medical Leave Act (FMLA)   Act that entitles eligible employees to take up to 12 weeks of unpaid job-protected leave each year, with maintenance of group health insurance, for the birth and care of a child, for the placement of a child for adoption or foster care, for the care of a child, spouse, or parent with a serious health condition, or for the employee's serious health condition.

fast track contract   A contract that provides for starting construction before all the plans and drawings are complete.

financials   An outline of the funds that are needed to achieve the goals established in the business plan.

first aid   Any one-time treatment and any follow-up visit for the purpose of observation, of minor scratches, cuts, burns, splinters, and so forth, which do not ordinarily require medical care.

fixed asset   Property owned by the business that will not be converted to cash within one year. Fixed assets include land, buildings, equipment, furniture, and fixtures.

float time   Excess time on a project that results when a task is completed in less than the scheduled time.

flowdown clause   A statement in the general contract that any subcontractors must comply with certain conditions of the general contract.

foreman   Provides support to the site superintendent.

formal bid   A statement that the contractor agrees to build the project in accordance with the bid documents for the stated price.

full-time employee   An employee who works a minimum of 30 hours a week.

G

general and administrative costs   Costs incurred in the daily operation of a business.

general conditions   Outline the roles of the owner, contractor, architect, and engineer.

general contractor   Any person (contractors, laborers, mechanics, and material providers) who contracts with an owner or a contractor.

general journal   A record of non-cash transactions, such as depreciation of assets and corrections.

general ledger   A form that contains a monthly summary of information by numerical number, by entering the data from the journals.

general overhead   Represents all the operating costs of the company that are not related to any project.

general partnership   Business formed by two or more persons. Partners may share equally in the business or they may invest different amounts, have different responsibilities, and share different percentages of the profits.

goals   What the company hopes to achieve.

gross profit   The amount remaining after deducting direct and indirect costs from revenues.

H

hours worked   The time an employee must be on duty or at the place of business.

I

immaterial breach   Although technically a violation of the contract, is a minor or inconsequential violation.

Immigration and Nationality Act   Act that requires every employer to verify the nationality and employability of every candidate for employment.

income statement   Form that shows the financial position of a company for the year.

indemnification clause   A contractual obligation in which one person agrees to secure another person in cases of loss or damage from certain liabilities.

indirect costs   Costs that are not related to any specific job, such as the cost of company vehicles and their operation.

indirect labor costs   Unemployment insurance, workers' compensation insurance, health insurance, and similar costs, which are not a part of the hourly wage.

installation floater policy   An insurance policy purchased to protect against loss or damage to equipment or goods, whether owned or rented at the building site.

inventory control   The art of keeping inventory costs as low as possible.

invitation to bid   A document that describes the proposed project and states the manner in which the bid must be prepared.

J

job costs   All costs related to any single project.

job cost analysis   Facilitates financial management of existing projects and provides information necessary for preparing bids for future projects.

joint entirety   Gives a spouse ownership in a portion of the property so it can not be considered a company asset.

joint venture   A partnership of two or more individual companies joining together to work on a particular project.

journal   A blank book with lines and columns in which are recorded, by type, all the source documents.

K

key man insurance   A type of life insurance that provides monetary assistance to the company in the event of the death of essential staff.

L

land-disturbing activity   Any change to the land that may result in soil erosion from water or wind and the movement of sediments into state waters or onto other land.

law   A body of rules of action or conduct that has legal force. Laws are developed by state legislatures.

lead   A lustrous metal that is very soft, highly malleable, ductile, and a poor conductor of electricity.

lead pre-renovation education rule   Rule that requires distribution of the EPA pamphlet Protect Your Family from Lead in Your Home before starting renovation work.

liability   Any claim against the business' assets. Liabilities can be short-term (current) or long-term.

lien   A claim on the property of another as security against the payment of a just debt.

limited liability company (LLC)   Neither a strict partnership nor a corporation. The same structure as a partnership if the company is set up without a manager, otherwise it is like a corporation with the partners as shareholders.

limited partnership   At least one person is considered a general partner and has the responsibility and liability for the day-to-day operation and financial decisions.

liquidity ratio   A measure of the ability of a company to pay its current liabilities.

long-term liability   Any debt or obligation normally due over a period longer than one year and which is not a current liability.

lost workdays The number of days including the day of injury or illness during which the employee would have worked but could not do so because of the occupational injury or illness.

lump sum contract A contract that reflects the contractor's guarantee to the owner that the project will be completed for a fixed (contract) price.

M

market analysis An evaluation of market research that describes how the company is going to enter the market through identified goals.

marketing Identifying customers and attracting them to the company's products and services.

material breach A significant violation of the contract that gives the other party a right to stop further performance and sue for damages.

material costs The total of all costs for materials used by the contractor, including the price of the materials, the cost of delivery, and any storage charges.

mechanic's lien A lien placed on a property, usually by a contractor, subcontractor, or material supplier, for failure to receive payment.

mechanics' lien agent A person designated in writing by the owner who will receive notice of the lien (CoV 43-1 and 43-4.01). The agent must be one of the following:

- A licensed title insurance agent
- A title insurance company authorized to write title insurance in the Commonwealth of Virginia
- An attorney licensed to practice law in the Commonwealth of Virginia
- A financial institution authorized to accept deposits

medical treatment Treatment administered by a physician or by registered professional personnel under the standing orders of a physician.

memorandum of lien A general written statement specifying the type of labor or the materials furnished and the amount of the claim.

minimum wage The lowest possible rate that can be paid to an employee.

mission The foundation on which the business is built and is the company's primary reason for existing.

mission statement Identifies what the company is about.

monitoring The process of overseeing the work and overcoming any obstacles to timely completion.

N

negotiation When both parties discuss or bargain to reach an agreement.

net income The amount resulting after taxes are deducted from net income before taxes.

net income before taxes (NIBT) The amount left after subtracting general and administrative costs from gross profit. NIBT is shown on the bottom of the income statement.

net worth The value of all assets after deducting all liabilities.

non-exempt employees Employees who are typically paid hourly.

O

overhead Expenses that are not related to any project. These include building rent, utilities, office equipment, and salaries for management, supervisors, and full-time staff.

overtime pay Wages due an employee for hours over 40 worked in a workweek.

owner The person who holds title to the property.

owner's representative Representative that acts on the owner's behalf when any questions or issues arise about the project.

ordinance A law adopted by local jurisdictions. The city may adopt ordinances that govern everyday activities, for example, parking and speed limits.

P

partnership   A for-profit business operated by two or more people.

pass-through taxation   When no tax is assessed on the profits of the company but only on the amount of income distributed to the partners.

payroll journal   A logbook that tracks employee wages and provides the records necessary for state and federal reports.

percentage of completion   Accounting method that recognizes and records expenses and revenues as the project progresses.

permissible exposure limit   The limit to the concentration of lead that an employee is exposed to, averaged over an eight-hour period.

personal representative   A person that an employee has designated in writing as representing the employee's interests.

plans (blueprints)   The drawings that detail the job.

policy   A guideline for operation of an office that does not have the effect of law. For example, the local building department has a policy posted that all inspection requests for the next day must be received by the office no later than 2:00 P.M. the preceding day. This policy helps the office run more smoothly, but no laws are broken and no punishments incurred if the policy is not followed.

prepaid expenses   An expense that is paid before the material is actually used.

professional liability insurance   Insurance that covers errors or negligence in performing the normal duties of a contractor.

profit (markup)   Represents the money left over after all expenses are paid.

project documents   The plans and specifications prepared for the owner by an architect and/or engineer.

project manager   Person responsible for everything relating to the project.

project overhead   The costs, except labor, associated with a particular project.

project planning   The process of carefully looking at a project to determine the time sequence of the work schedule and the relationship of job tasks to each other.

project scheduling   The process of designating where each task or work unit fits into the project plan and when it will be completed.

property insurance   Insurance that covers fire, smoke, theft, vandalism, and so on and provides coverage on structures and their contents.

punch list   A list of deficiencies on a project, usually minor, that need to be corrected.

purchased equipment   Equipment bought as a long-term investment.

R

registered agent   The person designated by the company and named on papers filed with a state agency as acting as a public contact.

regulation   A rule or order that has been issued by a government. Regulations are normally adopted by state agencies.

Resource Conservation and Recovery Act (RCRA) of 1976   Act intended to protect people and the environment from potential hazards due to waste disposal, and to conserve energy and natural resources.

revenue   The operating income or income due to the normal activities of the business.

retainage   A certain percentage of the payment retained by the customer to ensure satisfactory completion of the project.

risk management   Identifying potential risks and taking action to protect the contracting company from those risks.

rule   A standard or guide for action or conduct. A rule may be issued by a judge.

S

sales and cash receipts journal   A record of all income.

Service Contract Act   Act that requires payment of prevailing wage rates and fringe benefits; however, this act refers specifically to contracts over $2,500 that will be using service personnel to provide services to the federal government and does not cover construction of buildings.

shop drawings   Drawings prepared to clarify the architect's drawings and specifications.

site superintendent   Person responsible for all the activities at the job site.

soil erosion   The removal of material from a site by water, wind, or gravity.

sole proprietorship   A business that is owned solely by the proprietor with no partners in the business.

source documents   All documents relating to income or expenses. Source documents may include check stubs, invoices received and sent, cash receipts, and time cards.

specifications   Describe the materials to be used and the quality of the construction required.

standard form of agreement   A summary of all the documents related to the contract agreement that confirms the scope of the project, assigns responsibility for the project, lists bonding and insurance requirements, and sets the price and payment details.

statutory bond   A bond, usually required for public projects, that has been required by law.

straight-line depreciation   The cost of the asset is divided by a certain number of years and each year this cost is charged as an expense.

strategies   How a goal is to be achieved.

subchapter S corporation   A business form for small businesses with less than 75 shareholders and modest revenues. It has the limited liability of a corporation while avoiding the double taxation of profits characteristic of a standard corporation.

supplementary conditions   Additions or modifications to the "boilerplate" general conditions that apply to the specific project.

surety bond   A legal document under which one party agrees to answer to another party for the debt, default, or failure to perform for a third party.

T

taxable income   Money received for work, and that is taxable.

time cards   Form that records hours worked.

time contingency   A time buffer incorporated into the schedule to provide allowances for unexpected delays.

timetable   When a goal is to be achieved.

total asset utilization (TAU)   Asset utilization method that measures how well a company uses or turns over it assets.

turnkey contract   A contract that gives the prime contractor responsibility for developing the entire project.

U

underground utility   A public service or utility that is buried below ground to prevent damage to the utility.

unemployment insurance   Insurance, usually paid for by an employer, that is offered for individuals who have lost their job for reasons other than poor performance.

unit price contract   A contract in which the job is priced by each unit that is required for the project.

unit price method   Relies on job costs from previous projects, with labor, materials, and overhead for similar items or sub-assemblies combined into unit costs for those items.

V

value engineering   A term applied to a contractor discovering and disclosing to the owner ways to save money on a project.

W

wage garnishment   The act of withholding money from an employee's paycheck when required by a court order.

Walsh-Healey Public Contracts Act   Act that requires payment of minimum wage rates and overtime pay on contracts in excess of $10,000 that provide materials, supplies, or equipment to the federal government.

wetlands   Generally include swamps, marshes, bogs, and similar areas.

workers' compensation insurance   Insurance, usually paid for by an employer, that offers income to employees who have become injured through an on-the-job accident or illness.

working capital   Cash or equivalent assets available to pay bills.

workweek   A period of 168 hours during seven consecutive 24-hour periods. It can begin on any day of the week and at any hour of the day.

Z

zero profit method   Accounting method used when the project is such that the profit is difficult to estimate, so it is determined to be zero until such time that the project has progressed sufficiently to make a determination.